Sartre's Existential Psychoanalysis

Also Available From Bloomsbury

Sartre and Magic, Daniel O'Shiel
The Parallel Philosophies of Sartre and Nietzsche, Nik Farrell Fox
An Existential Phenomenology of Addiction, Anna Westin

Sartre's Existential Psychoanalysis

Knowing Others

Mary L. Edwards

BLOOMSBURY ACADEMIC
LONDON • NEW YORK • OXFORD • NEW DELHI • SYDNEY

BLOOMSBURY ACADEMIC
Bloomsbury Publishing Plc
50 Bedford Square, London, WC1B 3DP, UK
1385 Broadway, New York, NY 10018, USA
29 Earlsfort Terrace, Dublin 2, Ireland

BLOOMSBURY, BLOOMSBURY ACADEMIC and the Diana logo are
trademarks of Bloomsbury Publishing Plc

First published in Great Britain 2023
This paperback edition published 2024

Copyright © Mary L. Edwards, 2023

Mary L. Edwards has asserted her right under the Copyright,
Designs and Patents Act, 1988, to be identified as Author of this work.

For legal purposes the Acknowledgements on p. x constitute
an extension of this copyright page.

Series design by Charlotte Daniels
Cover image: Psychological concept vector illustration (© Irakli Topuria / Alamy Stock Vector)

All rights reserved. No part of this publication may be reproduced
or transmitted in any form or by any means, electronic or mechanical,
including photocopying, recording, or any information storage or retrieval
system, without prior permission in writing from the publishers.

Bloomsbury Publishing Plc does not have any control over, or responsibility for,
any third-party websites referred to or in this book. All internet addresses given
in this book were correct at the time of going to press. The author and publisher
regret any inconvenience caused if addresses have changed or sites have ceased
to exist, but can accept no responsibility for any such changes.

A catalogue record for this book is available from the British Library.

A catalog record for this book is available from the Library of Congress.

ISBN: HB: 978-1-3501-7347-7
PB: 978-1-3503-3107-5
ePDF: 978-1-3501-7349-1
eBook: 978-1-3501-7348-4

Typeset by Integra Software Services Pvt. Ltd.

To find out more about our authors and books visit www.bloomsbury.com
and sign up for our newsletters.

To J. C. C.

Contents

Acknowledgements		x
List of Abbreviations		xii
Introduction		1
1	Sartre's theory of the self	7
	The transcendent ego	7
	A sense of selfness	11
	The constitution of the ego	18
	The evolution of the Sartrean self	22
	Anguish, shame and self-deception	26
	Bad faith and self-formation	30
	The possibility of self-knowledge	35
2	Knowledge of selves	41
	The problem of other minds	42
	Sartre's solution to the conceptual problem of other minds	46
	Shame and loneliness	50
	Philosophical therapy and knowledge of selves	52
	Existentialism and psychoanalysis: The very idea	54
	Consciousness and comprehension	60
	Existential ontology as psychoanalytic metatheory	63
3	Situated selves: The development of Sartre's psychoanalysis	67
	From discourse to dialectic	68
	Dialectical materialism	70
	Knowledge of dialectical objects	73
	Sartre's search for a new objective method	76
	Sartre's debt to Beauvoir	80
	The spirals of self-formation	83
	Knowledge of another self	87

4	*The Family Idiot* and the objectification of a self	91
	Being	91
	Flaubert's passive constitution	92
	The paternal curse	95
	Pessimism and religiosity without religion	100
	Comprehension	102
	Autism, femininity and autoeroticism	103
	A spectacle for his sister	105
	Conversion from idiot to actor	107
	Magical behaviour and imaginary acts	109
	Knowing	113
	The objective spirit	115
	Sex and death, eating and decay	119
	Flaubert's choice of the imaginary	123
	Flaubert's failure	125
5	Objectivity in Sartre's study of Flaubert	129
	Why Flaubert?	129
	Is Sartre's method objective enough?	133
	Madame Bovary: The missing fourth volume	136
	Style over substance	136
	The unlikely heroism of Charles Bovary	138
	'I am too small for myself'	140
	Sadism and laughter	142
	Emma's insincerity, Flaubert's truth	145
	Sartre's blind spots and their implications	147
	The positive counterpart to Flaubert's misanthropy	147
	Reading 'like a man'	150
	Implications	154
6	Imagining the selves of others	157
	Bodies and books: Analoga for the self	157
	Structure, language and Sartre's 'return to Freud'	162
	'Show me your metaphysics!'	166
	Literature as experience incarnate	170
	Imaginary lives	174
	A true novel: Knowing *through* imagining?	176

7	The future of Sartrean existential psychoanalysis	181
	Sartrean existentialism: A new metatheory	182
	Sartrean existential psychoanalysis in practice	187
	Existential principles for integrative psychotherapy	192
	Existential e-therapy	197
	Suggestions for further research	199
Notes		205
References		231
Index		248

Acknowledgements

This book develops some of the key ideas of my doctoral thesis, which was supervised by Julia Jansen and Angela Ryan at University College Cork. I am very grateful to Julia for her guidance in thinking about the philosophy of the imagination and all matters phenomenological, and to Angela for her wisdom on psychoanalysis in the French tradition and advice on studying French texts. The lessons I learned under their supervision have continued to help me in my postdoctoral research. I am also grateful to my external examiner, Kathleen Lennon, who first suggested that I write a book about Sartre and 'knowing others' after my viva.

In 2018, I took on what was initially meant to be temporary position at Cardiff University and, marvellously, I'm still there. I don't believe it would have been possible for me to have written this book without the support and encouragement of colleagues in The School of English, Communication and Philosophy. Special thanks must go to Jon Webber who has been a great 'Sartre mentor' to me. I am particularly grateful to him for his feedback on drafts of Chapters 2 and 6 of this book and for discussions about the problem of other minds, which led me to see how Sartre solves the conceptual problem. I am also grateful to Alessandra Tanesini for being an inspirational senior colleague and for giving me informative feedback on early drafts of sections of Chapter 1. Special thanks must go to my good friend and colleague Alex Dietz for his comments on Chapter 7 and for sending a large box of books from Cardiff to Co. Kerry in the midst of the 2020 Covid-19 pandemic. Thanks to Josh Robinson for helpful comments on my book proposal. And thanks to my students enrolled on French Existentialism and The Social Imagination modules I taught (2019–21) for many enjoyable and challenging discussions on themes developed in this book.

Another force in shaping my thinking since completing my PhD has been my experience as a trainee psychotherapist at Dublin City University, which has enabled me to gain a clearer sense of the potential clinical implications of Sartre's existential psychoanalysis. Special thanks are due to Aisling MacMahon for her instruction on humanistic and integrative psychotherapy approaches and for giving me such insightful comments on Chapter 7. Thanks also to Gerard

Moore for his instruction in traditional psychoanalysis and psychodynamic psychotherapy and to Gemma Kiernan for her warmth and wisdom as a personal tutor.

I had the opportunity to present material for this book at a workshop on 'Beauvoir and Sartre on Self and Others' organized by the Husserl Archives at KU Leuven in cooperation with Cardiff University in 2018, at the 2019 UK Sartre Society Conference and at a Cardiff University Philosophy Work-in-Progress seminar in 2020. I am grateful to each of the audiences for discussions following my talks. I am especially grateful to two fellow UK Sartre Society members: Kate Kirkpatrick – for her positive influence and for enlightening discussions on philosophy and biography in Cardiff, Oxford and Leuven, which have informed my approach to Sartre's biographical studies – and Marieke Mueller – for thought-provoking discussions on Sartre, Flaubert and psychoanalysis.

Many thanks to Lucy Russell and Liza Thompson at Bloomsbury for their initial and continued enthusiasm for this project and for all their support and advice throughout the writing and editing processes. I am also indebted to Bloomsbury's anonymous reviewers for constructive feedback on my book proposal and for a clear-sighted assessment of the first completed draft of the manuscript, which provided me the push I needed to revise the first chapters.

On a more personal level, I am thankful to friends both inside and outside of academia for discussions related and entirely unrelated to this project, which have provided me with a source of strength and energy: Victoria Wilde, Rebecca Whiter, Miriam Twomey, Rachel Warren, Josie and Mike Burnes, Bernie Cronin, Emer O'Connor, Mo Morris, Ritchie O'Connell, Brian O'Neil, Marie O'Mahony, Katie Cosgrove, Mikey Goodman, S. Orestis Palermos, Huw Rees, Liz Irvine, Anneli Jefferson, Richard Gray, Jonathan Mitchell, Alix Beeston, Danielle Petherbridge, Luna Dolezal, Arthur Rose, Clara Fischer and Vittorio Bufacchi.

Thanks to my parents John and Abbie Edwards for their love, support and patience with my scholarly pursuits, to my parents-in-law Johnny and Pauline Clifford for so much kindness and understanding, and to my cousins Fiona O'Connor and Kerry O'Connor for their encouragement regarding this project.

Finally, to my husband Jonathan Clifford: I cannot thank you enough for supporting me in everything I do, for proofreading almost all this manuscript, for picking up the domestic slack while I was writing it, and for putting up with the 'third person' in our marriage – 'ol' Jean-Paul'. This book is dedicated to you.

Abbreviations

For full bibliographical details, see the References.

B	Sartre, J.-P., *Baudelaire*
BN/EN	Sartre, J.-P., *Being and Nothingness: An Essay on Phenomenological Ontology/ L'être et le néant. Essai d'ontologie phénoménologique*
CDR I/CRD I	Sartre, J.-P., *Critique of Dialectical Reason I: Theory of Practical Ensembles/Critique de la raison dialectique précédé de questions de méthode, Tome I: théorie des ensembles pratiques*
CDR II/CRD II	Sartre, J.-P., *Critique of Dialectical Reason, Volume II (Unfinished)/Critique de la raison dialectique, Tome II (inachevé): L'intelligibilité de l'histoire*
CL/EC	Sartre, J.-P., 'The Childhood of a Leader'/L'Enfance d'un chef'
CW	Freud, S., *The Standard Edition of the Complete Psychological Works of Sigmund Freud*
E	Lacan, J., *Écrits*
EA/MA	Beauvoir, S. (de), *The Ethics of Ambiguity/Pour une morale de l'ambiguïté*
EW	Flaubert, G., *Early Writings: Gustave Flaubert*
FI	Sartre, J.-P., *The Family Idiot: Gustave Flaubert 1821–1857*
I	Sartre, J.-P., *The Imaginary: A Phenomenological Psychology of the Imagination/L'imaginaire. Psychologie phénémonologique de l'imagination*
IF	Sartre, J.-P., *L'Idiot de la famille: Gustave Flaubert de 1821 à 1857*

IOT	Sartre, J.-P., 'Itinerary of a Thought'
IWS	Sartre, J.-P., 'An Interview with Jean-Paul Sartre'
MB	Flaubert, G., *Madame Bovary: Provincial Manners*/'Madame Bovary: Mœure de province'
MT/HM	Sartre, J.-P., 'The Man with the Tape-Recorder'/'L'Homme au magnétophone'
Nov	Flaubert, G. *November*
OIF/SIF	Sartre, J.-P., 'On *The Idiot of the Family*'/'Sur « *L'Idiot de la famille* »'
OJ	Flaubert, G., *Œuvres de jeunesse*
S	Flaubert, G., *Salammbô*
SE/ES	Flaubert, G., *A Sentimental Education*/*L'Éducation sentimentale*
SG	Sartre, J.-P., *Saint Genet: Actor and Martyr*/*Saint Genet, comédien et martyr*
SM/QM	Sartre, J.-P., *Search for a Method*/*Questions de méthode*
SS/DS	Beauvoir, S. (de), *The Second Sex*/*Le deuxième sexe*
STE/ETE	Sartre, J.-P., *Sketch for a Theory of the Emotions*/*Esquisse d'une théorie des émotions*
TE	Sartre, J.-P., *The Transcendence of the Ego*/*La transcendance de la ego. Esquisse d'une description phénoménologique*
W/M	Sartre, J.-P., *Words*/*Les Mots*
WL/QL	Sartre, J.-P., *What Is Literature?*/*Qu'est-ce que la littérature ?*

Introduction

In 1969, psychoanalyst Jean-Bertrand Pontalis wrote, 'One day the history of Sartre's thirty-year long relationship with psychoanalysis, and ambiguous mixture of *equally* deep attraction and repulsion, will have to be written and perhaps his work reinterpreted in the light of it' (Pontalis 2008: 220). This book fulfils the need for a scholarly investigation into Jean-Paul Sartre's long relationship with psychoanalysis that Pontalis identified over half a century ago.[1] It traces the development of Sartre's psychoanalytical thought throughout his career and indicates how his philosophical work ought to be 'reinterpreted in the light of it'. Rather than treating Sartre's philosophical and psychoanalytical projects as separate enterprises, it proposes that his oeuvre can be read in a more coherent and productive way when his psychoanalytical project is recognized as an expansion of his philosophical one. To recognize this is not merely to see that his psychoanalysis is rooted in, or that it applies insights from, his existential philosophy, but also to appreciate how it 'does' philosophy in its own right. A principal aim of this book is to illuminate the philosophical work in Sartre's psychoanalytical studies by showing how they synthesize his theories of the self, the imagination, individual freedom and the situation, and complete some of his philosophical arguments.

A major challenge for a project such as this is the sheer vastness of Sartre's oeuvre. It is estimated that Sartre produced twenty pages per day of his working life (Eshleman 2020: 1) and of all the pages he produced, most belong to his psychoanalytic biographies (Collins 1980: 5). The largest of these, *The Family Idiot*, nears three-thousand pages. This makes the task of offering a comprehensive and definitive study of Sartre's psychoanalytic work impossible. This book does not aim to do that. Rather, it strives to highlight how the development of his existential psychoanalysis can be fruitfully read as an expansion of his philosophical inquiry by focusing on one question: Does Sartre's existential psychoanalysis provide us with a special way of knowing other people? The answer to this question clearly has philosophical implications, especially if it is in the affirmative. If Sartre's existential psychoanalysis provides us with a route to knowledge of others that is surer or higher yielding than others, then it is of importance to epistemology. But if it provides us with 'new' knowledge – i.e. knowledge about others that cannot be gained through any other means and which we can only have now thanks to it – then it is of *major* importance to epistemology. It is also metaphysically important if this new knowledge tells us something about others' existence, that is to say, if it can speak to the longstanding philosophical conundrum known as the 'problem of other minds': the problem that it seems impossible to know anything about the mental states of other people, including whether they exist.

The key claim of this book is that Sartre's existential psychoanalysis does indeed speak to the problem of other minds, as it represents the second phase of his novel response to it. Further, it contends that Sartre's response to the problem of other minds solves it, albeit not on its original terms, by revolutionizing our way of thinking about 'selves' and presenting existential psychoanalysis as the means to make knowledge of our own selves and the selves of others possible for us. By so doing, the book integrates Sartre's existential psychoanalysis into his overarching philosophical project. It also highlights how his determination to solve the problem of other minds drives him not only to incorporate insights from René Descartes, G. W. F. Hegel, Edmund Husserl, Karl Marx, Sigmund Freud and Simone de Beauvoir into his existential philosophy, but also to supplement and enhance his work in the field of theoretical philosophy through the development and applications of an existential psychoanalysis that delivers knowledge of selves.

To begin with, Chapter 1 elucidates Sartre's theory of the self by clarifying his interpretation of the relationship between consciousness and the self in his first major philosophical work, *The Transcendence of the Ego*; analysing the important revisions he makes to his understanding of this relationship in *Being and Nothingness*; and indicating how these revisions impact his first efforts to establish the foundations of an existential psychoanalysis. It also explores how Sartre's existentialist understanding of the role of anguish, shame and self-deception in self-formation provides him with strong normative motivations for the development of an existential psychoanalysis. In the course of its exposition, the chapter argues that Sartre's 'non-egological' account of consciousness enables him to reconceive of the self as an object outside of consciousness, remove the metaphysical divisions that dominant philosophical conceptualizations of the consciousness-self relationship place between the self of one person and the self of another, and to present 'consciousness-object' and 'consciousness-self' relations as having the same form, which lays the foundation for his claim that it is possible to gain knowledge of other selves. Although the chapter delves quite deep into some of the more complex aspects of Sartre's thought concerning the constitution and the knowability of the self, no prior knowledge of Sartre's existentialism is presupposed and definitions of technical phenomenological and existential terms are supplied throughout so as to ensure that its content is accessible to psychological and psychoanalytical readers who may be unfamiliar with Sartrean existentialism, as well as philosophical readers who are well-versed in it.

Chapter 2 contends that Sartre's theory of the self in combination with his ontology, or theory of being, enables him to offer a novel solution to the problem of other minds. It argues that the first phase of this solution challenges the terms in which the traditional epistemological problem of other minds is set by showing that dominant concepts of 'mind' conflate two things that must be treated separately: consciousness and the self. Consciousness, for Sartre, is the being that is prior to knowledge and therefore beyond the scope of epistemology, whereas the self is an object that we can conceivably know things about and, therefore, within the scope of epistemology. Sartre's recognition of this distinction between consciousness and the self leads him to deny that there is any epistemological problem about other consciousness, although he accepts that there are two other problems about others: a conceptual problem about other consciousnesses and an epistemological one about other selves. The chapter shows how Sartre solves the conceptual problem and provides the first phase of his solution to the epistemological one in *Being and Nothingness*. Then, it explains how the second phase of this solution expands into his psychoanalytic studies, where he aims to demonstrate the possibility of gaining knowledge of other selves by applying the existential method of psychoanalysis outlined in *Being and Nothingness*.

Chapter 3 tracks how Sartre's development of dialectical reason informs the refinements he makes to his existential psychoanalysis after *Being and Nothingness*. It explains how his discovery of the dialectic brings his existentialism into a productive dialogue with Simone de Beauvoir's and enables him to synthesize his existentialist conception of the individual with a Marxist-Hegelian account of history. It shows how his theorization of a radically new way of making sense of human being in the *Critique of Dialectical Reason* leads him to make significant revisions to his existential conception of self-formation and to his psychoanalytic approach. Finally, it shows how Sartre developed his psychoanalysis after *Being and Nothingness* by considering his application of a provisional revision of it to Jean Genet in *Saint Genet* – a work that expands his philosophy by allowing him to synthesize aspects of Beauvoir's existentialism with his through an analysis of Genet's psychological oppression.

Chapter 4 turns to examine Sartre's most exhaustive application of his revised psychoanalytic method in *The Family Idiot*. It shows that this multi-volume work is designed to generate a reader-experience that he believes will enable the reader to comprehend its subject, Gustave Flaubert's behaviour and to use this comprehension to convert the biographical facts about him into knowledge of his self. It discusses Sartre's central claim that Flaubert gained a passive 'constitution' due to the way he was nursed in his infancy, which then becomes part of the 'situation' that he must respond to through making his self out of what it makes of him. Next, it summarizes the case that Sartre builds for the view that Flaubert's nervous attacks (generally attributed to epilepsy) are best understood as his neurotic response to his oppressive situation within the Flaubert family because they can be comprehended in terms of his choice of the imaginary – a choice that both 'saves' him by enabling him to go on living and stifles him by preventing him from becoming anything other than the family idiot in his reality. Finally, it considers how Sartre synthesizes a 'regressive' analysis with a 'progressive' one to interpret Flaubert's most celebrated novel, *Madame Bovary*, as an expression of his personal neurosis *and* a crystallization of the 'neurosis' of his entire class.

Chapter 5 addresses the important objection that the method of analysis employed in the first three volumes of *The Family Idiot* does not appear to be 'objective enough' to make good on its promise to deliver knowledge of Flaubert's self. It defends Sartre's progressive-regressive method of approach by showing that the psychoanalytical critique of *Madame Bovary* Sartre intended to supply in the missing fourth volume would have provided him with a valid means of confirming (or disconfirming) the findings of the first three, as it would have provided him with a means of checking his findings against something external to the dialectic he constructs in them. Then, it puts *The Family Idiot* to the test by using the clues Sartre left behind about his intentions for the fourth volume to provide a sketch of what a Sartrean reading of *Madame Bovary* would have been like, so as to assess the extent to which it could have confirmed the key findings of Sartre's study as it stands.

Then, Chapter 6 aims to clarify the role of the imagination in Sartre's project of gaining knowledge of a self. It shows how Sartre's theorization of the self as an imaginary, 'dialectical' object in the context of his mature existentialism motivates his use of author-centred literary criticism in his analysis of Flaubert, as well as his choice to present the findings of that analysis in the form of a 'true novel'. It explains how Sartre's use of the imagination in his attempts to gain and communicate knowledge of Flaubert's self does not contradict the theory of the imagination he defended in *The Imaginary* (1940), which denies that it is possible to gain knowledge through imagining. Further, it contends that *The Family Idiot* (1971–2) is aptly described as a sequel to *The Imaginary* on the grounds that the earlier work argues that the pathological preference for an imaginary life can be comprehended as a choice, and the later work aims to show that it can through its exposition of how Flaubert's choice to lead an imaginary life is 'incarnated' in his literary works.

Finally, the book closes with a consideration of 'The Future of Sartre's Existential Psychoanalysis' in Chapter 7. This chapter argues that integrating Sartre's development and applications of his existential psychoanalysis into his overarching philosophical 'treatment' of problems about selves and others not only enables us to interpret his oeuvre in a more productive way, but also points to the potential of Sartrean existential psychoanalysis to make valuable contributions to psychotherapy. But, rather than considering it alongside well-known existential psychotherapies, such as those developed by Irvin D. Yalom (1980), Rollo May (1983) and Emmy van Deurzen (2012), it aims to highlight the value that a specifically *Sartrean* form of existential psychotherapy can bring to psychotherapy as a result of its difference from these approaches, which draw eclectically upon the work of a range of thinkers historically categorized as 'existential' – a categorization that is problematic insofar as it emphasizes 'superficial similarities' between a diverse range of thinkers and overlooks many, often profound, disagreements between them (Webber 2018: 1). The chapter focuses on showing how Sartre's existentialism can offer therapists a rich, coherent psychological metatheory in which to ground their practice and it makes some specific suggestions about how a Sartrean approach can enhance integrative and electronically mediated psychotherapeutic practice. Then, it closes by indicating some fruitful avenues for further research that are opened by the new understanding of Sartre's existential psychoanalysis offered in this book.

A final word: Before we begin this investigation into Sartre's existential psychoanalysis, it should be noted that Sartre is not a trained psychoanalyst nor was he ever analysed by one.[2] Writing of his relation to psychoanalysis, he aptly describes himself as a 'critical fellow-traveller' (MT/HM: 199/1813). This book does not deem Sartre to have any more psychoanalytic authority than that of a deeply interested outsider, who strives to reach some of the same ends as traditional psychoanalysis by different means. That said, Sartre is a psychoanalytic outsider who is especially well placed to offer constructive criticism. Not only does the evidence suggest that he is the existentialist philosopher who demonstrated the most interest in psychoanalysis (Cannon 1991: 6), his existentialism is, as Simone de Beauvoir points out, an upshot of his fundamental interest in 'people' and his aim to 'replace the dry-as-dust analytical philosophy taught at the Sorbonne with a concrete, hence synthetic, *apprehension* of individuals' (1962: 42). So, Sartre is an existential philosopher who takes the task of comprehending people, in all their particularity, as his top priority. This book does not present Sartre as a psychoanalyst but as a philosopher whose lifelong search for a non-reductive way of understanding people led him to look to psychoanalysis for answers to questions about people that, he believes, philosophy does not have the tools to answer.

1

Sartre's theory of the self

Before beginning this inquiry into Sartre's psychoanalytic approach to gaining knowledge of others, it is vital to clarify what the object of such knowledge is. What exactly constitutes knowledge of another person? Put briefly, the answer to this question is knowledge of that person's 'self'. But this brief answer is unhelpful because Sartre's concept of self is peculiar, if not idiosyncratic. Moreover, his attempt to revolutionize our understanding of how the self can be known through existential psychoanalysis commences from a denial that the self exists in the way that it is generally presumed to. If we wish to appreciate Sartre's unique contribution to psychoanalysis, then it is necessary to gain a clear understanding of his theory of the self. To this end, this chapter clarifies Sartre's construal of the relationship between consciousness and the self in his early work, analyses the important revisions he makes to his understanding of this relationship in *Being and Nothingness*, and indicates how these revisions impact his first efforts to establish the foundations of an existential psychoanalysis.

The transcendent ego

At least since René Descartes identified himself with a 'thing which thinks' in his *Meditations on First Philosophy* ([1641] 1997: 142–7), philosophers in the West have tended to take a Cartesian concept of mind for granted in their attempts to understand the self[1] and so what may be called 'the standard model of the self' in the Western tradition makes four Cartesian assumptions: (1) we are each identical with the mind that is distinct from, but connected to, our body; (2) mental representations exist inside the mind; (3) mental representations are the primary objects of both knowledge and conscious experience; and (4) the subject of consciousness has exclusive access to their own mental representations. The standard model thus construes the self as a mental thing that the subject has direct access to *through being* identical with it. Consequently, the term 'self' is typically taken to refer to a subject of conscious experience, who exists in a private, mental realm, and consciousness is often regarded as the seat of the self in the philosophical literature.

Sartre, however, rejects the standard model of the self. One of his earliest and most enduring philosophical convictions is there is no self inside consciousness,[2] and his first major philosophical work, *The Transcendence of the Ego* (*La Transcendance de l'ego*, 1937), provides us with an alternative to the standard model of the self. This work is divided into two parts. The first part aims to refute the standard model of the self by targeting the version of it that Sartre finds preserved in Edmund Husserl's work. The second argues for the view that the self is, entirely, an object for consciousness that is constructed by consciousness. As Sartre's critique of Husserl's theorization of the consciousness-self relation supplies the theoretical groundwork for his own, let us commence our exposition of the Sartre's theory of the self from an analysis of what he finds problematic in Husserl's.

Sartre's ambivalence towards Husserl's work is apparent in the very first pages of *The Transcendence of the Ego*. To begin with the positives, he recognizes Husserl as the founder of phenomenology, the discipline that can grasp consciousness as an 'absolute fact' instead of approaching it as an abstract 'set of logical conditions' (TE: 4/18). He notes that the performance of a *phenomenological reduction* – interpreted as a special form of 'pure' reflection on just what is given to consciousness in a moment of its lived experience (*Erlebnis*)[3] – makes it possible for us to access and examine a 'real consciousness' (TE: 4/18). Finally, Sartre is also in agreement with Husserl on the point that a phenomenological study requires the performance of the phenomenological reduction known as the *epochē*, which involves the temporary suspension of all beliefs about the existence of objects beyond their immediate appearance.[4] The performance of the *epochē* is crucial for Husserl because he defines the phenomenological attitude as one that abandons the 'natural' attitude that presupposes existence of an 'objective spatio-temporal fact-world' that is '*there for us all, and to which we ourselves none the less belong*' (Husserl [1913] 2002: 55). The result is that 'the whole of the concrete life-word' is no longer apprehended by the phenomenologist as something that is objectively *there* but as 'a phenomenon of being' that is *there for them* (Husserl [1931] 1960: 19).

However, Sartre then goes on to charge Husserl with failing to be consistent in his application of the key phenomenological principle that '*all transcendence must fall under the scope of the epochē*' in his treatment of the ego (TE: 14/34).

To understand the nature of this charge, it is necessary to clarify the terminology employed. As Sarah Richmond (2004) observes, the terms 'transcendent' and 'transcendental' do not carry a Kantian sense in Sartre's usage but, rather, the phenomenological sense that Husserl describes them to have in §11 of his *Cartesian Mediations*. Here, the transcendent is presented as the correlate of the transcendental and this correlation is 'derived exclusively from *our* philosophically meditative situation' (Husserl [1931] 1960: 26), which is to say that these concepts are solely concerned with relations of consciousness. 'Transcendence' is a feature of 'anything worldly' that appears to consciousness and which also 'necessarily acquires all the sense determining it' from consciousness (Husserl [1931] 1960: 26). As such, transcendence is part of 'the intrinsic sense of the world' for consciousness and, as consciousness carries 'the world as an accepted sense' within itself and is, in turn, implied by this sense, consciousness is characterized as the 'transcendental' being that constitutes a meaningful world through its awareness of 'transcendent' objects (Husserl [1931] 1960: 26). When Sartre writes that '*all transcendence* must fall under the scope of the *epochē*', then, he means that anything constituted by consciousness must be excluded from a phenomenological conception of consciousness itself.

As Sartre sees it, Husserl's failure to exclude all transcendence (or constituted being) from his concept of the transcendental (or constituting) being of consciousness is evinced in his claim to have discovered a pure, 'transcendental ego' as a 'residuum' of the *epochē* and the phenomenological reduction in *Ideas: General Introduction to Pure Phenomenology* (*Ideen zu einer reinen Phänomenologie und phänomenologischen Philosophie. Erstes Buch: Allgemeine Einführung in die reine Phänomenologie*) ([1913] 2012: 112).[5] What Husserl purports to find at the end of the phenomenological reduction to a transcendental consciousness is a part of his self: an ego purified of the empirical subjectivity that belongs to the world, an ego that is *the subject* of his experience which he also *is*. Sartre objects to the notion that an ego is the subject of experience by pointing out that 'the consciousness that says "I think" is precisely not the consciousness that thinks' (TE: 10/23). He traces the tendency to posit the existence of a substantial subject of experience to Descartes' originary conflation of his (constituted) image of his self with his (constituting) consciousness, which led him to (mis)identify himself with a 'thing' that thinks, and he posits that Husserl makes the same basic error as Descartes.

Sartre believes that his phenomenological approach avoids this error by commencing not from the Cartesian *cogito* – i.e. the premise that 'I think' – but from what he calls the 'pseudo-"cogito"' (TE: 16/34) – a clear precursor to the 'pre-reflective *cogito*' he will later describe as the condition for the Cartesian *cogito* (BN/EN: 12/19). This pseudo-'cogito' represents an improvement of the Cartesian cogito for Sartre because it concentrates solely on what is given to pre-reflective thought and is, hence, minimally contaminated by the processes involved in reflection.[6] It facilitates a form of 'pure' reflection, which Sartre believes yields apodictic[7] evidence concerning the form of consciousness reflected on because it limits its scope to just what is given to consciousness in the immediacy of its lived experience. To illustrate the possibility of pure reflection, Sartre observes how somebody who yells 'I hate you!' to a friend in anger can always correct themselves by saying 'That's not true, I don't hate you, it was anger that made me say it' (TE: 23/48). These two statements articulate 'impure' and 'pure' reflections, respectively. The former is impure because it transforms the repulsive appearance of the friend in an experience inflected by anger into an enduring state of hatred. Rather than focusing solely on the object of pre-reflective experience – e.g. the friend who appears repulsive in the 'heat of the moment' – impure reflection abstracts from it to contemplate an enduring relation – hatred – between two objects – 'self' and 'friend'.

Although it might seem as though all conscious experiences are 'endowed with an I' (TE: 10/27), Sartre argues that this is only because consciousness usually engages in impure reflection, which retroactively inserts an 'I' into experiences and interprets this 'I' as the subject of them. But the 'sure and certain' evidence delivered by the pseudo-cogito attests to the absence of an ego at the primary, pre-reflective level of experience. When 'I' check my email, observe one of Rothko's red canvases, run to catch a bus, for example, all that I am is consciousness of emails-awaiting-reply, of vibrating-hues-of-red, of the bus-to-be-caught. This brings Sartre to a 'non-egological' concept of consciousness which affirms that consciousness lacks an ego in its most primary form. It is only when consciousness engages in a reflective contemplation of the relation between itself (considered as an object) and (another) object that the 'I' appears. Then, I say to myself that 'I' am checking 'my emails', 'I' am observing 'this painting', 'I' am running to catch 'that bus' and so on. While there is an I-subject in these reflective experiences, it is on the 'object side' of the consciousness-object relation because it is what consciousness is contemplating, not the consciousness doing the contemplating. Here lie the grounds for Sartre's claim that phenomenological reflection on strictly what is given to pre-reflective consciousness shows that the ego ought not to be treated as part of the structure of consciousness and so Husserl's 'privileged treatment' of the self can only be explained by 'metaphysical or critical preoccupations that have nothing to do with phenomenology' (TE: 14/34). What is more, Sartre also maintains that Husserl's incorporation of an ego into his concept of consciousness refuses one of the most important implications of his discovery of the 'intentionality',[8] which is that consciousness is, fundamentally, a pure, pragmatic engagement with objects in the world.[9]

Sartre is nevertheless convinced of the existence of a personal, 'psychical and psycho-physical *me*' (TE: 4/18), which Husserl identifies as the 'empirical subjectivity' that cannot survive the phenomenological reduction to a transcendental consciousness because it belongs to the world (Husserl [1913] 2012: 112). For both Sartre and Husserl, this empirical subjectivity is an occasional, transcendent object for consciousness, not an essential feature of it. What Sartre takes issue with is the notion that there is *another* part of the self that survives the phenomenological reduction in virtue of being integral to consciousness. He questions the idea that we need to combine the empirical, transcendent self with a transcendental ego when his phenomenological investigations show the field of lived experience to be an impersonal one that only becomes personal upon reflection. As 'the *I* is not given as a concrete moment', he affirms that it cannot be 'of the same nature as transcendental consciousness' (TE: 14/35).

Thus, despite being deeply inspired by Husserl's phenomenology Sartre's own phenomenological approach departs from Husserl's in a way that enables it to sustain a comprehension of consciousness as an unmediated, impersonal apprehension of its objects. Husserl's and Sartre's different conceptions of the phenomenological reduction and what it is supposed to achieve,[10] along with the fact that Sartre seems to read Husserl's transcendental ego to be more substantial than Husserl describes it,[11] make it difficult to assess the success of Sartre's refutation of Husserl's concept of the transcendental ego in any definitive way. What is clear, though, is that through his departure from the phenomenology of Husserl, Sartre breaks with a long tradition of treating consciousness as inhabited by a thinking thing and begins to radically reconceive of the relation of consciousness to the self.

A sense of selfness

Against Sartre's non-egological view of consciousness, it may be contested that even if phenomenological reflection indicates that there is no ego in consciousness, a transcendental ego is the only thing that could explain a key phenomenal feature of consciousness: the sense of 'selfness' that results from the way that experiences are apprehended as part of a unified stream and also have a first-personal character – i.e. a sense of all its objects as 'mine' or appearing 'for me'. This is not a Kantian *a priori* claim that it must be possible for an 'I think' to accompany all our thoughts, which Sartre denies has any bearing on his inquiry into the *de facto* structures of consciousness (TE: 2–4/13–18). It is the empirico-inductive claim that the only thing that could give all our experiences a sense of selfness is a transcendental ego. Although Husserl discovers a transcendental ego within the phenomenological attitude rather than offering it as an explanation for why consciousness is the way it is, his conception of the transcendental ego as a 'glance' that unifies the stream of consciousness through the preservation of its own identity (Husserl [1913] 2012: 111) can clearly serve this function. It can provide consciousness with something that is both 'prior to presences' and unaffected by them, which can act as its stable core (Breeur 2001: 193).

At first glance, Sartre's non-egological view seems incapable of explaining how consciousness could be unified and 'mine' for each of us. However, in a passage that cites Husserl's theory of retention approvingly, Sartre writes that 'consciousness that unifies itself, concretely, by an interplay of "transversal" consciousnesses that are real, concrete *retentions* of past consciousnesses' (TE: 6/22, emphasis added). For Husserl, retention 'constitutes the living horizon of the now' through its preservation of that which is 'just past' (Husserl [1913] 2002: 117). It explains how consciousness can stretch across time to grasp the whole of a temporally extended object such as a melody through the retention of the previous moment, and the one before it, extending all the way back to the start of the melody. In this manner, the whole melody can be perceived even though 'only the now-point actually is' (Husserl [1913] 2002: 114). For Sartre, retention also explains how consciousness can be unified as it moves from one object to the next, so that 'consciousness' refers to a unified movement rather than a series of discrete object-consciousnesses. The unity of consciousness through retention is a consequence of its intentionality in Sartre's view, as the movement of consciousness from one object to the next is not arbitrary but driven by the significance consciousness sees in the objects on the horizon of its experience, which is determined by the meaning of the objects that preceded it that consciousness retains through the sense it perceives in the present object. Every object refers to all those that preceded it, and the past guides consciousness's movement towards the future in the present. Hence, we do not need to posit the existence of an immanent ego to account for the unified character of consciousness in Sartre's view.

Sartre could also explain the 'mineness' of consciousness as an upshot of intentionality. He could, for instance, say that while the same object might be the object of two different consciousnesses, it cannot have the same meaning for both because its meaning is partly determined by the past and each consciousness has its own distinct past. But he makes a much stronger claim than this; he holds that each consciousness 'constitutes a synthetic, individual totality, completely isolated from other totalities of the same kind' (TE: 7/23), which implies that the 'mineness' of consciousness is guaranteed by the nature of consciousness itself and is not contingent upon its capacity for retention, which could be compromised. But what, if not an immanent ego, could individuate consciousness in this way? Kenneth Williford strives to clarify Sartre's grounds for this claim by interpreting the individuality of the Sartrean consciousness as a result of its 'non-positional' consciousness of itself, or what he calls the 'self-manifestation of the stream' (2011: 203). The non-positional consciousness of consciousness is precisely what distinguishes it from its object on Sartre's account; it is consciousness's tacit awareness that it is separate from its object and it is 'not *positional*' because 'consciousness is not its own object' (TE: 8/24). So, Williford's proposal is that the non-positional consciousness that consciousness always has of itself also bestows upon its object the character of being 'mine'. If correct, this would justify Sartre's view that no two consciousnesses are ever the same; it would mean that even if two people suffering from transient global amnesia were suspended in a sensory deprivation tank and made to watch the same video, through the same kind of video-playing goggles, at the same time, their consciousnesses would not be 'the same' for the duration of the video as each would experience the video as appearing *for it* and would, therefore, have an experience that is *its own*.

However, there does not appear to be any feature of a non-egological consciousness that could make it non-positionally conscious of itself in the first place. If my consciousness is nothing but an empty movement towards its object, what could make the object of my experience 'manifestly mine' if not for retention or the fact that it is given to 'me', a subject who pre-exists it? Dan Zahavi holds that Sartre is unable to provide a satisfactory response to this question. He contends that while (pre-reflective) consciousness may be described as a 'non-egological' field, it cannot also be described as a non-'egocentric' one because to have an experience in the first-personal mode of presentation is to have an experience in which 'self-awareness' is built into the 'giveness' of the object of experience, so that the object is given as an object of *my* experience (2000: 64).

Sartre does not directly address this concern in *The Transcendence of the Ego*. He does, however, suggest that consciousness's psychical ego or 'I' has a distinct presence to it, which is unlike that of any object and which is also distinct from that of the self-as-object or the 'me'. Further, he writes that the 'psycho-physical *me* is a synthetic enrichment of the psychical Ego' (TE: 28), which suggests that the ego is more basic than the 'me' that only exists as a positional object for reflective consciousness. However, this idea problematizes Sartre's claim that the 'I' and the 'me' are merely 'two faces' of the same, transcendent ego (TE: 20/43). Being and appearance seem to come apart in the case of the ego in a way that they do not for self-as-object, for which 'to be' and 'to appear' are the same thing. For instance, Sartre explains that the ego does not disappear when we are not positionally conscious of it by drawing an analogy between the ego and the 'World', understood as 'the infinite synthetic totality of all things' (TE: 30/58). The World is always *there* for us; it is always on the horizon of the objects of our experience and all the objects around us 'appear merely as the extreme point of that world which surpasses them and envelopes them' (TE: 30/58). Similarly, Sartre submits, the ego is also always *there* for us and is 'to psychical objects what the World is to things' (TE: 30/58). But, while 'the appearance of the World in the background of things is quite rare', the ego 'always appears on the horizon of states' (TE: 31/58). Further, each of our states and actions are given as being attached to the ego and only separable from it by abstraction. Even if one manages to detach the 'I' from a state through a judgement such as 'I am in love', this separation can only be temporary for Sartre because it would have no meaning if the ego and the state were not synthesized in the movement of consciousness – through, for example, *attending* lovingly to the object of one's affection, *loving* their laugh, eyes, etc. (TE: 31/58).

Thus, Williford is right to suggest that the ego grants the Sartrean consciousness a 'unity and stability' by supplying it with a sense of continual presence (2011: 209). It seems that it is only due to the constant, horizonal presence of the ego that Sartre can present the mineness of experience as something built-in to experience itself. And yet, the notion that the ego is always *there* for consciousness appears to contradict Sartre's non-egological view because it indicates that the ego is necessary for consciousness to be the way that it is. In his attempt to avoid this problem, Sartre affirms that the ego *qua* transcendent totality 'participates in the dubious character of all transcendence' and that it is 'a *dubious* object' because it is 'the spontaneous transcendent unification of our states and our actions' and, hence, always subject to change (TE: 31/59). But it is, rather, Sartre's insistence that the ego is an object here that seems dubious.

The kind of constant, creative, unbounded presence that he attributes to the ego means that it cannot be aptly characterized as 'objectual' at all since objects are, by definition, passive, determinate beings, with clear boundaries, separate from other objects. What makes the object status of the Sartrean ego dubious, then, is its perpetual presence 'in' consciousness – albeit it as an object on the periphery of consciousness – since an impersonal, perpetual presence is what characterizes the Husserlian transcendental ego that Sartre's account of the self seeks to 'transcend'.[12]

Commentators have recognized that the characterization of the ego as an object in *The Transcendence of the Ego* is inapt. Vincent de Coorebyter observes that Sartre's ego is comparable to an object in the respect that it is an intentional object for reflective consciousness and a concrete existent because it is transcendent, but he emphasizes that its concreteness is borrowed because it synthesizes lived experiences to 'give itself a *real* pole of intentionality' (2020: 33). It approaches object status in Coorebyter's view, but it cannot be accurately portrayed as an object among other objects because it has no substance of its own. Accordingly, he reads Sartre to correct himself on this point when he refers to the ego as a 'quasi object' in *Notebooks for an Ethics*. Phyllis Berdt Kenevan also sees reason to deny Sartre's ego full object status. As she interprets it as 'a personalized account of the primary [impersonal] upsurge viewed as "object"', she maintains that can only be regarded as a 'pseudo-object' (1981: 201). For both Coorebyter and Kenevan, the Sartrean ego cannot be neatly classified as an object because it has no substance of its own and its lack of substance is only made into something substantial by an impure consciousness. However, this does not go far enough; it is not enough to say that Sartre's ego is not truly or fully an object because it not only lacks a substance that objects have, it also has a presence that objects lack and which we tend to associate with consciousness itself.

Kenevan attempts to explain how the Sartrean ego could possess this quality of presence while remaining transcendent. She suggests that we should not take Sartre's denial that there is a substantial self to entail the denial of what she calls a 'self-in-progress'. Although he affirms that there is no substantial self within or behind consciousness, Kenevan argues that there is still 'a self-as-temporal-process of which we are non-positionally conscious with every act of positional consciousness' (1981: 200). Or, put differently, there is a non-objectual process that creates the self, which we are constantly aware of, regardless of what the positional object of our consciousness is, and it is on account of this awareness that ego is perpetually present to consciousness without being 'in' consciousness. Provisionally at least, Kenevan's reading enables us to posit the ego as the pseudo-object of self-consciousness that does not disappear when it is not the positional object of consciousness. However, Kenevan shows that this solution to the problem that Sartre's transcendent ego seems to have a transcendental quality creates issues for other aspects of his existentialist theory. Significantly, it presents a challenge for the notion that consciousness can become 'authentic' by apprehending the true nature of its being as a freedom in 'anguish' (*angoisse*)[13] because it makes it difficult to identify the agent of choice and insight in anguish. It cannot be located in the ego, which is a pseudo-object and, hence, passive, not active. Nor can it be located in consciousness, which is impersonal and only conscious of itself in a non-positional, background way. Anguish thus poses a serious problem for Sartre because it seems to imply the presence of an agent and a subject of self-knowledge in consciousness, when he insists that consciousness can contain neither and that consciousness can only gain knowledge of itself by reflecting on itself as an object.[14] To resolve this problem in Sartre's terms, it seems as though we have to postulate the presence of two consciousnesses in anguish because anguish-consciousness appears to be positionally conscious of two different aspects of itself in two different ways: it is consciousness aware of itself as a consciousness that contemplates itself as an object that it is not.

If the self that is the object of positional self-consciousness is regarded as 'the indirect unity of consciousness in *temporal dispersion*', Kenevan notes that the ego emerges as a 'process self' and the problem of two separate consciousnesses ought not arise, as the consciousness that reflects on its (past) self is conscious *of* its self-as-object without being *one* with it. This is the case in ordinary, impure reflection where the self-in-progress becomes objectified in the self when it is reflected on. The problem of two consciousnesses arises in the context of anguish because it is the result of pure reflection, through which consciousness grasps the truth of its being as an always incomplete unity-in-progress that lacks self-identity. For Kenevan, this indicates that the form consciousness takes in anguish is irreducible to 'consciousness of a transcendent object' as it is conscious of itself as a transcendental consciousness and a self-in-progress, which is not identical with the self-as-object but responsible for it nevertheless. Her proposed solution to the problem of two consciousnesses is to suggest that there are not two consciousnesses here, but two kinds of intentionality operating within the same consciousness. This would mean that there is 'not only a positional intention of objects other than consciousness' in anguish but also, simultaneously, 'an *at*tention to the self that *in*tends objects' (1981: 206). Splitting intentionality in two directions in this way would, according to Kenevan, enable Sartre to construe the sudden revelation of a self-in-progress through pure reflection as the apprehension of freedom in anguish while avoiding the problem of two consciousnesses.

Such attention-intention-split is, as Kenevan notes, largely consistent with what Sartre says about the anguish and pure reflection insofar as it would demand a powerful and unsustainable concentration, which could only take the form of a 'momentary apprehension' in a healthy consciousness (Kenevan 1981: 206, cf. TE: 46–9/79–84). But it is wholly inconsistent with what he says about intentionality, both in *The Transcendence of the Ego* and elsewhere. Sartre's concept of intentionality goes far beyond Husserl's original, which denotes the essential character of consciousness as a being that is 'of' or 'about' something in virtue of existing as an 'intentional' relation or a directedness towards an object (Husserl [1913] 2002: 82). In Sartre's hands, intentionality also implies that consciousness is dependent on its objects for its own existence (BN/EN: 20–4/26–9).[15] In *The Transcendence of the Ego*, he gestures towards this view through his affirmation that everything 'in' consciousness is 'clear and lucid' because the object of consciousness always opposes consciousness 'in its characteristic opacity' (TE: 7–8/24). The thought here is that consciousness must be entirely 'non-substantial' and free of any opacity if it is to exist as a transcendental movement towards objects that transcend it. Further, if part of it were to turn back towards itself, this part would be cut off from all transcendence. This would create closed loop and, hence, a kernel of opacity within consciousness, which would amount to the 'death' of consciousness as a transcendental movement in Sartre's view (TE: 7/23); it would make consciousness *be* something else besides consciousness of an object. A Sartrean consciousness could not therefore be divided between 'intending' its object and 'attending' to itself in the way that Kenevan suggests.

Be that as it may, Kenevan is certainly correct to observe that some modification of the theorization of the consciousness-self relation in *The Transcendence of the Ego* is required to account for anguish as the basis for authenticity since the revelation that characterizes anguish seems to entail a profound kind of self-awareness that exceeds the non-positional consciousness of consciousness. If anguish must involve such an awareness, without compromising the integrity or the intentionality of the Sartrean consciousness, though, the modification needs to target Sartre's conception of the self, not his conception of consciousness.[16]

The constitution of the ego

One of the principal aims of *The Transcendence of the Ego* is to show that the self's appearance of being 'one' with consciousness is an illusion that results from the way it is constituted. To fully comprehend Sartre's initial conception of the relation of consciousness to its self in anguish, it is vital to examine his account of its constitution in the second part of *The Transcendence of the Ego*. In the first part, Sartre tells us that the ego is an ideal, as opposed to a perceptual, object and that the nature of its existence is distinct from that of other ideal objects such as 'mathematical truths' and 'meanings', but he maintains that it is 'just as real' as they are because it is given to us as transcendent (TE: 15–16/36). The ego is real because it has a concrete presence for us, even though, as Coorebyter reminds us, its concreteness is 'borrowed' from the lived experiences that reflective consciousness objectifies and, subsequently, makes into the substance of the ego (2020: 133). But how exactly does this process work? How does consciousness unify aspects of its lived experience and, thereby, bring an ego into existence without knowing that it is doing so?

To begin with, it is crucial to note that 'states and actions' are aspects of lived experience that Sartre takes to be unified in the self (TE: 39/69). He uses the term 'states' to denote transcendent objects that are produced by impure reflections on particular features of instantaneous consciousness. For example, I may take the affect of tenderness that accompanies the present appearance of my cat for an enduring state of love if it prompts me to say to myself 'Gosh, I really do love that cat'. 'Actions' facilitate the transcendence of consciousness in the present, but the actions that form the self are transcendent objects since that is what actions become the moment they are reflected on: my act of running yesterday, for instance, is an object for my reflective consciousness now. Although Sartre sometimes omits the term 'qualities' from his summations of what is unified in the ego (TE: 30, 39/57, 69), he regards qualities as optional unities of states that may also be constituents of the self. When they are incorporated into the self, qualities are apprehended as inherent dispositions and potentialities that are expressed through 'failings, virtues, tastes, talents, tendencies, instincts, etc.' (TE: 28/54).

If the ego is nothing other than the unification of these kinds of transcendent objects produced by consciousness in the reflective mode, though, how can it possibly appear to be *the subject* of consciousness? Sartre explains the deceptive appearance of the ego as the effect of a special kind of impure reflection that is made possible by the horizonal presence of the ego in all experience. This reflective process is described by Sartre as 'magical' because it inverts the logical and ontological order of the relations between consciousness and the ego (O'Shiel 2019: 13–18). For the ego to appear to consciousness as a subject who precedes all the transcendent objects that constitute it, he believes that consciousness must apprehend its states and actions through a 'magical procession' (TE: 33/61), which presents the process of self-formation as running 'in *completely the reverse direction* from that followed by real production' (TE: 34/63). The aim of this procession is to return the spontaneity of consciousness to it '*represented and hypostatized*' in the object it calls 'I' (TE: 35/63). In other words, the aim of this magic is to make the spontaneity of consciousness 'disappear'. And being bewitched by this magic is precisely what Sartre believes makes it possible for us to deny the truth of our being as a spontaneous consciousness and buy into the idea that the nature of the self is fixed in advance by external factors such as unconscious drives, evolutionary biology or a Divine Creator. Moreover, by playing this kind of magic trick on itself, consciousness appears to be guilty of precisely the kind of existential dishonesty that Sartre will later call 'bad faith' (*mauvaise foi*) in *Being and Nothingness* (*L'Être et le néant*, 1943). But it is unhelpful to read Sartre's early account of the constitution of the ego anachronistically through the lens of his later conceptual framework, not only because the revisions that Sartre makes to his theory of the self during the late 1930s and early 1940s turn out to be foundational to the concept of bad faith (as the next two sections explain), but also because viewing the ego of *The Transcendence of the Ego* as constituted in an attitude of bad faith distracts us from the central importance of the illusion of a stable self for psychological wellbeing that Sartre is keen to emphasize in this work. This can be brought out by attending to the fact that the attitude that Sartre associates with the constitution of the ego here is the natural attitude.

While it may be tempting to classify the appearance of the self as 'a typical illusion of the natural attitude' as Coorebyter does (2020: 136), this oversimplifies Sartre's position since he does not merely indicate that the appearance of the ego is an effect of the natural attitude, he construes it as a core component of the natural attitude in the course of his attempt to show that an important advantage of his account of the ego is that it can provide a motivation for the phenomenological *epochē*. He begins by pointing out that the natural attitude is 'perfectly coherent' (TE: 49/83), lacking the kind of contradictions that might push a philosopher to enact a radical conversion of their stance towards the world, and so the appearance of the *epochē* in Husserl's phenomenology has a miraculous air. Once we recognize the natural attitude as an upshot of consciousness's ongoing but ultimately futile effort to conceal its spontaneity from itself, though, Sartre argues that the *epochē* no longer seems like a miracle. For if consciousness continually projects itself 'into' an object-like image of itself, and if it merely takes a simple act of reflection for consciousness to apprehend itself as a spontaneity that is separate from this image, then the *epochē* is a manifestation of anguish. It is, at once, 'a pure event of transcendental origin and an accident that is always possible in our daily lives' (TE: 49/84). The permanent possibility of apprehending our ontological truth in anguish therefore gives us a reason to suspend the 'natural' view that we each exist in the world as a thinking thing among things because it reveals this view to rest upon the false assumption that we *are* thinking things.

The idea that the reality of world we experience in the natural attitude hinges on an image of ourselves as thinking-things-in-the-world, which we construct in an attempt to flee from our 'monstrous spontaneity' (TE: 44/80), explains why Sartre regards anguish as both the motivation for the *epochē* and a factor in the precipitation of certain psychopathologies such as 'psychasthenia' (TE: 47/80). Borrowing from Pierre Janet's *Les Névroses*, he illustrates the connection he sees between phenomenology and psychopathology through his discussion of a young bride who suffers from a terror that if she is left alone in her house, she will call out to passers-by on the street like a prostitute. He interprets this woman to suffer from a 'vertigo of possibility' because the source of her distress is her recognition that she *could do* precisely the thing she is terrified of doing as there is no virtue inscribed in her being, no internal constraint, that would bar her from doing it if she chose to. Instead of attributing the fear of this young bride to a cognitive dysfunction or disorder, Sartre maintains that it results from the 'fear of oneself' that constitutes a 'pure consciousness' in anguish (TE: 49/83); that is, he presents her distress as a consequence of *lucidity* not lunacy. She becomes ill, in his view, because she apprehends the truth of her ontological structure without having the means to cope with this truth. Although he does not specify what could enable her to cope with this truth, his proposal that anguish lies at the heart of her malady suggests that a more robust sense of self could have mitigated the distress that her existential revelation caused her, or perhaps even prevented her from having this revelation in the first place.

The illusory appearance of the ego thus turns out to have a protective function for Sartre; it may be regarded as 'a life jacket that keeps us from sinking into the depths of our own possibility' (Flynn 2014: 75). By bringing everything that individuates us together at the surface-level of our experience and, at the same time, concealing an oceanic emptiness that we cannot countenance, it shields us from apprehending our freedom in anguish, at least most of the time. In Sartre's words, it is

> exactly as if consciousness constituted the Ego as a false representation of itself, as if consciousness hypnotized itself before this Ego which it has constituted, became absorbed in it, as if it made the Ego its safeguard and its law: it is, indeed, thanks to the Ego, that a distinction can be drawn between the possible and the real, between appearance and being, between what is willed and what is yielded to.
> (TE: 48/82)

This passage illuminates the deep connection Sartre makes between the constitution of the ego and the 'sense of reality'.[17] Not only does he believe that we lose the reassuring sense of being one with ourselves in anguish, he also believes that it causes the divisions that structure our sense of the world as a modal space in which we can act to break down too. So, while he upholds that the 'natural' way that we conceive of ourselves in our everyday lives is based on a deception that misrepresents the existential facts of our condition, he nevertheless regards this deception as what enables us to experience ourselves as belonging to the world and to 'get on' with the process of self-formation through action in that world. Hence, *The Transcendence of the Ego* concludes that the ego is constituted through an inherently deceptive process without which human life would be unliveable.

However, we have already seen that this conclusion spells disaster for Sartre's initial attempt to account for the possibility of authenticity. It also puts the possibility of self-knowledge into question, for it is extremely difficult to understand how one could acquire knowledge of an ego that is constituted through an inherently deceptive process. And what would the object of such knowledge be anyway? Would it be the quasi-object that only falsely appears to be the subject of consciousness, or would it be the true self-in-progress which Sartre insists cannot be an object? Some clues about the answers to these questions may be found in his reasons for rejecting the view that the subject has privileged epistemic access to their ego (TE: 38–9/68–9). He proposes that since the 'me', or the objective face of the ego, is given as an object in the world, it is the only part of the ego that can be known. Also, he insists that the only way to gain knowledge of it is through objective methods: empirical observation, constructing and testing hypotheses, and so on. But because the subject is intimately familiar with the other, subjective face of the ego, these methods, 'which are perfectly suitable for the entire domain of the *non-intimate* transcendent' (TE: 38/68), are unreliable for a subject seeking self-knowledge. The term 'intimacy' here refers to the illusory sense that the ego is '*part of consciousness*' (TE: 37/67), which blinds us to our primary ignorance of it. The intimacy of each of us to our ego represents a positive, unavoidable obstacle to self-knowledge for Sartre because even when we try to examine our self objectively, by viewing it from a distance, it always accompanies us in our attempt to withdraw from it; it will always be the 'I' who is reflecting on the 'me'. If we wish to know ourselves well then, he recommends that we enlist the help of others and try, as best as we can, to examine ourselves from another point of view. Nonetheless, he affirms that this point of view 'is necessarily false' because it is another's (TE: 38/69). This can only mean that because the perspective that delivers the ego as an object of knowledge is one that necessarily excludes the subject's lived awareness of the ego, it can only deliver knowledge of the ego that may be objectively accurate but false because it misrepresents the ego as a 'pure' object in the world.

All this renders true self-knowledge impossible in the context of Sartre's initial theory of the self. Either we can gain knowledge of the self as an object from a foreign perspective that does not have access to its subjective face and therefore misrepresents it, or we can gain a true awareness of the ego as a self-in-progress, which cannot be knowledge since the self-in-progress is irreducible to an object of knowledge. Furthermore, this account of how the ego is constituted and how it is known generates a paradox. It implies that someone who is incapable of unifying their states and actions through the kind of magical, impure reflection that constitutes the ego – say, someone in a permanent state of anguish – would not have an ego. However, others would still be able to know this person in just the same way as they know other people who do have egos, through observation, etc. So, this gives us a non-existent ego that possesses an objective face that can be known.

The evolution of the Sartrean self

Sartre drops the concept of the ego as a constant, horizontal presence to consciousness in *Being and Nothingness*, where he only speaks of different 'ekstases' or modes of consciousness and the 'self', understood as the part of consciousness that can be observed. This self does not have a subjective face that is hidden from others. It is not a pseudo-object that unifies reflections on lived experience; it is a composite object that unifies a person's actions in the world. As such, Sartre's revised concept of the self has been purged of the presence that seemed to bestow a transcendental quality upon the ego. What is more, self-knowledge need no longer be posited as 'false' knowledge from a perspective that is incapable of apprehending the true nature of its object, since the self is an object that is entirely separate from, and 'outside' of, the process that constitutes it.

Even this cursory summary of the major change Sartre makes to his theory of the self between *The Transcendence of the Ego* and *Being and Nothingness* helps us to see how his revised theory makes knowledge of selves feasible. But before we can assess this feature of it, we must address the problem that it raises the question of how consciousness can have a sense of selfness once more. How can this self appear to be the stable core of our being if it is nothing more than an ideal object that disappears as soon as we cease to attend to it? We have seen that in *The Transcendence of The Ego* Sartre construes the intimate relation consciousness has to its self as a function of the perpetual presence of the subjective face of the ego on the horizon of experience. But what could supply consciousness with a sense of selfness in the absence of this?

In *Being and Nothingness*, Sartre explains that the emergence of the self is the upshot of a contingent social relation: 'the Look' (*le regard*). He illustrates this relation with a vignette of a jealous lover peeping through a keyhole in a hotel corridor. This may be considered a form of eidetic reduction through the exploration of a paradigmatic case (Flynn 2014: 207) since, through being narrated in the first-person, it invites you (the reader) to imagine that you are peeping through a keyhole because you suspect that your beloved is in the room on the other side with someone else. In striving to see the spectacle 'to be seen' and to hear the conversation 'to be heard' on the far side of the door, you *are* 'a pure relation to the instrument (the keyhole)' to these ends (BN/EN: 355/298). Your consciousness is fully absorbed in a 'situation' that reflects both your facticity – the objective facts concerning your body and surroundings – and your freedom – your chosen relation to these facts – which, together, make the whole scene meaningful for you: the fact of the door obstructing the view of 'the spectacle' is what makes the keyhole appear to you as 'the instrument'. While you are engaged in the activity of peeping, you *live* your jealousy, but you do not *know* it; your self is absent from the scene. Everything changes the instant you hear footsteps, though. This sound makes you suddenly aware of the spectacle you make on the near side of the door for any passer-by who might see you assuming such a compromising posture. You realize that you must look like some kind of pervert! And *voila*, you have discovered your *self* through shame.

Without divesting 'shame' (*honte*) of its emotional connotations, Sartre uses it in a technical way to refer to the primary form of our being-for-others (*être-pour-autrui*): the form consciousness takes when it apprehends its self as being *that* object which the 'Other' – i.e. another consciousness – is looking at, judging. This means that the self appears to consciousness as having already been constituted as an object by the Other who sees it from outside. The body is therefore apprehended as what others see of us, and it replaces the subjective face of the ego in supplying the terrain on which the magical procession that produces the self advances. The body becomes the 'ultimate magical object' for Sartre (BN/EN: 468/391) because it is the perpetual, observable 'outside' of our most intimate 'inside', which gives it a special function in his theory of self-formation as the physical object that stands for the self. This function of the body explains why Sartre designates it with the three ontological dimensions he does. First, it is a being-for-itself, which is not '*joined*' with consciousness but which is consciousness 'in its entirety' (BN/EN: 412/344). This is the body that is *lived* as my situation. Second, the body is a *body-for-others*, which may be characterized as the 'biographical' dimension of the body; it is the one in which the self is constituted because it is only through the body-for-others that consciousness realizes itself – albeit always incompletely – as an object in the world for others. In this dimension, the body is 'the ultimate psychological object' (BN/EN: 463/387) and it is through it that consciousness apprehends its 'life' and its 'character' (BN: 459–62/384–6, 465–8/389–91). Third, the body is a (non-psychological) *object-being-for-others*, in the dimension in which consciousness is most alienated from its own being. Here, the body is given as if it is a being apart from consciousness: it appears as 'an organism' or an object of science. It is no surprise that this dimension of the body is most apparent in the context of illness, as Sartre's example of a stomach ulcer illustrates. The 'pain "in the stomach" *is* the stomach itself, in so far as it is painfully lived' (BN/EN: 473/396), but the knowledge that this pain is due to a stomach ulcer is discovered only through others' knowledge of human anatomy, the symptoms of stomach ulcers in general, etc. When I undergo treatment for my stomach ulcer, Sartre writes that both 'stomach' and 'ulcer' become 'perspectives of alienation of the object I possess' (BN/EN: 474/396); I experience my body 'designated as *a thing outside my subjectivity*, in the midst of a world which is not mine' (BN/EN: 470/393).

Situated in between the chapter that analyses the significance of the Look ('The Other's Existence') and the one that analyses interpersonal relations ('Concrete Relations with the Other'), Sartre's phenomenological analysis of the body and the different ways that it can be present to consciousness bolsters his view that the illusory appearance of the body as the 'container' for the self is key to understanding what, according to him, is the most peculiar feature of the self: its tendency to be mistaken for a subjective being that animates the body from the 'inside' when, really, it is an object that unifies all the acts of the body from a perspective that is 'outside' of the body. Moreover, it enables Sartre to offer a more satisfactory account of the connection between non-positional consciousness of consciousness and the self. Some of the remarks he makes about the body in *The Transcendence of the Ego* do, however, anticipate the key role Sartre will later assign to it in structuring consciousness's relation to the world and to the self. For example, it is suggested that the reason why fluid switches from positional consciousness of an object (and non-positional consciousness of consciousness) to positional consciousness of self are always possible – i.e. why I can always easily respond to questions such as 'What are you doing?' with an answer that begins with 'I am' – is because the body 'acts as a visible and tangible symbol for the I' (TE: 41/72). This certainly hints at an awareness of one's embodied situation *vis-à-vis* the object of one's consciousness in the here and now *is* non-positional consciousness of consciousness – a view that Sartre later explicitly endorses when he affirms that consciousness is the body and that non-positional consciousness *is* 'consciousness (of) the body as what it surmounts and nihilates in making itself consciousness' (BN/EN: 442/369).

Attending more closely to the body, therefore, enables Sartre to offer a coherent and compelling account of the self as an object constructed in the mode of being-for-others, which provides consciousness with an image of its objective being by unifying the objectively observable aspects of its being. The shift from a conception of consciousness as being haunted by an ego to a richer appreciation of the necessity for consciousness to *be* a body dissolves the tension between the ego as a private presence and the ego as a public object that we observed in *The Transcendence of the Ego*, as a body is capable of being 'lived' and 'looked at', simultaneously, but only the body 'looked at' contributes to the constitution of the self. Another advantage of this shift is that Sartre need no longer trace the individuality and the 'mineness' of experience to presence of a dubious ego-object because the fact that consciousness is a body, situated in a specific place, means that, for consciousness, 'to be is to-be-there' (BN/EN: 332): *there* at this desk, *there* on the top of that hill, *there* at the table next to the window in *Les Deux Magots*, etc. The possibility of one consciousness being either qualitatively or quantitatively identical with another is therefore ruled out as a direct consequence of embodied nature of consciousness. Further, Sartre can now identify the body as the feature of consciousness that makes it non-positionally conscious of itself in the first place, as the situatedness of the body gives consciousness a specific point of view, which gives all experience its first-personal character. As consciousness is always situated somewhere, all its objects are given to it as standing in a particular relation to it, which incorporates a sense of separation and difference into them, so that they appear as being 'within arm's reach', 'beneath my feet', 'around the corner', 'up above', 'in my mind's eye', etc. According to Sartre's (revised) theory of the self, then, it is because my body is my perspective on the world that all objects appear as being the way that they are *for me* and all my experience is manifestly *mine*.

But what about the problem of authenticity? Understanding the lived body as non-positional consciousness of consciousness does not resolve the issue that there seem to be two consciousnesses in the experience of anguish. However, I submit that Sartre's revised conception of the relation of consciousness to its self does. This is due to Sartre's explicit theorization of consciousness as a 'nothingness', which enables him to affirm that consciousness is not just *not* identical with the self it makes it the world; it is *nothing* at all in-itself. Hence, the only real manifestation of consciousness is in the self which it is not, and so the self-awareness that characterizes consciousness in anguish is the apprehension of 'not being' the self. Or, if you like, anguish is the 'manifestation of the freedom it confronts' in and through the apprehension of its self as an object that it is separated from 'by a nothingness' (BN/EN: 73/70). As such, the form consciousness takes in anguish is that of an 'internal negation',[18] which is the same form consciousness always takes: it is consciousness (positionally) conscious of an object and (non-positionally) conscious of itself in its difference from that object. It is not that the non-positional awareness of consciousness is cognitive, but that the way that the self is given – i.e. in the form of a negation – is apparent to a pure consciousness reflecting on its self in anguish when it is ordinarily concealed in impure reflection. Anguish is a consciousness troubled not by a second consciousness that knows the nature of its being, or by a split between intending its self and attending to itself, but by its (non-positional) awareness that *it is not* its self – the same awareness that it has of all its objects – which is troubling in this context because consciousness presumes that *it is* its self most of the time.

Anguish, shame and self-deception

We have just seen how from the early 1940s onward, Sartre regards the self as a product of a social interaction, rather than an attempt to flee from anguish. This change has important implications for his understanding of the role of self-formation not just in masking freedom and contingency from consciousness, but also – and more importantly for our concerns – in the precipitation of psychological illness. So, let us now clarify the nature of this change by considering the relation of anguish to shame and self-deception.

Simply put, 'bad faith' is a form of self-deception that Sartre believes mediates our relation to others, the world and our selves. Such pivotal significance is assigned to the role of bad faith in structuring human experience in *Being and Nothingness* that this work may be regarded as a treatise on bad faith.[19] Although there is vast amount of secondary literature devoted to the topic of bad faith,[20] scholars continually point out that it remains rather poorly understood (Manser 1987; Eshleman 2008a; Levy 2020) and there has been much contention over issues such as whether bad faith is avoidable (Rorty 1972; Solomon 2006; Horton 2017) and how it should be theorized in relation to sociality (Stone 1981; Santoni 1995, 2008; Bernasconi 2006; Eshelman 2008a, 2008b; Webber 2011). Studies on the role of bad faith in self-formation are, however, surprisingly scant.[21] Rather than attempt to offer an exhaustive analysis of bad faith here, I aim to outline the function of bad faith within Sartre's (revised) theory of self-formation in this section, before establishing how it can modulate a subject's self-formation in the next, so as to gain a clearer sense of how bad faith can represent an obstacle for authentic self-formation, self-knowledge and psychological wellbeing.

First, it is vital to note that bad faith is initially defined as an attitude in which one attempts to flee from anguish. As anguish is a consciousness aware of its freedom through its awareness of its difference from its self, it is, evidently, not something that one can truly flee from. To the contrary, Sartre writes that one must 'constantly think about it' to ensure that one is not thinking about it (BN/EN: 84/79). Hence, the attempt to flee anguish in bad faith *is* anguish in the mode of fleeing from itself (BN/EN: 86/80). Although bad faith is a form of deception, it cannot function like a lie whereby one person deceives another through exploiting their ignorance about the truth of a given state of affairs because it occurs within the unity of a single consciousness, which means that consciousness cannot but be aware of what it seeks to hide from itself. To pull off its deception, Sartre tells us that bad faith must engage consciousness in a complex and ongoing project of distracting itself from attending to something it is already aware of, and that it must generate a '*Weltanschauung*' (worldview) that simultaneously supports and shrouds this project by structuring the whole of a subject's experience and reflection so as to trap the subject in bad faith, like a dreamer who cannot wake up without some external disturbance (BN/EN: 114/103).

The waiter in the café is, undoubtedly, the most famous example of Sartrean bad faith. The waiter is portrayed as being in bad faith because he tries to *make believe* that he *is* a waiter in the same way that a pencil *is* a pencil. His movements are rather too rapid, too precise, and he walks as though he is trying to 'imitate the inflexible exactitude of some kind of automaton, while carrying his try with the recklessness characteristic of a tight-rope walker' (BN/EN: 102/94). Through these actions, he aims to '*actualize*' (*réaliser*) his current, contingent situation as a waiter in a café as a fact of his being (BN: 103/94).[22] Whenever I discuss this example with students, it always inspires a lively debate. Questions about whether the waiter needs to be in bad faith to do his job well invariably arise, along with imaginative proposals about how his behaviour might change were he to suddenly apprehend his freedom *not to be* a waiter in anguish, which include freezing, gleefully hurling plates at the wall, giving the customers a piece of his mind, and running out of the café. But the very idea that the waiter's behaviour would have to be different were he not in a state of bad faith is hinged on what, to my mind, is a far too simplistic opposition between bad faith and authenticity – albeit one that is perfectly understandable given the location of this example at the very beginning of *Being and Nothingness* (Pt. I, Ch. 2), shortly after bad faith has been defined in relation to anguish.[23] As Sartre switches from a third-person description of the behaviour 'the waiter in the café' to a first-person analysis of his thoughts – e.g. 'it is precisely this person that *I have to be* and that I am not' (BN/EN: 103/94–5) – in the course of narrating this example, Jonathan Webber is right to maintain that the waiter need not be in bad faith to behave in the way that he does because whether he is in bad faith depends not on what he does, but on the attitude he takes towards it (2011: 184–5). This has two key implications. First, whether someone is in bad faith is not something that can be discovered through observations of their behaviour alone. Second, we can perform our social roles perfectly well without being in bad faith, as we can truly 'play' at being them while being cognisant of the fact that they do not define us. We can therefore be authentic without constantly being in anguish through a pre-reflective engagement with the world in the natural attitude, which enables us to respond to the exigencies of our day-to-day lives in a practical manner, but which should not be conflated with the attitude of bad faith since it only requires us to 'suspend' thoughts about the nature of our existence, not to deceive ourselves about it.[24]

At the time he wrote *The Transcendence of the Ego*, Sartre had not yet developed the concept of bad faith. In that work, it appears as though the process of self-formation is the sole means by which consciousness can escape from a crippling state of anguish. It seems as though there are only two options for consciousness: truth, anguish, and psychopathology *or* deception, a stable self-concept, and an ability to function in the world. In *Being and Nothingness*, though, Sartre separates self-deception from the process of self-formation so that self-deception about the nature of one's existence is no longer a condition for the possibility of the existence of the self. We do not need to be in bad faith for the self to appear in our experience, we only need to have experienced the Look. The experience of anguish, however, remains a condition for authenticity since we have to be aware of our condition in order to accept it. So, it follows that the possession of a concept of self emerges a condition for the possibility of anguish since we have to be aware of what we are objectively – i.e. a self-object – in order to realize that we are irreducible to that. This means that shame, a concept that is not introduced until Part III of *Being and Nothingness*, is ontologically prior to anguish, a concept discussed in the first chapter of Part I, because it is only in and through shame that I can conceive of myself as an object for another. The discovery of the self as an object in shame is a prerequisite for the revelation that one is irreducible to that object in anguish and the denial of the true nature of one's relation to that object in bad faith.[25] Thus, not only is it the case that bad faith is 'necessarily social' (Eshleman 2008b), anguish is too, and Sartre's whole phenomenological ontology turns out to be rooted in a deep appreciation of humankind's radical sociality. 'I need the Other to fully grasp all the structures of my being' (BN/EN: 309/260–1), and I also need the Other *to be* the complex kind of being that a human being is – one that is not just capable of experiencing anguish and shame, but which is structured by these experiences in the most fundamental way. Even though the interpersonal relation that generates the concept of the self is posited by Sartre as a contingent one, it lies at the very core of the human condition he analyses in his magnum opus. And, given his concentration on the way bad faith can mediate our relations in that work, it is reasonable to suppose that he views bad faith to have the potential to play an important role in self-formation. Once we recognize that the self is a product of human sociality for Sartre, the fact that all the concrete interpersonal relations examined in *Being and Nothingness* are rooted in a conflict wherein each consciousness strives to deny the true nature of their relation to the other in bad faith,[26] it is apparent that bad faith has the potential to inflect the relations that have a formative influence on us.

Being and Nothingness is, however, an essay on phenomenological ontology. Although it underlines the potential of Sartre's ontology to enhance both the accuracy and efficacy of psychoanalysis, it also affirms that psychoanalysis must commence from the point at which ontology 'abandons us' (BN/EN: 796/662). This explains the absence of any extended vignettes or case studies geared specifically towards illustrating how bad faith can modulate an individual's self-formation in that work: this sort of psychoanalytical investigation is, quite simply, beyond its scope.[27] Nevertheless, we may look to the literary and psychoanalytical works Sartre wrote around the same time as *Being and Nothingness* to gain a sense of his views about how bad faith can influence self-formation as these works give him scope to explore the effects of bad faith in the context of a life.

Bad faith and self-formation

For anyone interested in a Sartrean portrayal of a life shaped by bad faith, the short story *The Childhood of a Leader* (*L'Enfance d'un chef*, 1939) is most illuminating. It narrates Lucien Fleurier's conversion to an attitude of 'seriousness', a form of bad faith that involves interpreting values as facts that are independent of human subjectivity. The story is psychoanalytical in the classical sense insofar as it traces Lucien's development from infancy and emphasizes his relationship with his mother, his early discovery of his ambivalence towards her, and the distress this causes him. But it also anticipates Sartre's existential psychoanalysis because it prioritizes Lucian's response to his early existential awakening over the maternal relationship in shaping who he eventually becomes. In an early scene that sets the stage for the rest of the piece, young Lucian is shown to be experiencing the anguish of not knowing who he will be and, at the same time, making the discovery that he does not 'exist' in the way that things do; 'all I have to do', he thinks to himself, 'is plug my ears and not think about anything and I'll become a nothingness' (CL/EC: 154/334). From this point on, he looks for strategies for coping with this revelation, but he does not want to cope with it so much as forget that he ever had it and 'go back to sleep' (CL/EC: 154/334).

Notably, Lucien embraces Freudian theory as a coping strategy. The discovery of the unconscious is a welcome one for him as it enables him to attribute his existential troubles to a cause. The finding that he can interpret his 'strange feeling of not existing', the 'emptiness in his conscience, his somnolence, his perplexities, his vain efforts to know himself which met only a curtain of fog' as evidence that he has 'a complex' (CL/EC: 161/339), releases him from the worry that his intuition that he lacks a fixed character contains some fundamental truth about his being. He can now feel assured that a 'true Lucien' exists, even if he is 'deeply buried in his subconscious' (CL/EC: 161/339). Lucien's endorsement of psychoanalytic theory represents an important phase on his journey towards seriousness as it provides him with some relief from anguish and normalizes his mixed feelings towards his mother, although it ultimately proves unsatisfactory as a strategy of bad faith for him because it puts self-knowledge out of his reach. By positing that the subject must continually work to discover who they are through, for example, searching their experience and dreams for expressions of their unconscious, psychoanalysis deprives Lucien of the kind of 'metaphysical comfort' he desires: that of knowing who he is in advance.

Eventually, though, becoming a member of a right-wing political party and an anti-Semite provides Lucien with the peace of mind and the self-assurance he believes he needs to become a leader when he succeeds his father as the owner of a factory. He completes his journey to seriousness shortly after a party at which the host, Guigard, introduces him to a Jewish friend and, instead of shaking hands with the Jew, he thrusts his hands in his pockets and leaves. What is significant about Sartre's recount of this scene is that it reveals his behaviour to be motivated by his reflections on what a fellow party member had said about him based on his previous anti-Semitic behaviour, not ideological fervour. After he leaves the party, Lucien worries that he may have insulted Guigard, but his last traces of self-doubt are swept away the next day at school when Guigard apologizes to him. Lucien then responds 'generously' by saying, 'I was wrong too. I acted like a rotter. But what do you except – it's stronger than I am. I can't stand them – it's physical. I feel as though they have scales on their hands' (CL/EC: 214/383). This 'sorry, but ...' formula is telling in a few respects. First, what follows the 'but' excuses Lucien from the wrong he has just apologized for. It relieves Lucien of any responsibility for his wrongful behaviour because it presents his hatred for Jews as 'stronger' than he is and as something 'physical' that he has no control over. Nonetheless, we (the readers) know that Lucien is in bad faith because we have insight into his psychological state immediately prior to the act in question; we know that he was under no compulsion to act the way he did and that he could have done otherwise.

After receiving Guigard's apology, Lucien experiences an extraordinary sense of delight because it seems to him that he is no longer an empty, troubled consciousness; he is 'Somebody who can't stand Jews' (CL/EC: 216/385). In a word, he manages to make believe that he has become identical with his self. What is more, because he undertakes this pretence in seriousness, he feels as though he simply responds to the values he perceives in the world and, in light of these values, he feels confident that his 'innate' anti-Semitism is something 'sacred' (CL/EC: 217/385), which makes him superior to others. Although Lucien discovers that his 'real self' is to be found in the eyes of others, which from a Sartrean perspective is true, he makes believe that he can know himself, immediately, by seeing himself reflected in 'the frightened obedience' of others, 'the hopeful waiting of all those beings who grew and ripened for him', the 'young apprentices who would become *his* workers', etc. (CL/EC: 217/386), which is, of course, false from a Sartrean perspective.[28] The tale concludes with Lucien identifying with his vision of himself as a person whose destiny to rule over others was marked out for him 'long before his birth' and who has a 'right to exit', even if others do not (CL/EC: 218–19/387).

At the end of the story, Sartre describes Lucien's conversion to seriousness as a 'metamorphosis' (CL/EC: 219–20). As Sartre was a great admirer of Franz Kafka, I believe that the allusion to Kafka's depiction of Gregor Samsa's transformation from a man into an enormous, revolting insect in *The Metamorphosis* (*Die Verwandlung*, 1915) is intended. Indeed, Sartre seems to use it to mock Lucien, who no longer feels like a 'big, bloated bug' (CL/EC: 215/384) but a very important person. This is because seriousness represents the most problematic form of bad faith from an ethical perspective, and Simone de Beauvoir even ranks the serious man among the 'sub-men' in the existential ethical system she develops (EA/MA: 42/56).[29] Through his conversion to seriousness, then, Lucien becomes something less-than-human for the existentialist, although, unlike Gregor Samsa, he is to blame for his diminished status. This interpretation finds further confirmation in the very last line of the story in which Lucian looks in the mirror, observes that his countenance is not quite terrible enough, and resolves to grow a moustache because Lucien's future moustache is reminiscent of another moustache in Sartre's fiction. In a memorable scene from *Nausea* (*La Nausée*), the hero, Antoine Roquentin, is shown to detect a lack of (human) existence in the 'fine gentleman' whom he believes does not feel the burden of his existence in the way that he does. Of this 'fine gentleman', Roquentin makes the following observation:

> he exists Legion of honour, exists moustache, that's all; how happy one must be to be nothing more than a Legion of Honour and a moustache and nobody sees the rest, he sees two pointed ends of moustache on either side of his nose; I do not think therefore I am a moustache ... He has a Legion of Honour, the Bastards have a right to exit.
>
> ([1938] 1965/1981: 147/121)

The connection drawn between the moustache and the 'right to exist' in these two works indicates that the moustache has symbolic significance for Sartre as marker of the 'respectable' bourgeois male, whose bad faith and inflated sense of his own self-importance blind him to his existential emptiness.[30]

Clearly, then, the form of bad faith Lucien adopts makes him a bad person from an existential ethical perspective. When considered as an example of how bad faith can modulate a subject's self-formation, *The Childhood of a Leader* highlights how bad faith can be deployed by an individual to construct a false self-concept that obscures the ontological truth of his being. Although it is almost certain that he will derive great comfort from this, it mutilates him in his very being in Sartre's estimation. The serious person makes believe that they know who they are and what their purpose is *in advance* at the cost of stagnating – i.e. of ceasing to grow through stiving to become something that they are not (yet). Lucien's seriousness therefore prevents him from fully engaging with the fundamental human project of 'becoming' or what we might call 'authentic self-formation'. But does it also make him ill? Not according to the standards used to assess psychological health in his society.

However, it should be noted that, in *Being and Nothingness*, Sartre states that he believes seriousness 'reigns over the world' (BN/EN: 810/674) and also affirms that a principal goal of existential psychoanalysis is that of leading 'us', as a society, to 'abandon the spirit of seriousness' (BN/EN: 809/674). This shows that he regards the ability to engage in authentic self-formation as essential for the health of a human *being*, understood as an embodied consciousness. When coupled with the view that bad faith is a widespread phenomenon that can inhibit authentic self-formation, we can see how this supplies the early Sartre with a normative motivation for his attempt to establish the foundations for an existential psychoanalysis that can cure people of bad faith. The species of bad faith he calls seriousness is, at least, a sickness on his account because it projects values into objects 'in order escape from anguish' by obscuring the human goals that are true source of all values in the world (BN/EN: 810/674). Seriousness leads people to pursue being blindly by concealing the freely chosen projects that are really guiding them in this pursuit, which results in them relinquishing some of the control they have over their self-formation by experiencing themselves as 'passive' in the face of objects and events that they could change. Thus, I submit that, for Sartre, Lucien represents the picture of (male) health in a society that is sick because its norms and standards are a product of collective bad faith and which, also, tend to promote bad faith among its members who must find a way to live in it.

The idea that Sartre views bad faith as an attitude that can prevent authentic self-formation finds further support in his first psychoanalytic study, *Baudelaire* (1946), which interprets Charles Baudelaire's dandyism as a self-imposed trap that stymies his personal growth. (Sartre's) Baudelaire inflicts 'minute, finicky rules on himself primarily in order to put the brake on his bottomless freedom' and his rigid adherence to them distracts him from attending to 'his own inner gulf' (B: 133/124). His pursuit of the project of *being* a dandy meant that his 'psychic becoming could only take the form of incessantly *working on himself*' (B: 136/126); it inhibited his movement towards *becoming* something other than he was because it demanded him to continually scrutinize and reproduce his self-as-object – i.e. his past. Rather than embracing his existence as a self-in-progress, he continually strives to reiterate his past self in a vain effort to apprehend the fullness of a fixed, thing-like being in himself. Significantly, Baudelaire's bad faith prevents him from achieving authentic self-formation in Sartre's view, but it does not prevent him from achieving greatness. Indeed, Sartre suggests that it may have even helped him create outstanding art since his many 'strict and useless rules' enabled to develop exceptional skills in self-restraint and to concentrate his energies on his work (B: 134/125). Despite being a celebrated person in his society, though, Sartre contends that Baudelaire suffered in his very being because he concentrated his energies on the goal of self-possession instead of self-production. In the final analysis, then, Sartre interprets Baudelaire's existentially maladaptive bad faith to resemble Lucien's insofar as it expresses itself through behaviours that are 'adaptive' in his socio-cultural context.

From the way that Sartre depicts bad faith modulating self-formation in these early works, we can see that his conception of psychological health deviates significantly from standard medical and psychoanalytic ones which prioritize the subject's ability to function in their social milieu. By calling attention to the existential sickness of 'high-functioning' individuals such as Lucien and Baudelaire, he gestures towards the idea that we, as a society, need to radically revise our conception of health. Moreover, these two early attempts to explore the effects of bad faith of self-formation point to a key distinction between a self-concept that is forged in bad faith and the 'real' self for Sartre.[31] Both of them contrast the subject's self-concept with what 'we' (Sartre and his readers) know about him through observing him from another point of view: Lucien's final concept of himself as a born leader is contradicted by our comprehension of him as someone who chooses to be a racist and a bully so that he can make believe that his existence is 'justified', and Baudelaire's concept of himself as someone whose sensitive soul singles him out for membership in the artistic elite is revealed to us as part of the cover he tried to pull over his freedom. Without denying the subjective truth of these individuals' self-concepts, Sartre's contrasts between how they conceive of themselves and what we know about them demonstrate why individuals' self-concepts cannot be taken for self-knowledge on his account: they do not necessarily result from the kind of careful, objective analysis that could deliver knowledge of a self.

The possibility of self-knowledge

The very first paragraph of *The Transcendence of the Ego* states that 'the Ego is a being in the world, like the Ego of another' (TE: 1/13) and – the revisions to his theory of the self notwithstanding – Sartre remains committed to the view that there is no difference between the fundamental structure of my reflections on my self and my reflections on another person's self. In both cases, my consciousness is conscious of a self that it is not. But does it follow from the ontological equivalence that there are no epistemological differences between my reflections on my self and my reflections on another person's self?

One reason that might be offered in support of the view that the subject stands in an epistemically privileged position with regard to their own self, which also seems *prima facie* compatible with Sartre's theory of the self, is that the subject is the person who is 'closest' to their self and, therefore, the person who is best-placed, proximally, to acquire knowledge of it through the ordinary routes – i.e. observation and analysis. However, the challenge that the subject's intimate relation to the self presents for self-knowledge neutralizes any epistemic advantage that may result from the subject's proximity to the self, as the body as it is seen from the outside is mysterious to the subject who lives it 'from the inside'. Although it is right to expect that being intimately acquainted with the object one seeks knowledge of would put one in epistemically advantageous position, what we are intimately acquainted with through the lived body on Sartre's account is not the self that others see 'in' our body but, precisely, the aspect of our being that can neither be seen and nor known: our experience, which is a nothingness. Thus, our intimate acquaintance with the lived body is not an intimate acquaintance with the object of self-knowledge.

Further, there is not only an ontological gap between consciousness and the self on Sartre's account, there is also a temporal gap. He describes the constant striving of consciousness to overcome this gap as a circuit of selfness (*circuit de l'ipséité*) (BN/EN: 159/139), which communicates the view that consciousness experiences the self as a moving target that is always behind it in time. Like a dog chasing its tail, consciousness must constantly turn back to discover its self.

But it can never fully grasp it because the act of reflection that makes the self appear for it is another act through which consciousness transcends and changes its self. This inability of consciousness to unite with its self – to become what it is – through reflection motivates Sartre's recommendation that Descartes' memorable phrase, *cogito ergo sum* (I think therefore I am), be reformulated as 'I think, therefore I was' (BN/EN: 178/154). Self-knowledge necessarily excludes knowledge of what one is now (becoming) in his view because the process of self-formation requires consciousness to be its self in the mode of fleeing from it, and self-reflection is but another way of fleeing from the self through trying to grasp it.

Thus, we can see that there is an epistemological difference between my reflections on my own self and my reflections of the self of another person in Sartre's view. The difference is that the former are *less reliable* than the latter. The Sartrean subject therefore stands in an epistemically disadvantaged position with regard to their self. We are each better placed to know others than ourselves because we can see others from the outside and we can analyse them objectively from a distance. However difficult it may be to gain self-knowledge in practice, though, Sartre assures us that it is possible since the self can be known by others, and others' knowledge can become a 'knowledge-object' for us (BN/EN: 455/381).

An important objection to Sartre's view that it is only possible to acquire self-knowledge by studying the self objectively comes from an unlikely source: Richard Moran's influential and avowedly Sartre-inspired account of self-knowledge in *Authority and Estrangement: An Essay on Self-Knowledge*. Here, Moran proposes that our first-person access to our own thought processes about what to do and believe provides each of us with an exclusive claim to authoritative self-knowledge, which explains the intuition that the way that we know ourselves is different from the way that we know others, as well as our expectation that people can gain immediate insights into their self even if they lack the sort of justification that we would ordinarily expect to accompany knowledge claims. Another attractive feature of Moran's view is that it can account for why the inability to respond to questions concerning one's own intentions, beliefs and feelings immediately and without having to consider empirical evidence is often a good indication that there is something wrong. In the absence of something wrong, Moran argues that subjects can generate beliefs about themselves that are authoritative because they have the quality of 'transparency'. A belief is transparent, according to Moran, when it appears to be true from the subject's first-person perspective. So, a person's response to the question 'Do I believe that *p*?' is transparent if she can arrive at it simply by directing herself to the question of whether *p* is true. If somebody can only respond to this question by reviewing her past behaviours, statements, etc., then assessing whether she has justification for attributing that belief to herself, Moran argues that transparency has failed.

Moran's discussion of examples of transparency failure in cases of *akrasia* (weakness of will), repression and self-deception points to a link between an impaired capacity for generating transparent beliefs and interpersonal conflict. Notably, he offers his own interpretation of Sartre's example of an akratic gambler who has resolved to quit gambling (BN/EN: 70–7/67–70) as an illustration of exactly how interpersonal conflict can cause transparency to fail. The akratic gambler is, he argues, committed to the truth of his decision to quit gambling because he knows that this is what he has resolved to do. Still, the gambler cannot affirm in all confidence that he will quit gambling because he also knows that he has a long track-record of reneging on this kind of commitment. On the one hand, then, the gambler knows that the strength of his determination to avoid the bookmaker's shop provides him with theoretical grounds for the expectation that he will in fact do so. On the other, he regards this 'purely theoretical' point of view of his resolution 'as an ungrounded, inconstant thing on which to base any confidence about what he will in fact do' (2001: 79). Moran argues that we cannot attend to all the epistemically salient features of the akratic gambler's situation if we treat his inability to avow that he will quit gambling separately from his report of his will to do so since this will lead us to overlook the crucial point that, ordinarily, avowals and reports run together.

While the mere capacity to report marries with traditional understandings of a 'purely epistemic capacity', Moran contends that the capacity to avow is what gives ordinary self-knowledge its characteristic authority and immediacy; it is what enables subjects to declare for themselves without having to make any observations (2001: 91).[32] Accordingly, he takes the separation of these two capacities in the gambler's case to highlight two possible routes to knowledge of the self: the 'avowal route' and the 'empirical route'. The former is the way to ordinary, authoritative self-knowledge. It is immediate, and it allows the subject to bypass the longer, less reliable empirical route. The need to take the empirical route to gain knowledge of the self usually indicates that something has gone wrong for the subject epistemically, according to Moran. Although he acknowledges that this epistemic problem is unlikely to capture all that has gone wrong for the subject in such cases, he believes that it shows that at least part of what is wrong is that transparency has failed and that the ordinary route to self-knowledge is barred for them.

But what characterizes the knowledge acquired through the avowal route? If we consider what it is, in isolation from the route to it, there do not seem to be sufficient epistemic grounds for viewing it as a distinct form of knowledge. Even if we grant that it is transparent to the subject who possesses it, transparency is a feature of the subject's *experience* of knowledge, not of the knowledge itself. For if ordinary self-knowledge is to be a *sui generis* form of knowledge as Moran proposes, it must be irreducible to propositional knowledge about the self. Otherwise, it is simply propositional knowledge, acquired in a special way. Although Moran does not offer a sustained account of the positive epistemic features of self-knowledge,[33] it is apparent that one thing that makes it distinct from propositional knowledge for him is that it is both propositional and agential. It is propositional because it is knowledge 'about' the self and agential because it is arrived at via the avowal route, which Moran presents as a 'knowing' and a 'becoming' at once because he interprets avowal as a reflective act that also contributes to the ongoing formation of the self. The thought is that, even if the propositional content of my self-knowledge and another's knowledge of me is the same, my knowledge is authoritative in a way theirs is not, in virtue of also being agential or self-shaping and this is what makes ordinary self-knowledge irreducible to propositional knowledge.

We now can see that Sartre would object to Moran's account of self-knowledge on the grounds that it joins together what his phenomenological ontology pulls apart: being and knowing. For Sartre, agential being and knowledge exist on two incommunicable levels: the first on the pre-reflective plane in which consciousness 'is' a direct, pragmatic engagement with an object, and the second on the reflective plane in which it 'contemplates' an object. No knowledge whatsoever can be acquired *through being* on his account since knowledge is always a product of reflective thought *about* objects, which is ontologically secondary to the pre-reflective thought that *is* consciousness of them. Hence, his claim that 'to know one believes is to believe no longer' (BN/EN: 115/104). By the same logic, to avow what one believes is no longer to know it, for an avowal is not act that could yield knowledge but, rather, a pre-reflective act that articulates an idea delivered by a previous reflective act. There is no ontological distinction between an avowal and a report from a Sartrean perspective since both are acts that articulate a thought gained through reflective processes. And, so long as the content of an avowal and a report is the same, they are also epistemically indistinct.

Although Moran's account of self-knowledge may be regarded as 'Sartrean' insofar as it emphasizes the point that there is a 'self-transforming aspect to a person's reflections on his own state' (2001: 59), it does not preserve Sartre's ontological insight that knowledge may be realized, affirmed and communicated by avowing, but never gained 'through' it. This, to my mind, means that a significant advantage of Sartre's account of self-knowledge over Moran's is that it is rooted in a robust phenomenological ontology that draws a clear distinction between the relations of being and the relations of knowledge. Moran might defend his departure from Sartre's ontological foundations by contending that there is no way to account for how people can be authorities on their own decisions unless they can gain ordinary self-knowledge in the way that he proposes. He may, for instance, note that if I avow my decision about what to do in the presence of another, 'I do indeed provide him with a reason to expect something, a very good reason if I'm not too vacillating, or a liar; but what I possess myself is not an expectation, based on evidence, but an intention, based on a decision' (2001: 56). While it is obviously true that I alone can announce my intention in a way that is based upon my own reflective deliberation about what to do, it is mistaken to take my ability to announce my intention for evidence of my having self-knowledge 'in advance' since whether I will act on my intention necessarily eludes my knowledge. An intention announces a subject's commitment to doing something, but it does not close off the possibility of them doing something else. Indeed, this is the central message of Sartre's original discussion of the akratic gambler, which presents the gambler's problem as 'anguish in the face of the past' (BN/EN: 70/67). What troubles Sartre's gambler is that his earlier resolution to quit gambling remains 'there' for him, but only as part of his past, and he recognizes that it has no hold over him now. His problem is not that he lacks self-knowledge, but that he sees all too clearly the truth of his condition. His previous good resolution haunts him because *he knows* that is part of who he is in the mode of 'not-being' it now; he suffers because he is keenly aware of the fact that there is nothing that can be known about his past that will determine what he will do in the future.

The difference between Sartre's and Moran's treatment of the akratic gambler is telling. It allows us to see that Sartre's rejection of the primacy of knowledge is not 'merely theoretical' because he views it as a condition for understanding both the ontological structures of being and the concrete behaviour of individual human beings. His analysis of the akratic gambler shows that he too can account for what has gone wrong when a person is impaired in his capacity to declare for himself, but it also indicates that it is not possible to get to the root of what is wrong in these cases by remaining at the level of 'ordinary' knowledge. For Sartre, the akratic gambler has an existential problem, not an epistemic one: he knows that he has committed to quit gambling and what distresses him is his awareness that his past commitment does not bind him. From a Sartrean perspective, then, Moran's epistemic treatment of the akratic gambler is distortive: by lumping the agential and epistemic aspects of the gambler's akrasia together, it overlooks the crucial point that the akratic gambler is tormented by the fact that he cannot gain self-knowledge 'in advance'. Consequently, it fails to appreciate that the kind of knowledge that could help the gambler deal with his situation is not the same knowledge he already has (of his commitment), gained via the avowal route,[34] but knowledge that unifies his conflicted feelings about gambling at a deeper level; reveals the role of his agency in their generation; and enables him to accept what he is, who he can be and what he can never know. Far from being 'ordinary', though, such knowledge is an extraordinary achievement, one which Sartre believes his existential psychoanalysis makes possible.

2

Knowledge of selves

The previous chapter examined the rationale for Sartre's non-egological view of the self, which supplies the basis for his existential understanding of consciousness as being whose existence 'precedes' its essence (BN/EN: 737/613) because it holds that consciousness can only acquire an essence through *becoming* something – namely, a self. Thus, Sartre's existentialism radically reconceives of the consciousness-self relation in a way that has major implications for the extent to which we can know ourselves and others, implications which he explores through the development of his existential psychoanalysis.

Now, although psychoanalysis is, first and foremost, a clinical discipline that aims to cure psychological illness, it is also a methodological approach to the study of an individual's psychology because it aims to cure *through* the provision of self-knowledge in a therapeutic setting. More specifically, it works to supply the individual with insight into the source of their psychological distress, the cognitive resources to conceptualize it and the support they require to work through the distress it causes them. The potential of psychoanalysis to deliver new insights into human psychology greatly intrigued Sartre as a philosopher; yet, the philosophic significance of his psychoanalytical studies tends to be neglected by philosophers.[1]

The central aims of this chapter are to highlight how Sartre's interest in psychoanalysis intersects with his chief concerns as an existentialist philosopher and to show that his psychoanalytical work is best understood as an extension of his philosophical work. It contends that Sartre's development of an existential psychoanalysis represents the second phase of his novel solution to the conundrum about other minds that has long troubled philosophers. It explains that first phase of his solution aims to show that it is possible to acquire knowledge of other 'selves' in theory, and the second aims to show how it is possible in practice. The first phase is contained within *Being and Nothingness*, but the second extends far beyond it, into Sartre's later works, which refine and apply his existential psychoanalysis. While the first phase is well-researched, the second is not. As a consequence of this, I believe that Sartre's response to the problem of other minds has yet to be appreciated in its entirety and the philosophical import of his existential psychoanalysis has been largely overlooked because it has not been viewed as part of his philosophical enterprise.

The problem of other minds

How do we know that other people are not mindless zombies?[2] This is a popular way to introduce philosophy students to the problem of other minds. The question is intriguing, and the stakes are high. If you cannot provide a satisfactory answer to it, then you cannot reject solipsism: the view that you are the only being in the universe who has mental states such as thoughts, feelings and beliefs (hard solipsism) or that you cannot rule out the possibility that you might be (soft solipsism or 'other minds scepticism'). Solipsism is generally thought to be intolerable,[3] but we lack sufficient evidence to refute it conclusively. This is the traditional epistemological problem of other minds.

In the nineteenth and twentieth centuries, there have been two basic kinds of philosophical response to this problem in the Western tradition. The first is to start from one's own mind and to assess what is it possible to know about other minds from the first-person perspective. A paradigmatic example of this kind of response is the argument from analogy, which was also the 'standard' philosophical response to the problem of other minds in Anglophone philosophy up until the middle of the twentieth century.[4] Although it can be traced back to David Hume ([1739–40] 2000: 206–11), it finds its paradigmatic formulation in John Stuart Mill's *An Examination of Sir William Hamilton's Philosophy*, where the following justification is offered for the claim that others have minds: 'First, they have bodies like me, which I know in my own case, to be the antecedent condition of feelings; and because, secondly, they exhibit the acts, and outward signs, which in my own case I know by experience to be caused by feelings' ([1865] 1872: 243). This pithy passage exhibits all the definitive features of an argument from analogy: it affirms we each have direct knowledge of our own mental states through experience; it observes that we express at least some of these through actions, gestures, facial expressions, etc., which make them observable from the outside; it observes that others have a physical constitution and expressive repertoire that resembles ours; then, from these observations, it concludes that others must also have mental states.

By commencing from the first-person perspective, the argument from analogy acknowledges the subject-other asymmetry with respect to knowledge of minds that both shapes our experience of others and lies at the heart of the epistemological problem of other minds.[5] As I write this sentence, for example, I experience flow of my thoughts about what to write next, the texture of the keys beneath my fingertips, the sound they make as my fingers meet them, and so on. But I do not have such insight into other people's experience. I can observe the motions of another person typing but I cannot gain knowledge of their thoughts and feelings by so doing; I can only make guesses about them based on my observations. The recognition of this subject-other asymmetry as an experiential fact, combined with a Cartesian concept of mind, generates the presumption that knowledge of one's own mind is epistemically direct and 'self-intimating' because it results from the subject's non-observational, non-inferential, first-hand experience of being 'one' with it, whereas knowledge of other minds is epistemically indirect because it is based on inferences drawn from third-person observations of their behaviour. If we commence from this presumption, the likelihood of one person being able to make legitimate claims to knowledge of another person's mind looks slim, as three degrees of separation would need to be overcome to gain such knowledge – namely, all that which separates the subject's mind from their body, their body from the other's and the other's body from their mind.

The argument from analogy presents the analogy between the subject and other people as a means of overcoming the epistemological problem generated by the subject-other asymmetry. However, the obstacle to justifying our claims to knowledge of other minds that results from that asymmetry cannot be satisfactorily overcome by grounding said knowledge in an inference from analogy, since it is always possible to draw the wrong inference from the evidence available. As no inferential knowledge can be placed beyond doubt, the argument from analogy cannot eliminate the in-principle possibility of solipsism being true.[6] What is more, there is an even deeper issue with the argument from analogy, which arises because of its assumption of a Cartesian concept of mind. As Descartes' construal of the mind as a 'thing which thinks', which is isolated from, and capable of expressing doubt about, all things external to it (Descartes 1997: 142–7), it implies that one *knows* one's own mind *through being* identical with it, whereas knowledge of everything else is acquired through representations that mediate the relation between mind and world. The supposition that knowledge of one's own mind is self-intimating in this way, though, is problematic because it renders the origins of our mental concepts mysterious. If my sole source of knowledge of 'the mental' is my experience of my own mind, then I would seem to have no grounds for a concept of mind distinct from the concept of my own experience. What could possibly prompt me to conceive of certain 'objects' in my experience as other 'minded' beings, other *subjects* of experience? Although the view that we do not possess a general concept of mind and so cannot ascribe minds to others (conceptual solipsism) seems to be obviously contradicted by our ability to formulate questions about other minds, the argument from analogy cannot sustain an account of how we could have come to have a concept of mind that is general and dissociable from the 'mineness' that characterizes our own experience. It simply presumes that we have this concept from the start.

The second kind of response to the problem of other minds is motivated by the recognition that the argument from analogy becomes incoherent when it is pushed to its full conclusion since it presupposes a Cartesian concept of mind that both generates the traditional epistemological problem of other minds and makes it difficult, if not impossible, to explain how we could come to conceive of 'minds' in the first place (Avramides 2001: 218–30). Or, as Norman Malcolm puts it, the argument for analogy leads 'first to solipsism and then to nonsense' (1958: 974). To redress these problems with the Cartesian concept of mind, the second response commences from the 'neobehaviourist' concept of mind associated with the later work of Ludwig Wittgenstein and his followers.

In his later work, Wittgenstein strives to show that many, if not all, mental states manifest themselves as observable behaviours. To this end, he construes first-person psychological statements such as 'I am in pain' as behaviour that humans can use instead of 'primitive, natural, expressions of sensation' such as crying, grimacing and limping ([1953] 2009: §244). Rather than communicating knowledge of the subject's (private) mental states to others, Wittgenstein argues that such statements are themselves expressions of mental states that trade off the same basic human capacity for immediate, interpersonal understanding as other 'natural' behaviours. Taking their cue from Wittgenstein's diffusion of mental states into the world, neobehaviourists argue that observable behaviours are our criteria for the application of mental concepts, without necessarily denying that some mental states may be unobservable from a third-person perspective as behaviourists might do. Malcolm (1958), for example, contends that it is only possible to acquire mental concepts that are general by making associations between others' use of them and certain kinds of behaviour, and by taking observable behaviours as our objective criteria for the application of mental concepts. If this were not the case, he maintains that the words each of us use to describe our mental states would collectively amount to a 'private language' comprised of concepts whose sense is strictly subjective. As Malcolm sees it, the recognition that we must see others as the bearers of mental states, before we can even conceptualize our own, frees us of the illusion that we each learn what mental states are in the private theatre of our own mind. Another effect of the realization that others teach us what it means to be 'minded', according to neobehaviourists like Malcolm, is to dissolve the traditional epistemological problem of minds by showing that we must take others to be minded *before* we can even entertain the question of whether they are.

Instead of commencing from one's own mind, then, proponents of the neobehaviourist response to the problem of other minds start by showing that we can only understand what a 'mind' is in terms of other people's behaviour because minded others are the condition for our ability to think about and relate to one another in the ways that we do. Replacing the Cartesian concept of mind with a neobehaviourist one that views knowledge as tempered by action and, specifically, interaction thus solves the conceptual problem of other minds (Avramides 2001). But the claim that this move also renders the epistemological problem of other minds redundant is suspect because the neobehaviourist conception of mind is vulnerable to a version of the charge that is frequently levelled against functionalism – the heir to behaviourism in contemporary philosophy of mind, which, broadly speaking, interprets mental states as functional properties that play a causal role in behaviour. Despite being credited with saving the reality of the phenomenal from the eliminativist tendencies of classical behaviourism, functionalism has been criticized for overlooking essential subjectivity of the mind (Searle 1992; Strawson [1994] 2010; Chalmers 1996). It is entirely conceivable that what the functionalist calls 'mental states' are internal events that generate behaviour, without the attendant experience. But functionality without feeling is precisely what characterizes the 'mindless zombies' that populate the nightmare scenario used at the start of this section to introduce the problem of other minds! Like functionalism, neobehaviourism delivers others who are 'minded' in the sense they are involved in a shared world of action but who could still be 'mindless' in the sense that they act without consciousness.

The thought that others might be mindless zombies troubles us because we do not have direct access to other people's experience. While neobehaviourists rightly observe that we can only acquire mental concepts that are general through relating to others whom we take to be minded, reframing the ontology of subjective experience in terms that emphasize third-person-accessible behaviours does not dissolve the subject-other asymmetry that gives rise to the epistemological problem of other minds. As Barry Stroud points out, 'something's being so does not follow from it being thought or believed to be so' (1994: 241). Even if the belief that other minds exist is a necessary condition for the acquisition of a general concept of mind, this is no guarantee of its truth because it does not rule out the possibility that the (only?) subject could have acquired the belief in the existence of other minds through relating to beings she took to be conscious but were in fact zombies, deceptive androids, etc. Only the provision of a positive metaphysical result that proves that other conscious subjects exist could eliminate this possibility, and neobehaviourism provides no such result.

We can now see why many contemporary philosophers are resigned to the view that the epistemological problem of other minds is insoluble.[7] The attempt to solve it seems to place the investigator in a double bind: either she starts from her own mind and gets caught in a conceptual quagmire about other minds or she starts from the minds of others and leaves experience out of her concept of mind, which enables her to overcome the conceptual problem of other minds but renders her incapable of speaking to the very problem she set out to address: the problem that she cannot know for certain that others exist as subjects of experience like her. Sartre, however, escapes this double bind by offering a response to the problem of other minds that solves the conceptual problem without purging experience from its concept of mind.

Sartre's solution to the conceptual problem of other minds

The first section of the chapter on 'The Other's Existence' in *Being and Nothingness* is simply titled 'The Problem'. At first glance, one might suppose that the problem being addressed is the epistemological problem of other minds, reformulated to target other 'consciousnesses' as Sartre tends to avoid using the term 'mind' (*esprit*) due to the connotations of an 'internal' psychological realm it carries (I: 5–7/17–18). But this would be mistaken. The section that introduces 'The Problem' points out that the two forms of consciousness that Sartre has already described – pre-reflective and reflective consciousness – present consciousness as a being that is 'for-itself' (*pour-soi*), although lived experience reveals that there are also times when consciousness exists 'for-the-other' (*pour-autrui*) (BN/EN: 309/261). The problem for Sartre, then, is that the form of consciousness that apprehends its self as an object for another consciousness has yet to be accounted for.

The fact that Sartre articulates what he takes to be 'the problem' about 'The Other's Existence' without mention of any epistemological concern in the first section of the chapter raises the suspicion that he takes issue with the traditional epistemological framing of problems about others. This suspicion is then confirmed by the expansive critique of previous proposed solutions to the problem of other minds that spans the next two sections and covers realism, Berkeleyan idealism, Kantian metaphysics, as well as the phenomenologies of Hegel, Husserl and Heidegger. In the course of this critique, Sartre accuses almost[8] all his predecessors of mistakenly treating others as objects. But how, one might wonder, is it possible to treat others as objects in the context of an inquiry explicitly concerned with whether they exist as subjects of experience? Sartre's reply is that treating the question of the existence of other conscious subjects as a question about whether we can know that they exist is to be concerned with 'others-as-objects' – albeit psychological objects, other 'consciousnesses' – that are externally related to consciousness (see Figure 1).[9]

Although relating to others-as-objects is one form that our relation to others can take, it is neither the only nor the primary form of that relation in Sartre's view. Indeed, the central aim of his analysis of the Look is to show that the relation to the 'other-as-subject' he calls 'shame' is the primary form of our being-for-others.[10] It attempts to illustrate how the structure of consciousness is triangulated in shame: it is connected to the 'other-as-subject' and its object (the

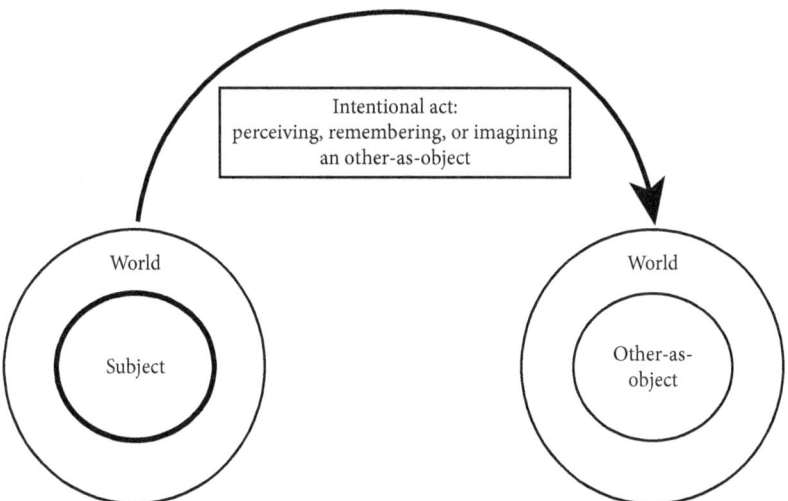

Figure 1 The Other apprehended as an object in an external relation to consciousness.

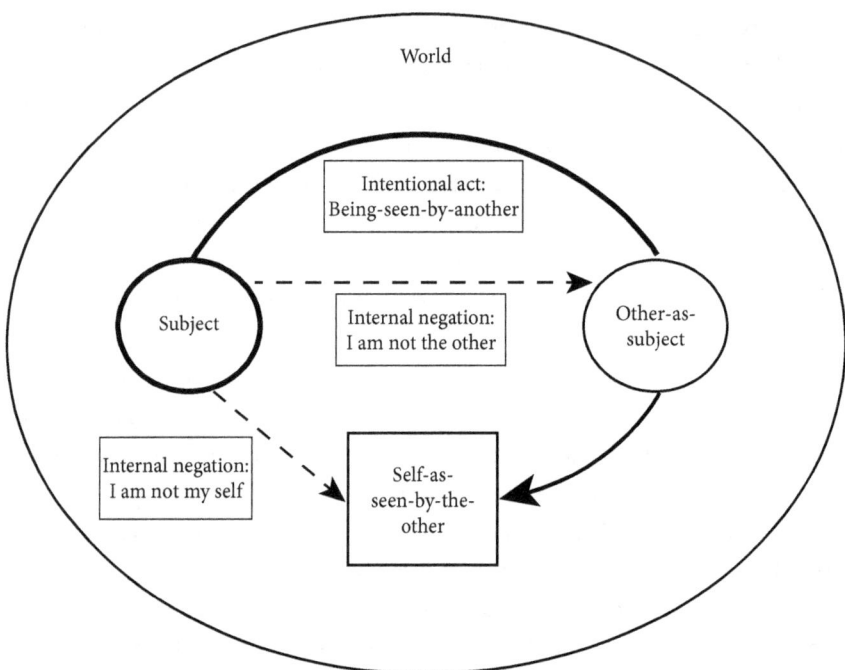

Figure 2 The Other apprehended as a subject in an internal relation to consciousness.

self-as-seen-by-the-other) by a double '*internal negation*' (BN/EN: 404/338, see Figure 2). The other-as-subject is therefore given to shame-consciousness as part of a structure that is its own, as the 'indispensable intermediary' between it and its idea of its self (BN/EN: 308/260); shame-consciousness *is* a consciousness apprehending its difference from both the other conscious subject who looks at it and its objective being – i.e. its self – which the experience of the Look reveals to it. The distinction between the other-as-subject and the other-as-object is therefore a distinction between primary and secondary relations in his view. Although he does not make this distinction explicit throughout his discussion,[11] it is what allows him to maintain that the other 'can in no way be known [*connu*]' and state that 'I can indefinitely increase my knowledge [*connaissance*] of the Other' without contradiction (BN/EN: 397/332). In the first case, he is referring to the other-as-subject who is given to shame-consciousness as a vital element of the internal relations that constitute it as an awareness of its self as an object in the world that is 'for' others. In the second, he is referring to the other-as-object in a world that is 'for' consciousness. All epistemological treatments of the problem of other minds that do not recognize the distinction between the other-as-subject and the other-as-object and the ontological primacy of the former are doomed from the very beginning, in his estimation, because they invariably fail to appreciate that another consciousness can never be the object of our consciousness (or knowledge) because other people's experience eludes ours in principle.[12]

Sartre's recognition of the fundamental inaccessibility of any experience beyond our own, including that which we take to be constitutive of other consciousnesses, leads him to see the need to account for how we can even conceive of an experience that is 'other' when the only experience we have access to is our own as the most basic philosophical problem about other minds. So, like the neobehaviourists, he prioritizes the conceptual problem of other minds over the epistemological one. But he grounds his solution to the conceptual problem in an analysis of first-person experience, not behaviour. Recognizing Sartre's analysis of shame as an attempt to derive a solution to the conceptual problem of other minds from experience helps us to understand why, on the one hand, he affirms that shame delivers the presence of other-as-subject to us as an experiential certainty while, on the other, he concedes that the epistemological problem concerned with the existence of other-as-object cannot be definitively solved.[13] As the other-as-subject and the other-as-object appear on two mutually exclusive and 'incomparable' planes of experience on his account, it is only '*probable*' that there is an other-as-object looking at me whenever I experience the Look even though the presence of other-as-subject in my experience of it is beyond doubt (BN/EN: 376/315). Sartre's analysis of shame-consciousness does not provide the kind of positive metaphysical result required to solve the epistemological problem of other minds – i.e. proof of the existence of the other-as-object – but it does demonstrate that the presence of the other-as-subject is a 'necessary condition of my objectivity' and, hence, my concept of self (BN/EN: 368/308). Indeed, we can only make sense of his claim that his solution to the problem of 'The Other's Existence' is '*worked out entirely on the level of the cogito*' (BN/EN: 291/307) if that problem is the conceptual problem of other minds, as his expansion of the Cartesian *cogito* beyond reflective consciousness to being-for-others discloses not the existence of two consciousnesses, but a particular form of consciousness that is constituted by a relation between it and two internally related concepts: the 'other-who-sees-me' and the 'self-as-seen-by-the-other'.

Thus, the first phase of Sartre's solution to the problem of other minds is complete. His analysis of shame reveals the concept of self as being internally related to the concept of another human perspective on the subject's being. He thereby solves the conceptual problem of other minds through the provision of a positive ontological result that reveals the concept of the other-as-subject as integral to the structure of shame-consciousness. Although this strategy is unable to solve the traditional epistemological problem of other minds on its own terms, it has important implications for it.

Shame and loneliness

Shame is revelatory for Sartre, not because it makes an addition to the things that I know, but because it is an 'original' reaction through which 'I recognize the Other as a subject out of reach' (BN/EN: 395/330). Through shame, I learn that I *cannot know* what the other person who is looking at me sees. It is precisely this lack of knowledge that gives shame its distinctive phenomenal character: 'unease' (*malaise*) (BN/EN: 375/314). Shame is uneasy for the very reason that involves the apprehension of myself as an object with a 'nature', which is not an observable fact in the world for me, but only for another. In shame, I apprehend my nature as something that 'escapes me and is unknowable as such ... I do not feel myself losing my freedom in order to become *a thing*; instead my freedom is over there, outside the freedom that I live, like a given attribute of this being I am for the other' (BN/EN: 360/302). So, shame is a discovery of one's self and of one's alienation at once; it shows me that I am alienated both from my self and from the Other who holds the secret of my 'nature'. This points to what is probably the most singular feature of Sartre's treatment of problem of other minds: its foregrounding of 'human loneliness' as an existential problem (Kirkpatrick 2017: 141). In fact, it is Sartre's emphasis of the ontological root of human loneliness that motivates his departure from the social ontology of Heidegger. Despite following Heidegger in rejecting the traditional epistemological framing of problems about others, Sartre argues that the German philosopher's notion of being-with-others (*Mitsein*) is an upshot of an unfounded assumption of 'ontological solidarity' between human beings that is flagrantly contradicted by the phenomenology of social experience (BN/EN: 338/284) and which is also incapable of helping us to resolve 'the psychological and concrete problem of our recognition of the Other' (BN/EN: 341/287). In contrast to Heidegger, Sartre grounds his social ontology in a phenomenological analysis that highlights the impossibility of a 'we' at the primary level of being. Each of us experiences our being as one that is originally and inescapably 'alone', he maintains, because the presence of others in our experience has the nature of a 'contingent and irreducible fact' (BN/EN: 344/289). Our being neither requires nor constitutes the being of others; we simply encounter others and react to this encounter with essential modifications in the form of our own being. Our ontological isolation is what Sartre posits as the ultimate source of the profound sense of our separateness from others, that 'great metaphysical solitude which is the lot of each and all of us' (B: 54/52).

This ontological isolation is the source of our epistemological isolation on Sartre's account. My fundamental inability to experience any experience apart from my own is the reason why it is always possible for me to be mistaken about what others are thinking and feeling and, indeed, about whether they are thinking and feeling at all. When I am all alone in a certain space, no aspect of my situation escapes my awareness, but the arrival of another introduces a new aspect 'of which I am not master, and which escapes me as a matter of principle – because it is *for the Other*' (BN/EN: 363/304). This new aspect is the '*reverse side*' of situations in which others are present – the side we cannot see – that Sartre calls 'devil's share' (BN/EN: 363/304–5) on account of its potential to give us hell[14] as a key component of shame and all varieties of what we might call 'epistemic social anxiety' (Bering 2008).[15] Without denying that others' emotions feature in our experience, he stresses the point that emotions *as they are experienced by others* do not. He appears to allude to the work of phenomenologists such as Edith Stein, Max Scheler and Theodor Lipps when he notes that 'modern theories of *Einfülung* [empathy], of *sympathy,* and *forms* ... improve the description of our means of presentifying the Other' but do not put the debate about what we can know about others from our experience on its true ground (BN/EN: 311/263). Insofar as these theories represent precursors to recent 'perceptual responses' to the epistemological problem of other minds, this swift dismissal of them gives us a good sense of how Sartre would assess them. These responses argue from the phenomenological insight that we can sometimes perceive emotions, such as anger, in the faces of others to the conclusion that, at least in some favourable circumstances, perception provides us with direct epistemic access to others' mental states (McDowell 1998; Overgaard 2012). Sartre's remark that theories about the potential for empathetic forms of perception to yield knowledge do not treat questions concerning our knowledge of others on their 'true ground' indicates that he would categorize perceptual responses to the problem of other minds alongside others that he believes fail because they do not differentiate between other-as-subject and other-as-object. As the recognition of this difference shows that the other's body is a secondary structure that belongs to the other-as-object in his view, the knowledge of others' emotional experience that perceptual responses take to be gained directly through the perception of others' expressions, gestures and the like is 'purely and simply conjectural' knowledge of the other-as-object (BN/EN: 312/263).

Here we see why Sartre refuses to view the epistemological problem of other minds as a 'special' epistemological problem. Because he believes the only aspect of human being that can be the object of knowledge – for any consciousness – is the objective aspect of it, he contends that the only true object of our knowledge of others is the other-as-object, which is not mysterious. There is no such thing as 'direct epistemic access' to a consciousness, or an other-as-subject, in his view, as a consciousness can only become known by being reflected upon as an object it is not: a 'self'. Accordingly, he affirms the traditional interpretation of the epistemological problem of other minds is premised upon a mistaken conflation of the other-as-object – which can be the object of knowledge – with the other-as-subject – which necessarily eludes knowledge – in its concept of 'mind' and that this generates the illusion that people have 'mental states' that they know directly through being identical with them. Once we see that knowledge of people is not a special kind of knowledge but knowledge of objects (selves) in the world, which is empirical just as all knowledge is,[16] then, Sartre upholds that others are not necessarily mysterious to us. This gives us grounds for interpreting Sartre's response to the problem of other minds as 'therapeutic', as it suggests that it is possible to overcome our epistemological isolation from others though gaining knowledge of their selves.

Philosophical therapy and knowledge of selves

The philosophy of later Wittgenstein is renowned for its 'therapeutic' ambition and is often regarded as the paradigm of therapeutic philosophy, and Wittgenstein's and Sartre's approaches to philosophy have been recognized as similar insofar as they both aim to instigate a therapeutic shift in the way that we view the world and, thereby, 'change the way we *live*' (Morris 2008: xiii). As we have seen that Sartre's solution to the problem of other minds cannot be characterized as Wittgensteinian in the sense of being neobehaviourist, it is important to recognize how Sartre's and Wittgenstein's philosophical-therapeutic responses to the problem of other minds aim to be therapeutic in very different ways.

In his later work, Wittgenstein searches for discoveries that bring philosophy 'peace' by saving it from the torment of questions it cannot answer ([1953] 2009: §133). He aims to achieve this by exposing the philosophical concerns that trouble us as nothing but confused ideas that result from language 'idling' and not doing its work properly, as opposed to the deep and serious problems they seem to be (2009: §132). As James Peterman notes, Wittgenstein is principally concerned with the way that the same viewpoints that give rise to traditional philosophical problems also seem to put us at odds with 'the human form of life' and so he strives to use philosophy as a means of providing 'a therapeutic clarification of the human form of life', which, he hopes, will bring our viewpoints into agreement with our life (1992: 116). For Wittgenstein, a therapeutic change of viewpoint has the potential to have a double effect. First, it can promote an acceptance of our human form of life. Second, it can inoculate us against 'pathological' modes of philosophical thinking that attempt to justify certain uses of language by an appeal to standards that are external to the facts of human life, which are, for the most part, readily available to us.

One of the main causes of 'philosophical diseases', according to Wittgenstein, results from a 'one-sided diet' that nourishes one's thought 'with only one kind of example' (2009: §593). Philosophy of mind, he argues, has become ill by placing too much emphasis on introspection, which does not play a great role in the ways that we ordinarily think about our minds, as evinced by the fact that questions such as 'How do you know that you believe that?' and answers such as 'I find it out through introspection' very rarely make sense in the course of everyday life (2009: §164). Thus, problem of other minds is the upshot of a 'one-sided diet' in his view. Rather than taking the fact that dimensions of others' experience will always elude our knowledge – and the fact that it 'plays hell with us' (Wittgenstein 1968: 276) – as the starting point of his response to the problem, then, he sets this aside and focuses instead on what we can know about others on the basis of observable behaviours. He offers the shift from the first- to the third-person perspective on human relations as a 'cure' to the 'sickness' that is solipsism. And, as we have seen above, this shift in perspective does enable us to solve the conceptual problem about other minds. Nonetheless, the first-person perspective that reveals the unknowability of others' experience to us is not an optional perspective on human life that we can simply abandon; it is the perspective of lived experience. So, Wittgenstein's therapeutic solution to the problem of other minds would be unacceptable to the existentialist philosopher, since it soothes through sanctioning an avoidance of the troubling fact that others are first given to us as beings beyond our epistemic reach, which motivates the problem in the first place.

Although Sartre's existentialist treatment of the problem is similar to Wittgenstein's in that it prioritizes the conceptual problem, it is therapeutic in an entirely different way. In accordance with the existentialist principle that it is only through a clear-sighted appreciation of how we are limited by the facts of our situation that we can avoid the trappings of bad faith and apprehend the full extent of our freedom, Sartre's response to the problem of other minds commences from an appreciation of our epistemic isolation from others as a concrete fact, rooted in the very structure of our being. Through his insistence upon the conceptual distinction between experience that is other than my own – i.e. the other-as-subject – and the objective being of another person – the other-as-object – Sartre's approach allows us to reconcile our theoretical understanding of others as observable, potential objects of knowledge with our lived experience of them as radically 'other' and unknowable. Moreover, Sartre does not stop at providing us with concepts that furnish us with perspicuous representations of our social experience[17]; he also derives a conclusion from his analysis that may help us cope with the fact of human loneliness: that everything about another person that matters is objective and, hence, potentially knowable by anybody.

In summary, Sartre not only believes that an understanding of the ontological basis for human loneliness enables us to accept it as an inevitable feature of our form of life, he also takes it to illuminate something that the typical conflation of the other-as-subject with the other-as-object in philosophical discourse blinds us to: the in-principle possibility of knowing everything there is to know about another. This possibility emerges as a consequence of the realization that what cannot be known about another is precisely *nothing* because the subjective aspect of their being is their consciousness, which has no self or mind inside or behind it and which is also no *thing* in itself. Sartre's solution to the problem of other minds does not inoculate us against solipsism at the level of abstract philosophical reflection; yet, it shows that everything that really matters about others, every concrete aspect of their being, is potentially knowable. It is therefore therapeutic in virtue of presenting the complete knowability of other selves as a salve for human loneliness.

Existentialism and psychoanalysis: The very idea

Sartre believes that existential psychoanalysis (*psychanalyse existentielle*) is the discipline that can deliver knowledge of selves and he outlines its guiding principles and key methodological features in *Being and Nothingness*. Before we can assess whether and how Sartre's existential psychoanalysis might work, we first need to establish its possibility in principle. This is because the term 'existential psychoanalysis' might seem to be oxymoronic insofar as it combines an analytic method whose chief goal is to make discoveries about the unconscious[18] with a philosophy that rejects the unconscious. For existential psychoanalysis not to be an impossible chimera, psychoanalysis must be able to withstand the loss of the postulate of the unconscious, which its founder presents as its most fundamental premise (CW XIV: 166, CW XIX: 13). But how could psychoanalysis yield insights into the psyche if no part of it is unconscious? To respond to this question, it is prudent to first establish the definitive features of the classic psychoanalytic unconscious. Although the task of defining and delimiting the unconscious is complicated by the fact that Freud changed his views frequently – most notably when he traded his topographical model of the mind in for the structural model in *The Ego and the Id* (1923) – our interest in establishing the extent to which the unconscious is integral to psychoanalysis is best served by concentrating on its core features, which endured the various changes Freud made to his model of mind.

Freud's early topographical model distinguishes between two types of nonconscious thoughts, located in different systems in the mind. The first are those which are not conscious right now but are capable of becoming so, should attention be directed towards them: the name of one's favourite primary school teacher, for instance. These are 'preconscious' thoughts, located in the 'Preconscious' system, which consciousness can access with relative ease. The second type are 'unconscious' thoughts, which express animalistic or infantile wishes, some of which are 'repressed' due to their potential to cause psychological pain. These are stored in the 'Unconscious' system, which is off limits to consciousness. Freud's subsequent structural model of the mind is more complex because it accommodates the idea that thoughts in *any* part of the mind could be unconscious, even those in 'the ego', which denotes the rational, agential part. Despite these significant changes, Freud continued to concentrate on thoughts that are 'dynamically unconscious' – i.e. those that are unavailable to consciousness because some part of the psyche is opposed to them – since these are what he believes to be responsible for psychological illness.[19] Let us then take the psychoanalytic concept of the unconscious to refer to instinctual, nonconscious thoughts that can 'drive' our action and find expression in dreams and parapraxes, but which cannot become conscious without the aid of psychoanalysis.

Now that we have a sense of what the psychoanalytic unconscious is, a good place to start our inquiry into whether psychoanalysis could become existential is Sartre's argument that the postulate of the unconscious is incapable of solving the puzzles of self-deception, which arise from the fact that people appear to be unaware of thoughts that their neurotic behaviour, parapraxes, jokes, etc., attest to; since, in order for a person deceive themselves about their own minds, they would need to both know and not know what they are deceiving themselves about and engage in the activity of self-deception without being aware of it (BN/EN: 90–7/84–9). Although, at first glance, Freud seems to avoid this puzzle by positing that the deception of self-deception is unconscious, Sartre contends that the notion of unconscious thoughts presupposes the existence of a censor within the mind that allows some thoughts to enter consciousness and blocks others. To be able to apprehend some thoughts as thoughts 'to be repressed' (BN/EN: 94/87), though, he maintains that this censor must possess both a project to shield consciousness from thoughts of a certain sort and a rather sophisticated degree of understanding to be able to discern which thoughts are of that sort and find effective means of keeping them out of consciousness. As the understanding of how to effectively pursue projects is the hallmark of rationality and the pursuit of projects is what defines agency, it seems as though the activity of intrapsychic censorship could only be undertaken by a rational agent. This gives rise to a serious problem for psychoanalytic theory in Sartre's view since no part of the Freudian psyche appears to be a fitting candidate for the role of the censor; it cannot be the rational, agential ego, since that would imply that consciousness has an awareness of its unconscious thoughts, and it cannot be the id, since the id is not rational.

The operations performed by Freud's censor imply that it must have self-awareness for Sartre and, because self-awareness is what distinguishes consciousness from non-conscious things for him, he believes that the censor must be a consciousness. While the presence of another consciousness within the psyche could lead to concerns about the proliferation of consciousnesses, this is not necessarily a problem for Freud's account, which could potentially accept that there are multiple consciousness within the mind. However, as Sartre reads Freud to attribute rationality and self-awareness only to the ego that consciousness identifies with, he concludes that censor-consciousness would have to be just like ego-consciousness:

> [W]hat type of consciousness (of) itself can the censor have? It must be consciousness (of) being conscious of the drive to be repressed, but precisely *in order not to be conscious of it*. What is left to say, other than that the censor must be in bad faith? We have gained nothing from psychoanalysis since, in order to eliminate bad faith, it installs between the unconscious and the conscious mind an autonomous consciousness in bad faith.
>
> (BN/EN: 94/87)

If Sartre is correct to claim that Freud must posit the existence of another consciousness that is just like ego-consciousness within the psyche, then his psychoanalysis only appears to solve the puzzle of self-deception by dissociating 'deceiver' from 'deceived' in the ego's consciousness only for them to be united once more in the consciousness of the censor.

But this is a big 'if' because Sartre's representation of Freud's psychoanalytic theory in *Being and Nothingness* is riddled with inaccuracies and misleading in some respects. Notably, it has even led commentators to accuse Sartre of bad faith in his reading of Freud (Neu 1988; Askay and Farquhar 2006). This accusation appears to be well founded if the species of bad faith referred to here is 'faith', understood as an epistemological attitude of 'unwarranted certitude' towards one's own view and a bias against any evidence that contradicts it (Webber 2009: 96), as Sartre does indeed focus on the 'bad Freud', the scientific reductionist who posits meaningless biological forces as the ultimate source of our behaviour, and ignores 'good Freud', who was a master in the hermeneutics of human experience, as Stuart Z. Charmé submits (2020: 256). It is hard to imagine that the Freud Sartre depicts could be the same Freud who, in his case study of the Rat-Man, describes how he learns that his patient could not accept his clinical interpretation of his (the Rat-Man's) unconscious feelings of resentment towards his father until it became emotionally meaningful for him.[20]

Further, while Sartre parses his account of the inability of Freud's theory to resolve the puzzle of self-deception in terms that refer to Freud's later structural model – i.e. 'ego' and 'id' – it seems only to apply to the earlier, topographical model, which locates unconscious thoughts in a discrete system, as Freud's later structural model introduces the notion of the 'super-ego', which, ostensibly, enables him to present the ego as the chief agent of unconscious intrapsychic censorship. This has led one commentator to charge Sartre with contriving 'to ignore' Freud's later writings (Howells 1988: 149) and another to read him as being 'dead wrong' about Freud's theorization of repression and other forms of ego-defence (Soll 1981: 590). At first glance, these charges seem correct, especially as the term 'Superego' appears only once in this part of Sartre's discussion (BN/EN: 94/87). Webber, however, contends that Sartre's objection to the unconscious targets the conceptual dualism that underpins both Freud's topographical and structural models of the mind: a dualism between 'rational' and 'arational' mental items. As Webber explains, rational mental items are responsive to evidence about the way the world is, and they form part of a logically coherent system, which means that they are 'available for beliefs to be formed about them, beliefs that can be linguistically articulated' (2018: 80). As such, they can be conscious or preconscious but never unconscious because the subject identifies with them and can easily become aware of them. In contrast, arational mental items are 'structured in a way that they do not stand in any rational relations with one another or with anything else' (2018: 80). Put simply, they are primitive 'wishes' whose organization is determined by arational biological forces. Such wishes can enter consciousness and motivate the subject to engage in acts that satisfy them, such as having sex, eating or sleeping. But if the subject is opposed to a wish or to the act that would satisfy it, it will be consigned to the unconscious. This reading underlines Freud's tacit commitment to the view that any 'rationally structured' mental item is 'consciously accessible' (Webber 2018: 81). This then leads Webber to conclude Freudian psychoanalytic theory is, as Sartre suggests, incapable of solving the puzzle of how the inherently rational activity of the censor could elude consciousness.

At this point, we might raise the concern that Webber seems to overlook Freud's discussion of the 'the unconscious sense of guilt' in *The Ego and the Id* (CW XIX: 26–7, 49–54), which strongly suggests that he abandons the conceptual dualism between rational and arational mental items. After all, Freud's finding that unconscious guilt is a precipitating factor for many forms of psychological distress leads him to argue that some of the highest intellectual processes may be unconscious because guilt is the result of critical self-reflection – a rational process *par excellence*. He then introduces the concept of the super-ego (*Über-Ich*) to account for phenomena like unconscious guilt. He also believes that it enables him to respond to many of his philosophical dissenters by solving the puzzle of how rational processes 'can remain to a great extent unconscious' (CW XIX: 39). As the super-ego is theorized by Freud as an element of the psyche that develops as a result of the individual's internalization of social norms and, eventually, comes to take on the parental role of censoring socially unacceptable wishes, this would explain the possibility of there being 'rules without reason' within the psyche. Further, Freud's concept of the super-ego enables him to identify the ego as the usual agent of unconscious policing of thoughts as he can now say that it performs this role 'in the service and at the behest of its super-ego' (CW XIX: 52). So, while the ego is the systematic organization of rational mental items, and the part of the psyche that the subject identifies with, the scope of the ego's activity exceeds the scope of conscious awareness because it can also become the pawn in the play of the super-ego. But, here, Freud's account runs into trouble again because for the super-ego to use the ego to serve its own agenda, it must have an agency and an understanding of its own, which it cannot have if it is nothing more than a repository of internalized rules. The super-ego could not conceivably take hold of the ego by being part of the ego that is 'less firmly connected with consciousness' (CW XIX: 28); it has to be a consciousness to do this.

Contrary to the view that Sartre's objection to psychoanalytic theory neglects Freud's later ideas about how intrapsychic censorship occurs, it demonstrates why *both* of Freud's models of the mind are incapable of explaining how it occurs because both require there to be a censor *somewhere* in the mind, which also must be a rational, agential consciousness. Although the dualism of rational and arational mental items does not map neatly onto an antithesis between consciousness and the unconscious in Freud's later work, due to the introduction of the concept of the super-ego, it persists there nonetheless, and this is why the notion of the super-ego is of no help to Freud in solving the puzzle of self-deception. The rational activity of the super-ego needs to be inaccessible to the rational ego, but this is inexplicable if the ego and the super-ego are simply functionally defined regions of one mind. There seems to be no way for the super-ego to be rationally structured and inaccessible to the conscious part of the ego unless it is effectively another, separate mind within the conscious mind, within which the puzzle of self-deception re-emerges.

So, here we see that Sartre, the philosopher, succeeds in identifying a flaw in Freud's theory of mind that renders it incapable of solving the puzzle of self-deception. But this criticism misses the crucial point that Freud's theory of mind was not developed to solve this puzzle but, rather, to act as a metatheory that provides his psychoanalysis with a foundation that is 'non-empirical' but scientific nevertheless (Askay and Farquhar 2006: 29). It is not geared towards solving abstract theoretical puzzles but towards providing a picture of the mind that most accurately reflects the findings delivered by the empirical research and explains how psychoanalysis works in the way that it does. As Freud sees it, his aim to provide a scientific basis for his clinical approach prevents him from producing 'a complete and ready-made theoretical structure', 'like a philosophical system', because it means that he must move 'step by step along the path towards understanding the intricacies of the mind by making an analytic dissection of both normal and abnormal phenomena' (CW XIX: 36). Therefore, the most important issue with Sartre's critique of Freud in *Being and Nothingness*, in my view, is that it does not consider debate about the unconscious on what Freud and his followers would consider to be its 'true ground'. While we may take the internal coherence and the explanatory force of Sartre's account of bad faith as a reason for preferring it to Freud's picture of the psyche, Freud's picture of the psyche is more credible from a scientific perspective because it was developed in response to the findings of case studies and other empirical research. Although, in the next chapter, we shall see that Sartre makes a compelling argument for the view that psychoanalysis should not measure itself by the standards of empirical science, he fails to consider and respond to the possibility that Freud's psychoanalytic metatheory may be able to account for empirically observed phenomena that his own theory cannot.

Putting the issues with Sartre's criticism of Freud aside, what we can learn from it is that psychoanalysis is, at least in theory, compatible with Sartrean existentialism since Sartre's argument that his notion of bad faith enables him to solve the puzzle of self-deception, which he believes Freud's hypothesis of the unconscious is incapable of solving, shows that he can account for how psychoanalysis could uncover insights that are concealed from the subject. As Sartre submits that bad faith can prevent consciousness from gaining knowledge of its own (necessarily conscious) thoughts, psychoanalysis can still pursue the end of enlightening subjects about their thoughts without hypothesizing the existence of the unconscious.

Consciousness and comprehension

Sartre begins the section 'Existential Psychoanalysis' with an illustration of how our experience usually coincides with a comprehension of its object in terms of a specifically human meaning by examining an experience in which it is made to be conspicuous by its absence: reading Paul Bourget's explanation of Gustave Flaubert's literary ambition. Bourget's description of Flaubert's ambition as an upshot of the 'exhilaration [*effervescence*] in his young blood' (BN/EN: 724/603) – a pseudo-biological condition Bourget takes to be common among precocious 'types' around eighteen years of age – inspires feelings of 'resignation and dissatisfaction' in the reader in Sartre's view (BN/EN: 727/605). It does so because our intuition tells us that ambition is not something 'received' ready-made from a platonic heaven or something that certain 'types' of people possess in the way that some rocks have moss on them, and others do not. Sartre maintains that the concept 'ambition' tells us nothing about *Flaubert's* ambition, which is not the same as that of Charles Baudelaire, Artemisia Gentileschi or Aretha Franklin. If Flaubert was ambitious, it is because he chose to act in ways that made it appropriate for others to describe him that way. 'Ambition' cannot therefore be part of the explanation for Flaubert's behaviour; it merely identifies a pattern of behaviour that requires explanation.

Sartre takes the lack of explanatory force of 'traits' and 'types' illuminated by psychological 'explanations' like Bourget's to show that the ultimate term of a psychological explanation cannot be some unintelligible physiological factor – bubbling of the blood and such like. It must, rather, be a psychic 'irreducible', whose irreducibility will be self-evident, not because it meets criteria determined by a theory of mind, but because it will be accompanied by a 'feeling of satisfaction' when it is reached (BN/EN: 728/606). Initially, the claim that a feeling of satisfaction is what should signal the endpoint of a psychological explanation seems odd, and it is certainly unorthodox. However, it is not itself an upshot of a 'mere intuition' or a hunch that Sartre has; it is a claim that is firmly grounded in his phenomenological ontology. He is critical of psychological interpretations that attempt to explain acts by placing them in sequences that are 'empirically observed' but literally 'unintelligible' (BN/EN: 726/604) because he is committed to the view that all actions, unlike spasms or reflexes, are comprehensible phenomena. And yet, no action can be comprehended in terms of factors that are external to lived experience – be they unconscious thoughts or the 'objective' features of the environment that elude the subject[21] – but only by continually asking *why* the subject acts. This view is not some childish quest for a 'because' that admits of no further 'why?' but, rather, a demand based upon a 'preontological' comprehension[22] of 'human-reality' and a 'related refusal to consider man as something that can be analyzed or reduced to basic givens' (BN/EN: 728/606).

Now, Sartre borrows the term 'preontological' from Heidegger to denote an innate comprehension of being, which is prior to any reflective knowledge. Preontological comprehension on Sartre's account is the primary, nonthetic understanding that consciousness necessarily has of all acts. But how might preontological comprehension be related to a refusal to explain a person in terms of 'basic givens' in this context? The answer, I believe, lies in Sartre's notion of 'human-reality' for which he is, again, indebted to Heidegger because 'human-reality' resembles Heidegger's notion of *Dasein* (literally: 'there-being') insofar it echoes the idea that human being is thrown into a temporal world. But Sartre also puts a Bergsonian[23] twist on his conception of 'human-reality' through his affirmation that, once thrown into the world, human being then throws itself towards the future by choosing projects to pursue, which makes 'existing' and 'choosing itself' the same for it (BN/EN: 752/618), as it continues to exist only in and through continually choosing what it is to be. It follows that each individual realizes themselves as a human being only through the pursuit of a fundamental project to realize an 'original choice' (*choix originel*) of Self. The capitalized first letter of 'Self' ('Moi' in the original French) is used by Sartre to distinguish the real 'self' one is for others from the ideal 'Self',[24] which is the unattainable end of the process of self-formation (BN/EN: 82–3/77–8): the fusion of consciousness with its ideal self in a being 'in-itself-for-itself' that is not constituted by freedom but possesses freedom as an attribute, which would amount to being God (BN/EN: 796/662). This makes Sartre's notion of 'original choice' original in the double sense that it is the origin of all other choices and that it is always an original creation of consciousness as each consciousness chooses the nature of the Self it aspires to be.

Having a source in an original choice is what makes *every* human act – even those that seem trivial, irrational, self-destructive, or pathological – comprehensible in terms of projects and, ultimately, in terms of a fundamental project on Sartre's account. It guarantees that every human act is motivated and that anybody who has an awareness of its motive can comprehend its meaning. This underpins Sartre's claim that psychological understandings must exploit the comprehension 'of being that is a characteristic of the enquirer' inasmuch as they too are participants in the creation of 'human-reality' (BN/EN: 745/620). The capacity of the enquirer to comprehend the subjective sense of an agent's acts is, for him, as important as their capacity to be objectively observed since this is what enables the enquirer to grasp the agent's motives. This explains why Sartre objects to Freud's views about the meaning of human behaviour and where it is to be found. Even though Sartre praises Freudian psychoanalysis for recognizing that each act refers 'immediately to deeper structures' and for refusing to set up a 'horizontal psychological determinism' that explains acts by the antecedent moment (BN/EN: 599–600/502), he argues that it sets up a 'vertical', libidinal determinism through its aim to trace acts back to a biological cause. He concludes that this effectively reduces the psychological significance of the acts examined by Freudian psychoanalysis to a function of their cathetic[25] charge, which is determined by arational instincts,[26] and ignores the role played by projects and 'the dimension of the future' in motivating acts and making them meaningful (BN/EN: 480/502–3).

As Sartre sees it then, Freud fails to follow his ground-breaking discovery that we make more meaning than we know through to the proper conclusion that all human action is meaningful *all the way down* to its source in an original choice. While he believes psychoanalysis has the potential to uncover the full meaning of behaviour, he maintains that if it is to be true to Freud's theory it must invariably switch from asking *why*-questions to *what*-questions to discover a 'cause' of behaviour it examines, which prevents it from realizing its potential to fully explain behaviour in terms of human meaning.

Existential ontology as psychoanalytic metatheory

If Sartre holds that the ultimate source of human action is an original choice and that we each have an immediate, primary comprehension of all our acts in terms of that choice, what kind of insights can his psychoanalysis deliver? We are now able to see why Sartre's answer is 'insights into the self'. Introspective reflection on lived experience may supply a crude expression of some of the meaning of acts in terms of the agent's known preferences and projects, but it is not a viable route to self-knowledge for Sartre because it does not employ the kind of 'instruments and techniques' necessary to isolate the choice embodied in the act, 'to determine it in concepts and place it on its own in the full light of day' (BN/EN: 740/616). At best, then, such reflections can deliver 'quasi-knowledge' (BN/EN: 740/616). While the Sartrean consciousness comprehends all its acts and can reflect upon any of them, the problem is that it retains all the details of its experience in a wholly disorganized way, with the result that when it reflects on its experience, it grasps a multitude of meanings without a sense of their 'salience' or 'proportion' in relation to one another (BN/EN: 740/616). So, when left to its own devices, consciousness is generally incapable of turning its innate comprehension of its acts into self-knowledge.

Here we see how Sartre uses his distinction between consciousness (*conscience*) and knowledge (*connaissance*) (BN/EN: 8–16, 740/16–23, 616) to bolster his view that psychoanalysis can, and should, become 'existential'. Insight cures for him as it does for Freud, although for Sartre curative insights are insights into the 'real self' we are for others, as opposed to a 'deep self' within us. The contrast between the metaphors Freud and Sartre use to describe the psychoanalytic process illuminates what is perhaps the most fundamental difference in their approach. Freud describes psychoanalysis as the 'archaeology' of the mind (CW XII: 12, Bernfeld 1951); he takes the task of the psychoanalyst to be that of digging in dark depths of a buried past to unearth the supressed wishes that torment the analysand in the present. Sartre, however, borrows a Barrèsian metaphor to present the task of the psychoanalyst as that of solving a 'mystery in full light' (BN/EN: 740/616).[27] He sees the analysand's original choice (of Self) the key to solving this mystery, as it is their solution to the 'problem of being', understood as the problem of being thrown into the world without any preordained purpose. Although he characterizes human being as a 'useless Passion' because it aims to solve the problem of being through the pursuit of a fundamental project to become its Self, which is doomed to failure (BN/EN: 797/662), the pursuit of this project results in the production of a real self. Establishing the nature of an analysand's Self in the context of an existential psychoanalysis thus discloses 'the real aim' of all their pursuits in Sartre's view (BN/EN: 810/674–5), and this is precisely the insight that could enable them to transform their innate, disorganized comprehension of their original choice into knowledge of what it has made them – i.e. self-knowledge. Hence, for Sartre, psychoanalytic interpretation does not cause the analysand to '*gain consciousness* of what he is: it makes him *gain knowledge* of it' (BN/EN: 745/620) and his enlightenment can only be explained if he has always been 'conscious of his deep tendencies' (BN/EN: 745/620). If consciousness – and its innate comprehension of all its acts – is a necessary but not sufficient condition for self-knowledge, then there is no contradiction in denying that anything is hidden from consciousness and affirming that people often lack self-knowledge.

The supposition that the ultimate source of psychopathological symptoms is an arational source outside of consciousness led Freud to deem it appropriate to attempt to approach the study psychopathology in a purely objective manner, as the natural sciences study their objects. However, Sartre believes that this restricts Freudian psychoanalysis to accruing empirical knowledge about the analysand, which means that it does not also explicitly aim to comprehend the 'subjective' meaning of the analysand's acts in a way that would allow it to solve the mystery of what motivates them. This leads him to conclude that Freudian psychoanalytic explanations of behaviour can only amount '*probable*' hypotheses, whose probability positively correlates to the 'amount of behaviour' they explain (BN/EN: 594–5/619),[28] because they do not exploit the analyst's and analysand's ability to intuitively apprehend the human meaning of human action.

An existential psychoanalysis, though, can draw upon a phenomenological understanding of the structures of being in general to guide its 'objective'[29] analysis of the '*ontological meaning*' of concrete objects in the world for individuals in Sartre's view (BN/EN: 777/645). Further, Sartre's phenomenological ontology gives psychoanalysis a non-arbitrary endpoint. This is because once the analysand's original choice (of Self), which drives their fundamental '*project of being*', has been grasped, Sartre writes that we arrive at 'the point from which we can reach back no further ... for evidently one can go back no further than being' (BN/EN: 733/610). His ontology posits that human being is 'fundamentally a *desire to be*, and the existence of this desire is not to be established through empirical induction' because it 'comes out of an *a priori* description' of consciousness's being, since consciousness apprehends itself as 'its own lack of being' (BN/EN: 733/610). On the one hand, then, Sartre's phenomenological ontology has an edge over Freud's as a psychoanalytic metatheory insofar as it gives psychoanalysis a clear end-point and enables the analyst to offer clinical interpretations that are humanly meaningful all the way down to an original choice at the core of the human being. On the other hand, it rejects the premise of the unconscious from the very start through its affirmation that 'psychological facts are coextensive with consciousness' (BN/EN: 740/616), which means that its stance on the unconscious is neither falsifiable nor responsive to new discoveries. Hence, it cannot supply psychoanalysis with a *scientific* metatheory. Moreover, as Richard Askay and Jensen Farquhar observe, Freud could reject the idea that Sartre's ontology represents a viable alternative metatheory for psychoanalysis on the grounds that it begs the question of whether unconscious processes exist (2006: 276–80). Although, from a phenomenological perspective, Sartre's *a priori* dismissal of the unconscious is justified – since phenomenology aims to provide all other disciplines with a robust foundation through commencing from the apodictic evidence yielded by reflections on experience and Sartre sees no evidence for the existence of unconscious processes in experience itself – from a scientific perspective it certainly is not.

Even though Freud's psychoanalysis has a better claim to knowledge of psychopathologies and their presentation because of its empirical basis, Sartre's arguably has a better claim to knowledge of *selves*. Sartre upholds that his existential psychoanalysis provides the surest route to knowledge of selves because it is 'a method that aims to bring to light, in a strictly objective form, the subjective choice through which each person makes himself a person, i.e., acquaints himself with what he is' (BN/EN: 745/620). The thought is that once analysand can make sense of all the acts considered during the existential analysis in terms of projects, she will then be able to identify the original choice that unifies all her acts by pulling them all towards the same end. The method of existential psychoanalysis can therefore be conceived of as a form of eidetic reduction to the essence of a self, where the 'essence' of a self is nothing other than the subject's original choice of Self. As is the case in a Husserlian eidetic reduction, the discovery of an essence in the context of an existential analysis is confirmed by intuition of the subject(s) involved in the analysis, who will experience a feeling of satisfaction – an 'aha!' moment if you will – when they have arrived at the 'strictly objective' articulation of the analysand's original choice of Self that makes the primary orientation of their *being* comprehensible. Further, as Sartre's existential psychoanalysis treats behaviour as intelligible all the way down to an original choice, its interpretations of the meaning of behaviour do not involve an inference to 'a causal influence' from the existence of a 'theme' or human meaning, which generates epistemological problems for Freudian psychoanalysis (Meehl 1995: 1021).

Let us now take stock. We have seen that the first phase of Sartre's response to the philosophical problem posed by the presence of minded others in our experience solves the conceptual problem of other minds by showing that the discovery of the self in shame involves the certain apprehension of another conscious subject, therefore, explains the emergence of a conception of consciousness that is general. Sartre does not solve the traditional epistemological problem of other minds on its own terms, though, because he rejects those terms. He takes the appearance of the other-as-subject to shame-consciousness as a fundamentally unknowable being to reconfirm the basic principle of his phenomenological ontology: that no consciousness can ever be the object of knowledge because it is no *thing* in-itself. This, for him, shows that there is no problem about knowledge of other consciousnesses because consciousnesses are simply not the kind of beings that can be known. There is a problem about knowledge of selves, though, since selves are objects; yet, Sartre denies that this problem is a special epistemological problem because selves are not the subjects of an internal life but objects in the world. The problem is that the discipline that yields knowledge of selves – existential psychoanalysis – has not yet been developed.

The second phase aims to solve what Sartre identifies as the real epistemological problem about other 'minds': the problem that we do not yet have a sure-fire route to knowledge of 'selves'. Hence, the philosophical point of his provision of a sketch of an existential psychoanalysis in *Being and Nothingness* is to indicate that a discipline that delivers knowledge of selves is 'possible' in principle (Moati 2019: 266–7). And, as Sartre notes at the end of this sketch, certain 'especially accomplished biographies' already attest to this possibility (BN/EN: 746/620). All of Sartre's psychoanalytical works after *Being and Nothingness* can therefore be read as part of his project to complete this second phase of his solution to the problem of other minds by showing exactly how we can gain knowledge of selves.

3

Situated selves: The development of Sartre's psychoanalysis

We have now seen that Sartre's existentialism interprets all behaviour as having its *raison d'être* an original choice (of Self) and that it construes this choice as the 'essence' of the self in virtue of being what determines the shape of each person's process of self-formation. From this, it follows that knowledge of a self can only be gained via a comprehension that can make sense of all the acts that constitute that self in terms of the subject's original choice, which makes it possible to understand the subject's acts as part of a coherent whole – i.e. a self.

During the 1950s, however, Sartre came to see that an entirely new form of reason is required to deliver knowledge of selves because he realizes that we do not simply make our selves, we make them out of what has already been made of us (SG: 49/64; SM/QM: 97/127). This means that if we are to gain knowledge of a self, not only must we be able to comprehend the subject's acts in terms of their original choice, we must also synthesize this comprehension with an understanding of the extent to which the subject's capacity to choose is constrained by their situation. None of the dominant methods of interpreting human behaviour enable us to do this in Sartre's estimation, not even his initial form of existentialism.[1] This is because the form of reason that all established systems of thought rely on is one that, he believes, precludes an understanding of human being as simultaneously free and constrained, subject and object, constituting and constituted. A radically new rationality is therefore required to understand human being in its full complexity, one that can preserve and make sense of the contradictions inherent in it. Sartre supplies a detailed account of this rationality, which he calls 'dialectical reason' (*raison dialectique*), in the *Critique of Dialectical Reason* (*Critique de la raison*, 1960, '*Critique*' hereafter). This articulation of a new way of interpreting human being represents a major breakthrough for Sartre and it has significant implications for his existential psychoanalysis. So, let us now establish what dialectical reason is and how it drives the changes Sartre makes to his psychoanalytical approach after *Being and Nothingness*.

From discourse to dialectic

Philosophers have employed 'the dialectic' as a method of dialogue since the time of Socrates/Plato. This method works by considering a thesis and its antithesis, then synthesizing them in a new thesis. In *Phaedrus*, for instance, Plato's Socrates recounts two speeches about love: one which argues that it is undesirable and one which argues for the contrary view. He then describes how each speech contains a partial truth about love. One reveals its jealous, troublesome 'left' side, while the other reveals its heavenly, generous 'right' side (265e–266b). He therefore concludes that the only way to the truth about love is the dialectician's way, via the synthesis of the contrary partial truths contained in both speeches, as this way leads to an understanding of love in its full complexity – i.e. its potential to bring us joy and happiness on the one hand and misery and torment on the other.

When the dialectic is understood as a discursive method in this way, Sartre can be interpreted as having been a dialectical philosopher long before he wrote the *Critique* (Cumming 1981). His discussion of the stutterer in *Being and Nothingness* provides a particularly fine example of what may be considered an early Sartrean dialectical analysis. Here, Sartre's initial thesis is that the stutterer's stutter is behaviour that manifests the choice *to be* inferior before others. If, as often happens, the stutterer was to visit a psychoanalyst to cure his stutter, Sartre denies that this would undermine his initial thesis. Even though visiting a psychoanalyst is behaviour that ostensibly manifests the choice *not to be* inferior before others, it is not necessary to dismiss the stutter's claim to behavioural status to understand the stutterer's motives. Instead, Sartre shows that both behaviours can be understood when they are traced back to a choice that establishes their harmony at a deeper level. The choice of inferiority achieves this end, he contends, as it allows both the stutter and the attempt to cure it to be interpreted as part of the same inferiority-project, which is pursued directly through stuttering and indirectly through visiting an analyst in the hope of confirming that the stutter is 'incurable' (BN/EN: 620/519) and, hence, his appearing inferior before others, inevitable. The synthesis of these contrary choices therefore makes the full range of this stutterer's conduct intelligible. It also suggests that Sartre was already employing the dialectic to explain how 'we try, on the one hand, to actualize something which, on the other hand, we refuse' in the early 1940s (BN/EN: 619–20/519).

In light of this, Sartre's insistence that he did not discover the dialectic until later in his career is surprising. Although he admits to having known of the dialectic since his student days at the École Normale Supérieure (1924–9), he claims not to have employed it himself until after *Being and Nothingness*. And while he accepts that some parts of that work 'resemble the dialectic', he states that the approach of this work 'was not dialectical in name' nor was he aware of a dialectic in it at the time of writing it (IWS: 9). According to these remarks, then, Sartre only became aware of the potential of the dialectic to provide a new means of interpreting human being after he undertook a serious, independent study of Hegel in 1945. So, 'the dialectic' that enables Sartre to see that there is another way of interpreting human being is a Hegelian one. Despite the key terms in *Being and Nothingness* – i.e. 'being-for-itself' and 'being-in-itself' – indicating a strong Hegelian influence on his initial existentialism,[2] I believe we ought to take Sartre at his word on this point for two main reasons. First, his remark that 'my relations toward the Other are not dialectical but circular' in *Being and Nothingness* (BN/EN: 482/403) stands in clear tension with his later interpretation of the dialectic as 'indistinguishable' from 'the relations which each person has with everyone through inorganic materiality' (CDR I/CRD I: 36/55). Second, as I endeavour to show in this chapter, it is only in works written after 1945 that Sartre begins to analyse human being with the explicit end of revealing a concrete synthesis in it.

But what does the Hegelian dialectic represent for Sartre and how does his discovery of it alter his understanding of human being? According to Alexandre Kojève's interpretation, which Sartre largely followed,[3] Hegel does not present the dialectic 'as a philosophical *method*' but rather as a process that is being continually effected through history (Kojève 1969/1947: 183/460), which means that task of the Hegelian philosopher is not to construct the dialectic but to disclose it. This makes the Hegelian dialectic less 'dialectical' in the traditional sense of the term than it is descriptive and phenomenological since its chief aim is to comprehend the dialectic 'in' being exactly as it reveals itself. Sartre evidently agrees with (Kojève's) Hegel that the dialectic 'must be recognized *where it is there to be seen*, instead of being dreamed of in areas where we cannot yet grasp it' (CDR I/CRD I: 34/152) and he interprets dialectical reason, which aims to do just this, as the 'living logic of action' (CDR I/CRD I: 38/156). Hence, he motivates his investigation into dialectical reason with the bold claim that 'absolutely no one, either in the East or the West, writes or speaks a word about us or our contemporaries that is not a gross error' because the dialectical reason present in the movement of history has yet to be identified or properly understood (SM/QM: 111/155–6).

What we ordinarily think of as reason simpliciter is just one kind of reason, according to Sartre. It is 'positivist' or 'analytic' reason, which has a much more limited scope of understanding than the more primary, 'dialectical' reason that human history conforms to. If the notion that the movement of history conforms to reason strikes us as odd, Sartre explains that this is only because we are so firmly anchored in the positivist tradition, and he reassures us that the existence of dialectical reason will be demonstrated through its capacity to 'reveal certain structures, relations, and meanings which necessarily elude all positivism' (CDR I/CRD I: 58/173). Although this idea appears to be latent in Sartre's acknowledgement that the stutterer's behaviour is unconstrained by the analytical logical principle of non-contradiction in *Being and Nothingness*, his treatment of the stutterer there would not qualify as 'dialectical' in the sense that Sartre later uses the term as it neglects to attend to the dialectic between the stutterer's choice and history – including his own developmental history.

Even though Sartre views history as ongoing process of 'totalization', rather than a teleological progression towards an absolute 'totality' as Hegel does, thinking about history in terms of the dialectic is productive for him, as it enables him to further substantiate his claim that all human acts are comprehensible by revealing them as irreducible constituents of the intelligible, totalizing movement of history. The discovery of the dialectic is also instrumental in leading Sartre to a greater appreciation of the role of culture in the constitution of selves as it enables him to present every human act as a consequence of an original choice *and* 'centuries of history' and, specifically, the way that history has been preserved in the culture through which the agent interprets their experience (CDR I/CRD I: 54/170).

Dialectical materialism

Despite the usefulness of the Hegelian dialectic for Sartre, it is an unlikely source of inspiration for him because it is both idealist and anti-individualist. Sartre's existentialism is fundamentally opposed to idealism because it affirms that we are capable of effecting change in a world beyond thought and idealism is a metaphysic that deprives us of this capability by denying there is anything beyond thought. What is more, Sartre argues that idealism also fails to appreciate the double character of human being as both an embodied subject who acts and a body that is acted upon, which effectively blinds it to the basic, material source of antagonism between individuals: '*scarcity*' (CDR I/CRD I: 113/225). As he sees it, the permanent possibility of scarcity is the bottom line of the explanation for why conflict is the primary relation between human beings. I first apprehend other people not simply as other consciousnesses but as other human organisms with the same material needs and anxieties as me. I am also always aware that, in the context of scarcity, they could take what I need to survive. Hence, others embody an existential threat to me at a primal level. Although I may overcome that threat and develop positive reciprocal relations with others, if I respond to that threat by attacking another, Sartre explains that 'it is myself that I try to destroy in him, so as to prevent him from destroying me in my own body' (CDR I/CRD I: 133/245).

Another problematic feature of Hegel's dialectical idealism for Sartre is that it offers no way of confirming or disconfirming interpretations of the dialectic against something that is external to the thought of the investigator. As the movement of being and the process of knowledge are one and the same for the idealist philosopher, there are no true 'unknowns' because nothing is truly 'other' than consciousness. This has the effect of making all knowledge – be it of objects or persons – a form of 'self-Knowledge' (*Savoir de soi*) because it is nothing other than thought knowing itself (CDR I/CRD I: 22/141). In the context of Sartre's existentialism, though, we have seen that all knowledge – even self-knowledge – is knowledge of objects that are other than consciousness. Indeed, Sartre's insistence upon the otherness of objects and the irreducibility of the embodied individual stands in such stark contrast with Hegel's dissolution of the object in consciousness and of consciousness in Spirit (*Geist*)[4] that it is legitimate to wonder whether his existentialism is compatible with *any* interpretation of the Hegelian dialectic. And although it is undoubtedly a key aim of Sartre's mature existentialism to show that dialectical reason can furnish us with knowledge of objects that analytic reason cannot provide us with, but which is also grounded in an 'objective' analysis and verifiable,[5] we may have reservations about whether the dialectic is fit for this purpose, given its origins in Hegel's idealism.

To show that the dialectic can be interpreted to manifest itself through history in such a way that it can be apprehended by reflective thought, while always also being other than thought, Sartre looks to Karl Marx's materialist reinterpretation of the Hegelian dialectic. Here, he finds a balance between Hegel's 'epistemologization' of being and Søren Kierkegaard's subjectivism. He regards Kierkegaard's insistence upon the primacy, specificity and irreducibility of lived experience to undercut the 'dogmatic' absolutizing[6] that leads to the absorption of the being into knowledge in Hegel. Although Kierkegaard's conclusion that *any* abstraction from the concrete particulars of lived experience amounts to falsification goes too far in Sartre's view, as it precludes the possibility of philosophy – which must abstract from the concrete in order to uncover truths that are general – he believes that Kierkegaard's treatment of lived experience teaches us that the opposition between what can be known (objects) and what eludes knowledge (the being of consciousness itself) is rooted in an indissoluble opposition between two ontological structures (SM/QM: 10–13/16–20).

Sartre finds an implicit Kierkegaardian reproach of Hegelian idealism in Marx's dialectical materialism because he reads it to underscore the lived reality of history by asserting that the objectification processes that all people are involved in are processes of 'opening out', through which they develop their own lives and transform themselves 'by changing nature' (SM/QM: 12/20). This is what he believes enables Marx to affirm the irreducibility of being to knowledge and to present the dialectic as discoverable in '*both*' being and knowledge (CDR I/CRD I: 23/142). The superiority of Marx's interpretation of the dialectic over the Hegelian original for Sartre is therefore an upshot of what he takes to be its tacit ontological commitments. It is because Sartre reads Marx's dialectical materialism as an 'ontological monism' that is also '*dualist because it is monist*' that he believes it can explain how the logic of thought can map onto the logic of being '*without idealism*' (CDR I/CRD I: 25/144). In short, it is because Sartre reads the Marx's Marxism to contain an implicit 'demand for an existential foundation' (SM/QM: 177/245) that he finds Marx's interpretation of the dialectic compatible with his existentialism.[7]

Sartre aligns his mature form of existentialism with a 'realistic materialism' (*matérialisme réaliste*) (CRD I: 148),[8] which, he believes, supplies Marx's dialectical materialism with the existential foundation it demands. This new alignment serves as the rationale for the changes Sartre makes to his key ontological terms the *Critique*, wherein 'being-for-itself' and 'being-in-itself' are replaced with 'praxis' and 'practico-inert'. These changes are not merely terminological. While Sartre's mature existentialism still subscribes to a dualistic ontology that construes existence as comprised of two components in an internal relation, it assigns different features to these components.

The Ancient Greek term 'praxis' is often translated as 'realization' or 'action' and Marx uses it to refer to distinctively human activity in his first thesis on Feuerbach. In the *Critique*, 'praxis' refers any purposeful action. However, Sartre's realistic materialism leads him to interpret praxis as material change that refers to a project and involves a passage from one objective state to another through 'interiorization' – i.e. through being mediated by the thought of the agent (CDR I/CRD I: 71/185). Unlike being-for-itself, praxis cannot be used interchangeably with 'consciousness' or 'thought' because it has to have a material manifestation.

'Practico-inert' is distinct from being-in-itself because all that can be said of the latter is that *it is*: it is the being that is identical with itself, whereas the practico-inert designates the world of worked-on matter in which praxis obtains. The introduction of the concept of the practico-inert is perhaps the most major development in Sartre's social theory (Caws 1992), due to how its recognition of the way that matter imposes necessities upon human being because of what it is, and because of its indifference to human being, facilitates a nuanced appreciation of how socio-material structures mediate between the aims of individuals and their ability to accomplish them. The presence of 'practico' in the practico-inert signals that there is no 'pure inertia' anywhere in the human universe, as material things possess a kind of automatic or agentless agency, which makes the material world capable of acting upon the action of agents in it. This explains the existence of 'counter-finalities': the by-products of praxis that transform it into 'antipraxis'. Sartre illustrates this idea by considering the floods that occurred in China as a result of agricultural deforestation. The Chinese peasants' positive pursuit of greater yield from their harvests through the creation of more arable land, he explains, blinded them to the consequence of negative aspect of their pursuit (the removal of trees): the increasing lack of protection from floods provided by forestry. Although the Chinese peasants could not have foreseen the consequences of deforesting their land, the terrible history of the Chinese floods can be regarded as 'an intentionally constructed mechanism' through which agents' need-satisfying intentions became counterfinalized, as their praxis was stolen, reversed and handed back them in an unrecognizable form (CDR I/CRD I: 162/273). The practico-inert thus incorporates far more than the brute physical facts of the environment; it also refers to the potential of the environment to act upon us. (It is also indicative of the kind of ecological awareness that is associated with the term 'Anthropocene' today, as it construes nature as having been irrevocably touched by culture.)

Knowledge of dialectical objects

We have already seen why, for Sartre, everything that can be known about another person pertains to their objective being, their 'self'. He reaffirms this view in *Search for a Method*, but he formulates it somewhat differently. Here, he argues that subjectivity exists only in its objectification, so that 'the objectified truth of the objectified subjective must be considered the *only truth of the subjective*' (SM/QM: 98n./136n. emphasis added). This claim is consistent with Sartre's earlier view that even if it were possible to experience another's experience, no knowledge of them could be gleaned from such an experience because the truth of their being lies in the objective world. However, it should be noted Sartre's conception of truth in his later work is decidedly more Hegelian. Hegel illustrated his conception of truth by pointing out that the 'bud disappears in the bursting forth of the blossom', which is then superseded by the fruit; yet, it is nonsense to claim that each of these forms – bud, blossom, fruit – falsifies the previous as 'the truth' of the plant when each form is necessary to it and 'this mutual necessity alone constitutes the life of the whole' (Hegel 1977: 2). Sartre's later conception of truth is also dialectical in this way. In *Search for a Method*, he affirms that 'truth is something which becomes ... a totalization which is forever being totalized' (SM/QM: 30/45). This means that no fact in isolation can be true since facts only become truths through their relation 'to the totalization in process' (SM/QM: 31/45). So, while the facts themselves are not subject to change, and no fact can be excluded from the totalization, the truth of the relation between the facts is subject to change with the emergence of new facts within the developing totalization.

Although this Hegelian conception of truth as a relation might initially appear to be a form of relativism, Sartre denies that this is the case. He even presents dialectical reason as a corrective to what he calls 'the relativism of the positivists' which regards the reconstitution of an object 'in its totalising movement' as an impossibility on the grounds that dialectical reason makes this possible (CDR I/CRD I: 23/143). Just as the bursting forth of the flower and the fruit does not falsify the bud, the claim of dialectical reason to deliver 'certain totalising truths – if not the whole Truth' cannot be disqualified by the way that the facts are reorganized from one moment to the next (CDR I/CRD I: 23/143). Hence, Sartre views truth as relational but not relative; it is a function of the relation of all the facts to one another at a given moment, which means that the truth of any given moment is not merely valid from a particular perspective at a specific time and place, it is 'valid for all the particular cases which recreate it' in a way that discloses its dialectical necessity (CDR I/CRD I: 37/156).

Sartre's Hegelian conception of truth does not imply that he abandons his conception of knowledge as (empirical) knowledge of objects, but it does give him a more sophisticated conception of the totalizing, imaginary objects that allow human beings to make sense of their experience. In what follows, I will use the term 'dialectical objects' to refer to such objects, which are both constitutive of and constituted by the historical dialectic. As the historical dialectic 'can only be the totalisation of concrete totalisations effected by a multiplicity of totalizing individualities' (CDR I/CRD I: 37/155–6), dialectical objects refer to the concrete totalizations of which it is composed and which represent the proper objects of dialectical investigations: namely, particular histories and selves. Only a dialectical analysis can deliver knowledge of such objects in the context of Sartre's mature existentialism, not because it can uncover any new facts about them but because it provides the key to the proper organization of the facts and knowledge of a dialectical object must be an 'organization' not an 'inventory' (CDR I/CRD I: 23/143).

The first major epistemological implication of Sartre's discovery of the dialectic is that knowledge of a dialectical object, such as a self, requires the knower to configure all the facts concerning that object in a way that renders each fact intelligible in terms of the 'totalization' of all of them. The second is that it is possible to communicate knowledge of dialectical objects via the production of representations that facilitate 're-totalizations' of them. This should not be read to reintroduce an intellectualist conception of truth as correspondence between representation and reality, though. Sartre's mature existentialism affirms that it is possible to communicate knowledge of dialectical objects through language, not because it takes the intelligible structure of language to correspond to that of dialectical objects but because it views the language we use to describe them as nothing other than their intelligible structure, since our conceptual comprehension of human-reality is, simultaneously, an 'immediate existence' in our consciousness of objects and the basis for 'an indirect knowing of existence' (SM/QM: 170–1/236). The very idea that our being and knowledge are dialectically related in this way is, Sartre stresses, 'contradictory to the intellectualist idea of knowledge' (SM/QM: 175/242).

One further point is, I believe, crucial to understanding how Sartre adapts his epistemology after his discovery of the dialectic. In a lengthy footnote in *Search for a Method*, Sartre observes that Marx can only present his materialist conception of reality as capturing its absolute truth by supressing his own subjectivity and imaging himself 'an *objective observation*' (SM/QM: 32n./47n.). The suppression of subjectivity in the work of Marx and his followers has, Sartre argues, resulted in the production of materialist perspectives that exclude the 'human' from the 'matter' they are concerned with. To highlight the error of this approach, he draws an analogy between microphysics and dialectical analysis on the grounds that 'the revelation of a system' in both kinds of investigation is only effected 'in and through' human acts that change it (SM/QM: 32n./47n.). Just as

Heisenberg's uncertainty principle holds that any attempt to measure the velocity of a subatomic particle will interfere with its motion in an unpredictable way, Sartre's mature existentialism holds that the contemplation of an object changes it by reintroducing it into the dialectic at a new stage and 're-totalizing' it there. Even if Marxist analyses often neglect to situate knowledge within the dialectic, Sartre nevertheless finds 'the rudiments' of the 'realistic epistemology' in them (SM/QM 33n./49n.), which he goes on to develop by emphasizing knowledge as part of the dialectic.

Sartre's search for a new objective method

Freud coined the word 'psychoanalysis' by coupling 'psychology' and 'analysis'. He brought these two terms together to emphasize the analogy he sees between the discipline he founded and 'chemical analysis' in terms of its scientific rigour and methodological approach. He therefore conceived of psychoanalysis as a sister to chemical analysis in the psychological realm, with the idea being that just as chemical analysis strives to isolate the 'fundamental substance' from the salt in which it is combined with other substances and initially 'unrecognizable', psychoanalysis strives to isolate the pathological 'instinctual impulses' from the complex mental formations in which they are embedded (CW XVII: 160).[9]

However, Freud recognized the subjective dimension of psychology as a clear obstacle to psychoanalysis being ranked among the natural sciences. The tendency of his case histories to read like novels particularly concerned him. In the Prefatory Remarks to *A Case of Hysteria*, for example, he criticizes physicians who read psychoanalytical case studies not as contributions 'to the psychopathology of the neuroses', but as novels 'for their private delectation' (CW VII: 9). Obviously, Freud is most disturbed the exploitative nature of this practice in the context of studies that detail patients' sexual experience. But his insistence that the value of these studies lies in their provision of clues to the answers to scientific questions about 'the internal structure of the neurosis' and 'the relation between the mental and the somatic' (CW VII: 13) also betrays his concerns about the mere possibility of his psychological studies being read in a literary manner, as opposed to a source of facts about natural phenomena. Freud is, I believe, troubled by the fact that his case studies afford literary readings because he knows that if psychoanalysis is to be recognized as a scientific enterprise that generates knowledge about nature beyond 'the subjective', its subject needed to be recognized as a natural one. He therefore strove to 'naturalize' the subject of psychoanalysis by connecting the thoughts of the patients he studied to a natural object – the unconscious – whose physical operations are potentially observable.[10] Hence, his insistence that it will always be possible to discover the presence of 'an unquestionably organic factor' in the aetiology of even the mildest psychological disorders – 'the neuroses' (CW XIII: 175).

Although Sartre agrees with Freud on the point that the subject of psychoanalysis must be an object in the world, he regards Freud's approach to objectifying the subjective as unhelpful because it reduces the subjective to a mere effect of arational, causal processes within the natural order. By taking the thoughts it takes to be the ultimate source of psychopathological symptoms to be an upshot of natural processes, Freud's psychoanalytic theory dismisses the significance of meaningful connections between thought contents that its analyses often uncover because it supposes them to be the result of rationalizations that occur at a relatively superficial level and, therefore, incapable of shedding any light on the deeper, unconscious, arational, natural mechanisms that ultimately cause psychological problems. This effectively excludes the intelligible relations between thoughts from the causal processes that count for Freudian psychoanalysis, at least in terms of its scientific agenda. And this, in Sartre's view, leads Freudian psychoanalysis to interpret behaviour as if it emerged from a thing-like substance rather than a totalizing movement – i.e. a human being. Although the analytic approach it employs allows it to explain thought in wholly objective terms by tracing it to a biological source, Sartre describes it as a 'logic of ambiguity' insofar as it affirms the significance of the subjective at the empirical-therapeutic level of patient analysis only to deny it at the level of aetiological theorization (CDR I/CRD I: 17n./137n.). From the perspective of dialectical reason, this ambiguity can be attributed to Freud's failure to recognize that the proper object of psychoanalysis is not a natural, 'analytical', purely objective object but a dialectical object that is partly constituted by subjectivity.

In a lengthy footnote that spans over two pages in the *Critique*, Sartre illustrates his understanding of the relation between dialectical and analytical objects through the example of a picture of a line intersecting a circle. A child or an uneducated person, he writes, can look at this picture and intuitively grasp the truth that a straight line which intersects a circle at one point must also intersect it at another. This, he believes, is because the picture is first dialectically intelligible in terms of praxis – as an abstract representation of movement, in which the circle 'as the abstract idealisation of enclosure, *confines*', while the straight line 'as the idealisation of a disciplined journey, *shatters obstacles in its path*' (CDR I/

CRD I: 62n./177n.). A mathematician, however, would not be satisfied by merely apprehending this truth this way; she requires proof. But the proof pushes the 'circle-as-sensible-object' into the background and defines it by only 'one of its properties' (CDR I/CRD I: 62n./177n.) – the property of being radially oriented around a centre point – which allows the relation between the line and the circle to be expressed algebraically (in terms of simultaneous quadratic and linear equations). Sartre concludes that the mathematician's analytic process 'destroys the sensible and qualitative unity of the *circle-gestalt*' in order to interpret it in a purely geometrical schema (CDR I/CRD I: 62n./177n.). The analytical truth concerning the relation between the circle and the line is, therefore, only a partial truth of the dialectical object, which it can only be arrived through the suspension of the rich, primary comprehension we first have of it.

Rather than regulate the primary, lived comprehension of experience to the background by treating the subject of psychoanalysis as an analytical object, Sartre uses dialectical reason to incorporate the subjective into the objective process of self-formation and to, thereby, preserve its significance to psychoanalytic investigations. So, while in *Being and Nothingness*, Sartre notes that existential psychoanalysis has yet to find its 'Freud' (BN/EN: 745/620) – meaning someone who could develop an objective method appropriate to the study of selves – once he discovers dialectical reason, he realizes that he can be existential psychoanalysis's 'Freud'. Dialectical reason provides him with the tool he needs to work out how Freudian psychoanalytic techniques can be adapted and incorporated into an existential analysis. In *Search for a Method*, he construes them as belonging to the 'regressive' part of his proposed 'progressive-regressive' method of analysis and, contra Freud, interprets them to be chiefly concerned with uncovering the 'subjective' significance of the biographical facts for the analysand. He then presents the 'progressive' part as being concerned with gaining an 'objective' understanding of the analysand's socio-material situation. By bringing these two parts together, his revised method of existential psychoanalysis works to synthesize a comprehension of the action of 'childhood' on shaping the analysand's choices with an understanding of the effects of the 'objective structures' and 'material conditions' upon them in a 'dialectical totalization' (SM/QM: 64/90).

This progressive-regressive method is geared towards highlighting the individuating features of the subject's objective being – i.e. those that cannot be explained as a result of the objective conditions – as this allows the choices that contribute to their self-formation 'to emerge from the background of the *general* contradictions of productive forces and relations of production' (SM/

QM: 57/81–2). Sartre's explicit aim to push the progressive analysis from a general understanding of the analysand's socio-material situation all the way through to the discovery of the choices that individuate them is what makes his revised psychoanalysis both Marxist and existentialist. Although Sartre reads Marx himself to have often pushed his analyses close to this point, he holds that contemporary Marxists leave the task of establishing the particulars of a person's life to other disciplines, which lack the means to do so satisfactorily because Marxism is 'the only philosophy which can really grasp the complexity of human being' (SM/QM: 53/76). So, Sartre's progressive-regressive method is 'objective' insofar as it can, in principle, be applied to any human being by any other, but it is also 'subjective' insofar as the analyst must regard their subjectivity as a tool to be used in the analysis, rather than as an impediment to it. This is because, for Sartre, our basic capacity to comprehend the primary, human significance of biographical facts is essential for the acquisition of knowledge of a self, as it is what allows us to apprehend them as part of a totalization.

A word on the body: It would be absurd to ascribe to Sartre the untenable view that biochemical factors never play a role in precipitating psychological illness. Although his initial existentialism has, however, been rightly criticized for not having taken the potential for the body to constrain freedom seriously enough (Wider 1997; Howells 2011) and although I believe this problem is redressed in Sartre's mature existentialism through its emphasis of need as a central force in structuring human-reality, I will not belabour this point here because Sartre's crucial point is that the self, not the body, is the proper object of psychoanalysis. So, Sartre can, for example, accept that behavioural and personality changes may be the only symptoms of a brain tumour (Madhusoodanan et al. 2015), although he would affirm that such symptoms are psychologically significant only insofar as the subject can choose the way that these symptoms manifest themselves and/or the stance she takes towards them. When there is no scope for the subject's choice to oppose the facts of their situation, there is no dialectical process of self-formation in play, only causal determination. Sartre's discussion of the wounded soldier in *The Family Idiot* illustrates this point well. This solider is marching away from the enemy and he knows that if he continues to march alongside his comrades, he will escape. But he suffers more with every hour that passes, he becomes less able to endure it, and, consequently, he loses interest in joining with the regiment, outwitting the enemy in pursuit and being nursed back to health. This is because the strength of his choice is reduced by the 'violent', unchosen desire 'to give up, to leave his comrades, to let himself fall, to lie passively, awaiting disaster and death', which will eventually become 'irresistible' (FI I/IF I: 36/46). Once this happens, the soldier's choice drops out of the equation; his physiological state deprives him of the power to make himself anything other than a wounded soldier who is going to die if his comrades do not carry him. Thus, all 'psychological' symptoms that are truly the effects of organic illness fall within the purview of medicine not psychoanalysis on Sartre's account because they are not part of the dialectic that constitutes the subject's self, although they will be reintegrated into this dialectic when the subject regains their capacity to choose.

Sartre's debt to Beauvoir

How can society shape selves? Sartre's initial form of existentialism cannot provide a satisfactory answer to this question. The only notion it can draw on to explain how people can be constrained in their self-formation is bad faith. But bad faith is a tool for coping with the human condition that is developed at the individual level, so it can neither account for how people can come to behave in ways that are typical of certain social groups, nor for how members of socially oppressed groups typically develop 'inferiority complexes', which manifest themselves in various self-sabotaging behaviours. Although we have seen that bad faith *can* explain how an individual could conceal the choice of inferiority from themselves – as in the case of the stutterer considered above – it *cannot* explain how many members of marginalized social groups could make the same choice of inferiority and express it similar in ways.

If the freedom of consciousness to choose its Self and the meaning of the world for it is without any external constraints, the fact that people who belong to the same social group or who have been similarly exploited or abused often display similar qualities seems to be an 'unexplainable coincidence' (Webber 2018: 123–5). Without an appreciation of how environmental factors can constrain subjects in their capacity to choose, there is no way to account for the well-documented effects of oppression upon the behaviour of members of oppressed groups.[11] Feminist philosopher Sandra Lee Bartky uses the term 'psychological oppression' to denote the covert, systematic, social processes of fragmentation and mystification that mediate oppressed people's relationship to their self. In this context, 'fragmentation' refers to the social mechanisms that effectively split the subject's image of her self into parts. Stereotyping, for example, incites a conflict between a 'true' and a 'false' self by presenting the subject with an image of her self that has no basis in her actions, whereas sexual objectification presents the subject with a 'degrading' image of her body instead of her self (1990: 23). 'Mystification' then refers to the systematic obfuscation of these processes of fragmentation, which work to ensure that the members of the groups targeted by them will blame themselves for their depreciated self and live out their relation to it as 'destiny, guilt, or neurosis' (1990: 23). A final result of psychological oppression, according to Bartky, is to deprive the subject of 'an autonomous choice of self' (1990: 31). Although Bartky concentrates on highlighting the function of psychological oppression in Western patriarchal societies, she also suggests that psychological oppression can occur within the family unit.[12] In what follows, I shall take up this suggestion by using the term 'psychological oppression' to refer to the process through which social macrocosms – i.e. societies at large – and social microcosms – families, friendship groups, workplaces, etc. – make their members oppress themselves.

Sartre's mature form of existentialism can account for the phenomenon of psychological oppression because it can explain how the subject's interpretation of their self and their possibilities can be constrained by the objective features of their situation. The change in Sartre's conception of the situation from his initial to his mature existentialism is perhaps best illustrated by the change in the way that he describes the composition of 'hodological space' – a concept he borrows from Gestalt psychology to signal the difference between the space that human beings live in and Euclidian geometric space. Hodological space is composed of pragmatic pathways towards ends determined by the subject: I apprehend the space between the door and my body as 'space-to-be-traversed' if I am to realize the possibility of leaving of the room, not as 'three metres'. This leads to a conception of the world as a 'hollow that is always in the future' (BN/EN: 433/362), which hints at the idea of a 'mould to be filled' without any suggestion that this mould is set by anything other than the subject's original choice. In the *Critique*, however, Sartre offers an example of a situation in which 'hexis' (*ëxis*) – i.e. inertia-like action that does not transcend the situation – 'was primarily a hodological determination of the lived space' (CDR/CRD I: 358–9/462): the Réveillon riots of 1789, in which the lack of unity and organization among the protesters, combined with the topographical configuration of the Quartier Saint-Antoine, all but guaranteed that troops would enter the district and massacre the protesters there. There was already a clear pathway in the hodological space for the troops, which 'predestined' their action. In Sartre's mature existentialism, then, the situation can no longer be considered as brute matter for subjects to mould into a meaningful shape; it is more like a pre-prepared mould for their selves. But what motivates this dramatic shift in his understanding of the situation?

Sartre began to revise his initial existentialism in the wake of the Second World War,[13] and his 'conversion' to Marxism during the 1950s was obviously instrumental to the development of his dialectical materialism. However, the extent to which Simone de Beauvoir's existentialism influenced his transition from his initial to his mature form of existentialism is also beginning to be brought to light (Simons 1986; Kruks 1995; Webber 2018; Kirkpatrick 2019a, 2019b; Edwards 2021). Notably, Beauvoir was the first to combine existentialism with psychoanalysis *and* dialectical materialism to explain how women can be made to accept a feminine destiny as their fate in *The Second Sex* (*Le deuxième sexe*, 1949). Moreover, she integrates insights from psychoanalysis and historical materialism into her existentialism *after* pointing out that women's subjugation cannot be accounted for in terms of a Hegelian Master-Slave dialectic (SS/DS I: 6–17/18–34). Hegel, Marx, Freud: the very same triumvirate that guides the development of Sartre's existentialism after *Being and Nothingness* first appears in Beauvoir's existentialist analysis of women's psychological oppression, where she synthesizes insights from the Hegelian dialectic, Freudian psychoanalysis and Marx's (and Engels's) historical materialism to show that the source of what she calls the 'feminine inferiority complex' (SS/DS II: 627/443) lies in the systematic, social processes that fragment women's selves and mystify their consciousness during their transition from girl to woman.

Beauvoir's analysis of 'Women's Situation and Character' in *The Second Sex* is especially noteworthy in that it may have supplied Sartre with a blueprint for his progressive-regressive method. The aim of this chapter is to offer a '*synthetic point of view*' of women's situation to comprehend the 'eternal feminine' as an upshot of women's 'economic, social and historical conditioning as a whole' (SS/DS II: 653/477, emphasis added). In it, Beauvoir examines specific features of women's situation within a patriarchal society to make the interplay between the socio-material forces of domination and individual choice in their experience comprehensible and to show that 'woman's whole "character"' can be explained by 'her situation' because her situation impairs her capacity to choose for herself (SS/DS II: 677/511). As Michel Kail points out, it is through this endeavour that Beauvoir supplies the foundation for a 'new epistemology' (2006: 117), one that indicates how we can acquire knowledge of others through synthesizing an objective analysis of their situation with an empathetic comprehension of it, which, I believe, bears a striking resemblance to the 'realistic epistemology' that Sartre turns his mature existentialism to support (see pages 73–6 above).

In the *Critique*, Sartre recognizes the possibility of 'transcendence failures' through acts that amount to no more than hexis, which does not effect any positive change. His discussion of the working-class man who seeks to better himself by taking up boxing as a profession shows that he also regards such transcendence failures as a key symptom of oppression. This working-class man's exploitation in the market system 'de-realizes' his physical power in the ring, in Sartre's view, by making it a symbol of his 'radical powerlessness' outside of it; yet, all this is mystified in his experience because he lives his violence 'in its explosive power', even while it alienates him from his 'sole emancipatory power' (CDR II/CRD II: 46/56). His acts in the ring are hexis because they are co-opted by the bourgeoisie and transformed into another commodity sold on the market. Beauvoir's concept of negative action is a clear precursor to Sartre's 'hexis'. In *The Ethics of Ambiguity*, for example, Beauvoir argues that a 'transcendence condemned to fall uselessly back upon itself' because it only engages in negative action is 'what defines the situation of oppression' (EA/MA: 81/102). Then, in *The Second Sex*, Beauvoir offers the example of the housewife who dusts, sweeps, mops, cooks, polishes and tidies but nevertheless 'does nothing' (SS/DS II: 487/264) because the patriarchal institution of marriage dooms her to repetition, routine and experiencing transcendence only in its 'negative aspect' (SS/DS II: 488/265).

This strongly suggests Sartre is greatly indebted to Beauvoir for having provided the first model of how existentialism can be adapted to accommodate the phenomenon of psychological oppression, support a realistic epistemology and to appreciate the key significance of childhood for subjects' self-formation. And it is his later appreciation of how our conditioning during childhood constrains what we can imagine, choose and become in our adult life which represents the most important difference between Sartre's initial and mature forms of existentialism from a psychoanalytic perspective.

The spirals of self-formation

Sartre's first psycho-biographical study was published in 1946 and its subject was the poet Charles Baudelaire. This rather unflattering portrait of one of France's national institutions caused a scandal (Contat and Rybalka 1970: 143), and the lack of objective measures in Sartre's initial version of his existential psychoanalysis led commentators to dismiss the study as a work of 'subjective criticism' that reveals more about its author than its subject (Roditi 1950: 100).

Sartre also quickly dismisses *Baudelaire* as 'inadequate' when asked about it in a 1969 interview for *New Left Review* (IOT: 50). But we should not be so quick to dismiss the significance of this first application of his psychoanalytical method, as it offers important insights into the development of his psychoanalytical thought.[14]

Firstly, *Baudelaire* supplies what, to my knowledge, is Sartre's first depiction of a circular process of self-formation. As if anchored to a fixed point, Sartre's Baudelaire suffers because he cannot become 'other' than what he is; he cannot progress, only go round and round in circles, reaffirming that he is what he is. However, Sartre presents this suffering as a result of Baudelaire's own choice of an unchanging, statue-like Self. Had Baudelaire not been in bad faith about this choice, Sartre contends that he would have been able to move 'forward' in his project of self-formation but, instead, he stifled the positive aspect of his freedom 'to experience it in its negative form of non-satisfaction', which effectively meant that 'the loop was looped' in his life's trajectory (B: 98/91) and he cut himself off from new possibilities at the age of twenty-one, after which he did nothing new. Herein lies one of the first major achievements of Sartre's analytical method in practice: the provision of an account for the so-called compulsion to repeat that does not make recourse to the unconscious because it shows how bad faith can lead a subject to become trapped in a circular movement.[15] Although Beauvoir's summation of *Baudelaire* as 'a phenomenological description', which 'lacks the psychoanalytical dimension that would have explained Baudelaire on the basis of his body and the facts of his life history' is accurate (1963: 52), certain aspects of it indicate that Sartre was already beginning to see the potential for the situation to play a more active role in subjects' self-formation. Most notably, *Baudelaire* describes two traits that Sartre will later present as symptomatic responses to psychological oppression: a 'complex' that constrains the subject in their self-formation (B: 56/53) and a tendency towards escapism that is self-destructive.[16]

It is not until he writes *Saint Genet: Actor and Martyr* (*Saint Genet, comédien at martyr*, 1952), however, that Sartre traces a circular form of self-formation to the subject's childhood conditioning. As a Parisian orphan being raised by foster parents in a village community, Sartre proposes that Jean Genet was 'condemned to theft' (SG: 58/73). Being both dimly aware of his own abandonment and inculcated to see property as a cipher for goodness and legitimacy, young Genet began to steal at an early age in order to feel like a legitimate member of his community by acquiring property. However, Sartre argues that when Genet is eventually caught in the act at the age of ten, this plunges him into the 'crisis' that led to him to make his original choice to be what this crime made him in the eyes of others: 'evil' (SG: 59/74). If Genet was already a thief, though, why is this incident the 'crisis' that sets the mould for his self? In brief, Sartre's answer is that it makes him shamefully aware of what he is for others for the first time. Genet had not previously experienced his pilfering in defining him in any way; it did not even seem real to him, as it had never had an adult witness. But as soon as he is caught stealing, everything changes: his secret, unknown 'inwardness' becomes an objective, shameful quality of his self with a name: 'thief' (SG: 18/27).

Two features of this event make it a crisis. One, Genet is not caught by one of his parents but by another member of the community. If he had been caught by his father, Sartre explains that he would have soon been able to overcome his sense of shameful isolation because it is easy to dismiss stealing from one's own family as not really stealing and because his father's critical Look would, eventually, have given way to a loving Look. But because it is someone from outside the family who exposes him, they expose him as a thief *and* a foundling simultaneously by revealing an 'evil' principle within him, which can only be 'explained' by his shady origins outside the community along the following lines: 'That little thief, where does he come from? He surely takes after someone. Only a slut would abandon her son. A chip off the old block' (SG: 19/28). So, this shameful revelation appears to Genet as proof of what he had always suspected: he does not belong. Two, Genet is caught at the tender age of ten, an age at which adults still appear to be gods and children lack the ability to challenge parental values. Had somebody called Genet a thief at the age of seventeen, Sartre says that he would have by then had the means to reject other people's opinions of him. But at ten, Genet has no way to defend himself from the damning judgement of the 'honest folk' who surround him; he is 'trapped like a rat' because he cannot question their morality and so he becomes his own most zealous tormentor because they 'have penetrated to the very bottom of his heart and installed there a permanent delegate which is himself' (SG: 21/31).

Rather than describe Genet's choice to be what his situation made him as a form of bad faith, Sartre presents it as a choice he had to make to continue to live in his situation, as the only alternative was to allow it to crush him. He interprets it as a form of 'defensive aggressiveness' that enables Genet to gain some sense of autonomy in a situation that stifles it through determining 'the inner meaning of his pilfering' (SG: 58/73). Notably, Sartre compares Genet's defensive aggressiveness to that which Beauvoir identifies in adolescent girls who make themselves touch and eat revolting insects in performances that anticipate and symbolize the 'deflowering' that they know they will have to endure, but which they experience as a result of their own initiative (SG: 57/72 and see SS/DS II: 377–8/122–3) because he believes that what these young girls and Genet have in common is that 'their only recourse is to will what is'; their future is carved in stone and they cannot refuse it, they can only 'refuse to *undergo* it' (SG: 57/72). But to accept a destiny imposed upon one in an attitude of defensive aggressiveness is 'to place oneself in a prison without bars' in Sartre's view (SG: 69/85), since its only effect is to make this destiny bearable through the affirmation of choice in it when there was originally none. Acceptance in defiance is still acceptance, and the final result of defensive aggressiveness is to allow oppressed subjects to comply with society's expectations of them, without feeling as though they are complicit. Sartre proposes that the psychological mechanisms that facilitate this in Genet's case are 'whirligigs' (*tourniquets*) (SG: 333/372).[17] Thinking through whirligigs that trap his thought in circles enables Genet to conceal his continued complicity with his destiny from himself by distracting him from hoping for something different, better. He does not dare imagine 'that he will someday write', for instance, because he has learned to make his life liveable by locking his thoughts in a 'circular prison' (SG: 339/379). His psychological whirligigs are therefore a consequence of his oppressive situation and a creative strategy for surviving it at once.

What is most remarkable about (Sartre's) Genet, then, is that he manages to break free of the whirligigs that lock him in a vicious cycle of hexis. In the second volume of the *Critique*, Sartre provides further clarification of his concept of hexis when he describes it as 'the mere interiorization of conditionings' (CDR II/CRD II: 199/210), which is externalized through actions that are in accord with how the 'common individual' of that society would be expected to act (CDR II/CRD II: 200/210). Genet's life of crime before he became a writer thus represents hexis insofar as it is entirely in accord with his social conditioning and others' low expectations of him. But Genet finds a way to break the mould his society made for him through the entirely unexpected production of great literary works. To achieve this, Sartre argues that Genet's attitude towards others had to undergo a 'radical conversion' (SG: 425/473). Crucially, though, Genet's conversion is not attributed to a marvellous 'instant' of radical freedom wherein Genet abandons his original choice for a new one,[18] but to Genet's ability to develop new ways of pursuing the same original choice, which, eventually, lead him to a way of being that enables him to play a more creative role in his self-formation and thereby become something other than the criminal he was conditioned to become. Genet's writing does not evince a new choice of Self, then, but a new behavioural interpretation of his original choice to be the no-good troublemaker society told him he was. So, he is still, if only for himself, being 'evil' when he writes because he conceives of his literary works as artful 'snares' (SG: 370/413), designed to allure the reader so that they may infect them with the same evil principle that Genet's society found in him. Even though writing enables Genet to 'transcend *all* his contradictions', to break free of his whirligigs, and to partake in 'pure freedom' of the artist that knows neither Good nor Evil (SG: 422/470), he writes when it is too late to change who he fundamentally is, as that matter was settled for him when he was ten years old. Moreover, it is thanks to a 'whirligig', rather than a positive choice to change, that Genet starts writing, since he writes his first poem and reads it in public to inspire the contempt of others whom he holds in contempt, so that he can take pride in their mockery of and contempt for him and thus prove that 'he who loses wins' (SG: 430/478).

Although Sartre denies that he had all the 'keys' of his progressive-regressive method of psychoanalysis when he undertook his study of Genet (IOT: 51), what is present in this study that was missing in *Baudelaire* is the inclusion of an objective, 'progressive' dimension. Sartre still understands transcendence as a vertical movement, an 'original arising' of freedom that negates the facts of the deterministic universe through its positive movement towards a chosen possibility (BN/EN: 250/212), but he now situates transcendence in a socio-material world, within that universe, where it is almost always bent, twisted or even inverted by the mould that society makes for its members' selves. Thus, *Saint Genet* represents a milestone in the development of Sartre's existentialism insofar as it portrays Genet as a victim of psychological oppression, whose situation imposed an original choice of Self upon him that he struggled to live with.

Knowledge of another self

In Sartre's mature existentialism, reciprocity replaces conflict as the fundamental form of human relation. 'Reciprocity' simply describes the relation between two persons 'who *recognise each other* in their freedom' (CDR I/CRD I: 110/222). It can either be positive – in relations of love, friendship and solidarity – or negative – in relations between rivals and enemies. In any case, it is the basis for comprehension. Regardless of whether I wish another well or ill, recognizing them as a free agent in pursuit of projects is what allows me to see their behaviour as purposive. However, the 'mutual recognition' that Sartre now considers the primary form of sociality tends to be corrupted by the socially determined responses to scarcity: seriality and struggle among individuals, which, in a capitalist society, lead to 'exploitation and oppression' (CDR I/CRD I: 110/222). After writing *Saint Genet*, Sartre states that he regards love 'more positively' (IWS: 13) and, hence, sees more possibilities for escaping the sadomasochistic circles described in *Being and Nothingness*. But he also sees the potential for the structures of domination in a socio-material world to crush individuals by turning their attempts to transcend their situation into circular hexis that only embeds them deeper in it. Hell is not other people for later Sartre,[19] it is the circle that characterizes the experience of oppressed persons whose acts are only hexis,[20] whereas the living struggle is represented by a spiral that both preserves and transcends the *status quo*.

Sartre's views about the sources of interpersonal misery have changed. But the problem of human loneliness remains a central concern for him as two consciousness that look at one another still lies at the heart of his social ontology. Reciprocity represents both the basis for, and the limit of, 'unification' between people, since no matter how many projects two people share or how intertwined their 'synthetic totalizations' (i.e. selves) become, *'there will always be two of them*, each integrating the entire universe', separately (CDR I/CRD I: 113–14/226). So, by producing psychoanalytical biographies that aim to demonstrate the possibility of gaining knowledge of another self, Sartre calls upon his epistemology to mitigate the negative implications of his social ontology. The view that Sartre's biographies are at least partly intended to assuage the reader's loneliness is substantiated by his remarks in the conclusion to *Saint Genet,* where he underlines the anguish we are likely to experience 'when certain minds open before our eyes as yawning chasms' to reveal 'what we considered to be our innermost being' – our selves – as a mere 'fabricated appearance' and that nothing prevents us from having the qualities 'that repel us most in others' (SG: 589/650). By imaginatively engaging with the processes through which Genet formed his self, then, we become aware of the fundamental basis for our empathetic comprehension of other people's experience: our ontological selflessness. That is, we realize that 'Genet is we' precisely because he is 'our solitude carried to the point of Passion' (SG: 599/661). But, through gaining knowledge of Genet, we can feel less alone without being any less alone.

However, Sartre's biographical study of Genet makes for strange reading when one realizes that Sartre and Genet were friends and that Genet read it. In a late interview with Beauvoir, Sartre describes Genet's reaction to the manuscript: 'He read it, and one night he got up and went over to the fireplace with the intention of burning it. I believe he did throw some pages in and then plucked them out'

(1986: 273). He then notes that his relations with Genet 'diminished' afterwards (1986: 274). Somewhat sadly, then, Sartre's attempt to mitigate human loneliness through supplying knowledge of a self had the effect of estranging him from the very person he sought to know. His psychoanalytic 'remedy' for human loneliness thus, arguably, increased his own personal loneliness by straining his friendship with Genet. It is important to note that Sartre's application of his existential psychoanalysis to Genet was not intended as therapy for Genet. Certainly, insofar as the conversion of 'hexis into praxis' can be regarded as a major therapeutic goal of Sartre's (revised) existential psychoanalysis (Cannon 1991: 171), it seems that one of the reasons why Genet interested Sartre as a biographical subject was because he believed that Genet had achieved this goal by himself. Genet was, for Sartre, an example of someone who was not in need of existential psychoanalysis. So, he applied his method to Genet to prove a point: that 'freedom alone can account for a person in his totality' (SG: 584/645). Nonetheless, Sartre's insertion of himself into the totalization-in-progress that was Genet's process of self-formation was evidently – and understandably – experienced by Genet as an unwelcome intrusion. Indeed, Sartre's observation that *Saint Genet* 'disgusted' Genet because he felt that he was as described there (1986: 273) suggests that reading the book supplied Genet with insights into his self, but without the kind of trusting, caring relationship that supports the subject in processing such insights in the context of psychotherapy. Despite his plea that we, the readers of *Saint Genet*, 'use Genet properly' (SG: 584/645), Sartre seems to have been oblivious to how inappropriate it is to 'use' any person in this way.

As noted in the Introduction, Sartre never underwent any formal psychoanalytic or psychotherapeutic training, nor had he been analysed or completed his own self-analysis at the time he wrote *Saint Genet*. So, his (mis)treatment of Genet in this work results from him approaching the project as a purely theoretical enterprise. He treats Genet as an object because his principal aim is to deliver knowledge of Genet and 'one can only know objects' (SG: 589/650). But the living Genet is still a subject and his self, still an intimate object for him. Putting aside the ethical issues involved in applying existential psychoanalysis to another living person outside of a contracted therapeutic relationship, the choice of a living subject creates problems for the epistemological claims of the analysis too, given Sartre's mature understanding of selves as dialectical objects. As a living person plays the central creative role in the formation of their self during their lifetime, the living Genet can still undermine Sartre's assessment of him through his acts, which do not merely become new facts that can be 'added' on to the end of the biography because they also re-totalize his self. It is due to the profound unknowability and unpredictability of the human being that makes its self that Sartre will later say that 'psychoanalysis is not knowledge nor does it claim to be, save when it hazards hypotheses on the dead' ([1964] 2008/1972: 145), which is to say that psychoanalysis can only make claims to knowledge of the dead for the reason that, in death, the subject passes the responsibility for the continued totalization of the dialectical object that is their self to others.

Sartre's final and fullest application of his psychoanalytic method, *The Family Idiot*, responds to the question: 'what, at this point in time, can we know about a man?' (FI I/IF I: ix/7). It aims 'to prove that every man is perfectly knowable as long as one uses the appropriate method and as long as the necessary documents are available' (OIF/SIF: 123/106) by communicating knowledge of a dead man's self. In this study, Sartre aims to present the results of years of intensive historical, biographical, socio-political and psychoanalytical research into Gustave Flaubert's (1821–80) life and times in a book, which, he believes, will enable the reader to gain knowledge of Flaubert's self through a re-totalization of it.

4

The Family Idiot and the objectification of a self

If we think of human history as a tapestry and the life of an individual as a single thread, then we can say that *The Family Idiot* aims to examine the constitution of Flaubert's being, which may be likened to the fibres that compose a single thread (Being); chronicle his psychological development as he weaves his way through the structures that surround him, so as to facilitate an empathetic understanding of the subjective meaning of his choices (Comprehension); and, finally, to trace the pattern he made on history's tapestry to establish the objective meaning of his acts and illuminate the full dialectical significance of his situated choices (Knowing).

This chapter concentrates on showing how Sartre's application of his existential psychoanalysis in *The Family Idiot* combines these three approaches to understanding Flaubert's self-formation, treating each separately under the titles 'Being', 'Comprehension' and 'Knowing'. It is not intended as a substitute for the experience of reading *The Family Idiot* – the narrative of which plays a crucial role in making Flaubert's lived experience comprehensible. Rather, it aims to show how this multi-volume biography represents the completion of Sartre's solution to the problem of other minds, as well as the most rigorous application of his existential psychoanalysis, through its effort to synthesize the objective and subjective aspects of Flaubert's life and work and to, thereby, yield knowledge of Flaubert's self.

Being

Sartre identifies three fundamental relationships, formed at different stages of Flaubert's childhood, as having played a central role in shaping of his experience at all levels. These are: 'his relationship with his mother (action, language, sexuality), his relationship with his father (being looked at by the Other), and his relationship with his sister (spectre or the epic performance)' (FI II/IF II: 15/665). This section focuses on Flaubert's relationships with his mother and father. It elucidates Sartre's view that Flaubert's parents 'constitute' him, before going on, in the next section, to explore Flaubert's process of becoming, through which he responds creatively to his situation and to what his parents made of him, a process which his relationship with his sister is integral to.

Flaubert's passive constitution

The claim that Flaubert had a passive constitution is central to *The Family Idiot*. As the notion of 'constitution' is entirely new to Sartre's thought, it is vital to have a clear understanding of what purpose it serves in his psychoanalysis. Further, as Sartre presents Flaubert's constitution as partly a result of how he was nursed by his mother, the introduction of this notion represents a significant progression in Sartre's understanding of psychological development. Never before has Sartre acknowledged the paramount importance of the mother-infant relation to a person's capacity for growth. As Hazel E. Barnes observes, prior to his analysis of Flaubert, Sartre's existential accounts of self-formation seemed to imply that people 'sprang forth from the ground of being in full maturity – like Athena from the forehead of Zeus' (1981b: 24). But the idea that the way we are treated in our infancy could constitute us seems to run counter to the rejection of psychological determinism at the heart of Sartrean existentialism, so it is important to establish how Sartre integrates it into existentialism.

First of all, it is important to recognize that even though Sartre describes Flaubert's passive constitution as something he 'received from his mother' (FI I/IF I: 223/231), it is not something he was born with; it is an *almost* inevitable result of the situation he was born into. Gustave Flaubert was born in Rouen on the 12th of December 1821 to Anne Justine Caroline Flaubert and Dr Achille-Cléophas Flaubert, the director of the Hôtel-Dieu, a major hospital in Rouen. In the nine-year interim between Gustave's birth and that of his elder brother, Achille, the Flauberts had two other sons, and both had died at an early age. Another son arrived shortly after Gustave, only to die within a few months. Sartre asserts that Caroline was not emotionally invested in Gustave, her fourth son, partly because she feared that he might expire as quickly as his brothers and partly because she longed for a little girl. Apart from the fact that Caroline's frequent pregnancies only ceased after she gave birth to a female, there is no 'hard' evidence to support the Sartre's claim that she longed for a daughter. Hazel E. Barnes regards it as plausible, though, but notes that Sartre is at his 'most fascinating' and 'least excusable' when he draws conclusions about Caroline's treatment of baby Gustave on the basis of these three infant mortalities (1981b: 38), as he does in the following passage:

> Certainly infant mortality was severe at the time. However, the death of those three young males has always seemed suspect to me. Without 'mothering' an infant declines, in one month or three. Can we imagine that the virtuous and 'glacial' Caroline *senior* was the cause of their precipitous retreat? Struck by the previous mournings, she would have made an effort in Gustave's case. It is to this that he owed his life. Just barely. But afterward, she might have cried: 'Another one!' and the newborn, in the face of such a welcome, would have beaten a quick retreat.
>
> (FI II/IF II: 70n./723n.)

Although Barnes is certainly right to advise us to approach this kind of speculation about Caroline's mothering of her sons with caution, Sartre makes no attempt to conceal the fact that he is voicing a suspicion in this excerpt, which is taken from a footnote. In the main text, his analysis is more careful and, importantly, the conclusions he draws from the picture he paints of Flaubert's infancy are corroborated later on, through the dialectic of *The Family Idiot*. With this in mind, let us consider Sartre's discussion in the third chapter of the first volume on 'The Mother'.

Sartre assures his readers that Caroline loved her sons, but with the qualification that her love of them was secondary to, and derived from, her love of her husband. It was out of duty to her husband that she cared for *his* sons. Her love of them was, therefore, general, for 'whatever the child, the seed was the same' (FI I/IF I: 85/95). 'More a wife than a mother': Sartre states that this epithet fits Caroline Flaubert but suggests that 'incestuous daughter' is more apt (FI I/IF I: 86/95). A brief biographical analysis of Caroline Flaubert is offered in support of this rather startling idea. It underlines the facts that Caroline's mother died giving birth to her in November 1793 and that her father, Dr Fleuriot, died ten years later, as key to comprehending Caroline's character. What Sartre infers from these facts is that Caroline's earliest years must have been characterized by a double-frustration. Without a mother, she would have adored her father; yet, as his health began to deteriorate after his wife's death, he was most likely inattentive towards the daughter whom he seemingly did not love enough 'to want go on living' (FI I/IF I: 73/82). While widowers may harbour feelings of bitterness towards the child that 'killed' their wife, Sartre warns that there is no way of knowing that this was so in Caroline's case. Nor, he adds, is it possible to know how Caroline experienced being orphaned at ten years old. What we can know, though – because it is confirmed in the dialectic of Caroline's life – is that when her father died, Caroline decided that 'she would marry only her father' (FI I/IF I: 73/82) and hoped to have a daughter, so that she could compensate for the frustrations of her own childhood by vicariously experiencing the happiness of her daughter. This hypothesis explains many aspects of Caroline's relationship with her husband[1] and it motivates Sartre's claim that she reserved her tenderness for the little girl that would follow Gustave.[2]

Although the evidence for Sartre's conclusions about Caroline's mothering is somewhat slim, a remarkable piece of testimony seems to confirm them. Caroline's granddaughter states that, whenever they passed the Flaubert family's first home, 8 rue de Petit-Salut, in Rouen, her grandmother would declare that it was there that she spent the best years of her life (FI I/IF I: 76/85). When one realizes that the Flauberts lost two out of three children at their first address but only one out of three at their second, it seems odd that Caroline would consider the time she spent at the first address her happiest, as a crude arithmetic comparison would lead us to expect her to have experienced twice the amount of grief there. Sartre maintains that this mother's nostalgia for her first residence only makes sense if she did not truly suffer as a result of these first bereavements because her happiness depended entirely upon her husband. If this is correct, then Caroline's closeness with her husband during the first seven years of their marriage, before he took on a more senior role and the family took up residence in the Hôtel-Dieu, would explain her sentiment.

There are some good reasons to accept Sartre's view that Caroline Flaubert nursed Gustave with proficiency but without tenderness. Although, arguably, Sartre needed only to emphasize the point that Gustave arrived after two dead sons, as it is almost self-evident that a mother trying to protect her infant from death, but fearing that he might die all the while, would have been overly cautious and somewhat remote from him. What remains to be shown is whether this could cause her to 'constitute' her child in the way that Sartre argues she does. Sartre's argument for this view runs as follows. During his infancy, Gustave would have been diligently handled, changed, washed and fed at regular intervals, which meant that he would have never felt his physical needs urgently and so he would not have had the impetus to cry out or break out of 'the magic circle of passivity' (FI I/IF I: 131/138). Without tears or revolt, Gustave would have felt a very particular frustration: 'want of tenderness' (FI I/IF I: 129/136). What baby Gustave lacks is precisely the kind of reassurance regularly provided by less efficient mothers, who respond lovingly when their infant cries while they try to determine what is wrong. He is handled as a delicate 'thing' without having the compensation of also being recognized as a cherished subject.

As Sartre sees something like 'the rudimentary form of a project and consequently of action' in infants' expressions of their desires (FI I/IF I: 130/137), he argues that Gustave's situation deprived him of his earliest opportunity to realize himself as an agent because it did not allow him to feel desire long enough for him to learn how to communicate it through gestures and sounds. Gustave would not have felt desire as a call to action but as 'a prelude to an agreeable an imminent surfeit' (FI I/IF I: 130/137), so his response to desire was simply to wait. Rather than bursting into the world of action with wails and wordless demands, he lingers quietly outside of it. Sartre's conclusion that Caroline's style of parenting[3] is the source of Flaubert's passive constitution is in line with D. W. Winnicott's influential theory that a 'good-enough' mother's (or primary caregiver's) active adaption to the needs of her infant 'gradually lessons' (1971: 13), so as to give the infant the opportunity to adapt to the reality of being separate from the mother and to bring forth creative gestures to communicate their needs to her. It is also dialectically confirmed insofar as Flaubert's later passive behaviour becomes comprehensible when considered in relation to Sartre's picture of his infancy.

The paternal curse

Though Flaubert's relationship with his mother is effective in explaining Flaubert's passivity, it is not, in Sartre's view, enlightening with regard to Gustave's later expressions of defensive aggressiveness, his preference for the imaginary over the real, or his eventual decision to become a writer. Sartre's examination of Gustave's relationship with his father aims to shed light on these matters.

Sartre starts out by establishing what kind of man Dr Flaubert was. His depiction of him as a good, irreligious, well-respected man of science, whose short temper was infamous, seems accurate. Flaubert's biographer Benjamin F. Bart characterizes the hospital director similarly, noting that he might 'have been considered a saint, had it not been for the bite of his wit and the keenness of his mind, which made him feared as the devil' (1967: 6). Barnes agrees that Dr Flaubert was 'certainly anticlerical' but queries Sartre's ascription of the 'atheistic materialism of the eighteenth century' to him due to a lack of grounds (1981b: 40). However, it is worth noting that the 'loving portrait'[4] Gustave provides of his father through the character of Dr Larivière in *Madame Bovary* suggests that

Flaubert, at least, saw his father as one who subscribed to the philosophy of an earlier time that replaced religious worship with a principled commitment to physical science, since Dr Larivière is described as a man who belonged to 'that generation, now long gone, of philosopher-practitioners who cherished their art with fanatical devotion' (MB: 285/618).

The critical question for Sartre is, however, whether this great surgeon was also a good father. Sartre's response is ambivalent: yes and no, or rather, yes, then no. He tells us that during the first few years of Gustave's childhood, when Achille-Cléophas is fooled into thinking that Gustave's education is under control, he was relatively affectionate. The period that lasted from Gustave's third year until his seventh is Gustave's Golden Age (*Age d'Or*), in which he experienced being the primary object of his father's affections.[5] This ended abruptly when, as a consequence of his prolonged illiteracy, Gustave fell out of his father's favour. As all the love and validation in Gustave's childhood came from his father, he would have experienced Dr Flaubert's turn away from him as a terrible blow. Moreover, as his brother Achille was nine years his senior and absent most of the time, little Gustave had forgotten to envy him during his Golden Age. However, Gustave's Fall commences from the moment that unflattering comparisons between him and his scholarly elder brother begin to be made and it, therefore, coincides with Gustave's realization that he ought to envy the brother whose share of the paternal heart is larger than his own. As Dr Flaubert was an old-fashioned paterfamilias, Sartre affirms that the status of firstborn in the Flaubert family is not merely a 'minimal advantage that dims and disappears in bourgeois families when the brothers had both reached adulthood' (FI I/IF I: 334/345): the firstborn was 'born to be' his father's successor and so Gustave's secondary status was an immutable fact.

In addition to the obstacles presented by Flaubert's passive constitution, Sartre argues that Gustave sought to extend his Golden Age for as long as possible and, as written language symbolized the first step on the path towards being sent away to school for him, he 'challenged this symbol with a symbolic refusal' to learn his letters (FI I/IF I: 355/367). Now, Gustave's intention is not to vex his parents but his awareness of his intention in his inability to learn his letters plunges him into feelings of guilt and self-loathing. These feelings are intensified by Dr Flaubert's response to his learning difficulties, which is to take his son's education into his own hands. Though Achille-Cléophas succeeds in correcting the deficiency in the son that had humiliated him (Gustave learned to read within a few months), Sartre accuses him of having 'bungled' everything else in the process since the memories of this private tutelage would haunt Flaubert for the rest of his life (FI I/IF I: 355/367).

Sartre identifies overt submission (FI I/IF I: 376–86/388–99), combined with passive resentment (FI I/IF I: 386–409/399–422), and envy (FI I/IF I: 409–38/422–52) as the key features of Gustave's response to his early humiliation before his father. And, as Barnes notes, Sartre's analysis of Flaubert's juvenilia 'does much' to assuage the misgivings we may have about his hypothetical reconstruction of Gustave's Golden Age (1981b: 53). Further, Sartre maintains that because his analysis of Flaubert's juvenilia is the first to illuminate it in the 'black light' (*lumière noire*) of his earliest years (FI I/IF I: 46/57), it is also the first to highlight its psychological significance as the chronicle of how Flaubert experienced his Fall. As he puts it, 'we are frankly learning what – as far as I know – has escaped the experts on Flaubert: Gustave is subjectively certain that he has lived the most atrocious and rigid life from the age of seven to twenty-three ... for having been exiled, frustrated, and tortured from the age of seven by his family – in other words, by his father' (FI I/IF I: 184/194). In Flaubert's adolescent writings, Sartre finds evidence that his experience of his illiteracy 'as trauma' was pivotal to his eventual project to become a literary great. He singles out *Whatever You Want* (*Quidquid volueris*, written in October 1837) as being particularly useful for facilitating a comprehension Gustave's determination to 'overcompensate for the humiliations he could not forget' (FI I/IF I: 30/41).

Whatever You Want is a story about a half-man, half-ape creature called Djalioh, who is the issue of the rape of a slave-girl by an orangutan, orchestrated by a gentleman, M. Paul, ostensibly in the name of science.[6] Djalioh is raised by M. Paul and his associates in Brazil until he reaches the age of sixteen, when he is brought to France by M. Paul. In France, Djalioh passes for a man, even though his strange appearance and mannerisms inspire aversion in all who meet him. Djalioh does not speak in the story, except for once near the start, where he utters a word so quietly that it is mistaken for a sigh. Chief among the things Djalioh cannot communicate is his love for Adèle, M. Paul's fiancée. This causes him great distress. On the day of M. Paul and Adèle's wedding, the pain of seeing the couple exit the church triggers a seizure in Djalioh, in which his lips 'became animated as though he were mimicking rapid speech ... and his eyeballs rolled in his socket like those of an idiot' (EW/OJ: 87/255).

After their wedding, M. and Mme. Paul de Monville move to a fashionable district of Paris, where Djalioh lives with them for almost two years. One day, however, he picks up the Monville child from his cradle and launches him at the floor with all his might, killing him instantly. Then, he makes his way to the salon, where Adèle is reading a novel. Again, he experiences extreme frustration at not being able to communicate his passion for her; he stammers and strikes his head in rage, as if to say: 'What, do you mean I can't even say one word to her or detail all my torture and suffering, with nothing to offer her except the tears of an animal or the cries of a monster!' (EW/OJ 99/269). Djalioh's display frightens Adèle, who is evidently repulsed by him. After she shouts at him to leave her alone, he sexually assaults her and kills her in the process. He then proceeds to run around the room in a mad frenzy and to kill himself by running headfirst into the marble fireplace. Flaubert concludes the tale by telling us[7] that Adèle was buried, Djalioh's skeleton was put on display by the Ministry of Zoology, and M. Paul remarried.

This ghastly tale certainly has a general adolescent appeal, but Sartre also finds peculiarities in it which he reads to indicate that Flaubert, at fifteen, is still reeling from the humiliations he endured at the hands of his father when he was seven. He reads Djalioh to represent Gustave's idea of his former self as asinine child, 'easily superior to the members of our species with regard to the depth of his tender feelings' (FI I/IF I: 22/32). Despite being unable to communicate his emotions, Djalioh feels them so intensely that they affect his physical health. Importantly, Sartre believes that when Gustave describes how Djalioh's somatizes his emotional response to the Monville wedding, he is re-imagining one of his own childhood stupors (*hébétudes*) as seen '*from the outside*' and that he qualifies it as such by using the same words that were used to describe him when he had them: 'like an idiot' (FI I/IF I: 24/34). Creating Djalioh, in Sartre's view, is Gustave's means of indirectly denouncing the criminal thoughtlessness of his parents, who had simply taken his stupors to evince idiocy and internal vacancy, without realizing how they masked the most violent storms. In brief, it is his way of saying 'here is what took place inside me!' (FI I/IF I: 24/34). Flaubert regards the storms that rage inside Djalioh/Flaubert when he looks like an idiot to others as 'poetry' (*poésie*), according to Sartre, because adolescent Flaubert has a peculiar conception of poetry as 'a silent adventure of the soul' that operates not through language but 'against' it (FI I/IF I: 25/35). Djalioh is a poetic being because, in him, '[l]ogic had given way to poetry' (EW/OJ 82/250). It is as if there is a finite amount of space for logic and poetry to share, so that more logic means less poetry. What is more, the implication in *Whatever You Want* seems not to be that Djalioh wants to speak and cannot, but that he refuses to try because he knows that the poetry of his soul cannot be communicated through language. This leads Sartre to conclude that, for adolescent Flaubert, language involves the application of a reductive logic that 'kills' poetry by making it commonplace – 'words de-compose' the poet's exquisite sentiments (FI I/IF I: 27/37).

Barnes agrees with Sartre that the themes of 'paternal malediction' (in the characterization of M. Paul) and 'fraternal jealousy' (in Djalioh's murder of the Monville child) are present in *Whatever You Want* (1981b: 54). Despite accepting that Flaubert denigrates M. Paul's character to the point that it becomes a literary fault, though, she rejects Sartre's claim that Dr Flaubert is the primary target of young Flaubert's attack. Instead, she takes M. Paul to embody 'rational science' and Djalioh, the 'feeling soul' (1981b: 55). This reading is largely based on the comparison Flaubert invites between Djalioh – a natural monster, with limited intelligence and an expansive, tormented soul – and M. Paul – a monster of civilization, with great intelligence and a shrivelled soul – in which Djalioh emerges as superior. This interpretation fits with Flaubert's post-romantic disdain for scientific materialism. That said, I believe that Sartre's interpretation is preferable to the one Barnes recommends because it does a better job of explaining an important feature of this tale, as well as a particular feature of Gustave's response to his situation.

First, consider Sartre's point that Gustave (mistakenly) holds his father entirely responsible for the passive constitution he inherited from his mother and the misery it causes him because it is only when he makes a serious effort to enter into language that he begins to feel culpable and idiotic, and because he has 'neither the means nor the desire' to explain the suffering he endures as a result of his mother's behaviour (FI I/IF I: 225/233). This appears to be confirmed in Flaubert's decision to present M. Paul as the source of Djalioh's *pathos*: Djalioh is passive because he is part ape, he suffers because he is part man 'and this explosive mixture has been willed by his creator' (FI I/IF I: 225/234). If resentment of his father was not at the heart of this tale, Sartre maintains that some tragic accident would have been presented as the cause of the unnatural union that produced Djalioh. It is significant that it is M. Paul's will, not chance, that creates a subject who can only suffer. And Sartre's explanation of this significance is convincing: just as M. Paul 'was not afraid to father that anthropoid', Achille-Cléophas was not afraid to father 'a younger brother' (*un cadet*); just as Djalioh is 'irremediably brutish', Gustave is irremediably a younger brother (FI I/IF I: 225/234).

Second, if we read Djalioh as representing 'a possible Gustave' as Sartre suggests (FI I/IF I: 211/219), parallels between Gustave's Fall and Djalioh's misery become apparent: Djalioh's agony begins as soon as he enters France, which Sartre argues signifies culture in the tale because Djalioh was not made to imitate a man in his childhood home of Brazil (FI I/IF I: 208/217). But while culture is the catalyst for the realization of Djalioh/Gustave's misery, M. Paul/ Achille-Cléophas is presented as the cause. Djalioh's suffering thus results from a 'paternal curse' (*malédiction paternelle*) that mirrors Flaubert's own (FI I/IF I: 400/413). Hence, the pessimistic message of Djalioh's story: it is of little consequence *when* you discover a failing in yourself if this failing 'is a congenital defect' (FI I/IF I: 327/338–9). And, as we shall see, Sartre's analysis explains how Flaubert's belief that he suffered from a paternal curse cements his passive constitution by leading him to resign himself to his 'fate'.

Pessimism and religiosity without religion

Sartre argues that Gustave, like everyone else, must interpret his experience through the ideologies that are available to him and that, for him, these were: Christianity (from his early education, which Sartre attributes to his mother) and scientism (from his father) (FI I/IF I: 439/453). He observes that, in nineteenth-century France, genuine religious faith was no longer socially acceptable for the bourgeois male, as it was regarded as the preserve of the irrational, the naïve and the proletariat. A public show of religiosity was acceptable, though, and it was required of the Flaubert family because a large proportion of Dr Flaubert's clients were Catholic, and he would have lost many of them if his family had refused the holy sacraments. Flaubert's father was, therefore, an atheist within the Christian religion. He hypocritically observed religious rites, and he expected his sons to follow suit.

Dr Flaubert's decision to baptize Gustave would have been 'unforgivable' had he known the consequences it would have in Sartre's view (FI I/IF I: 492/508), for it enabled Gustave to gain a sense of purpose that would be brutally snatched from him when Achille-Cléophas felt the time was right to make his second son swallow the antidote to faith: 'the healthy principles of analytic atomism' (FI I/IF I: 493/508). Exposing Gustave to the autopsy was part of Achille-Cléophas's project to disabuse him of his religious beliefs. Sartre couches his discussion of Flaubert's early encounters with the autopsy in terms of alienation because he claims that taking on his father's 'objective knowledge' of bodies leaves Gustave feeling alienated from what he feels he understands of himself 'from the inside', as it leads him to view people, including himself, as 'unsuspecting cadavers' (FI I/IF I: 459/474). Consequently, he comes to apprehend his self as unreal because he has been made to believe that only the material objects that his father can see and dissect are real.

Further, the time that Dr Flaubert thought was the 'right time' to rid his younger son of his religious beliefs was quite possibly the worst time: around the time of the Fall. So, just as Gustave becomes aware of his inadequacy in the eyes of his earthly father, his heavenly Father is exposed as a myth. If Gustave was made to experience the Death of God while he was grieving his Golden Age, Sartre contends that these two events would have seemed to him to be fundamentally connected, with the result that the only things about him that would have seemed real would be his failure and his stupidity, which his father had discovered in him and which his father punished him for by killing his God. Religion could have saved Flaubert from the neurosis he goes on to develop in Sartre's view. For had he believed in God, he could have substituted the 'absolute Eye' for the 'surgical eye' and regarded his self not as an 'unreal' side-effect of material events, but as the reality of his being in its 'native transcendence' (FI I/IF I: 497/513).

Further, Sartre contends that Flaubert must have comprehended his great need for faith because religion remained a 'permanent *temptation*' for him (FI I/IF I: 496/511) and that this leads him to interpret his inability to acquire faith as both an extension of the paternal curse and confirmation of his pessimistic belief that 'the worst is always certain' (FI I/IF I: 512/529). What could be worse than God not existing? God existing for everybody *except you*. Again, Sartre finds support for this view in Flaubert's adolescent work, particularly in *Rage and Impotence* (*Rage et Impuissance*, written in December 1836), the tale of a man buried alive who knocks on the wood of his coffin lid when he hears footsteps above but is not heard and dies blaspheming. Sartre's reading of this tale as an analogy for Gustave's own relation to God is apt. The man in the coffin needs to attract the attention of those above him or die but, precisely because he has been put into a coffin and buried, he cannot be heard. Compare: Gustave cannot reject his father's atheism if God does not reveal himself, but God only reveals himself to the faithful so, precisely because he is in the thrall of his father's atheism, God will never exist for him. Nonetheless, Sartre contends that Gustave attempts to reconcile the scientism of his father with the remnants of his faith by fetishizing it, so that he comes to understand himself as 'a piece of cursed matter' (FI I/IF I: 460/475).

By the end of Part I of *The Family Idiot*, Sartre has completed his exposition of how Flaubert's passive constitution is a consequence of his familial situation. Flaubert was constituted as a passive agent by his mother during his infancy. He could have re-constituted himself with the support of a father – earthly or divine – whom he believed loved him unconditionally. He was unable to do this, though, because Dr Flaubert showed him that his love was conditional, and that God does not exist. Flaubert's awareness of his father's role in cementing his passive constitution leads him to hold Dr Flaubert entirely responsible for it and for the suffering it causes him, and to imagine that he is a victim of a paternal curse, which then enables him to 'justify' his passivity by believing that he was born to suffer. Still, Sartre maintains that 'no one can be alive without creating himself' and 'going beyond what others have made of him' in a way that manifests his original choice (FI I/IF I: 627/648). Thus, constitution is not predetermination. Let us now turn to consider how Sartre strives to comprehend Flaubert's response to his situation, including his constitution, by interpreting his process of self-formation in terms of an original choice.

Comprehension

As Sartre interprets the pinnacle of Flaubert's self-formation[8] to be 'the novel he published' (FI II/IF II: 7/658), the main objective of *The Family Idiot* is to account for how Flaubert managed to make himself into The Author of *Madame Bovary*. Having established how Flaubert suffers because of his passive constitution, Sartre asserts that Flaubert's self-formation must have continually revolved around his attempt to integrate this malady 'on the level of stress' (FI II/IF II: 9/659). Here, 'stress' refers to the disharmonious unity that results from the apprehension of a 'nonassimilable [*inassimilable*] element' in the self, as well as the subject's 'global defense' against it (FI II/IF II: 5/656). Sartre compares the fusillade of attacks deployed against a nonassimilable in stress to the antibodies that charge through a transplanted organ, which ultimately do more harm to the organism they seek to protect than the 'threat' they attack. Despite the vast amount of collateral damage it causes, stress is effective because, although it neither neutralizes nor eliminates the nonassimilable aspects of the self, it allows the subject to oppose and surpass it. Hence, Sartre construes stress as the typical response to a nonassimilable,[9] which gives the process of self-formation its typical spiral shape[10] as subjects must continually strive to assimilate nonassimilables through a totalizing movement that both surpasses and preserves them. So, by retracing the circular pathways that brought Flaubert to a nervous crisis in January 1844, then to the production of a masterpiece in 1856, Sartre believes that he can organize the biographical facts about Flaubert in a way that provides the basis for a re-totalization of his self. To comprehend the particular form of stress that characterizes Flaubert's self-formation, Sartre relies on the imaginative self-expansions he finds in Flaubert's fictional works, which, he believes, enabled Flaubert to gain a deep comprehension of his self that he was unable to convert into self-knowledge.

Autism, femininity and autoeroticism

From testimonial evidence, Sartre deduces that Gustave must have eventually succeeded in learning to read and write between the age of seven and eight (FI I/IF I: 6/16). As we have seen, he attributes Gustave's early difficulties with language not to any cognitive defect but to his constitution and to a related desire to prolong his Golden Age. But he holds that Gustave's passive constitution still made learning how to read and write more difficult for him than for other children. He defends this view by dividing the understanding of language into two phases. The first is passive: recognizing the meaning of the words uttered. The second involves a kind of action: reconstituting the meaning of the utterance and making contextual adjustments. Unsurprisingly, Sartre's contention is that, before he learns how to read, little Gustave gets by without this second, active phase of understanding. His passive constitution, which prevented him from seeking to express himself as an infant, also prevents him from interpreting the acts of others as expressions because his limited awareness of his own agency makes it difficult for him to comprehend the intentions in the acts of others.

This theory that Gustave's passivity is the source of his trouble with language is not irrefutable, but it is compelling. If his passive, incomplete understanding of words causes him to regard words as 'things' in themselves as opposed to 'signs' that point to something else, this would account for the reports of his extreme gullibility in his early years.[11] If little Gustave mistakes words for things, it would not occur to him to consider the intentions of others as a factor in determining their meaning. Moreover, if Sartre is correct about Gustave's passivity being the source of his infantile autism because it causes him to receive words rather than interpret them, then it is no small wonder that written language eluded him for so long. Although the gap between spoken language and written language is significant for most children, oral communication is already an activity. But for a child who had managed to participate in oral communication – albeit poorly – for years, without applying the 'reducing agent' that would allow him to appreciate speech as action (FI I/IF I: 156/163), the leap from spoken to written language would be enormous because actual activity cannot be avoided in the interpretation or the production of written language.

Flaubert had managed to make this enormous leap by the time he went to school at the age of eight years, but Sartre argues that his constitutional passivity continues to structure all his relationships and that this is clearly apparent in his *'perverse'* sexuality (FI II/IF II: 32/684). Describing Flaubert's sexuality this way is not meant to indicate any negative moral judgement, however, as Sartre uses the term 'perverse' to refer to 'any erotic attitude that implies an unrealization geometrically multiplied', meaning any desire to push erotic imagining to the limit in reality (FI II/IF II: 42/694). Because Flaubert feels that his self is a thing in the hands of others, Sartre submits that he strives to reclaim it by making it 'a fascinating object for his executioners and simultaneously for himself' (FI II/IF II: 32/684). To become this kind of sexual object, Sartre argues that Flaubert believes that he requires a change of sex, because it is women who derive pleasure from being 'taken' (FI II/IF II: 33/685). If Flaubert fantasizes about being 'taken' as a woman, does this mean that he desires a man as a sexual partner? Is Flaubert a homosexual? Sartre anticipates such questions and reminds us that a commitment to 'nominalism' precludes us from resorting to 'classifications' as a means of explanation (FI II/IF II: 34/686). It will not do to simply label Flaubert a 'homosexual', as the aim of psychoanalysis is to understand Flaubert's sexuality in its particularity. Sartre's efforts to comprehend *Flaubert's* sexuality then reveal why the label 'homosexual' is unsatisfactory, as they lead him to conclude that Flaubert chiefly desires to be caressed by a 'mother-goddess' (*déesse-mère*)[12] and that if he sometimes desires a man, this is because he 'endeavours to convince himself *in front of his mirror* that he is of the other sex' (FI II/IF II: 351/704).

To be sure, Sartre's interpretation of Flaubert's sexuality makes some problematic, out-dated heteronormative assumptions. However, the idea that Flaubert's erotic desire is an upshot of a deeper, general preference for the imaginary over the real is what is most important here. Sartre's key claims are that Flaubert desires the specific kind of sexual partners he does *so that* he may imagine himself as a woman and that he takes most pleasure in playing 'at *being masturbated*' (FI II/IF II: 43/695). These claims find strong support in Sartre's exposition of the theme of the mirror and the fetish in Flaubert's literature (FI II/IF II: 32–60/684–712) and in his analysis of Flaubert's uncomfortable relationship with reality. For a taste of the latter, let us briefly consider Sartre's discussion of Flaubert's fetishization of Louise Colet's slippers alongside Léon Dupuis's theft of Emma Bovary's glove in *Madame Bovary*.

In the novel, Léon theft of Emma's glove occurs during the period in which he is infatuated with her but regards her as the virtuous wife of another, whom he can never have any real romantic relationship with. To compensate for unattainability of the real Emma, he turns to fetishizing things connected to her, such as a rug she made and even her husband (!), whom he regards as the 'unconscious support for the crystallization his wife has worked on him' (FI II/IF II: 65/718). One day, when Emma is sewing at Homais's house, she drops one of her gloves and Léon sneakily pushes it under the table. Later, when everyone else is asleep, he returns for the glove and takes it to bed with him. Reading between the lines of Flaubert's text, Sartre deduces that Léon then proceeds to masturbate with the glove, imagining that hand inside it is 'Emma's virile hand', which illustrates the fetish of the 'female hand and the phallus merged' through Emma's glove functioning as a *'transcendence object'* (FI II/IF II: 66/719). Then, Sartre proceeds to argue that Louise Colet's slippers served the same function for Flaubert. Flaubert avoided meeting Colet in person whenever possible because when she was there in person, she always 'disturbed his dreams' (FI II/IF II: 67/719). Hence, he much preferred the company of his mistress's little brown slippers since, through the aid of these objects, he could find her in the imaginary, 'reduced to the muteness of inanimate matter and at the same time, active, devouring, tractable' (FI II/IF II: 67/719). Accordingly, Flaubert's sexuality is 'perverse' (in the Sartrean sense) because it is centred on his desire to control the object that he is for the other by imagining the other being embodied in an object, which, unlike a real other, does not hide its vision of him behind a Look. In a word, Gustave is an 'onanist' because he desires to discover his 'femininity in sexual excitement' and while the other is the means to this end, his eroticized, feminized image of his self disappears 'if the other is too real' (FI II/IF II: 62/714–15).

A spectacle for his sister

The false belief that human being is justified in advance is necessary for children's psychological wellbeing in Sartre's estimation, as it protects them from discovering the existential truth that their being is unjustified before they have had the opportunity to learn two other truths that enable them to cope with it. The first of these is that humans are agents and the second is that human being has a (human) meaning, even if it lacks a preordained purpose. Children who learn the existential truth before having discovered to these two 'protective' truths are, Sartre believes, likely to view themselves as superfluous objects in an absurd universe, without a *'mandate to live'* (*mandat de vivre*) (FI I/IF I: 133/140). They may also fail to discover their positive power to infuse the world with meaning. Sartre submits that an unhappy consequence of Flaubert's Fall and loss of faith occurring together is that he was one such child.

The belief that only objectively observable things are real is a key factor in alienating Flaubert from his self on Sartre's account. In ontological terms, Flaubert's 'I' is 'another' for him because he mistakes his being-for-others for the primary form of his being. As he knows that he is real for others, he seeks to discover his self by witnessing the object he is for others. But since nobody can see their self from the outside, Flaubert needs something to 'reflect' his self back to him. Sartre traces Flaubert's fascination with mirrors to the period that followed the Fall when he saw in the mirror the promise of being able to see himself as others do. However, he holds this first iteration of 'Operation Reflection' (*l'Opération Reflet*) was doomed to fail (FI II/IF II: 107/762) because one cannot truly apprehend oneself as an object in the mirror, because one can always anticipate (as a subject) the movements reflected.

What Gustave needs, then, is a human mirror, and he can find none better than his little sister, Caroline. As a girl, Caroline is naturally inferior in the eyes of the paterfamilias so, unlike Achille, she is not considered a rival. And while she may be 'docile and fascinated', she is nevertheless 'active', which is enough to allow him to 'lose his reflection' (FI II/IF II: 108/762). So, little Gustave acts before Caroline and Sartre tells us that acting came naturally to him because he believes that the only meanings he can make are those that he can make others believe. With Caroline, Operation Reflection has a greater chance of success. But success in this operation will not solve the problem of Flaubert's alienation from his self because he can never know for sure that his meanings are affirmed in consciousness of another; the best he can hope for is to 'believe' that he is believed (FI II/IF II: 22/673). More worryingly, this iteration of the operation further alienates him from others precisely because it involves him acting, which means that he apprehends his self as a being for others in the third person, which precludes him from experiencing reciprocal relations in the second person; Flaubert is for himself a 'he' who puts on a show for 'them'. Sartre therefore compares Flaubert's experience during this second iteration of Operation Reflection to that of the celebrated Shakespearian actor Edmund Kean[13] as he plays Hamlet insofar the intimate 'you' is impossible for each of them since they both are 'separated from their audience by the blaze of the imaginary that envelops them even more than footlights' (FI II/IF II: 109/764).

Sartre states that Caroline could have saved Flaubert from his miserable alienation after his Fall, as well as from his eventual neurosis, as his performances for her could have been the prelude to reciprocal love. But, because Caroline was her mother's pet, she needed no further love or validation; she did not need Gustave as he needed her. She was content to let Gustave amuse her and to receive his affection as a 'delicious luxury', but she did not feel a need to give him anything in return (FI II/IF II: 80/733). This plunges Gustave deeper into the imaginary because he is always aware that his sister's gratitude is addressed to the character he plays when he says 'I' and this crystallizes his image of his self as a 'He' instead of a 'me'.

Barnes contests this interpretation and notes that, even if we grant Sartre his premises, his conclusion about Caroline and Gustave's relationship is too pessimistic because Caroline gave Gustave something very precious indeed: a positive role to play within the Flaubert family. Through his performances for her, he chooses the acts through which he objectifies his self for the first time. While Caroline did not prevent her brother's crisis, Barnes makes the point that she is, most likely, 'one of the influences that led him to make of it a beginning and not an end' (Barnes 1981b: 97). Indeed, by Sartre's own admission, to act upon oneself in order to act upon others is 'passive action', but action nonetheless (FI II/IF II: 21/672), and Caroline gave Flaubert an incentive to act in this way. Hence, Barnes's concern that Sartre understates Caroline's positive influence upon young Gustave is well founded, since it is in his relationship with Caroline that Gustave gains his first opportunity to express himself as an agent, even if his response to this opportunity is consistent with his passive constitution. It is Caroline who facilitates Flaubert's conversion from a silent, suffering 'poet' to a child actor because playing the fool for her enables him to realize that, as well as escaping into the imaginary, he can also turn reality into the imaginary. And this realization puts him on the path that will eventually lead him to become a creative writer.

Conversion from idiot to actor

Although Flaubert's first project to become an actor is quickly abandoned, Sartre considers it to be of tremendous significance for comprehending Flaubert since the core element of this choice endures the first revolution of the spiral of Flaubert's self-formation and every one that follows: his original '*choice of the unreal*' (*choix de l'irréel*) (FI II/IF II: 10/660).

What is unusual about Gustave's first choice of vocation,[14] according to Sartre, is that it represents a choice not to *be* but to pretend. His elder brother, for example, wants to be 'that heroic doctor' and the fiction in this case – the imaginary self as heroic doctor – holds the promise of future realization; it anticipates a 'passage from being *toward being*' (FI II/IF II: 10/661). Flaubert's theatrical ambition, however, reverses 'the "normal," "healthy," *practical* order of things by making the real a means to unreality' (FI II/IF II: 11/661). This first choice to be an actor reveals the Flauberts' younger son as 'a suspicious character' because it shows that his first major move in his self-formation is to place himself '*outside* humanity' (*FI* II/*IF* II: 11/661). Although following his first vocation could have saved Flaubert 'at least some of the stress' that would later make him a writer (FI II/IF II: 118/773), Sartre argues that he was prevented from following his dream of becoming an actor by his family's silent disapproval. There was no need for them to actively forbid little Gustave from following this dream, as the son of a chief surgeon does not become a 'buffoon' (*bateleur*), he becomes a lawyer or a physician '*by force of circumstance*' (FI II/IF II: 214/873–4). So, it was not long after Gustave's entry into school that he abandons his project to become an actor.

The death of Flaubert's dream to become an actor was, however, promptly followed by the birth of the Garçon: a giant boy character that he and his schoolboy friends invented to laugh at the follies of humanity. Flaubert once described the Garçon as embodying 'the spoof of materialism and Romanticism' (FI III/IF II: 151/1257), and Sartre finds this description telling not only in relation to Flaubert's response to the two dominant and conflicting ideologies of the time, but also in relation to why this character gained general popularity among Gustave's schoolboy friends, who took turns at playing him. Sartre explains that, for these boys, caught between the Romantic ideals of the books they read and the materialist principles of the bourgeoisie in their lived experience, it would have seemed to them that 'the spoof of materialism is Romanticism and the spoof of Romanticism is materialism' (FI III/IF II: 152/1257). Hence, he reads the popularity of the Garçon as an indication that Flaubert and his classmates were united in their struggle with the same two ideologies, as the Garçon's laughter provided them all with an imaginary solution to 'the antinomy of the century' (FI III/IF II: 152/1258). To take one example of the Garçon's antics that Sartre analyses: every time the schoolboys passed Rouen cathedral, one would remark that this fine example of Gothic architecture 'elevates the soul', then whoever was playing the Garçon would laugh loudly, agree that it is beautiful and announce that so too is Saint Bartholomew's Day, the Edict of Nantes and the massacres of Louis XIV's dragoon's. Against the Goncourts, who see in the Garçon a prefiguration of Homais in *Madame Bovary* and judge him to mock the bourgeoisie who would call upon 'a few massacres' to condemn 'Holy Religion and the works of art it inspires' (FI III/IF II: 152/1258), Sartre maintains that the Garçon's laughter cuts both ways, attacking bourgeois materialism and Romantic sentimentalism at the same time; it laughs at all human projects by reducing its grandest to folly. For if the religious instinct is the highest in humankind but it can only find 'fulfilment in fanaticism which leads inevitably to genocide', then human beings must be so monstrously constructed that their 'love for Being' drives them to annihilate it (FI III/IF II: 156/1263). The Garçon is therefore simultaneously sadistic, masochistic and nihilistic for Sartre. He even describes him as the 'reverse image' of Jesus because while Jesus strives to save us, the Garçon strives to reveal our damnation to us (FI III/IF II: 162/1268).

Although it brings them much joy, Sartre argues that the schoolboys' creation of the Garçon only provides them with an imaginary solution to the ideological difficulties they face, which is to say no real solution at all. Moreover, by playing the Garçon they do not enjoy an immediate, reciprocal relation with one another since it is mediated by the imaginary. The imaginary functions as the basis of a real bond for them; it 'governs and vampirizes the individuals who perpetuate its being' (FI III/IF II: 215/1323). Playing the role of the Garçon may allow Flaubert and his classmates to experience being part of a 'group-in-fusion' (*groupe en fusion*) (FI III/IF II: 221/1329), but the Garçon is ultimately a trap because it only brings those who create him together through imaginary action. Further, Sartre infers that Flaubert's anomalous relation to reality makes playing the Garçon particularly damaging for him. Through an examination of what he calls the 'ego-ology' of the Garçon (FI III/IF II: 186/1293), he concludes that this giant boy is a caricature of the young Flaubert, which means that playing the role of Garçon is yet another iteration of Operation Reflection for him, through which he dissociates himself from his lived experience by assuming the imaginary perspective of another consciousness. As Flaubert is likely to have been one of the chief creator-curators of the Garçon, Sartre proposes that the Garçon represents 'a new spiral' in the movement of his self-formation, for the function of impersonating the Garçon is more specific than acting: 'It tends to make everyday reality a materiality without being' (FI III/IF II: 341/1453). The Garçon and his avatars become a permanent fixture in Flaubert's life and works, in Sartre's view, because it is only through imagining himself as another that he can approach the task of comprehending his experience. Despite the failure of Flaubert's initial project to become an actor, then, Sartre claims it drives first revolution of his spiral and continues to play 'a leading role' in Flaubert's self-formation ever after (FI II/IF II: 118/773).

Magical behaviour and imaginary acts

Flaubert's nervous crisis[15] is the primary focus of Part Three of *The Family Idiot*, entitled 'Elbehnon, or the Last Spiral'. Sartre borrows the 'Elbehnon' from the title of Mallarmé's prose piece, *Igitur or Elbehnon's Folly* (*Igitur ou la folie d'Elbehnon*), which details its protagonist's (Igitur's) journey into nothingness, death and spiritual discovery as he descends into a tomb. As Bettina Knapp points out, circular symbols of eternity are associated with 'Elbehnon', or the number eight (1977: 204). So, Sartre's title hints that Flaubert's 'Last Spiral' is a 'looping of the loop' that locks him in a closed, repetitive circuit. The reference to Mallarmé's piece is therefore an apt indicator of Sartre's purpose in this part: to present Flaubert's illness as his means of becoming a great artist through an intentional withdrawal from the world, which spells the end of the spiral motion of his active life.

Flaubert's nervous attacks are usually attributed to epilepsy, despite their atypical presentation.[16] However, Sartre concentrates on the atypical features of Flaubert's illness to arrive at an alternative understanding of it. He notes that Dr Flaubert initially diagnosed his son with a minor apoplexy and only much later settled on the diagnosis of epilepsy, due to the cyclical recurrence of Gustave's attacks. Dr Flaubert's initial mistake was, he believes, 'imposed on him by the illness itself' since 'nature of hysterical diseases is to look like what they are not' (FI IV/IF III: 113/1885). So, Flaubert's psychological illness is certainly 'hysterical' in Sartre's view, but he refuses to subsume it under any more specific nosological category[17] in a way that would preclude his analysis from unveiling its full meaning for Flaubert. Indeed, as Sartre is concerned only with the human meaning of Flaubert's attacks, the medical title ought not concern us either. What is important for us to consider here is the evidence for Sartre's claim that Flaubert's illness *has a meaning*.

As we know, Sartre posits the human meaning of behaviour lies in its motive. If he is to show that Flaubert's illness is not the mere effect of a meaningless mechanism, then he needs to establish a 'motive' for it – i.e. a reason why Flaubert becomes ill that he is necessarily conscious of but not necessarily thetically aware of. The 'motive' he proposes is that Flaubert's family were pushing him towards a future he wanted to resist but had no means to resist. 'Doctor, barrister, solicitor, magistrate, notary, subprefect, judge': this is the range of family-approved professions, which, due to his passive constitution, he deems to delimit 'his destiny' (FI III/FI III: 366/1478). Despite holding this 'motive' to uncover the presence of intention in Flaubert's neurosis, Sartre is adamant Flaubert did not knowingly will to become ill. As Flaubert's constitution robs him of the possibility of actively refusing anything his family imposes on him, revolt could only have appeared to Flaubert as an impossibility and necessity at once since he had to take up one of the family-approved professions but none of them would enable him to pursue his own fundamental project. He cannot disobey his parents, so the only way for him to escape the destiny they are forging for him is to magically change 'his being' (FI III/IF III: 369/1482). Unlike voluntary and rational behaviour that results from deliberation about how to act, 'magical behaviour' (*conduits magiques*) is Sartre's term for a behaviour of escape that aims to change a situation when all ordinary behavioural routes to change seem to the subject to be blocked: fainting in terror is a prime example, as it aims to 'eliminate' a threat by eliminating the threat in the subject's experience (BN/EN: 584/489).[18]

After establishing the 'motive' and the magical means, Sartre argues that Flaubert's neurosis was also 'planned' by showing that his crisis was prefigured by at least two years in *November* (*Novembre*), a novella that Flaubert completed in the winter of 1842. He highlights many similarities between this tale of a life illuminated in the tragic light of the apparent necessity of an early death and the particulars of Flaubert's first attack in 1844. The accuracy of Flaubert's description of the depression suffered by the unnamed hero of this work has been remarked upon (Unwin 2004: 46), but Sartre places special emphasis on a peculiar feature of Flaubert's description of the hero's malady: his 'deculturation' (FI III/IF III: 610/1730), evinced by his neglect of basic human rituals of self-care such as shaving, washing, changing his shirt, removing shoes if one's feet get wet, etc. He affirms that this deculturation is distinct from the kind of apathy usually associated with depression, as it appears to be more of a symbolic refusal than an effect of a general loss of desire. The unnamed hero of *November* also achieves a remarkable death 'by thought' (FI III/IF III: 633/1754), which Sartre reads to signal the presence of an intention in Flaubert's later collapse. One of the reasons for this is that the sudden, silent death of the hero, who is also first narrator, gives way to the discourse of a second, who emerges 'from nothingness' to comment on and publish the hero's incomplete work (FI III/IF III: 600/1721). The schizophrenic character of this break in *November* is also noteworthy as it invites the question of whether Gustave is already ill. For Sartre, it certainly indicates that Flaubert is 'preneurotic' if not yet ill. Though transitions from third- to first-person narration were common in the epistolary and confessional novels of the time – e.g. Goethe's *The Sorrows of Young Werther* (*Die Leiden des jungen Werthers*), which Flaubert had read before writing *November* – *November* breaks the rule of this convention, which is that the second character must be introduced at the beginning and return at the end. Further, as the narrative of *November* repeats itself at various intervals and does not appear to conform to any plan to offer clarity to the reader, Sartre thinks it reasonable to conclude that the introduction of a second a narrator at the end is an *ad hoc* addition, which testifies to its author's disordered state of mind.

Sartre also suggests that Flaubert may have had a secondary, economic 'motive' for his crisis since being incapable of work would allow him to claim his inheritance in advance. Though he anticipates the objection that he may be going too far here, as this motive seems like a rational one, he maintains that Flaubert's illness cannot be understood at all unless it is interpreted primarily as 'the "stress" of a *son of a good family* for whom money *earned* is necessarily vulgar and who can only accept *bequeathed* wealth' (FI IV/IF III: 110/1881). Of course, Gustave became a chronic patient, not an aristocrat, and Sartre readily acknowledges that Flaubert's crisis and continued illness reduced him to the condition of a perpetual child, extreme dependence, and, all in all, to an existence drastically dissimilar to – and, for most, significantly less desirable than – that of an aristocrat. Nonetheless, he maintains that aristocratic-being and patient-being were similar enough in a crucial respect for Flaubert: both aristocrats and patients are excused from having to earn a living.

Additionally, Sartre finds the fact that Dr Flaubert had to forbid his younger son from doing disturbingly accurate impressions of an epileptic beggar as further evidence of Flaubert's neurotic 'planning'. Dr Flaubert, he explains, would have been keenly aware of the fragility of the mind and would not have doubted that mental illness 'is catching' (FI III/IF III: 615/1736), and, as Gustave would have deferred to his father on all medical matters, we can infer that he was testing his capacity for autosuggestion by aping an epileptic. Or, in other words, he was '*doing what he had to do* to become mad' (FI III/IF: 615/1736).

Comprehending the meaning of Flaubert's first attack is key to comprehending the meaning of his illness as a whole in Sartre's view, as it results from Flaubert's intention to reject the future that was being made for him, which is reaffirmed by all the later 'referential attacks' (FI IV/IF III: 16/1784).[19] The first attack occurred one night in January 1844, when Gustave and his brother were returning from Deuville, where they had been to view the plot of the family's future country house. Gustave was driving the carriage when, suddenly, a wagon emerged from the darkness and passed the carriage on the right, somewhere near Pont-l'Evêque, after which Gustave let go the reigns, fell to his brother's feet and remained motionless. Achille, fearing that his brother might be dead or dying, carried him to a nearby house, gave him emergency treatment, and drove him back to Rouen that same night, once he had regained consciousness (FI IV/IF III: 3/1771). The stimulus for the first attack appears to be the waggon that burst out of the darkness and disappeared again. This event would have undoubtedly given Gustave a fright, but there was no threat of an accident once the waggon has passed. So, Sartre deduces that Gustave must have realized how devastated he was that there was no accident after he overcame his initial shock. If a fatal accident could have satisfied Gustave, it is most likely to be because death is an irreversible and a state from which he could never return to his miserable situation. Madness is also irreversible and if Gustave's intention is to 'cut himself off from his future being by a moment of irreversibility', it serves his purpose equally well (FI IV/IF III: 70/1840).

What is more, Sartre contends that Flaubert's illness provides Flaubert with a means of retribution for the paternal curse via passive, symbolic parricide because, by martyring himself through his obedience to his father, he forces his father into devastating grief and guilt over his son's symbolic-social death. To support this view, Sartre points to evidence in the correspondence that suggests that Flaubert '*quite consciously*' experienced his father's death as a deliverance (FI IV/IF III: 123/1895), reports that the frequency of Flaubert's attacks reduced drastically after his father's death in 1846 (FI IV/IF III: 124/1896), and interprets Flaubert's late work, *The Legend of Saint Julian Hospitator* (*La Légende de Saint Julien l'hospitalier*, 1877), to express his guilt for having wished for his father's death and for having symbolically killed him two years in advance (FI I/IF III: 128–38/1900–10).

Altogether, this leads Sartre to conclude that although the catastrophic nature of Flaubert's first attack may give the impression that it was accidental and without reason, Flaubert's nervous crisis becomes fully comprehensible when it is treated as a conversion rather than a physiological affliction. Although Sartre's commitment to nominalism generally leads him to eschew diagnostic categorization, he uses the term 'neurosis' to designate 'an intentional adaptation of the whole person to his entire past, to his present, and to visible forms of his future' and a way 'of making oneself bearable' (FI I/IF I: 168/176). Thus, he presents Flaubert's conversion to neurosis as an intentional adaption that enables him to make his situation bearable through the passive-aggressive-defensive acceptance of his self as the 'loser who wins',[20] because being incapable of pursuing a suitable bourgeoise profession allows him to devote all his time to writing. Becoming a 'man-failure' (*homme-échec*) therefore allows Flaubert to 'win' by becoming an artist (FI V/IF 3: 7/13).

Knowing

Sartre contends that Flaubert comprehends himself 'better than most people do, though not better than those who *know themselves*' (FI II/IF II: 68/721). This is because he sincerely reflects upon his experience when he imagines his self embodied in another – e.g. Djalioh, The Garçon, Emma Bovary. So, while Flaubert only makes an insincere show of his self when he speaks or writes about himself in real life, he expresses the subjective truth of his experience when he creates 'fabrications' (FI I/IF I: 150/157). Reliving his lived experience through the imaginary experience of imagined others may allow Flaubert to gain an exceptional comprehension of the meaning of his experience, but it also enables him to avoid turning this comprehension into self-knowledge because as soon as he comes close to grasping an aspect of his self through this medium, he starts to generalize and presents what he discovers as an aspect of human nature.[21] Hence, Flaubert's strategy of comprehension 'through fabrication' only ever furnishes him with the dawning of a reflection that could lead to self-knowledge, since his projection of his own intentions onto others prevents him from engaging in thetic self-reflection (FI III/IF III: 429/1544). Here is a remarkable passage in which Flaubert appears to testify to this view:

> I am a strange character … I thought to know myself for a time, but by dint of analyzing myself, I no longer know at all what I am; also I have lost the silly pretence of wanting to grope about in that obscure chamber of the heart that is lit from time to time by a brief flash that reveals everything, it is true, but in return it blinds you for a long time. You tell yourself: yes, I have seen this or that, oh yes, I shall certainly find my way, and you set off and run up against all the corners, you lacerate yourself on all the angles. If I know where this analogy came from, I'll be damned. It has been a long time since I have written anything, and from time to time I need to exercise a little style. (Flaubert as quoted by Sartre FI III/IF III: 433–4/1548)

Although it is taken from Flaubert's correspondence, Sartre does not question its sincerity. This is perhaps partly because it is taken from a letter Flaubert wrote to his sister and Sartre concedes that there is 'some truth' in Flaubert's relationship with her (FI II/IF II: 110/764). But what more than anything else would signal Flaubert's sincerity here from a Sartrean perspective is the fact that he generalizes what he says by switching to the second person towards the end, so as to present what he has just described as if it were something everybody experiences. Further, Flaubert also strives to retroactively 'fictionalize' what he has written this experience by describing it as an exercise in 'style'.

What precedes Flaubert's dismissal through generalization and fictionalization is, Sartre believes, a truthful admission, whose importance to a study of Flaubert cannot be overstated. Of particular interest to Sartre is the way that Flaubert describes the brief flashes of clarity he experiences as something that 'happens' to him because it reveals his conception of moments of luminosity, of personal revelation, as 'visitations' rather than intellectual achievements (FI III/IF III: 436/1551), which shows that he does not conceive of himself as an agent, not even when he pursues self-knowledge. Moreover, as the bursts of light that invade Flaubert's psyche are described as blinding, Sartre reads this to suggest that Flaubert identifies comprehension of lived experience with the '*denial of self-knowledge*' (*IF* III: 1551/*FI* III: 436), since all that is revealed is almost simultaneously concealed, before it can be analysed, thetically understood and known.

Nevertheless, Flaubert's 'fabrication approach' to self-analysis is partly successful in Sartre's view since, without applying any psychoanalytical method, Flaubert manages to deepen his comprehension of his lived experience through the creation of stories about 'others'. As Sartre sees it, Flaubert has already gone as far as it is possible to go in terms of comprehending the subjective significance of the acts that constitute his self via his literary form of 'self-analysis'. Once his analysis of Flaubert has 'comprehended the comprehension' contained in Flaubert's literature, then, Sartre believes its next task is to understand Flaubert's self 'objectively', so that the 'subjective comprehension' can be synthesized with an 'objective understanding' of him.

The objective spirit

After uncovering the subjective meaning of Flaubert's neurosis over the course of the first two (original French) volumes of *The Family Idiot*, Sartre aims to determine, objectively, whether Flaubert's neurosis harmed or benefitted him in the third. Although there are certainly some objective-progressive elements in the first two volumes, the discussions of objective structures – e.g. the institutional whole, historical contingencies, social class and the bourgeois family structure – are, by Sartre's own admission, 'highly particularized' there as they are only examined insofar as they impacted the 'familial intersubjectivity of the Flauberts' (FI V/IF 3: 4/10). Sartre also purposely refrains from passing any judgement on Flaubert's neurosis in the first two volumes to concentrate on gaining an empathetic comprehension of it, before assessing the objective facts of his situation. From the (mainly) subjective-regressive analysis in the first two volumes, Sartre concludes that *Madame Bovary* is the work of a neurotic. This provides the objective-progressive analysis with its main question: How can the tremendous popular success of *Madame Bovary* be explained if it is a work of 'neurotic literature'[22] that would ordinarily have a limited, psychological appeal? A satisfactory objective evaluation of Flaubert's neurosis must, in Sartre's view, account for the 'strange reciprocity' between Flaubert and the French reading public of his era that made it possible for a product of his neurosis to make him the most celebrated author in all of France upon its publication (FI V/IF 3: 32/40).

To this end, Sartre considers it necessary to gain a sense of 'the Objective Spirit' (*l'Esprit objectif*) in France during the second half of the nineteenth century. He assures his readers that while the notion of the Objective Spirit has its origins in Hegelian idealism, it does not refer to anything intangible when it is reinterpreted within the context of historical materialism. In this context, it denotes 'nothing more than culture as practico-inert' (FI V/IF 3: 35/43). Or, more specifically, 'the totality to this day (in any day) of the imperatives imposed on a man by any given society' (FI V/IF 3: 39/47). Sartre's notion of the Objective Spirit is perhaps best understood as a further development of the notion of '*bewitched matter*' (*matière ensorcelée*) discussed in the *Critique* (CDR I/CRD I: 219/329), since it posits that every object of cultural significance appears with objective 'directions for use as an order', as well as a subjective sense (FI V/IF 3: 39/47). Everyone's basic, pragmatic interpretation of the objects that populate their world is informed by the Objective Spirit, which may issue imperatives such as 'Shake before use' if the object is a packaged consumer product, 'Slow down' if it is a pedestrian crossing, or 'Admire me' if it is a celebrated artwork. The Objective Spirit, then, appears everywhere in human experience as a 'practical seal imposed on the raw material' (FI V/IF 3: 39/47).

In *The Family Idiot*, Sartre confines his analysis to just one dimension of the Objective Spirit: the domain of literary production. He combines insights from *What Is Literature?*[23] with those of the *Critique* by drawing an analogy between literary works and canned goods. The irredeemable changes that living thought undergoes when it is transformed into a material product (the literary text) are likened to those undergone by fresh fruit when it is immersed in syrup and canned. The totality of ideas that the author unites to create a literary work represents 'a multiple and contradictory comprehension of our species as a product of history, of present circumstances, and of the future that it is preparing for itself', but once this totality transformed into a literary text, it becomes 'canned thought' (*pensée de conserve*) (FI V/IF 3: 40/48), awaiting re-totalization at some later time by readers who will interpret it in new situations and find new meanings in it. However, just as the processed peach still resembles the fresh peach it once was, certain elements of the original living thought are preserved in the literary text – 'a skeleton of imperatives' remains intact and directs the reader's thoughts (FI V/IF 3: 46/54). This understanding of the literary text supplies the theoretical basis for Sartre's analysis of how the Objective Spirit influenced Flaubert and his generation of aspiring writers by delivering a series of imperatives concerning 'literature-to-be-written' (*littérature-à-faire*) through 'literature-already-written' (*littérature-faite*) (FI V/IF 3: 49/58).

Sartre's exposition of the literary face of the Objective Spirit as it would have appeared to the group of French, male, middle-class creative writers born between 1820 and 1830 that he calls 'Postromantics' begins by reconstructing the series of givens that situate this group in relation to culture and, specifically, literature. The Postromantics, he argues, would have studied many celebrated writers from the seventeenth century and earlier at school, such as Racine, Bossuet and Shakespeare but these authors would have had little influence on them, for they would have seemed 'quite dead' (FI V/IF 3: 57/66). The eighteenth century marks the beginning of 'living literature' for the Postromantics (FI V/IF 3: 58/67). Although the great authors of this era were also dead, they were still relevant – the Postromantics would have admired them because their parents did, even if they found their works somewhat dated. Hence, Sartre compares the imperatives the Postromantics encounter in the great works of the previous century to grandfatherly advice and he argues that the overarching message of it is 'Transcend your class if you want to write' (FI V/IF 3: 98/110).

The advice of the grandfathers, however, was not all the Postromantics had to go on. Another set of authors, whose work published in the first half of the nineteenth century, held even more sway over them: the Romantics. Sartre considers the influence of the Romantics comparable to that of older brothers. But here he identifies a problem: the sanction issued by the older brothers contradicts the imperative of the grandfathers. The grandfathers instruct the budding artists of the 1840s to transcend their class by writing, but the older brothers tell them that they cannot write because they are not aristocrats. As the imperatives issued by literature-already-written about literature-to-be-written are contradictory, they cannot be reconciled by ordinary, rational means. Thus, Sartre proposes that, in order to become the authors that their class membership bars them from becoming, the Postromantics were forced to make recourse to 'magic' – i.e. they were forced to adopt a neurotic attitude towards literature. As Sartre understands it, the '*art-neurosis*' (*Art-Névrose*) (FI V/IF 3: 35/43) of the Postromantics is a form of stress and, as such, it is an effort to assimilate a nonassimilable with the means at hand. More specifically, it is the Postromantics' effort to assimilate their class-being (the nonassimilable) into their selves by manipulating their class ideology (the means at hand).

What was the class ideology the Postromantics had to work with? According to Sartre, the bourgeoisie of the 1840s required a new form of 'humanism' for their ideology to 'justify' their continued exploitation of the proletariat. As the humanism of the previous century had affirmed the equality of all men, it was clearly unsuitable. Thus, the new ideology that the bourgeoisie of the mid-nineteenth century came to endorse is described by Sartre as 'a black humanism' (*l'humanisme noir*) (FI V/IF 3: 264/286), on the basis that it is less a humanism than a thinly disguised misanthropy, combined with aspects of Darwinism (FI V/IF 3: 236/258).[24] Briefly, the thought is that black humanism enabled the bourgeoisie to affirm that they deserved to belong to the ruling class because they had risen above their animal needs. The wretched conditions of the disadvantaged classes then become 'justifiable' on the grounds that the people in them were either incapable of or unwilling to transcend the animal condition. From the perspective of black humanism, the proletariat represent '*pure nature*', which is not human nature but 'animal nature in its pure inhumanity' (FI V/IF 3: 229/249). The bourgeoisie therefore sought to emphasize their 'distinction' from the working classes through their 'ostentatious denial of human animality' (FI V/IF 3: 230/249) – through uncomfortable attire, through strict routines, through 'moderation' pushed to the point of deprivation, and so on.

Having been conditioned as young bourgeois males, the Postromantics have internalized black humanism. But they adapt it so that it 'justifies' their disdain for 'bourgeois nature', which they imagine that they have risen above through having developed a superior artistic-aristocratic sensibility. Accordingly, Sartre's Postromantics initiate themselves into an imaginary, aristocratic order that he calls the 'Knights of Nothingness' (*chevaliers du Néant*) by refusing the bourgeois utilitarianism of their fathers and vowing to write '*for nothing* and *no one*' (FI V/IF 3: 136/150). Their art-neurosis thereby allows them to 'unrealize' their lived reality as young bourgeois males.

Sartre supports this interpretation of the Postromantics with a rich study of their works, which highlights key points of harmony in their artistic output that transcend the differences between individual artists and the formal features of their works. One of the most significant points of harmony emphasized here is the perspective of a 'panoramic consciousness' (*conscience de survol*), which describes the human world from an inhuman 'Absolute' point of view (FI V/IF 3: 333/358). But what belies the inhuman nature of the Postromantic panoramic consciousness is its expression of two 'all too human' attitudes: misanthropy and misogyny. Further, the way that these attitudes are expressed in the work of the Postromantics invariably exposes the author as a bourgeois male writing in the middle of the nineteenth century. The very desire to portray the world from the perspective of a panoramic consciousness is misanthropic in and of itself, as this perspective trivializes every aspect of human reality. Further, the technical difficulties involved creating an artwork that describes the world from this impossible perspective expose the misanthropy of the Postromantics as being unmistakeably bourgeois in virtue of asserting the 'primacy of the ideal and of the human thing over the humble lived experience of daily life' by demanding the 'sacrifice of the man to his product' (FI V/IF 3: 352/379). Unlike the art of the Romantics – who might claim to have written their masterpiece in one night, 'mingling ink with the tears they shed' (FI V: 96/107) – the art of the Postromantics requires painstaking labour.

The kind of misogyny present in the work of the Postromantics is also 'typical of the midcentury', according to Sartre, because it demonstrates an inability to reconcile 'the sensual relations of the body with the human relations established between couples' (FI V/IF 3: 338/364). As sex and love were largely relegated to separate spheres in this era, many bourgeois males (even those that were married) would have used prostitutes to satisfy their sexual needs 'in the shadow', because it was forbidden to 'treat one's wife like a mistress' (FI V/IF 3: 338/364). Among the toxic effects of the prevalent dichotomic conception of 'woman' as either 'angel' or 'beast' (FI V/IF 3: 339/365) is the potential to render all women despicable in the eyes of a nineteenth-century bourgeois, heterosexual male, who is already ashamed of his sexual desires and frustrated by the fact that he cannot satisfy them without feeling still more shame. It would not be surprising, Sartre states, if this male should come to detest both kinds of woman: 'the whore in the name of the angel' whom he is permitted to love but not to make love to, and 'the angel in the name of the whore' he shamefully makes love to but is forbidden from loving (FI V/IF 3: 339/366).

With this objective understanding of Flaubert's situation as a Postromantic writer in place, we can now turn to the question of whether Flaubert's neurotic literature is, in part, a 'solution' to the problem of his class-being is substantiated by the way that Flaubert objectified himself in his literary works.

Sex and death, eating and decay

Sartre posits that the misanthropy and the misogyny discoverable in Flaubert's literature have a basis in a very bourgeois disgust with human bodily needs. A definitive feature of this disgust as it manifests itself in Flaubert's work, though, is that it is rooted in the recognition of a fundamental relationship between sex and death. To take just one example of this attitude in one of his earliest works, the narrator of *Whatever You Want* (1837) remarks, seemingly with pride, that although Lord Byron may have felt revulsion at the sight of a beautiful woman eating, he cannot even look at one without imagining her cadaver (EW/OJ: 96/265). Rather than being a temporary, adolescent preoccupation, this is a recurring theme in Flaubert's work. An excellent example is even discoverable in one of his very last works, the final version of *The Temptation of Saint Anthony* (*La Tentation de Saint Antoine*, 1874), where a graphic exchange between 'Death' and 'Lust' exposes their unholy allegiance:

> I hasten the dissolution of matter!
> 'I facilitate the scattering of the germs!'
> 'Thou destroyest that I may renew!'
> 'Thou engenderest that I may destroy!'
> 'Active my power!'
> 'Fruitful my decay!' (Flaubert 1926: 158)[25]

In the last line of this excerpt, the word 'fruitful' (*féconde*) – which usually has positive connotations: fertile, nourishing, life-giving, etc. – is linked directly to decay. If Flaubert's intention is to demoralize his reader, as Sartre argues it is, then this line serves him well. Fertility and decay are typically conceived in opposition to one another: one is productive, the other destructive; one gives life, the other takes it; and so on. But, by assuming the imaginary perspective of death, Flaubert shows that this opposition is only apparent; he reveals decay as the 'ultimate truth' of organic life and living fruit as merely a temporary structure in the cycle of decay.

Further, Sartre contends that the motif of shameful procreation[26] in Flaubert's literary work indicates that sex has a deep association not only with death for him, but also with defecation when it results in childbirth. As we have seen, Sartre's subjective-regressive analysis indicates that young Flaubert's feelings of helplessness, guilt and self-loathing led him to the conviction that his birth was the result of wilful cruelty on his father's part. This, Sartre believes, leads Flaubert to believe that the sexual act becomes positively shameful when it results in conception. So, while Flaubert's misogyny may allow him to deflect his shame about his sexual exploits onto women,[27] Sartre proposes that if he had procreated, he would have felt as though he had '*made excrement* – because his father did when he engendered him' (FI I/FI I: 208/216). And, indeed, Flaubert certainly seems to express genuine terror at the prospect of Louise Colet being pregnant with his child when he urges her to take the nineteenth-century equivalent of emergency contraction – a 'remedy to bring on the Redcoats' – because she knows 'how that monster lies in wait for his victims' (1982/1973: 109–10/337–8).

Nutrition also has negative connotations in Flaubert's literature, which Sartre finds unsurprising since eating implicates the eater as an active participant in the cycle of decay when considered from the perspective of death. The amount of textual evidence in support of Sartre's contention that pleasure in digestion functions as an indicator of 'spiritual mediocrity' (FI I/IF I: 441/445) in Flaubert's literature is almost overwhelming. Characters portrayed as enjoying their food include Ernest, the traitorous lover (EW/OJ: 110/282); Homais, the figurehead of bourgeois mediocrity (MB: 286–7, 297/619–20, 630–1); Bournisien, the priest who failed to save Emma's soul (MB: 100, 297/427, 630–1); Dr Larivière, the ineffective medical expert (MB: 286–7/619–20);[28] Charles Bovary, the cuckolded husband (MB: 39/363); Hannon, the self-serving Carthaginian general (S: 99/176); and the hypocritical Elders in *Salammbô* (S: 222/372). When these characters take satisfaction in their digestion, they appear grotesque because Flaubert uses gustatory satisfaction as a cipher for negative qualities such as ignorance, complacency or self-absorption. Of special interest is Flaubert's tendency to depict representatives of religion as having 'a fundamental relation to food' (FI IV/IF III: 173/1945), which Sartre reads as an upshot of Flaubert's resentment about his inability to take solace in faith. The feasting of the Elders in *Salammbô* renders them particularly deplorable, as they gorge themselves 'on the pretext of some devotion', while the other citizens of Carthage starve (S: 22/372). Their eating thus symbolizes their hypocrisy and their complacency with the suffering of others at once.

According to Sartre, Flaubert's tendency to link the gratification of bodily desires with the prolongation of suffering or the creation of new subjects of suffering in his work evinces the depth of his comprehension of his own struggle to live because it works on the assumption that life is suffering. However, Sartre seeks to progress from the comprehension of the subjective meaning of Flaubert's disgust to knowledge of the role it plays in his self-formation. By explaining Flaubert's peculiar aversion towards biological processes as a consequence of his early encounter with the autopsy, his fetishized materialism, and his internalization of his class ideology, Sartre reveals that the ties between Flaubert's literary expressions of disgust towards the organic and his bourgeois social conditioning run deep, and this is perhaps most apparent in the way that Flaubert's characters 'distinguish' themselves through suffering. As Sartre observes, the only sentiments that find grace with Flaubert 'are those that shatter the individual' (FI I/IF I: 322/333). Again, there is a vast amount of evidence to corroborate this view, and the feelings that find grace with Flaubert may be considered under two categories: (1) Masochistic devotion, which involves self-denial and the desire to degrade, deprive or sacrifice oneself for another, either earthly (romantic masochistic devotion) or divine (religious masochistic devotion); and (2) Insatiable desire, which cannot be satisfied by earthly things and which may be manifested through hedonistic behaviour, extreme *ennui* (if the subject realizes that nothing on this earth can satisfy them), or it can evolve into masochistic devotion.

Romantic masochistic devotion is a common theme in Flaubert's fiction. It is apparent in many of the early works Sartre analyses in *The Family Idiot*, especially *Passion and Virtue* (*Passion et vertu*, 1837), where the female protagonist, Mazza, murders her husband and two children to be with her lover, then kills herself when she discovers he is engaged to another woman. It is also evident in *Whatever You Want*, through Djalioh's adoration for Adèle.[29] There are also clear examples of romantic masochistic devotion in Flaubert's mature work, such as: Mâtho's slavish devotion to Salammbô,[30] Justin's adolescent worship of Emma Bovary[31] and Louise's adoration of Frédéric[32] in *A Sentimental Education*. All these characters suffer for their love of another and their suffering seems to distinguish them from other characters. Similarly, religious masochistic devotion is a central theme in Flaubert's portrayals of the hermit saints (in *The Temptation of Saint Anthony* and *The Legend of Saint Julian Hospitator*), as well as in *A Simple Heart* (*Un Cœur simple*, 1877), the story of Félicité, a servant who devotes herself to others all her life, then, finally, to Loulou, a parrot that appears to her as the incarnation of the Holy Spirit.[33]

Masochistic devotion appears to result from an insatiable desire that serves as the hallmark of a superior soul in Flaubert's fiction. Sartre reads 'Great Desire – or infinite privation' to be the hallmark of a noble kind of dissatisfaction with the world in Flaubert's literary-metaphysical schema (FI II/IF II: 435/1103). He examines how it presents itself in the character of Mazza, before it evolves into masochistic devotion, to show that Mazza represents a 'black saint' (*Sainte noire*) for Flaubert by the rule that 'if impossible gratification is the painful mark of election for great souls, it is because they desire nothing less than the *infinite*' (FI I/IF I: 421/434), Mazza suffers because of the boundlessness of her desire. Flaubert likens her to 'those who drink seawater to quench a thirst that it only increases' (EW/OJ: 127/300) and, as it seems that nothing on earth could quench her thirst, she will only find peace by destroying herself. Emma Bovary appears to be a black saint like her predecessor Mazza, although, unlike Mazza, she is unable to transform her insatiable desire into masochistic devotion. We will return to this issue in the next chapter but, for now, it is worth noting that one of the indicators of Emma's greatness-blackness is her ambivalent, even pathological, relationship with food, which illustrates her dissatisfaction with the life it sustains.[34]

Naturally, Sartre argues that Flaubert considers himself a '*black saint*' (FI I/ IF I: 428/442). Flaubert's choice to represent himself through black saints in his literature would certainly follow from him having a conception of himself as both a victim of the paternal curse and one of the literary-aristocratic elect, as black souls are victims of the 'profound injustice' of being born into a world that is too small for them and they are doomed to suffer this injustice 'like the most agonizing passion' due to their superior sensibilities (FI I/IF I: 438/452). Hence, one lesson we may draw from Sartre's analysis of Flaubert's literature is that Flaubertian black saints suffer on account of their great desire for more than the earth could ever provide them with, and that they will be driven to self-destruction, unless they can channel their energy into religious masochistic devotion, like Félicité and Salammbô (before she falls in love with Mâtho),[35] or to art, like Flaubert.

Flaubert's choice of the imaginary

From the very beginning of *The Family Idiot*, Sartre affirms that understanding the meaning of Flaubert's childhood stupors (*hébétudes*) is key to understanding his genius, since they are the condition for his eventual crisis at Pont-l'Evêque, which enabled him to become a creative writer. Sartre's idea is that if Flaubert is constituted in such a way that the smallest demand, the slightest discomfort, could plunge him into a daze through which he escapes his reality, then it is possible to comprehend Flaubert as having a fundamental relationship to the imaginary. This is not to say that Flaubert does not experience the world as real in the same way as everyone else, only that he escapes it more frequently than most because imagining is his default response to difficulty and discomfort. This 'inclination' towards the imaginary would also have to have been something that Flaubert lived with and worked on in the years between his illiteracy and the production of his masterpiece, *Madame Bovary*.

After revealing Flaubert as a Postromantic who writes to escape his reality, Sartre calls attention to the irony in the fact that the Postromantics, who produce artworks so that they may 'transcend' their class-being in the imaginary, produce class literature in reality.[36] He also underlines the point that their works were erroneously received by the nineteenth-century reading public as works of 'realism'. It is extremely telling that the 'sham desituating' (*désituation feinte*) (FI V/IF 3: 278/301) of these writers who attempt to adopt the perspective of a panoramic consciousness is taken for realism by the bourgeois readership, in Sartre's view, since it highlights an affinity between these authors' literary means of 'desituation' and the bourgeoisie's means of 'distinction'. What seemingly escapes the Postromantics' first readers is that the 'realist', 'disinterested', 'objective', perspective of the panoramic consciousness is, in fact, the derealized, misanthropic, self-loathing, perspective of a disillusioned member of their class. Sartre explains that the 'enlightened' elite could only mistake the bleak perspective offered by the Postromantics for 'the' objective perspective if there were strong parallels between their own perspective and that of the Postromantic panoramic consciousness. That is, the 'black' literature produced by the Postromantics could only have been received as 'realist' if its readers had been '*blackened*' (*noircies*) by the history they had made (FI V/IF 3: 307/331).

Though both the Postromantics and their first readers were deceiving themselves about the nature of their class-being, Sartre contends that the presence of bad faith in both author and reader is not enough to explain the kind of rapport that existed between Flaubert and the first readers of *Madame Bovary*, who fitted together like 'hand in glove' (FI V/IF 3: 396/426). This could only have been possible, he suggests, if both Flaubert and his first readership shared the same ultimate concern, which allowed them to discover their synchronism at a deeper level. Sartre's suggestion is that not only does black humanism provide the bourgeoisie with an excuse for their moral failure (i.e. their continued exploitation of the proletariat) and – with a few adaptations – Flaubert with an excuse for his personal failure (being the 'idiot' of the family), but both Flaubert and his readership had a history they sought to forget as they had both experienced a moment that had pushed them into hatred, guilt and self-hatred. This is why the nineteenth-century reader of *Madame Bovary*, who reads this text as the realist work it was never intended to be, can take reassurance in its black message: he can use this portrayal of a radically evil world to excuse himself 'in his own eyes, and to present his own intentional hatred as an innocently *other* intention (of that *other*, the author)' (FI V/IF 3: 313/337).

Although the two failures that unite Flaubert with the bourgeois reading public reach different points of crisis at different times – namely Flaubert's nervous crisis at Pont-l'Evêque in 1844 and the massacres of the of lower classes during the June Days uprising of 1848 – Sartre asserts that Flaubert's neurotic response to his crisis represents 'a *real* anticipation' of the bourgeoisie's response to theirs, so that the particularity of his neurosis is suppressed in 'the singular universality of the work in which it is recounted' (FI V/IF 3: 398/427). This is what allows Sartre to answer the question of how *Madame* Bovary, a neurotic artwork, could have such popular appeal. It is because both Flaubert and his first readers need to assimilate similar nonassimilables in a similar way, and it is enough for them to have been conditioned by the same factors for the same neurotic 'solution' to work for both of them. Therefore, Flaubert's objectification of his neurosis in *Madame Bovary* enables both him and his first readers to relieve their stress, as well as their feelings of hatred, guilt and self-loathing by imagining that this world is objectively wicked.

Flaubert's failure

After assessing Flaubert's neurotic solution to a situation that was unliveable for him 'objectively', Sartre concludes that, until 1870, 'Flaubert's relation to the (bourgeois) real is *imaginary destruction*' because his commitment to 'art for art's sake' is nothing other than an imaginary 'cover' that he and his fellow Postromantic writers drew over their class-being (FI V/IF 3: 619/658). Flaubert was in need of such a cover, Sartre maintains, because he had to conceal the nonassimilable aspects of his self from himself – his humiliation, his failure in the eyes of his family, his class-being, etc. – in order to have the self-esteem he needed to pursue his fundamental project and to make art. The society of the Second Empire had provided Flaubert and other Postromantics with security, validation and – importantly – a means of keeping their cover over their bourgeois-being intact. During the liberal period of the Second Empire, Flaubert was able to live his dream of *déclassement*[37] by playing 'the role of a great writer recruited by the nobility' (FI V/IF 3: 496/529) and he was as happy as he could possibly be, according to Sartre, since his public success seemed to validate his life-philosophy: the loser wins.

However, when the Second Empire fell in 1870, Sartre argues that it left the Postromantics exposed. They were forced to integrate themselves back into the reality that they had laboured to transcend in the imaginary. They had to take ownership of their class-being and recognize that they shared in the fears of their class: fears of occupation, of physical violence and of losing their property. For Flaubert specifically, Sartre contends that the outcome of the Battle of Sedan had the effect of unravelling the imaginary cover that had shielded him from having to deal with his real self since 1844 and of returning him to 'the primal scene', where it is as if the paterfamilias, resurrected, and looks at him once more with 'icy scorn' (FI V/IF 3: 556/592). Sartre argues that Flaubert wakes up in 1870, as if from a long dream, to the realization that he still is – and never stopped being – 'the family idiot' (FI V/IF 3: 556/592).

After this awakening, Sartre describes how Flaubert became melancholy and came to regard his former hopes of achieving a place among the literary elite as nothing other than 'the *dated* dreams of a parasite nourished by a mirage society' and his books as 'false masterpieces that a false elite pretended to admire' (FI V/IF 3: 477/510). During the Prussian occupation of France in the early 1870s, Flaubert believes he has taken ill with stomach cancer. He did not have cancer, but Sartre argues that his real, physical symptoms provide even further evidence for the view that Flaubert is neurotic. He interprets Flaubert's sickness in the 1870s as another important instance of his disposition towards magical behaviour. He compares Flaubert's almost daily bouts of vomiting during this period to the way a pregnant woman 'spits into the ashes' when she refuses to accept her condition on the grounds that it manifests a denial that Flaubert strives to make with his 'entire person', including 'his underlying reality' (FI V/IF 3: 460/491). What is it that Flaubert is attempting to deny here? Sartre holds that Flaubert's letter to his friend Ernest Feydeau, dated 28th October 1870, provides an important clue. Here, Flaubert writes: 'Never, my dear fellow, have I felt such a colossal disgust. I would like to drown humanity in my vomit' (FI V/IF 3: 460/491). As is the case with Flaubert's nervous attacks in the mid-1840s, Sartre argues that Flaubert's *'pithiatic belief* (*croyance pithiathique*) that he is ill is his attempt to 'get out of the game' (FI V/IF 3: 460/492). This time, however, Flaubert's denial comes hand in hand with some admission of guilt since, while he takes revenge on humanity by vomiting onto them, he also vomits 'himself', which appears to signal recognition of his culpability as a beneficiary of the imperial regime. This, coupled with the fact that Flaubert took part in elections in 1871, leads Sartre to conclude that – for the first time in his adult life – Flaubert has become a *'realist'* in the sense that he recognizes his need to safeguard his 'material interests' and his position as a landowner in order to write (FI V/IF 3: 468/500).

This analysis of Flaubert's illness in the 1870s certainly offers more evidence to support Sartre's claim that Flaubert's nervous attacks in the 1840s were hysterical. This is important as the success of Sartre's project in *The Family Idiot* hinges on his account of Flaubert's nervous crisis in 1844 as meaningful, since his claim to have gained knowledge of Flaubert' self through his existential psychoanalysis rests upon the claim that this most decisive event Flaubert's self-formation originates in an intention and is, therefore, comprehensible in terms of an original choice. Although Sartre accepts that Flaubert's choice to fall at his brother's feet that night in January 1844 was 'irrational' in the ordinary sense, he refutes the idea that it is 'arational' by showing that it makes more sense to interpret it as Flaubert's intentional response to his situation and contending that it is also a 'dialectical necessity' within the totalization that is Flaubert's self.

Sartre's describes his analysis of Flaubert's illness in *The Family Idiot* as a kind of 'antipsychiatry' (*antipsychiatrie*), since it treats Flaubert's illness not as the problem, but as 'the solution to the problem' (OIF/SIF: 118/100). Having now surveyed this analysis, we are now able to see why Sartre believes that Flaubert's neurotic 'solution' to his problem in 1844 ultimately did him more harm than good. If we can roughly summarize Sartre's dialectical understanding of Flaubert's crisis thus: 'Flaubert made himself a failure in reality so that he may achieve superiority as an artist in the imaginary', then we can summarize his objective understanding of it thus: 'Flaubert made himself a failure.' Even though Flaubert achieved real success as a writer during the Second Empire, which allowed him to imagine himself as a member of the literary elite for over a quarter of a century, Sartre compares Flaubert's relation to the imaginary to that of a man in a room that is on fire and whose only exit leads him back into the same inferno. Flaubert's imaginary traps him because it gives him the 'crazy false hope' that he can escape from his situation by imagining that he is in another (FI V/IF 3: 480/517). Putting an imaginary cover over his self for himself allows Flaubert to live but it also, tragically, has the effect of allowing the inassimilable features of his self to be the ones that most define him for those whom he makes his self for: his 'original others'. Although it is obviously false to say that Flaubert is 'a failure' for us, his readers, his biographers, or for the many writers who have been inspired by his work, Sartre's key point is that Flaubert could never feel authentically proud of who he really was due to his psychological oppression within the microcosm of the Flaubert family who, collectively, looked at him through the critical gaze of the paterfamilias and saw only an idiot.

5

Objectivity in Sartre's study of Flaubert

Perhaps the most serious objection to Sartre's analysis of Flaubert in *The Family Idiot* is that it cannot satisfactorily support its claim to deliver knowledge of Flaubert's self. Sartre's progressive-regressive approach to gaining knowledge of a self is radically new. It aims not merely to collate the biographical facts about its subject, but also to highlight their subjective meaning in a way that facilitates the 're-totalization' of the subject's self. On the one hand, this way of knowing 'through re-totalization' potentially dissolves the epistemological barriers that have long been presumed to exist between 'subject' and 'other' by allowing us to gain direct knowledge of other selves. On the other hand, it seems to grant the subject doing the 're-totalization' too much power in determining the nature of their object for it to be regarded as an object of knowledge as opposed to a subjective image.

This chapter addresses the objection that the method of analysis employed in the first three volumes of *The Family Idiot* does not appear to be 'objective enough' to support its claim to deliver knowledge of Flaubert's self. It defends Sartre's progressive-regressive method by showing that the psychoanalytical critique of *Madame Bovary* he intended to supply in the missing fourth volume would have provided him with a valid means of confirming (or disconfirming) the findings of the first three. Then, it uses the clues Sartre left behind about his intentions for the fourth volume to provide a sketch of what a Sartrean reading of *Madame Bovary* would have been like. Finally, it uses this sketch to assess the extent to which this reading could have confirmed the findings of *The Family Idiot* as it stands.

Why Flaubert?

At first glance, Gustave Flaubert appears to be a bad choice of subject for Sartre's project of showing that the self of another can be the object of our knowledge. First, Flaubert was dead and had been dead for quite some time. Approximately three-quarters of a century had elapsed since Flaubert's death in 1880 and the mid-1950s when Sartre commenced serious work on his study on Flaubert. This ruled out the possibility of Sartre being able to interview anyone who had known Flaubert directly. We have already seen why Sartre believes that psychoanalysis can only deliver stable knowledge of a self if the subject is dead in Chapter 3. However, the inability to interview the subject or people acquainted with them also removes the 'obstacle' of testimony that may oppose the analyst's view of the subject – precisely the kind of obstacle that we would expect a balanced, objective analysis to have to overcome.

Another reason why Flaubert, in particular, appears to be a bad choice of subject for Sartre is that Flaubert actively contrived to make the task of any future biographer a difficult one. He expressed a desire to make prosperity believe that he never existed as a man distinct from his art, and he sought to achieve this by cultivating a particular style of writing that works rigorously to remove any traces of the author's personality – a style which many of his first readers mistook for 'realism'. As Enid Starkie observes, writers of the Realist school in the mid-nineteenth century aimed to be 'locally and chronologically true to their own age, so that the characters they created could not have lived at any other time or in any other place', but Flaubert 'wished to depict what did not pass, what was the same for every age, what was eternal' (Starkie 1967: 351). Flaubert adhered to the principle that the author must be 'present everywhere and visible nowhere' (1982/1980: 238/204), precisely because he wanted his works to transcend the particular, and he believed that authors who betray their own opinions, preferences and sentiments run the risk of reflecting prejudices peculiar to their era and rendering their work irrelevant to readers of the future.

Further, although a vast amount of Flaubert's correspondence has been published, Sartre regards it with a considerable degree of mistrust because he believes that Flaubert is incapable of being sincere while being himself. If Flaubert extracts himself from his fiction and his insincerity effectively fictionalizes his non-fictional writings, then it would seem that he left no reliable accounts of his personal experience behind and, hence, no material for a Sartre's 'regressive' analysis to analyse. This might lead us to think that the dialectical object that is Flaubert's self is unknowable for the Sartrean analyst because there is insufficient evidence about Flaubert's lived experience for them to synthesize with the biographical facts. As a phenomenologist, though, Sartre is acutely aware of the bad faith implicit in Flaubert's attempt to narrate fictional worlds 'from nowhere' because he understands the assumption of a 'desituated' perspective as impossible for any human being. It is even impossible to offer a desituated perspective on fictional world in Sartre's view because, to construct a fictional world, one must use this world (and one's comprehension of it) as a model, which means that literary authors invariably reveal idiosyncratic aspects of their 'conception of the world' in their work (SM/QM: 141/196). So, Sartre is not deterred by Flaubert's impersonal writing-style. To the contrary, we have seen that he believes that the pretence of 'falsification' allows Flaubert to disclose more truths about his lived experience in his fictions than in any other context and that this is a significant part of Flaubert's appeal to him as a biographical subject.

There are, however, other reasons, not publicized, for Sartre's choice of Flaubert. In his Preface to *The Family Idiot*, Sartre teasingly remarks that the first reason for his choice of subject is 'very personal', but, rather than elaborating, he hastens to add that it has 'long ago ceased to be as salient as it once was in the origin of this choice' (FI I/IF I: x/8). On the basis of Sartre's remarks about Flaubert in his autobiographical work, *Words*, one could speculate that the 'very personal' reason he alludes to here is a desire to avenge himself on the author he believed 'poisoned' him in his youth.[1] Harry Levin, for one,[2] is convinced that *The Family Idiot* 'marks the end of a lifelong vendetta' (1972: 643), and he is extremely critical of it as a consequence in his review essay, 'A Literary Enormity: Sartre on Flaubert'. Levin's essay begins by drawing an analogy between the presence of Flaubert in Sartre's writings and that of King Charles' head in those of the befuddled Mr Dick in *David Copperfield* (1972: 643). Now, we must concede that this analogy is apt insofar as Flaubert's name appears at regular and often surprising intervals throughout Sartre's oeuvre, outside of his actual study on Flaubert. Sartre's *War Diaries* recounts his critical reading of Flaubert's *A Sentimental Education* in December of 1939 ([1983] 1984/1995: 101–4/304–8). In *Being and Nothingness*, a psychoanalytical biography of Flaubert is evidently already under consideration. Fyodor Dostoyevsky is also suggested here as a potential subject, but, as Dostoyevsky's name only gets two mentions in this text (BN/EN: 71, 746/67, 620), and Flaubert's name appears twenty-one times (BN/EN: 725–8, 746, 762/603–6, 620, 634), it already seems clear which of these candidates will prevail. Further, Flaubert is mentioned twice in Sartre's posthumously published *Notebooks for an Ethics* (1983 [written *c.* 1947–8]: 108–9), seven times in *What Is Literature?* (WL/QL: xxii, 93, 95,

96, 100, 124, 139, 175/11, 128, 130, 131, 136, 165–6, 183, 227), where one of his characters (Charles Bovary) is also discussed (WL/QL: 163/212). Sartre discusses Flaubert at various points in the *Critique* (CDR I/CRD I: 199, 226, 754/309, 335, 833; CDR II: 408, 413/398, 412) and at length in *Search for a Method* (SM/QM: 85–166/119–230). In Sartre's autobiographical work, *Words*, Flaubert is cited five times (W/M: 42, 43, 45, 101, 113/ 55, 56, 58, 131, 146) and his novel, *Madame Bovary*, three times (W/M: 37, 43, 67/48, 56, 89). Although Flaubert's name does not appear in Sartre's fiction, his influence is often apparent. Perhaps the most-striking example of this is Sartre's famous description of Roquentin's encounter with the chestnut tree in *Nausea*, which recalls the training exercise Flaubert assigned to the young Guy de Maupassant, which Sartre we know that was aware of since he describes how Flaubert sat Maupassant 'in front of a tree and gave him two hours to describe it' in his autobiography (W/M: 101/131).

What is more, in a late interview entitled 'Justice and the State', Sartre admits to having spent 'the last seventeen years' engaged in a study on Flaubert 'which can be of no interest to the workers' but which he is 'committed to', meaning, in his words, 'that I am sixty-seven years old, I have been working on it since I was fifty, and before that I dreamed about it' (1978a: 185). This, together with Sartre's numerous references to Flaubert, indicates that Sartre probably did believe that he had a score to settle with Flaubert and that he was determined to do so in his final major work. Hence, in his popular novel, *Flaubert's Parrot*, Julian Barnes has his fictional Flaubert biographer compare Sartre to 'some brawny, desperate lifeguard' who 'spent ten years beating on [Flaubert's] chest and blowing into his mouth; ten years trying to yank him back to consciousness, just so that he could sit him up on the sands and tell him exactly what he thought of him' ([1984] 2009: 86). Even though Barnes' work is a fiction, this remark nicely captures the consensus among critics that Sartre's personal reasons *for* choosing Flaubert as the subject of his biographical study should have struck him as reasons *against* choosing him, as they compromised his ability to approach Flaubert as a disinterested observer. Regardless of whatever Flaubert meant to Sartre personally, though, what is certain is that Sartre goes to great lengths in *The Family Idiot* to ensure that his method is as rigorous and as objective as possible and, while he admits that there are elements of himself in the book, he maintains that 'the essential thing is the method' (OIF/SIF: 121/104). So, it is only fair that we assess Sartre's study on its own merit here as his most thorough attempt to apply the innovative method of psychoanalysis he developed throughout his career.

Is Sartre's method objective enough?

Although the preceding chapters have explained the rationale for Sartre's progressive-regressive method, the sheer volume of criticism levelled at Sartre's study of Flaubert for its alleged lack of objectivity (e.g. Mauron 1962; Bart 1967; Levin 1972; Barnes 1982) means that the concern that Sartre's method does not include enough measures to prevent its findings from being unduly influenced by the biases of the analyst must be taken seriously.

Sartre emphasizes the importance of methodological flexibility in psychoanalysis on the grounds that an adherence to strict procedures would necessarily preclude the revelation of certain meanings (BN/EN: 743/619). Even if we grant that methodological flexibility is required in the study of selves, though, this goes no way towards providing us with assurances of the reliability of Sartre's method as a route to knowledge of selves. Without some form of methodological standardization, what is there to assure us that all analysts who apply Sartre's method to Flaubert would arrive at the same conclusions? As the subject of psychoanalysis – be it the unconscious or the unknown dimensions of the self – is perhaps the most elusive subject matter conceivable, it is also the most vulnerable to misinterpretation and corruption by the analyst. Freud was acutely aware of this, which is why he hoped to claim for psychoanalysis the disinterested precision associated with the natural sciences and to prevent, as much as possible, the biases and the projections of the analyst from obscuring the evidence presented by the analysand. The assumption here is that the conclusions of psychoanalysis have a better claim to knowledge if its methods can hold claim to the same objective validity that the natural sciences have by preventing the subjectivity of the analyst from influencing the findings of the investigation.

Sartre's insistence that the course of the analysis should be determined by the conscious experience of the analyst emphasizes the importance of the very thing that Freud sought to exclude, as much as possible, from his psychoanalysis: the subjectivity of the analyst. But Sartre's denial that scientific objectivity should be viewed an aspirational goal for psychoanalysts is not 'unenlightened'. To the contrary, Sartre joins Husserl in affirming that naïve positivism can lead us to neglect to examine the fundamental structures of the life-world through which all objects are given to us (Husserl [1936] 1970). His view that the dialectical analysis of selves is, like phenomenology, concerned with the primary, internal relations that constitute the life-world, or a reality that is first of all 'for us', underpins his contention that while it is 'legitimate for the natural sciences to free themselves from anthropomorphism ... it is perfectly absurd to assume by analogy the same scorn for anthropomorphism where anthropology is concerned' (SM/QM: 157/218). And anthropology is most certainly concerned in investigations into objects whose essence is determined by the ongoing dialectic – i.e. by human being, as opposed to arational, natural forces. So, the standard of objectivity required in the study of selves cannot exclude the subjective; it must, rather, be intersubjective.

According to Sartre, the intersubjective validity of a dialectical truth can be established by its appearing '*as necessity*' within the investigation which reveals it and by its provision of the key to '*the intelligibility* of the process in question' (CDR I/CRD I: 37/156). This makes the subjective experience of the investigator 'the test' of the validity of a dialectical truth. Nevertheless, Sartre's articulation of two conditions for validity provides a clear demonstration of how his development of dialectical reason enables him to supply a more robust theorization of the processes that give rise to the 'feeling of satisfaction' which, in *Being and Nothingness*, he proposed would confirm that the analysis had reached its endpoint. Thanks to his theorization of dialectical reason in the *Critique*, Sartre can now explain how even though intuitions are unquestionably subjective, they have a claim to 'objective' status via intersubjective validity when they are experienced within the context of a dialectical study. The assumption here is that the capacity to comprehend the meaning of human action is universal among humans, which we have already seen to be firmly grounded in a Sartre's theorization of what human being is. So, altogether, this implies that the Sartrean analyst can find confirmation that they have not erred in their application of the progressive-regressive method if their conclusions allow for the analysand's acts to be interpreted as part of a coherent totalization in which each act emerges as dialectical necessity.

Even if it is granted that the standard of objective validity for claims to knowledge of selves is intersubjective, it still seems as though Sartre's biographical analysis of Flaubert in *The Family Idiot* might not be 'objective enough', in sense of being 'neutral' or 'unbiased', to support its claim to deliver knowledge of Flaubert's self. This is partly because it is heavily reliant upon hypotheses concerning matters about which there is little to no objective evidence – about how Flaubert's mother nursed him as an infant, how Flaubert felt when he looked at himself in the mirror, and so on. It is also partly because Sartre's means of qualifying his findings by revealing their dialectical necessity appears to be questionable because the dialectic Sartre develops over the course of the three published volumes is internally coherent *precisely because* it is both constructed and contained within them. That is to say, Sartre does not verify his findings in the first three volumes of *The Family Idiot* against something external to the dialectic he constructs in them. In the absence of such verification, most people would agree that Sartre's findings cannot be considered anything more than compelling hypotheses, so they cannot lay claim to intersubjective validity.

However, the very last lines of the published text of *The Family Idiot* note that Flaubert denied that he was a novelist and affirmed that he was a 'writer', even though he only wrote novels and *The Temptation of Saint Anthony*. Two questions are then posed. The first asks what the meaning of Flaubert's insistence that he is a writer could be. The second asks how the idea of 'pure art' that Flaubert shared with other Postromantic authors could have motivated him to produce the particular works he did. Then, *The Family Idiot* closes with a promise to attempt 'to answer these questions by reading *Madame Bovary*' (FI V/IF 3: 621/665). It is known that Sartre intended to write a fourth volume of *The Family Idiot*, which was to be a literary critique of *Madame Bovary* (1978b: 20; IWS: 22; OIF/SIF: 126/109; Beauvoir [1981] 1984: 33). In an interview following the publication of the first two volumes, Sartre states that an analysis of *Madame Bovary* would supply *The Family Idiot* with an additional 'objective' element (OIF/SIF: 110/92). In the same interview, he also remarks that 'a moment comes when the *text* must be confronted: this is the moment of victory. When I come to *Madame Bovary*, I will also find moments of defeat' (OIF/SIF: 125/108–9). Here, Sartre is speaking of the capacity of *Madame Bovary* to provide *Flaubert* with his 'moment of victory' by proving his genius; yet, *Madame Bovary* could have also provided Sartre with one too; his proposed critique could have confirmed the successes of his study of Flaubert and illuminated any defects. Much to Sartre's regret, deteriorating health and the onset of blindness forced him to give up writing before he could complete *The Family Idiot* as he had hoped to.

In later interviews, Sartre downplays the value of the missing fourth volume. In 1975, for instance, he states: 'Someone else could write the fourth on the basis of the three I have written' (1978b: 20). Nevertheless, his earlier insistence that *Madame Bovary* 'illuminates Flaubert, not the reverse' (CDR I/CRD I: 226/335), shows that he originally assigned a central significance to the study of *Madame Bovary* in understanding Flaubert. Further, the fact that a reviewer of Carol Cosman's English translation of *The Family Idiot* remarks that the fourth volume would have 'illuminated and dignified' the rest (Brown 1982) highlights how important the fourth volume would have been from a critical perspective. Finally, and most importantly for our concerns, a critique of *Madame Bovary* would have provided Sartre with a means of confirming the results of his dialectical analysis in the three published volumes of *The Family Idiot* against something external to the dialectic in them. It would have allowed Sartre to superimpose one of Flaubert's mature texts, which is not fully analysed in the first three volumes, upon those of his juvenilia, which are, and to, thereby, assess the extent to which Flaubert's objectification of his self in *Madame Bovary* aligns with his objectification Flaubert's self in the first three volumes of *The Family Idiot*.

Madame Bovary: The missing fourth volume

As Barnes notes, it would be 'idiotic' to attempt to reconstruct the missing fourth volume of *The Family Idiot*, despite Sartre's claims that someone else could do it (1981b: 341). Nonetheless, it is possible to use the information he left behind in his notes for the fourth volume, the remarks he made in the later interviews, his discussions of *Madame Bovary* in the first three volumes, alongside Barnes' research into the fourth volume (1981b: 340–87), to sketch in outline what a Sartrean reading of *Madame Bovary* might have been like. This section aims to do just this. Then the next will use this sketch as a tool for a coarse-grained assessment of the validity of the findings in the three published volumes of *The Family Idiot*.

Style over substance

In a late interview, Sartre states that the fourth volume would concentrate on the 'style of *Madame Bovary*' (1978b: 20). This is confirmed by the notes that he left behind for it. Now, although these notes do attend to some of the formally stylistic features of *Madame Bovary*,[3] it must be remembered that, in the first three volumes of *The Family Idiot*, Sartre argues that, for Flaubert, 'style' does not only refer to formal techniques, but also to a way of communicating aspects of lived experience that are otherwise incommunicable through '*indirect* expression' (FI III/IF III: 499/1616). Style is Flaubert's central discovery, according to Sartre, since the realization that it is not the 'the *saying* that manifests the artist's thought but the *way of saying*' enables Flaubert to see it that he is not confined to trying to tell his readers about what he imagines; he can also employ style to make them imagine what he imagines (FI III/IF III: 499/1615).

Further, Sartre holds that Flaubert comes to believe that style should dictate the content of a literary work, not the other way around, because writing only becomes beautiful when it employs style to offer an 'indirect sign and symbol ... of the unreal beauty of the world' (FI III/IF III: 500/1617). If this is correct, Flaubert does not use style to reflect the real world, which he finds to be mediocre and bad, but to institute an imaginary world, which is beautiful because it is 'bad to perfection' (FI III/IF III: 462/1578). He would thus create something akin to the Platonic Form of 'world', which this world is but an imperfect instantiation of. Sartre believes that this aim is what characterizes Flaubert's aesthetic once he discovers style, after which he has only one subject: 'radical Evil', and one mode of expression: 'style' (FI III/IF III: 500/1617). Baudelaire's interpretation of *Madame Bovary* lends support to this conclusion, especially as Flaubert is known to have approved of it (Barnes 1981b: 342). According to Baudelaire, *Madame Bovary* and *The Temptation of Saint Anthony* are analogous in that they are both products of Flaubert's ambition to write a book about nothing so that it may be governed by style alone,[4] although this ambition is more apparent in the latter work, whose subject is an anchorite who literally does nothing but suffers from imaginary temptations (Bart 1967; Starkie 1971). However, Sartre is the first to my knowledge to maintain that Flaubert's ideal of style is inextricably connected to the subject of evil. From both *The Family Idiot* and the notes for the fourth volume, it is clear that Sartre intended to investigate this connection further by discussing Baudelaire's interpretation of *Madame Bovary* in relation to Maxime Du Camp and Louis Bouilhet's criticisms of the first version of *The Temptation of Saint Anthony* and the genesis of *Madame Bovary* (FI III/IF II: 177/1285; Notes 165, 166/177, 169/179; Barnes 1981b: 371–2), so let us investigate this a little.

It is likely that the negative feedback Flaubert received from Du Camp and Bouilhet on the first version of *The Temptation of Saint Anthony* in 1849 brought him to the realization that he must commence from the particular if he is to realize his aesthetic goal of showcasing pure style, as style is best evinced through the transformation of something mundane into something extraordinary. This theory is supported by the difference between the fantastic nature of *The Temptation of Saint Anthony* and the 'realistic', if not truly 'realist', nature of *Madame Bovary*. Clearly, *Madame Bovary* has a particular subject: Emma Bovary, the adulterous wife of a country doctor, who lives in a particular region of France; yet, there is an important sense in which its subject is 'general', non-specific, indistinct. The theme of adultery was not new to the reading public in the nineteenth century,[5] nor were the specific kinds of events recounted in

Madame Bovary, as Flaubert's inspiration for Emma is thought to be Delphine Delamere, second wife to Eugene Delamere, a former medical student under Dr Flaubert (Bart 1967: 242). Even within the novel, the heroine is one of three Madame Bovarys and the banality of her life is a great source of frustration for her. Enid Starkie also suggests that Flaubert deliberately chose to set *Madame Bovary* in a 'vague locality, with no particular features', so that it 'could be anywhere in France' (1971: 389).

What is unique about *Madame Bovary* is the way it is told. Sartre describes it as a 'cosmic novel' (FI III/IF II: 177/1285), as he believes that it uses style to describe the events it relays from the panoramic perspective of an Absolute being. It is because Flaubert associates style with the cultivation of this kind of Absolute perspective that Sartre contends that subject of Flaubert's mature fiction – i.e. from 1856 onwards – is nothing other than evil. He asserts that the inspiration for *Madame Bovary* arrives when Flaubert realizes that 'an object is necessary for the macrocosm to become incarnate in it, and that the object is of no importance' and that the only story to be told is that of 'the tragic, grandiose emptiness of a Godless universe', but the only way to tell it is through the adventure of a particular subject (FI IV/IF III: 193/1967). In short, then, (Sartre's) Flaubert realizes that he can show that the world is hell by perching a saint on a summit and having a devil torment him, but he can also do it by taking the adulterous wife of a health official and describing how the world tortures her. Let us now assess whether *Madame Bovary* can be fruitfully read as a product of its author's aim to show that the world is hell through his distinctive style.

The unlikely heroism of Charles Bovary

In 1971, Sartre remarks that after some time studying Flaubert, he came to realize that Charles Bovary 'embodies' one of Flaubert's ideals (OIF/SIF: 110/91). This explains why Sartre's reading of Charles Bovary deviates from the standard one of him as a one-dimensional moron, whose 'bovine boorishness' drives Emma to look elsewhere for love (Orr 2000: 31). Sartre's reading takes the fact that *Madame Bovary* begins and ends with Charles' suffering to be of key significance. That Charles is the first character to be introduced in the novel would usually corroborate the idea that he is of central importance from an authorial perspective. However, the first impression we are given of him is that he is something of a fool; 'we' (*nous*) are even encouraged to join the narrator in mocking the new schoolboy whose hat slides off when he stands up to introduce himself to his classmates and who then garbles the pronunciation of his own name: 'Chabovari' (MB: 6/329). We are also invited to observe the affinity between him and his ridiculous piece of headwear, which is described as being 'of composite order, in which one recognises features of a military busby, a lancer's cap, a bowler hat, an otter-skin cap, and a cotton nightcap, one of those pathetic objects, in fact, whose mute ugliness reveals great depths, like the face of a halfwit [*imbécile*]' (MB: 5–6/328). While Sartre acknowledges that Charles' cap 'bespeaks the stupidity of its owner to such a degree that Charles himself is turned into a cap' (FI I/IF I: 597/617), he argues that Flaubert identifies with Charles to a degree. He interprets the mysterious 'we' at the start of the novel as a manifestation of Flaubert's strategy of 'aggressive defense' as it allows him to place himself alongside the schoolboys in the class – with those doing the deriding – and to distance himself from Charles, whose experience of isolation, humiliation and trouble with language in this scene resembles his own childhood experience (FI III/IF II: 96/1202). To comprehend the significance of Charles Bovary for Flaubert, Sartre considers it essential to note his frequently expressed sympathy for idiots. Though Charles is not truly an idiot, Sartre believes he embodies the 'profundity possessed by fools which Flaubert adores because it is *his own*' (FI III/IF II: 97/1203). Indeed, from a Sartrean-analytic perspective, there are striking similarities between Flaubert's presentation of Charles' difficulty with language and the comprehension of his own that he gains 'through fabrication' in *Whatever You Want*, especially as Charles' difficulty also later prevents him from communicating his love for his wife, who mistakes his want of vocabulary for lack of emotional depth.

Further, Sartre draws attention to the fact that it is Charles, not Emma, who 'looks like a *deflowered virgin*' the morning after their wedding night (Notes: 178/168). Evidently, this description is not meant to imply that Charles (having already been married) was a virgin until this point. Rather, it indicates that this couple's first intimate encounter had a greater effect on him than it did on Emma because he adores her, and his pure adoration of Emma is read by Sartre to elevate him above the other characters in the novel. In his notes, he affirms that Flaubert presents Emma as superior to her lovers but not to Charles (Notes: 187/175), which is almost certainly because he believes that Flaubert regards the state of adoration in which the subject considers himself secondary to the one he adores, or what I have called romantic masochistic devotion above, as 'profound' (FI I/IF I: 321/332–3).

Sartre also reads Charles' fatalism to resemble Flaubert's. When Charles asserts that fate is to blame for Emma's demise in a conversation with Rodolphe towards the end of the novel, the latter, who believes he orchestrated Emma's fate, finds

Charles' resignation as foolish and somewhat despicable. But it is Rodolphe who emerges as the fool in this scene not Charles in Sartre's view (FI I/IF I: 321/333). It is only because Rodolphe is utterly incapable of comprehending the depth of Charles' love for Emma – which enables him to sacrifice his pride and converse amicably with the man who cuckolded him – that Rodolphe takes Charles for a fool. That Flaubert depicts Charles as having just uttered his first-ever 'memorable phrase' (*grand mot*) in this scene – 'Fate is to blame' – testifies to this interpretation, as it suggests that Rodolphe is the fool for believing and that Emma would not have ended up the way she did if it were not for him (MB: 311/644). Both Charles' fatalism and his capacity to forgive Rodolphe signal his possession of Flaubertian wisdom for Sartre, as he appears to acknowledge that 'the worst is always certain' not because of forces acting on humanity from the outside, but because 'universal human wickedness' guarantees it (FI V/IF 3: 416/450).

Finally, at the end of the novel, Flaubert depicts Charles as being overwhelmed by 'the nebulous wafts of love that swelled his sorrowing heart' (MB: 311/645) and then being found dead by his daughter soon afterwards. The results of the post-mortem indicate that there was nothing wrong with him physically, so readers are left to conclude that he died of a broken heart. Or, put differently, Charles dies a 'death by thought' because the thought of living on without Emma kills him. On a Sartrean reading, this death is Charles' crowning glory, which places him among the Flaubertian 'saints'. He dies without any organ being damaged, just like the hero of *November*, who could only have gained his miraculous[6] deliverance from misery if some all-seeing, all-powerful Absolute deemed him worthy of it. Though Sartre might agree that Charles Bovary is 'the man with no imagination who is doubly destroyed by the imagination' (Barnes 1981b: 360), Charles' lack of imagination does not impair his capacity to suffer, which is what Sartre believes distinguishes him in his author's eyes.

Altogether then, Charles' hidden emotional depth, his suffering, his acquisition of Flaubertian wisdom and his marvellous death render him the unlikely hero of *Madame Bovary* on a Sartrean reading. Moreover, if Flaubert's pessimism dictates that 'the value of a soul is measured by the number of torments inflicted upon it' (FI I/IF I: 545/564), then Charles' suffering may be taken as evidence that his author thinks him too good for the world.

'I am too small for myself'

Madame Bovary may be described as an inverted fairy-tale: Emma marries first; then goes to the Vaubyessard ball, where she is charmed by the luxuries, the rituals and the deceits[7] of the aristocracy; then she lives miserably ever after.[8] Emma's memories of the Vaubyessard Ball work to exacerbate her melancholy by providing her with material for imaginary escapes into a fantasy world, which only highlights the paucity of her reality when she returns to it. After her experience at the ball, Emma believes that she is without hope of happiness, or of discovering 'that marvellous passion' that she has read of in novels, because she is married to Charles, and she concludes that she has suffered a terrible injustice at the hands of the almighty (MB: 60/352). Sartre reads this to imply that Emma Bovary, like her author, subscribes to the belief that she suffers not because of bad luck, or mistakes that she has made, but because she has been damned.

'I am too small for myself' (*Je suis trop petit pour moi*). This phrase functions as maxim for both Flaubert and Emma on a Sartrean reading (Notes: 185/174).[9] It captures one of the most important and enduring themes of Flaubert's works, and it is 'exhausted' in *Madame Bovary* (FI I/IF I: 551/570). Sartre presents this phrase as a Flaubertian twist of the title of Jean Sarment's play, *Je Suis trop grand pour moi* (*I am too grand for myself*, 1924),[10] which is also the proposed excuse for its lead character's failures. However, while Sarment's version contains the possibility of hope – since the subject may be able to grow into their self, their 'I' – Sartre regards it a triumph to Flaubert's pessimism that he manages to present this idea in such a way that it precludes the possibility of growth improving the subject's situation because 'it *is already accomplished*' (FI III/IF II: 89/1297).

In the glimpses the reader is allowed of Emma Bovary's stream of consciousness, she is often expressing disgust with her reality or fantasizing about escaping it. Throughout the first fifteen chapters of the novel, she feeds her Great Desire for more than she has on daydreams. However, following Léon's departure for Paris, she changes tact. Flaubert's account of this can be read as a fictional representation of the kind of 'instant' in which a subject's fundamental project is dropped and replaced with a new one, which Sartre believed to be possible in *Being and Nothingness* (BN/EN: 621/520–1). On this reading, the demise of Emma's fundamental project in this instant is marked by Emma's funereal mood and her experience of 'that kind of brooding which comes over you when you lose something forever, that lassitude you feel after every irreversible event, that pain you suffer when a habitual movement is interrupted' (MB: 110/437). What has so far constituted Emma's 'habitual movement', we might say, was her 'original' choice to compensate for a life that she finds intolerably dull by escaping into the imaginary, which, according to Sartre, is her 'one love', although she does not know it (Notes: 184/173). Again, this view finds robust support in the novel. Charles, for instance, falls in love with Emma in all her particularity and in spite of the flaws he perceives in her – e.g. he observes that her hand is 'not beautiful' (MB: 16/338) – but Emma strives to deceive herself that *through* Charles she might be able to grasp 'that marvellous passion which until then has hovered like a great rosy-plumaged bird in the splendour of poetic skies' (MB: 37/361). Love, for Emma, appears to an abstract ideal, not a movement towards a concrete other.

Léon's departure ruptures the delicate tissue of grandiose fantasies that had provided Emma with her imaginary 'cover' for her small, disappointing self, which had enabled her to cope with her situation hitherto. Rather than repair that cover, though, she endeavours to change her self. She resolves to *become* one of the Romantic heroines she had previously only fantasized about being. At the beginning, her new project seems to hold promise of success. During her first affair with Rodolphe, she experiences 'that poetic legion of adulteresses' singing to her 'with sisterly voices' and she makes believe that she is 'actually becoming a living part of her own fantasies' (MB: 145/474). At this moment, Emma is pleased with her self. Her pleasure is, of course, short-lived. But it is not her choice to commit adultery *per se* that sets her on the path to damnation from a Sartrean perspective; it is the fact that the betrayal of her husband also represents the betrayal of her one true love: the imaginary. Emma, by (Sartre's) Flaubert's reason, is 'the loser who loses' through her failure to recognize the superiority of the imaginary over reality. Unlike her author, she does not see that the loser wins by 'living through imagination' (FI IV/IF III: 239/2013). What secures Emma's damnation, then, is her attempt to realize her fantasies, without seeing that the mould that is set for her self in reality is 'too small' to allow her to satisfy her Great Desire.

Sadism and laughter

Flaubert's repeated invention of tormented characters, together with his concentration on the details of their suffering, has led him to become renowned as a sadistic writer (FI III/IF II: 221/1329; Tilby 2004). *Madame Bovary* seems to offer a prime example of Flaubert's sadism as its eponymous heroine is continually disappointed, denied the romance she craves and ends up taking her own life in the face of financial ruin. She also suffers an agonizing and gruesome demise from arsenic poisoning, and Flaubert exploits his medial knowledge to detail her symptoms with such precision that her deathbed scene is considered a paradigm of 'medicalized realism' (Rothfield 1992: 45). Further, any hope Emma has of reclaiming some dignity in her final moments is crushed by the loud, lewd lyrics of the blind man singing outside. Thus, Emma's suffering on her deathbed far exceeds what may be considered 'poetic' punishment for her infidelities: their abject failure and her financial ruin are sufficient for these purposes.

In addition to making Emma suffer exorbitantly, Sartre contends that Flaubert mocks her throughout the novel. In *The Family Idiot*, he pays special attention to Flaubert's decision to locate the prelude to the notorious taxicab scene, in which Emma and Léon consummate their love, in Rouen Cathedral (FI III/IF II: 168–80/1275–87), and he evidently intended to pick up this discussion again in the fourth volume (Notes: 186/175). In *The Family Idiot*, Sartre maintains that Flaubert invites his reader to draw a contrast between the shady, adulterous exploits of this couple and the holiness of place where they meet to degrade their relationship. He then emphasizes how Flaubert's refusal to grant this couple's first, long-awaited, experience of intimacy the dignity of any human perspective also has the effect of dehumanizing them, as it is described from perspective that sees only a shaky cab, rattling around the streets of Rouen. Even though Flaubert attempts to banish all expression of his own opinions in his work, Sartre holds that his 'pantagruelizing' (*pantagruélisant*)[11] in this scene betrays him (FI III/IF II: 178/1285): it shows that he cannot resist the temptation to make Emma and Léon appear '*objectively laughable*', so that he may distinguish himself from them (FI III/IF II: 177/1284), so he allows his alter-ego, the Garçon, to write this scene so that he may 'laugh for him' (FI III/IF II: 180/1287).

According to the theory of laughter Sartre outlines in *The Family Idiot*, the primary function of laughter is to cast the object of laughter as a sub-human 'permanently affected with the illusion of subjectivity' and to, thereby, affirm the humanity of the laugher, who recognizes the sub-human's show of humanity as a sham (FI II/IF I: 164/821). This means that laughter's primary social function is a conservative one, as the laugher's own conformance to social norms is the tacit basis for their claim to superiority over the 'object' of their laughter. Society is therefore whole and present in the defensive aggression that laughter is in Sartre's estimation; it attacks individuals who fall short of its standards, so as to defend those who meet them. However, Sartre affirms that Flaubert's laughter typically has a more complex function because he frequently makes himself the object of it so as to reverse the terms of the relation it ordinarily implies. By laughing at his own failure to meet social norms rather than feeling ashamed, Flaubert ridicules the standards of social seriousness that others apply to render such failures laughable (FI III/IF II: 106–7/1211). Flaubert's laughter functions as an instrument of his aggressive defensiveness because it undercuts the laughter of those who would laugh at him by announcing that he '*doesn't take himself seriously*' (FI II/IF II: 183/841). Flaubert's recognition that he is a sub-human pretending to be a human *just like everybody else* therefore elevates him above those who take their pretence seriously and who would laugh at him. After having worked so carefully to uncover the complex function of Flaubert's laughter,[12] it is surprising that Sartre interprets the authorial laughter in the taxicab scene as ordinary laughter. A more developed Sartrean reading of this scene ought to interpret the laughter in it differently.

The text of *Madame Bovary* supplies us with guidance on how to produce such a reading. The first thing to note is that laughter seems to have a peculiar function in the novel. Take what is perhaps the most memorable instance of it: Emma's 'ghastly, frenzied, despairing laugh' on her deathbed (MB: 290/623). Here, Emma's laughter seems to be an entirely inappropriate response to her situation. What makes it even more disturbing is that Emma seldom laughs. The only other time she laughs in the novel is after reading Rodolphe's farewell letter, which puts an end to their romantic relationship (MB: 182/513). On both occasions, Emma's laughter strikes the reader as a bizarre response. This suggests that a promising way to approach the laughter in this novel, including authorial laughter, is to appreciate it as a signal for something that is not funny at all.

Approaching the laughter in *Madame Bovary* this way suggests that Flaubert is reversing the ordinary terms of laughter here too, so as to make anyone who would laugh at Emma, on the presumption that they are superior to her, the butt of the joke. This makes it possible for us to detect a very human empathy for Emma behind the façade of cosmic laughter in the taxicab scene. As Sartre's notes indicate that he intended to investigate the laughter in *Madame Bovary* in some depth (Notes: 184/172), it is likely that he would have seen how this interpretation does a better job of synthesizing his interpretation of the specific function of Flaubert's laughter with his theory that Emma is a 'black saint', like her prototype Mazza. Further, it also allows us to read the difference between Flaubert's portrayals of Emma and Mazza as further evidence for Sartre's view that Flaubert would have deepened his comprehension of his experience considerably in the twenty or so years between his creation of these characters. His portrayal of Mazza is straightforwardly sadistic, but his portrayal of Emma is also masochistic, and consciously so, for Flaubert famously says of Emma that 'She is myself!' (FI I/IF I: 195/203). What is more, Emma is evidently more 'distinguished' than Mazza. This is perhaps most apparent in the way that she is occasionally granted the privilege of a panoramic point of view, usually reserved for the author himself, which is what enables her to laugh when it would be more appropriate to cry. Emma can find 'cosmic' relief in moments of profound despair because, in these moments, she seems to rise above her pitiful situation to see it from a perspective that resembles her author's 'Absolute' one. This would appear to be why Emma is able to have the literal and figurative last laugh in the novel; her recognition of the funniness of blind man's unwitting sabotage of her sham of religious seriousness on her deathbed allows her to claim a Flaubertian 'moral' victory before she loses her life.

Emma's insincerity, Flaubert's truth

Emma's displays of affection always seem to be affected. This is evinced by her prolonged mourning for her mother 'with no more sadness in her heart than wrinkles on her brow' (MB: 36/361) and almost all her interactions with Charles and her child. While she often succeeds in making a good show of religious devotion – at one point she even inspires fear in the curé that her religious fervour could progress to something that 'verged on heresy' (MB: 190/521) – she never manages to go beyond the representation to what is represented. She has only religiosity without religion. Significantly, one of her last acts is to kiss the crucifix presented to her by the curé: she thrusts 'her neck forward like someone parched with *thirst*, and, fastening her *lips* to the *body* of the Man-God, she bestowed upon it with every ounce of her dying strength the most passionate *kiss* of love that she had ever given' (MB: 288–9/621–2, emphasis added). The language in this passage fuses the spiritual with the sensual, which has the effect of cheapening Emma's display. The reader is not convinced that she has finally found faith. As Bart notes, Emma does not undergo a conversion on her deathbed, but she does drag 'the symbol of the cross down to her level' by using it as a prop (1966: 101). But this is not to say that she is entirely insincere in this scene. On a Sartrean reading, she is as sincere as a black saint can be: she sincerely *desires to feel* what people who are sincere in their faith *do* feel (FI I/IF I: 427/440).

Although, again, it may seem as though Flaubert has allowed the Garçon to narrate Emma's deathbed scene, it is also possible to detect empathetic undertones in Flaubert's description of her desperate and ill-informed attempts to establish a relationship with God in this scene and throughout the novel. It is significant that Emma's lack of faith does not appear to be entirely her fault. In one of her earlier moments of despair, she sought out the advice of a holy man, the Abbé Bournisien. It seems that he could have saved her if he were not such a stupid gourmand. When Emma seeks him out in her time of need, he rather remarkably fails to realize that it is spiritual, not medical, guidance she wants from him. Even after she tells him that she is not seeking 'earthly remedies'

(MB: 100/427), he attributes her emotional turmoil to indigestion. If finding faith could have led Emma towards salvation, then the foolishness she finds in this man could only have pushed her in the other direction. Though Emma's desire for faith is sincere, she is not given proper guidance in matters of faith and has only Romantic depictions of religious characters to work with. Hence, the only way to faith she can see is by imitating the beautiful displays of religiosity she has read of. As Sartre indicates some parallels between Flaubert's and Emma's failed searches for faith in *The Family Idiot*, it is likely that the fourth volume would have explored this point.[13]

Similarly, a sincere desire for love motivates Emma's decision to embark on an affair with Rodolphe, and subsequently Léon. She pursues this desire in the same way that she pursues her desire for faith: by making a good show of it. She works to convince her lovers, and herself, that she is in love, seemingly in the hope she will be rewarded with the feeling that is supposed to correspond to the expression if she does a good enough job of the expression. But all Emma's attempts feel through the expression of feeling fail. This is nowhere more apparent than in her relationship with Rodolphe. Her attempts to articulate the intensity of the love she longs to feel for him misfire because phrases such as 'You are my King! My Idol!' ring in the ears of this practised seducer as vain attempts to add flourish to flimsy affections (MB: 169/500). Though Emma sincerely strives to realize the intense passion she professes and would, as Sartre points out, undoubtedly do anything for Rodolphe (Notes: 187/175), all her attempts to communicate his importance to her fail. Again, the fault seems not to lie entirely with Emma. This time, language is partly to blame, as it supplies no adequate means of distinguishing between emotions that are called by same name. As Emma has not discovered style, she can only express herself through ordinary language, which Flaubert likens to 'a cracked kettle on which we beat our tunes for bears to dance to, when what we long to do is make music that will move the stars to pity' (MB: 170/500).

Sartre is convinced that insincerity 'from emotional alienation' is a trait that Emma shares with her author.[14] In *The Family Idiot*, he shows that Flaubert's passive constitution alienates him from his own desires in a way that makes him insincere when he is being himself, not because he seeks to conceal his genuine desires but because he genuinely does not know what they are. He contends that Flaubert finds his truth in Emma, though, because through his depiction of this specific form of insincerity through her experience, he supplies a sincere expression of his experience. We have just seen that Emma is not entirely responsible for her failure to connect with religion from a Sartrean perspective and, as Sartre's notes indicate that he also intended to explore the failure of language as a theme in *Madame Bovary* (Notes: 178–9/167–8), this gives us good reason to believe that his critique would have uncovered the evidence exculpating her for her inability to make sincere love connections too, especially given that he has already emphasized Flaubert's view of language as a hopelessly inadequate tool for conveying human emotion (FI I/IF I: 27/37).

On a Sartrean reading, then, the themes of the imagination and insincerity in *Madame Bovary*, combined with Flaubert's identification with its heroine, suggest that Emma Bovary can be read to represent something like what Flaubert imagines he would be like had he not discovered art. This means that *Madame Bovary* is less a work of sadistic fiction than its author's attempt to produce a 'stylized' counterfactual autobiography. What is more, its key message appears to be that, at least for superior souls (like his), the world is hell and the only way to 'win' in it is to recognize the superiority of the imaginary to the real. This message is clearly in line with Sartre's conception of Flaubert's original choice, as well as his interpretation of the function of style for Flaubert.

Sartre's blind spots and their implications

Now we have gained a sense of what a Sartrean reading of *Madame Bovary* might have been like, we may address the question of whether the proposed fourth volume of *The Family Idiot* could have validated the findings of the first three. To begin with, we can see that Flaubert's original choice of the imaginary finds its 'objectification' in what a Sartrean reading shows to be the key message of *Madame Bovary*: the (real) world is hell. Moreover, the way in which this message is communicated, through 'style', provides support for Sartre's specific understanding of how Flaubert pursued his original choice through his behaviour and his writing. However, there are two important features of Flaubert's objectification of his self in *Madame Bovary* that do not map onto Sartre's objectification of it in *The Family Idiot*. The next sections identify these features, before turning to assess their implications for the success of Sartre's study of Flaubert as a whole.

The positive counterpart to Flaubert's misanthropy

In 'Sartre's (Mis)Reading of Flaubert's Politics: An Unacknowledged Dialectic of Misanthropy and Utopian Desire', David Gross argues that Sartre acknowledges '*only* the misanthropy and pessimism, the *l'art pour l'art* escapism and the apolitical' in Flaubert's fictional work and misses the crucial subtext of Flaubert's ostensible pessimism and political apathy (1985: 132). This criticism is valid. Sartre presents Flaubert's love of beauty as the 'other side' of his misanthropy (FI V/IF 3: 353/380). However, his commitment to beauty cannot represent the positive dialectical counterpart to his misanthropy on Sartre's account because it holds that Flaubert identifies beauty with radical evil, that he attributes all evil to a self-interested (bourgeois) human nature, and that this is what explains his (masochistic-)sadistic treatment of characters that he deems not to be evil. Here we have not a dialectic but a circle in which Flaubert's conception of beauty feeds into the misanthropy he expresses in his literature, rather than opposing it.

Furthermore, Flaubert did not miss his 'rendez-vous' with Revolution in 1848 as Sartre claims (FI V/IF 3: 413/447). Gross calls attention to the fact that Flaubert was engaged in political activities in 1847 and even went to Paris specifically to witness the Revolution in 1848 (1985: 139). Although these activities may well have left Flaubert feeling disillusioned and provided him with the inspiration for his social critique in *A Sentimental Education* (1869),[15] they point to his hope for political progress, which represents an obvious dialectical counterpart to his publicized misanthropy, especially because Flaubert appears to have taken pains to conceal it. Instead of fully unpacking the significance of Flaubert's misanthropy in relation to its counterpart in his 'utopian' desires though, Sartre neglects some of its complexities and contradictions. Clearly, this runs counter to the aims of his progressive-regressive method, so it is curious. Why is his dialectical exposition of Flaubert's misanthropy in *The Family Idiot* wanting in this way? Gross' suggestion is that it is possibly because Sartre's own fiction, *Nausea* in particular, 'is so much a part of the negative, critical modernist movement he describes, his criticism is one-sided, his view incomplete' (Gross 1985: 128). Sartre's later desire to distance himself from his early uncommitted literature may certainly have contributed to his inability to see the traces of political commitment that belie Flaubert's expressions of misanthropy. However, this can only be part of the explanation, as Sartre also seems to have been convinced that Flaubert represented the epitome of the uncommitted[16] writer, long before undertook his study on Flaubert, and this may have rendered him susceptible to 'confirmation bias'[17] with respect to Flaubert's political stance.

Over twenty years before the publication of *The Family Idiot*, in a note to *What Is Literature?* Sartre states that he has so often been charged with 'being unfair to Flaubert'[18] that he 'cannot resist the pleasure' of supplying extracts from Flaubert's correspondence to buttress his interpretation of Flaubert as the uncommitted writer *par excellence* (WL/QL: 124n./165-6n.). These include: 'I'm worth twenty Croisset voters' (1871); 'I have no hatred for the communards for the reason that I don't hate mad dogs' (Croisset, Thursday, 1871); and 'I believe that the crowd, the herd, will always be hateful. The only ones of importance are a small group of spirits' (Croisset, 8 September 1871) (WL/QL: 124n./165-6n.). To be sure, these remarks are counter-progressive, bigoted even. But it is vital to remember that a key finding of Sartre's application of progressive-regressive method to Flaubert is that Flaubert is incapable of being sincere while he is being himself, which means that anything that he writes in his correspondence must be cross-checked against his fictional work to establish 'whether it contains a biographical truth' (SM/QM: 143/199, see also FI I/IF I: 150/157). However, in the third volume of *The Family Idiot*, Sartre again relies chiefly on remarks from Flaubert's correspondence to support his hypothesis that Flaubert writes novels not to promote progressive ideas or incite change but to demoralize his readership (FI V/IF 3: 413-34, 468/443-65, 500). Arguably then, Sartre's analysis of Flaubert's misanthropy in *The Family Idiot* fails to match it with its true dialectical counterpart because Sartre's view on this matter was fixed long before he applied his analytical method to Flaubert, and this effectively blinded him to important evidence contradicting it in both Flaubert's life and works.

A possible challenge to this idea may be found in Rhiannon Goldthorpe's examination of how Sartre's interpretation of Flaubert's late work, *The Legend of Saint Julian Hospitator* (*La Légende de Saint Julien l'hospitalier*, 1877), can support the 'potentially surprising claim' that Flaubert may be considered a committed writer (1992: 140). Goldthorpe argues that Sartre's analysis of *The Legend of Saint Julian Hospitator* in *The Family Idiot* reveals how, for Sartre, Flaubert's writing can be 'at once a revelation of his own and his reader's situation', which 'not only demoralizes but may also energize readers', who may experience solidarity with him and work to constitute the world that he invites them to imagine (1992: 174). Although this shows that Sartre can see *some* evidence of engagement in Flaubert's work, it is only of the most accidental kind, as he denies that Flaubert is thetically conscious of having any political agenda when he writes fiction. Moreover, as this late work comes after Flaubert's 'conversion' between 1870 and 1871, through which, Sartre argues, he becomes a 'realist' (FI V/IF 3: 468/500), Sartre can even accept that Flaubert had a political agenda in mind when he wrote *The Legend of Saint Julian Hospitator* but still remain blind to evidence of conscious political engagement in all of Flaubert's works written prior to 1870, including *Madame Bovary* (1856). So, the question for us is whether a reading of

Madame Bovary can substantiate the claim that *if* Flaubert's literary work written prior to 1870 is committed, it is not committed on purpose.

Sartre recognizes that if Emma 'were merely a *déclassée* provincial woman who had made a poor match, *Madame Bovary* would not have been worth an hour's effort in the eyes of its author', but he argues that Emma holds great significance for Flaubert because she is a 'beautiful' artistic creation (FI III/IF III: 473/1589). And yet, Flaubert's commitment to beauty alone cannot explain why he would go to great lengths to show that the suffering and lovelessness of the human beings at the heart of the novel, Emma and Charles, have their source in their decidedly bourgeois society. Emma's immersion in Romantic culture, in particular, gives her unrealistic expectations about love and about where human happiness is to be found, which prevents her from finding anything loveable in Charles, who truly loves her. Her internalization of the materialist values of her society also leads her to attempt to assuage her misery with the purchase of luxury items – a project that plunges her into debt. What is more, neither the published volumes of *The Family Idiot* nor Sartre's notes for the fourth pay much attention to the character of Monsieur Homais, who is widely recognized among Flaubert scholars as a caricature of the bourgeois male (Starkie 1967: 375–77; Tanner 1979: 273–84). Homais is a pharmacist who practises medicine without a licence; pretends to befriend the Bovarys as he continually poaches Charles' patients; and pushes Charles to undertake risky, experimental surgery on a clubfoot, the terrible failure of which ruins Charles' credibility as a medical professional. So obvious is the critique of bourgeois ideology worked into Flaubert's portrayal of Homais that Tony Tanner even reads Homais as less of a person than 'a toxic mental atmosphere that is pervading more and more of the world around it' (1979: 275). As Flaubert was a meticulous writer, who constantly drafted and re-drafted his works, and the drafts for *Madame Bovary* alone total over four-thousand pages (Bart 1967: 65), it is impossible that he could have been only 'non-thetically aware' of the social critique implicit in his portrayals of Emma's and Charles' suffering and the despicability of Homais. A reading of *Madame Bovary* therefore shows that it is mistaken to interpret Flaubert simply as a Postromantic who believes he writes '*for nothing* and *no one*' (FI V/IF 3: 136/150).

Reading 'like a man'

Sartre's dialectical analysis of Flaubert's misogyny in *The Family Idiot* is also one-sided. Although a great deal evidence from both Flaubert's life and literature is supplied for the view that Flaubert's masochism is related to his misogyny in *The Family Idiot*, masochism cannot be the dialectical counterpart to his misogyny as proposed because Flaubert is presented as being 'a woman' in his experience (FI I/IF I: 432/445), which means that masochism would feed into his misogyny. Thus, again, Sartre offers us a circle in place of a dialectical opposition: Flaubert hates women because he is one and he hates himself because he hates women.

Further, the notion that masochism is what dialectically opposes misogyny in Flaubert's experience provides no means of accounting for the nuanced understanding of the systemic nature of women's oppression demonstrated in *Madame Bovary*. Sartre rightly observes that Emma suffers because she desires far more than she can realistically hope for. But, while Flaubert's rendering of Emma's situation does seem to make her suffering inescapable, we have seen that it does not imply that her suffering is all her fault. Even Homais notices how Emma's unusual talents are doomed to be wasted due to the lack of opportunities that her situation as the wife of a provincial health officer afford her (MB: 96/423). Emma's *situation* is what makes her self too small for her, and her reasons for wanting a son indicate some awareness of this:

> [B]earing a male child was like an anticipated revenge for all the powerlessness of her past life. A man, at least, is free, free to explore all passions and all countries, to surmount obstacles, to indulge in the most exotic pleasures. But a woman is constantly thwarted. At once passive and compliant, she has to contend with both the weakness of her body and the subjection imposed by law. Her will, like the veil attached to her hat, flutters with every breeze; always there is desire inviting her on, and, always, convention holding her back.
>
> (MB: 79-80/405-6)

Observe how Flaubert's use of free indirect discourse here masks the intrusions of his narrator in a way that give the reader cause to question whether the thoughts expressed here are all Emma's. This invites the reader to consider the extent to which the sources of her oppression are mystified in her experience.

Sartre, however, reads Flaubert's treatment of Emma Bovary to betray his misogyny in a straightforward way. He characterizes Flaubert's misogyny as the view that women are costumed beasts playing a role, who trick men into believing that they have spiritual depth when they do not because they are deceitful whores 'by nature' (FI V/IF 3: 576-7/613). Sartre's Flaubert therefore takes sadistic pleasure in mocking Emma's womanly beastliness by showing that all the splendour of Rouen's Notre-Dame Cathedral could not move her towards virtue; yet, Léon's remark that 'Everyone does it in Paris!' is enough to steer her into vice (MB: 216/547). Even though adultery is a grave sin in the eyes of Emma's Catholic God, Léon's reassurance that having (extra-marital) sex with him in a taxicab cannot possibly be degrading because sophisticated Parisians do it all the time is effective because it allows her to superficially reconcile this act with her Romantic-aesthetic ideals. Or, as Sartre crudely puts it, it allows her to 'take her ass for her heart' (FI III/IF II: 169/1276). Further, although both Emma and Léon are dehumanized and rendered objectively laughable in the scene that follows, through their absorption into an absurd object of the taxicab, Sartre suggests that it is only Emma who is mocked at an existential level because becoming the butt of this vulgar joke signals the failure of her fundamental project to become the heroine of her own great Romance – a feminine project *par excellence*.

Sartre's view that Flaubert experiences his reality as if he were an oppressed woman (FI I/IF I: 431–2/445–6) implies that Flaubert's ability to successfully portray female characters is due to a *felt* identification with them, rather than due any intellectual achievement gained through reflections on women's situation. But Flaubert's diatribe against marriage in *November* counts against this view. At just fifteen years old, Flaubert observes:

> [T]he man who, basing his actions on the Civil Code, forcibly enters the bed of a virgin who has been given to him that same morning, thereby carrying out a legal rape, that is protected by authority … [has] no counterpart among apes, hippopotami, toads; they at least, male and female, copulate when common desires lead them to seek out each other and unite, in such a way that there is neither terror and disgust on the one side, nor brutality and obscene despotism on the other.
>
> (Nov/OJ: 91–2/824)

This shows that Flaubert recognizes marriage as a patriarchal institution that harms women.

What is more, Flaubert's imagining of married life from a woman's perspective in *Madame Bovary* displays a keen awareness of how sexist structures in nineteenth-century France tended to preclude women from leading fulfilling lives. The fact that Emma is married *to Charles* is merely a contingency, although she mistakenly identifies it as the source of her misery. Her presumption that other women are blissfully happy by virtue of having husbands who are not like Charles (MB: 41/365–6) emphasizes, for the reader, the mystification of women's oppression and the romanticization of marriage in her society. Part of Emma's tragedy is that she fails to see that she already has the most that she could realistically hope for, which is to be a second-class citizen as a someone's wife, as the only realistic alternative for her is to become a sub-citizen, through falling into poverty or prostitution.[19] Such an astute depiction of a woman's socially engineered misery, which exposes precisely the kind of mystifications that Simone de Beauvoir shows 'keep women in their chains' (SS/DS II: 772/638), cannot be adequately explained by a crude 'felt' identification with women. Feminism, understood as a critique of patriarchal society, does a far better job of synthesizing the contradictions apparent in Flaubert's treatment of Emma. It also allows us to give Flaubert credit for the social critique implicit in a novel that mocks principles of patriarchal society and grants a mystified woman who suffers for pursuing what seems to be the highest good available to her in the context of that society – Romance – the last laugh.

Why does Sartre not detect Flaubert's feminism when other commentators have?[20] Sartre may have had preconceptions about Flaubert's attitude towards women before he commenced work on *The Family Idiot*, but there is also reason to believe that he may have had an emotional investment in emphasizing Flaubert's femininity, which may have blinded him to the positive, feminist 'other side' of his misogyny. This reason is that Sartre may have been biased against acknowledging the similarities between Flaubert and himself. In a late interview, Sartre says: '[Flaubert] began to fascinate me precisely because I saw him in every way as the contrary of myself' (IOT: 52). Moreover, Sartre is a self-avowed 'macho' (1986: 298), whom psychoanalytical commentators have found to embody a somewhat anxious masculinity (Doubrovsky 1995; Boulé 2005). Hence, Sartre may have had some emotional investment in reading Flaubert as the 'feminine opposite' of himself. A remarkable scene from Sartre's childhood recounted in his autobiography lends support to this view, as it highlights an important similarity between Sartre and Flaubert (although without explicitly alluding to this similarity). Here, Sartre writes that he believed his mother had wished he was a girl because she strove to give him 'the sex of angels, indeterminate but feminine around the edges' by preening his long blond curls (W/M: 65/86). One day, though, Sartre's macho grandfather decided that he could tolerate the ambiguous gender of his grandson no longer and took it upon himself to take little Jean-Paul to get a haircut more befitting a boy. Upon seeing 'the new *him*' when he arrived home, Sartre's mother shut herself in her room and wept because, Sartre believes, her precious little girl had been changed into a boy. This is also the moment that reveals Sartre's 'ugliness' to him, as his pretty curls had hidden his exotropic right eye. After this haircut, Sartre recalls going through something akin to 'the agonies of an ageing actress' (W/M: 66/88). He discovered that his new, 'ugly' and unquestionably male appearance meant that he could no longer please others by his presence alone: he now had to make an effort. From this, it is reasonable to conclude that Sartre's entry into masculinity was fraught. His first male haircut could even have been the 'original crisis' that put him on his path to becoming a writer, for it taught him that he must act if he is to justify his existence and, later, this imperative became more specific: he must 'write in order to be forgiven for being alive' (W/M: 121/157).

Taking all this together suggests that Sartre's constellates writing within a network of interrelated, gendered binaries that serve a heuristic function for him: feminine/masculine, passive/active, apathy/activism, imagination/reality, reading/writing. If his self-esteem is hinged upon always being on the 'right side' of these binaries and if he views Flaubert as the opposite of himself, then Flaubert must always fall on the left. Further evidence in support of this idea can be found in the contrast between Sartre's conception of his writing and Flaubert's. Sartre states that he conceives of his reader as a person 'on whose duration I act' (1986: 211). However, he describes Flaubert's writing as a passive activity, more like 'a dream of the pen' than an act (FI IV/IF III: 223/1997). The gendered aspect of Sartre's interpretation of Flaubert's writing becomes most apparent when he portrays Emma Bovary and Flaubert switching places *and* (hetero)sexual roles in Flaubert's imagination as he writes *Madame Bovary* in the following remark: 'la Bovary, *this* penetrates him from the outside and is discovered to be himself in passivity; or, if you like, he is himself that great creature lying between the lines, a creature that only the act of another will awaken' (FI I/IF I: 166/174).

Implications

The first three volumes of *The Family Idiot* certainly reveal many aspects of Flaubert's character that find support in a Sartrean reading of *Madame Bovary*, such as his passivity, his aesthetic, his identification with his characters, his masochism, his misanthropy, his misogyny, his aggressive defensiveness and, crucially, his original choice of the imaginary. However, Sartre's view of Flaubert as the apolitical, feminine opposite of himself, which he held long before he applied his existential psychoanalysis to Flaubert, appears to have burdened him with confirmation biases that effectively blinded him to the evidence for Flaubert's political commitment and feminism. Although Sartre's critique of *Madame Bovary* could have brought this to his attention and he could have adapted the dialectic of *The Family Idiot* in the fourth volume, the sketch of a Sartrean reading of *Madame Bovary* provided here shows that *The Family Idiot*, as it stands, fails to provide the reader with a satisfactory basis for re-totalizing Flaubert-the-author-of *Madame-Bovary*'s self.

But this by no means implies that Sartre's existential psychoanalysis is not a viable route to knowledge of selves. Having put Sartre's most rigorous application of his analytical method to the test that he himself recommends, this chapter has shown only that it is incomplete, which we already knew. The fact that Sartre was unable to complete his study on Flaubert makes it difficult to assess the success of this project in a definitive way. It has been remarked that the unusual value of *The Family Idiot* in its unfinished state is that it demonstrates the overwhelming difficulty of the task it takes on since, despite nearing three thousand pages, this book 'seems too short', precisely because Sartre goes into such detail and tries to make all of his theoretical assumptions explicit (Grimaud 1982: 209); his attempt to re-totalize Flaubert through the production of a monumental text illuminates how much of Flaubert's self is excluded from it. In a response to the remark that the notion of lived experience is quite vague and not fully theorized in 1975, Sartre replies: 'I think that it would have come, little by little, in the volume on *Madame Bovary*. But it is difficult to go very far into this area, because it means really "breaking into" the other. I can talk about my lived experience [*mon vécu*], but only at risk can I reconstitute yours' (IWS: 22). This suggests that Sartre may have come to acknowledge the overwhelming difficulty involved in gaining knowledge of a self. Indeed, it may be impossible for any human – even Sartre – to succeed in gaining complete knowledge of a self. Hence, *The Family Idiot,* the work whose incompletion weighed upon Sartre like a kind of 'remorse' (1978b: 20), may be necessarily incomplete.

The necessary incompleteness of *The Family Idiot* does not render Sartre's attempt to show that everything about a self can be communicated a failure, though. Certainly, *The Family Idiot* succeeds in communicating many aspects of Flaubert's lived experience that have historically been thought to be incomprehensible and incommunicable. Therefore, the greatest accomplishment of this work may be that it succeeds in showing that all aspects of a self are potentially communicable, even if it is impossible to communicate them all. Sartre once said that even if his study on Flaubert was a failure, he hoped that it would 'give others the idea of re-doing it, better' (IOT: 51). In thinking about what can be learned from his example by those who have this idea, it is worth recalling Thomas R. Flynn's remark that 'if the moral of Sartre's stories is that there is always a moral to the story, their epistemological lesson is the ancient one that methods determine the content; in other words, that one notices only what one looks for' (1997: 263). This ancient lesson appears reconfirmed by Sartre's final 'story' about Flaubert. Even though Sartre may have been able to address the oversights in the first three volumes of *The Family Idiot* identified above had he been able to write the fourth, the fact that these oversights appear to result from his personal biases is instructive. It shows how the biases of the analyst can blind them to evidence concerning their subject's character, even when they are adhering strictly to Sartre's (revised) method of existential psychoanalysis. Of course, the problem of analyst-bias is a general one, and Sartre's existential psychoanalysis does appear to avoid the problem about confirmation bias towards psychoanalytical explanations that traditional psychoanalysis faces (Lacewing 2018: 100), as it does not have any ready-made explanations. Nevertheless, Sartre's application of his psychoanalytic method in *The Family Idiot* teaches those thinking about 're-doing it, better' of the importance of putting additional checks and measures in place to ensure that their biases do not blind them to the evidence before them.

6

Imagining the selves of others

The previous chapters have illuminated the central role of the imagination in Sartre's existential psychoanalysis. This chapter aims to clarify that role. Crucially, it will demonstrate how Sartre's view that gaining knowledge of another self requires us to 're-totalize' it in our imagination does not conflict with the theory of the imagination that he defends in *The Imaginary*, where we find the claim that 'one can never learn from an image what one does not know already' (I: 10/27). Further, it aims to make sense of Sartre's view that *The Family Idiot* is *The Imaginary* 'at seventy years of age' instead of 'thirty' (IWS: 15) by showing how *The Family Idiot* develops key ideas from the earlier work about the implications of different uses of language and the imagination for self-formation and analysing how Flaubert's 'retreat' into the imaginary shaped the person he became.

Bodies and books: Analoga for the self

Psychoanalytical commentators have criticized *The Family Idiot* for the excessively rationalistic philosophy of consciousness that they believe underpins it (Mouchard 1971; Pontalis 1985). Indeed, the very idea that one can psychoanalyse a dead person seems to overlook the fact that a person is an *embodied* consciousness. In the context of current psychotherapy and psychoanalysis, the direct experience of empathizing with another who is present tends to be a theorized as an experiential way of knowing: an 'unmediated and visceral knowing of the other' (Ginot 2009: 301; see also Greenberg 2008: 51). Although we have already seen that Sartre would deny that we can learn anything about another merely through being in their presence since he denies that any knowledge whatsoever can be gained 'through being', this is not the point of the concern being raised here. The point is that knowledge that is – somehow – based on observations of someone's actions and gestures would appear to be essential to a re-totalization of their self for the very reason that their self is their objective being, their being *as seen from the outside*. As Sartre upholds that others have an advantage over the subject with regard to knowledge of their self precisely because they see the subject from the outside, it seems surprising that he would uphold that it is possible to gain totalizing knowledge of a self through analysing the records they made of their thoughts and the historical evidence about them but without any first-hand observations of how they 'live' their body, especially as Sartre was influenced by Gestalt psychologists (Mirvish 2020), who emphasize the importance of attending to what subjects say through their body and how this may belie what they actually say in order to gain a holistic understanding of them.

For Sartre to be able to respond to the objection that his existential psychoanalysis unduly neglects to attend to the embodied dimension of its subject's being, he must be able to show that first-hand observations of the subject in the flesh are not essential for gaining totalizing knowledge of their self. To begin to see how he can do this, let us recall that in *Being and Nothingness* he affirms that we can gain self-knowledge despite being unable to observe our body from the outside because our selves are objects of others' knowledge and so they are capable of being the object of ours (BN/EN: 455/331). He then offers a tantalizing hint about how exactly we can learn about our selves towards the end of his analysis of the Look, when he states that through language we can gradually learn what others think of us and thereby gain knowledge of the object that is at once 'a source of fascination and of horror' (BN/EN: 362/304): the object that we are for them.

If the self is nothing other than the ideal unification of knowledge of the subject's objective being that is projected 'into' their body as Sartre contends, then it would be possible to gain knowledge of a subject's self without observing their body because the body and the self are separate objects that exist in mutually exclusive modes of experience. I submit that the conception of the body-self relation that *The Family Idiot* presupposes may be accurately captured in terms of Sartre's early theory of the imagination thus: the body is an analogon for the self. In *The Imaginary*, Sartre uses the term 'analogon' to refer to the 'matter' that acts as the 'equivalent of perception' for an image (I: 18/42). Now, physical objects, such as photographs, portraits, as well as the bodies of actors and impersonators, can function as analoga. Sartre explains how different kinds of analoga can serve as the matter for the same image by arguing that the form of the imaginary act through which I aim to make the face of the same absent friend present is the same, regardless of whether its matter is a photograph, a caricature or 'something' that emerges 'out of the void' to fulfil my imaging intention (I: 18/43). Although the photograph and the caricature are physical things, with properties that may be observed, whereas the matter for purely mental image is consciousness itself,[1] the experience of the image formed in each case will have the same form so long as the object aimed at by the imagining intention is the same.

Now, the view that physical analoga can serve as the matter for imaginary objects does not contradict Sartre's claim that perceptual and imaginary objects do not mix in our experience because the analogon is not the intentional object of the imaginary act, as the matter for the image is precisely what is negated and surpassed by the imaginary act that brings forth an absent object. I can therefore form an image of Princess Diana through the aid of a painting of her, but I cannot observe the features of the painting and have an image of Princess Diana at the same time; the disappearance of the painting before my eyes is the condition for the appearance of her image. Moreover, Sartre's theorization of the analogon, combined with his view of the self as an imaginary object and his understanding of the body as 'the ultimate magical object' (BN/EN: 468/391), implies that a similar process occurs when we are in the presence of others, with the difference that the bodies of others seem to present us with their selves 'in the flesh'. My meeting with Victoria yesterday, for example, may supply me with the matter for my image of her today (e.g. a photograph), through which I aim to experience her presence as I did yesterday. But I did not perceive Victoria's self during our meeting yesterday; I perceived her body, which seemed to be animated by her self from the 'inside'. Further, I can no more be conscious of Victoria's self when observing the features of her body than I can be conscious of my image Princess Diana when observing the way that her face, eyes, hair, etc. are depicted in the painting that is the matter for my image of her. Therefore, if we accept a Sartrean understanding of the self, then the role of the body in social experience must be that of a physical analogon for the self. Although Sartre acknowledges that letters, photographs, memories, etc. are all poor substitutes for the physical presence of loved ones, he believes that this is because we use these analoga to try to 'replace the weakening affective analogon' that can only be rejuvenated by the presence of the loved one in person (I: 145/279). This suggests that the bodies of others are the most effective analoga for selves because of how we feel when we are in their presence. But how can we explain this feeling if the self is not really present in the body? I propose that, on a Sartrean account, it can be explained as a result of the body being the primary analogon for the self in combination with the illusion that the self animates the body we see before us 'from within'.

This illusory appearance of the self 'inside' the body can then be attributed to the body's other function as the subject's instrument of self-formation – as the object *through which* the subject makes their self – which obscures its analogical function for us and causes us to project the self 'into' it.

Although Sartre does not explicitly defend this view of the body as the primary analogon for the self in *The Imaginary*, his exposition of how the body of one subject can serve as the analogon for the self of another takes us part way to this conclusion. Sartre describes how the whole body of the female performance artist Claire Franconay becomes an analogon for the absent Maurice Chevalier – despite the obvious disanalogies between her physical appearance and his – for the observer who ceases to perceive her body and, instead, 'reads' her gestures as part of a 'signifying synthesis' (I: 26/59). To read Franconay's body this way, though, Sartre contends that the observer must already possess knowledge of how the real Chevalier comports himself, as this is what facilitates the synthesis of the protrusion of her lower lip, the tilt of her head, the angle of her hat, etc. in an image of Chevalier. Understanding this sort of prior knowledge as a prerequisite for the ability to read Franconay's performance this way enables Sartre to build his case for the view that our prior knowledge shapes our perception of objects by predisposing us to project certain affective qualities onto them, which we then perceive 'in' them. Prior knowledge of Chevalier causes the subject to perceive his body as having a specific affective 'sense' – a sense of 'Chevalierness' if you will. And so, what happens when an observer experiences Franconay's performance as an imitation of him is that their prior knowledge awakens the affective reaction that constitutes the sense of Chevalier for them, which then enables them to see her body *as if* it were 'possessed' by Chevalier (I: 29/64).

This discussion points to analogical function of the body in social experience more broadly, which I believe his later study of Flaubert assumes in order to hold that the 'affective sense' of Flaubert, which allows us to synthesize the biographical facts about him in an imaginary re-totalization of his self, can be gained by means other than direct observations of his behaviour. This is chiefly because Sartre gives us no reason to deny that the body functions in same way in ordinary interpersonal interactions as it does in Franconay's impersonation, except that we read others' behaviour to express who they really are 'inside', their real self, in ordinary interpersonal interactions. Of course, Sartre emphasizes the phenomenological difference between seeing Pierre 'in the flesh' and forming an image of him from other physical or psychical matter. However, a difference in the phenomenological character of experiences is not always indicative of a difference in their form on Sartre's account. When I form an image of Pierre based on a portrait, I incorporate all that I perceive 'into a projective synthesis that aims at the *true* Pierre, a living being who is not there' (I: 22/51, emphasis added). But it seems that a projective synthesis must also be involved in my experience of Pierre, the living being who is there too. Even though I can perceive and interact directly with the body that symbolizes and creates Pierre, what constitutes the 'true' Pierre for me – i.e. his self – is not really 'there', inside his body, in this case either. This means that our ordinary experience of others' presence 'in person' results from a form of 'reading' that resembles the reading of Franconay's body discussed above: the prior knowledge we have of others – even if it is only the minimum knowledge gained via our first impression of them – enables us to read their acts and gestures as expressions of their 'inner' selves.

An appreciation of the body's function as an analogon for the self allows us to understand how other bodies and other objects can serve as analoga for the same self. If our experience of other people in person is deceptive, insofar the imaginary constitution of them has phenomenal character that resembles perception, and if the self is nothing more than an ideal totalization of knowledge that is projected 'into' the body, then a subject's body is not the only possible matter for their self. Indeed, the potential of other objects to serve as analoga for the self is a condition for the possibility of self-knowledge on Sartre's account since no subject can view their own body as the object it is for others. For us to be able to form an accurate image of our selves based on what others tell us about how we appear to them, then, it must be possible for words to function as linguistic analoga for selves. Sartre writes of the power of a single word to prompt an imaginary act: the word 'moon', he proposes, can represent the 'central core' of the analogon for the image of the moon if it is invoked as part of an intention to synthesize the subject's knowledge of the moon in an image of it (I: 85/169). If a single word can feed into imaginary objects in this way, then it follows that a series of words, all describing the same object can collectively function as the analogon for an imaginary object such as a self. That is to say, we may be able to read the self of another 'in' a book just as we read it 'in' their body. This is precisely the view that, I believe, underpins Sartre's later belief that a successful biography can stand in place of the body and, hence, communicate knowledge of its subject's self in the absence of their body.

Still, a major obstacle for the claim that a book can stand in place of the body as an adequate analogon for its subject's self is the fact that other people's gestures, expressions and intonations play a significant role in conveying that specific 'sense' of them as individuals, which is what allows us to comprehend their actions and synthesize them in a coherent totalization.[2]

Sartre acknowledges as much towards the end of his early study of Baudelaire, when he states that just a 'glimpse' of the living Baudelaire 'could make us feel that the characteristics mentioned here, one after the other, are in fact built into an indissoluble synthesis in which each of them expresses itself and all the others at the same time' (B: 185/172). This remark testifies to Sartre's acute awareness of how it is much more difficult to comprehend someone who is not present in person than it is to comprehend someone who is. The rest of this chapter will be geared towards defending the Sartrean view that it is at least theoretically possible to gain the kind of experientially based comprehension of another person required to synthesize the biographical facts about them in a re-totalization of their self without ever having seen them 'in' the flesh.

Structure, language and Sartre's 'return to Freud'

To assess Sartre's claim that a body of words can stand in place of another person's physical body as the basis of our knowledge of them, it is vital to gain an appreciation of the special significance he ascribes to language as both an objective structure in the world and a tool we use both to make sense of it and to make our selves in it. As he regards human beings as radically social beings who use language to acquire knowledge and whose perception of the world is shaped by their prior knowledge, he treats language not as a medium through which we relate to others and objects indirectly, but as a mode of direct access to certain objects: objects of knowledge. He even describes language in biological terms as a 'third eye' that enables us to see 'into our neighbour's heart' because we 'perceive' the language of others 'as we perceive the limbs of others' (WL/QL: 12/26). Language takes on even greater significance in the context of his mature existentialism, where it is theorized not just as a tool but as part of the fabric of the world, alongside other 'already signifying material' such as 'iron' and 'marble', 'which others animate with their movement from beneath, like stage-hands creating waves by crawling around under a piece of canvas' (CDR I/CRD I: 182/293). Alongside marble and iron, then, language forms part of the raw material out of which we, collectively, make the world through acts that awaken meanings latent in it. And although language is a general structure that precedes the individual, its inexhaustible potential for variation at the individual level allows Sartre to uphold that it is one of the most important instruments of self-formation. Language is therefore the focal point of his psychoanalysis and so it is unsurprising that his rapprochement with Freud in his later work is made via Jacques Lacan's 'return to Freud'.[3]

Lacan's psychoanalysis develops Freud's by interpreting the unconscious as embedded in language and having its most important manifestations in language. Sartre hints at the influence of Lacan on his psychoanalytical thought in an interview in 1969 when he states that 'Lacan says that the unconscious is structured like language, I would say that the language which expresses it has the structure of a dream. In other words, comprehension of the unconscious in most cases never achieves explicit expression' (IOT: 49–50). This telling remark shows that, by 1969, Sartre has come to see that language not only plays a key role in structuring lived experience and knowledge, but that it is also what separates what is known from what is 'unconscious' insofar as it is comprehended but unknown;[4] language is the means through which we objectify our lived comprehension of our experience and comprehension can only become an object of knowledge by first being objectified. This allows Sartre to buttress his hypothesis that people make more meaning than they know because it allows him to hold that a primary, linguistic comprehension of lived experience can influence what people do, say and write, without them knowing about it on the grounds that 'nothing precedes language' as a means for interpreting the world as meaningful (FI I/IF I: 38/49). It also brings him closer to Freud's position on the capacity of the subject to thetically understand their experience and their behaviour by enabling him to account for what we might call the phenomenon of the unconscious 'in' lived experience without construing the unconscious as a source of psychic causality outside consciousness.

Betty Cannon has, however, warned against overstating the influence of Lacan on Sartre by showing that many of the apparent similarities between these two thinkers' psychoanalytical theories are merely apparent (1991: Chs. 6–7). Cannon is certainly right to emphasize the point that Lacan's psychoanalytic theory replaces Freudian biological-physicalist determinism with a structural-linguistic determinism in a way that makes it fundamentally incompatible with Sartrean existentialism. Nonetheless, thinking with – and against – Lacan was instrumental in leading Sartre to a fuller appreciation of how we relate to others and our selves through language. To bring this out, it is helpful to briefly consider Lacan's views on the Mirror Stage in human psychological development, which he believes occurs between the ages of six and eighteen months. Lacan attributes the infant's jubilant response to the recognition of their reflection in the mirror to the capacity of this image to allow them to anticipate a mastery over, and a unity with, their body, which they lack.[5] Upon the apprehension of their mirror-image, the infant's self enters into their experience 'in a primordial form', without the function of an *I*-subject it will take on once the infant acquires language (E: 76/94). Put simply, the infant's mirror-image serves a roughcast of their self in Lacan's view: it is a 'gestalt' that simultaneously symbolizes 'the *I*'s mental permanence' and provides the template for 'the *imago of one's own body* in hallucinations and dreams' (E: 76/95). Crucially, though, Lacan understands the infant's identification with her mirror-image as a fundamental '*misrecognition*' (*méconnaissance*) that serves as the foundation for the whole process of self-formation. He interprets it as the first form of the stance of 'not-knowing' *vis-à-vis* the (real) self and paranoically identifying with the (imaginary) other that the '*I*' signifies, which represents the (languaged) human stance for him.

This summary of Lacan's account of how the self enters lived experience allows us to see that both Lacan and Sartre construe the subject-self relation as one founded on alienation, although they each have different accounts of the source of this alienation. For Lacan, it originates in the subject's misidentification with another person, whereas for Sartre it is an upshot of the unbridgeable ontological gap between the being that reflects and the being that is reflected upon. So, while Lacan regards the unification of subject and self as a possibility – with 'catastrophic' implications (E: 379/454)[6] – and self-knowledge as an impossibility, Sartre regards the contrary to be true: unification with self is impossible but self-knowledge is possible. Despite this difference, both Lacan and Sartre regard the intrusion of inert factors in the subject-self relation as a major source of psychological distress. Lacan writes that the 'inertia characteristic of the *I* formations' can be taken to supply 'the broadest definition of neurosis, just as the subject's capture by his situation gives us the most general formulation of madness – the kind found within the asylum walls as well as the kind that deafens the world with its sound and fury' (E: 80/99). So, just as oppressive situations capture subject and drive them to madness, the signifiers that capture the self drive the subject into neurosis. Now, although Lacan is not cited in *Saint Genet*, this insight can be seen to underpin Sartre's analysis of how 'thief' functions as the 'dizzying word' that captures Genet (SG: 17–48/26–60), and it clearly influences Sartre's analysis of how language shapes Flaubert's relation to his self in *The Family Idiot*, where Lacan is cited at an early stage (FI I/IF I: 15/25).

Unlike Lacan, though, Sartre is not concerned about the possibility of inert, thing-like factors entering the subject-self relation through language because he believes that they can further alienate the subject from the other whom she (mis)takes for herself, but because he believes they can extend the ontological gap between the subject and her self by disempowering her as the agent of her self-formation. This is because inert factors in the subject-self relation are unchosen traits imposed upon the self from outside; in a word, they are 'nonassimilables' that must, somehow, be assimilated into the self because they already define it for others – prime examples are the traits signified by the words 'thief' and 'idiot' for Genet and Flaubert, respectively. An excess of nonassimilables in the self may be regarded as the hallmark of psychological oppression in Sartre's mature existentialism, since the more inert factors present in the self, the less scope there is for the subject's choice to influence their self-formation. And, as we have seen from the examinations of *Saint Genet* and *The Family Idiot* in the previous chapters, the stress of having to assimilate many nonassimilables into the self is what typically drives oppressed people to develop neuroses in Sartre's view.

Although Sartre does not develop a satisfactory account of psychological oppression until he writes *Saint Genet*, he first attends to the connection between oppression and the inferiority complex in *Anti-Semite and Jew*, where he writes that it is acceptable to use the term 'Jewish complex' to refer to the specific inferiority complex that is peculiar to Jews. Although he qualifies this by saying that it is only acceptable if the term 'complex' is not taken to refer to something 'received from the outside' since the Jews who have this complex also create it insofar as they have allowed themselves 'to be persuaded by the anti-Semites' of their inferior nature and live out their situation in bad faith (1948/1954: 94/114). In the context of his initial existentialism, then, Sartre recognizes the inferiority complex as a response to an oppressive situation but interprets it as chosen response, rather than one imposed upon the subject.[7] In *Saint Genet*, however, he holds Genet's society accountable for burdening him with numerous psychological complexes but cautions against interpreting his complexes in standard psychoanalytical way,[8] as he believes that to do so would preclude a comprehension of them by explaining them in terms of 'impulses' and overlooking the crucial fact that Genet continually acts 'against these impulses' in his attempts to regain his autonomy (SG: 157/180).

Sartre's refusal to interpret subjects' behaviour in terms of predefined psychoanalytical complexes continues into *The Family Idiot*, where it seems almost stubborn in relation to *The Legend of Saint Julian Hospitator* since, as William J. Berg notes, the parallels between this tale and the Oedipus myth are so obvious that 'even the most cautious critics have acknowledged them' (1982: 10). In fact, Sartre reads this tale to attest to Flaubert having been 'Freudian in advance' because it evinces his comprehension of his hero's remorse as resulting from the knowledge he has 'in his heart' that the parricide who kills his father by accident is not innocent if he had hoped for his father to die (FI IV/IF III: 131/1903). So, Sartre is certain that Flaubert had a complex that regulated his relationship to his father and made him long for his father's death but, rather than tracing Flaubert's 'Oedipal' desires to an Oedipus complex, he works to comprehend them in relation to the humiliations his father subjected him to as a little boy and to use this comprehension to make sense of the specific mixture of guilt and relief Flaubert felt after his father died. Even though the Oedipus complex can be used to describe a wide array of 'loving and hostile wishes which the child experiences towards its parents' (Laplanche and Pontalis 1973: 282–3), Sartre resists the move to employ this form of categorization as a means of psychological explanation and his comments in later interviews indicate that the reason for this resistance is that he views psychoanalytical complexes to function in an analogous way to analytical concepts that permit only 'interpretation without contradiction' (IOT: 57). So, when a subject's acts are interpreted to instantiate the Oedipus complex, they become subdued under a general concept and the potential of language to pick out the specific sense they have for the subject is lost because concepts can only communicate part of its dialectical truth.

This points towards Sartre's main misgiving about Freudian (and Lacanian) psychoanalysis in his mature work: its lack of dialectical reason. Despite accepting a version of the unconscious and becoming 'convinced that complexes exist' (IOT: 47), he remains unconvinced that the source of our desires, emotions and dispositions is fundamentally arational and unstructured. Neuroses and complexes are, for him, rooted in reasons because he rejects the Freudian view of reason as something that only appears at the surface-level of experience. Here lies the limit to Sartre's 'return to Freud' via Lacan: his refusal to abandon his existential commitment to the view that all human acts are comprehensible all the way down to their source in an original choice, no matter how mystified the agent is or how limited their options are.

'Show me your metaphysics!'

Sartre agrees with Freud that works of creative literature are a fecund source of psychoanalytical material but disagrees with him about why. Freud compares the creative writer to the daydreamer because he believes that dreams and imaginative works originate in an unconscious wish. As Freud's psychoanalysis aims to make the unconscious conscious and regards the interpretation of dreams as the 'royal road' to knowledge of the unconscious processes of the mind (CW V: 608), it posits the psychoanalytical value of creative works to result from their similarity to dreams insofar as they originate in a 'strong experience in the present', which 'awakens in the creative writer a memory of an earlier experience (usually belonging to his childhood) from which there now proceeds a wish which finds its fulfilment in the creative work' (CW IX: 151). Thus, for Freud, the same model used for interpreting dreams can be applied to interpret creative works to reveal the unconscious wish that they seek to fulfil.

Sartre, however, denies that dreams are a privileged site of psychological revelation. Dreams hold a psychological interest for him only insofar as they offer insight into the operations of a consciousness detached from its situation but, for the very reason that they are 'desituated', they hold little psychoanalytical interest for him as the dreaming consciousness is one that is 'captured' by the imagination and cut off from the world. Locked in an imaginary of its own making, it has nothing to negate or transcend and its actions have no consequences. This means that the freedom of dreamer has no dialectical opposition: it has 'lost its being-in-the-world', which is the necessary condition for making any meaning in the world (I: 170/329). While the waking subject's reactions to their dreams may well have important psychoanalytical significance for Sartre, the dreams themselves do not. This means that he cannot follow Freud in explaining the great psychoanalytical significance he attributes to creative works in terms of a straightforward analogy between the creative writer and the dreamer.

As Sartre sees it, literary works are an invaluable resource for a psychoanalytical study of their author for the reason they result from the effort on the author's part to relay events that transpire in an imaginary world and to use language to construct analoga for the worlds that they imagine.[9] Unlike the dreamer, then, the writer of prose is a free agent, engaged in an activity that aims at the creation of a 'free dream' for their readers (WL/QL: 37/57). To succeed in constructing an object – a text – that can be used by others as a physical analogon for an imaginary world, the author must make decisions about what the world they want to communicate is like and they must also work out how to describe its specific features to others. As the real world is the only model of a world that anybody has, it seems that authors must draw upon their own experience of how this world works to construct their own worlds in the imaginary.

This idea appears to motivate Sartre's claim that it is possible to discover and an author's metaphysics in their literary works:

> Criticism is a discovery, a certain manner of seeing the world, a way of discovering how the fellow whose work you are reading and criticizing saw the

world ... For me that was the critical idea. Finding out how the men who wrote saw the world, each separately. They described the world, but they saw it in different ways. Some in its plenitude, others from the side, narrowly ... As I see it, criticism is a double process. It must be an exposition of the author's methods, rules, and techniques, insofar as these techniques show me his metaphysics.

(1986: 208–9/297–9)

Here, Sartre uses the term 'metaphysics' in a peculiar way: to designate the specific framework a subject uses to make sense of the world.[10] Although he does not offer a sustained defence of this view that an author's literature reveals their metaphysics in his philosophical work, the claim that literature is a special mode of metaphysical communication is explicitly defended by Simone de Beauvoir in her essay, 'Literature and Metaphysics'. Because Sartre uses the term 'metaphysics' in the passage quoted above in the same peculiar way as Beauvoir does in that essay, it is highly likely that he is building upon the argument she offered there to propound his more radical view that literary works can provide insight into their authors' metaphysics. Therefore, I believe we can construct a Sartrean argument for this view by taking Beauvoir's argument in this early essay as our point of departure.

Beauvoir commences from the premise that metaphysics is something irreducible to abstract concepts because it is not a theoretical enterprise that is concerned with objects of knowledge but a way of comprehending forms of experience through being. More specifically, metaphysics is concerned with the 'attitudes' or perspectival stances through which we relate to the world. These attitudes shape our experience in ways that cannot satisfactorily be expressed in ordinary language because experience invariably exceeds what can be grasped through reflective thought about it and, hence, anything that can be said about it. However, Beauvoir holds that novels can communicate metaphysical attitudes because they use language 'to reconstitute on the imaginary plane this experience itself as it appears prior to any elucidation' (2005/1946: 270/1154), as opposed to theoretical texts that use language to articulate thoughts produced by reflection. If a novel succeeds in furnishing the reader with an experience, then it will present the reader with a 'flesh-and-blood presence' (2005/1946: 270/1154); it will give the reader an experience complete with a primary, pre-reflective comprehension of it from a(nother) perspective. A novel can therefore acquaint its readers with different metaphysical attitudes by furnishing them with the opportunity to experience 'foreign' experience in the imaginary – i.e. to apprehend and comprehend the irreducible, unsayable dimensions of an experience that is not originally *theirs*. Novels that achieve this end may appropriately be described as 'metaphysical' in Beauvoir's view as they offer a 'disclosure of existence' in a manner that is unlike other forms of expression; they use language to mimic life in its opacity and ambiguity (2005/1946: 276/1163).

In *What Is Literature?* Sartre argues for a specific ontological conception of the literary work, which makes a sharp distinction between the 'literary text' that is perceived and the 'literary work' that is created. Here, he takes literary texts to be defined by the specific form of language that constitutes them: prose. This form of language, he argues, functions in the same way as ordinary spoken language does insofar as it has a specific meaning relative to a specific context.[11] If we are sketching a tree together and you have an eraser in your hand and I say, 'Can you pass me that, please?' then the context tells you that by 'that' I mean the eraser you are holding. The words in literary texts also refer to specific objects in Sartre's view, but to specific objects that populate an imaginary world. This means that if the reader takes the author up on the invitation to work collaboratively with them to construct to the imaginary world they describe, then the reader will experience the literary work as a 'disclosure-creation' (WL/QL: 45/67). Thus, Sartre views the literary text as a physical object that invites the reader to treat it as an analogon for an imaginary world and to, thereby, bring the literary work into existence as 'a subjective thing which reveals itself under the aspect of the objective, a discourse so curiously contrived that it is equivalent to silence' (WL/QL: 22/38). Accordingly, we can see that he agrees with Beauvoir that literary texts can communicate metaphysical attitudes because, like her, he believes they can 'give' imaginary objects to readers in a manner analogous to that in which the world gives perceptual objects to us in real life – namely, as impregnated with a specific sense, which is a function of the subject's metaphysical attitude.[12]

But how does Sartre move from the view that it is possible to communicate *a* metaphysics to the more controversial one it is possible to discover *the author's* metaphysics in their literary works? Before responding to this question, it should be noted that this view was especially controversial when *The Family Idiot* was published in the early 1970s, when the influence of structuralism[13] – the movement that pronounced the author dead – was at its peak. As structuralism rejects the long-standing assumption of authorial 'authority' on the meaning of their text not as merely as a falsehood, but as a falsehood generated by an oppressive ideology, it is perhaps unsurprising that Sartre's gargantuan study on Flaubert was received by many as the product of an outmoded, 'bourgeois' interest in the person of the author. However, Sartre's remarks in the later interviews reveal his ambivalence towards structuralism and indicate why he believes literary works invariably betray their author's metaphysics. On the one hand, he admits that 'a moment comes in the research when the *text* must be confronted ... I want to do a totalizing critique: this is why the last volume [of *The Family Idiot*] will be a textual or "literary" study of *Madame Bovary*, and in it I will try to use "structuralist" techniques' (OIF/SIF: 125–6/108–9). This shows that he appreciates the value of certain structuralist insights *vis-à-vis* the literary text and regards the use of certain structuralist techniques, which examine the text in isolation from its origin, as an essential ingredient in his proposed critique of *Madame Bovary*. On the other hand, when he is asked whether he would still attempt to reconstruct Flaubert if all that remained of him was *Madame Bovary*, he replies as follows: 'I am completely opposed to the idea of the text, and that is precisely why I chose Flaubert. By leaving us juvenilia and an abundant correspondence, he offers the equivalent of "psychoanalytic discourse"' (OIF/SIF: 123/106). This shows that he is opposed to the structuralist idea of a text as something that has broken free of all its connections with the subject who wrote it. His response to the potential structuralist objection to his psychoanalytical treatment of literary works may therefore be captured in his reminder that 'writers are alive before being dead' (WL/QL: 23/40).

Because Sartre takes the language of literary texts to function in the same way as speech does, believes that the author must draw on their comprehension of this world to construct an imaginary one, and views the literary work as a collaboration between one subject (the author) and another subject (the reader),[14] he asserts that – at least for the psychoanalytic reader – the author silently communicates the metaphysical dimensions of their own lived experience through the 'free dream' of literary work in the reader's experience. In relation to *Madame Bovary*, in particular, Sartre affirms that the reader who knows where to look can find within that work 'a style of living' that is 'infinitely condensed' in a style of writing and, though this reader may not yet comprehend Flaubert, they will divine that he is comprehensible because the work conveys something of his peculiar '*flavor*, which is sensed immediately' and which can 'be reconstituted by the end of a long acquaintance or biographical study' (FI II/IF II: 8/658).

Literature as experience incarnate

As we have seen, much of the theoretical groundwork for Sartre's revised existential psychoanalysis is supplied in the *Critique*, which strives to identify the conditions for the possibility of 'knowledge *of a History*' (CDR I/CRD I: 40/158).

One of the conditions it identifies is the ability to breathe life into concrete past events by gaining a comprehension of how they would have been experienced by those who lived through them. It is only by attending to 'incarnations' of specific historical moments that Sartre believes it is possible to grasp their dialectical truth and thus incorporate knowledge of historical facts into totalizing knowledge of a history. The 'incarnation' of the social ensemble is prioritized over the concept of it because it is realized through events, which are not 'instantiations' of concept but concrete moments in which the 'totalization is individuated' (CDR II/CRD II: 28/37). As individuation is the definitive feature of reality for Sartre,[15] the analytical concept can never express the 'synthetic unity of an event' because it must abstract from the concrete particulars of the lived dialectic (CDR II/CRD II: 48). Be that as it may, Sartre expresses the hope that the 'conceptual formulation' employed in totalizing analyses of a history will be dissolved in the dialectic they reveal in the *Critique* (CDR II/CRD II: 41).

The Family Idiot pushes Sartre's demand for the formal abstractions of history to be 'concretized' to its full conclusion (Flynn 2014: 351). This work, which responds to the question of 'what, at this point in time, is it possible to know about a man' (FI I/FI I: ix/7), appears to implicitly concede that knowledge of a history can only be acquired by way of a comprehension of how the historical facts are totalized in and through the life of an individual. This is not to say that Sartre abandons the idea that the movement of history is intelligible but, rather, that he comes to question the idea that historical truths can be grasped through the 'disappearing *self*' (moi *qui disparaît*) of the investigator (CDR I/CRD I: 52/168), as the analysis of various historical moments in *The Family Idiot* suggests that it is only through the re-totalization of another self that we can fully comprehend the sense of a historical moment that we ourselves have not lived through. Further, as Sartre interprets Flaubert's life as an 'oracular' one that also crystallizes the crisis of his entire class in advance (FI V/IF 3: 409/440), he believes that the sophisticated comprehension that Flaubert gained of his lived experience through his production of literary works offers the psychoanalytic reader special insight into the sense of his life *and times*. For this reason, Sartre denies that the sense of Flaubert's lived experience is wholly peculiar to him. To be sure, it results from, and can only be comprehended in terms of, his original choice of the imaginary as a means of fleeing his unbearable reality. But, as the rest of his class also find the reality of their class-being unbearable and are equipped with the same tools as he is for responding to it, Flaubert's way of relating to the world is original without being unique. Hence, Sartre's remark in the Preface to *The Family Idiot* that no one is truly an 'individual' because everyone is a '*universal singular*' who is universalized by their epoch because they must internalize its general structures in order to make their selves within it (FI I/FI I: ix/7).

In a late interview, Sartre states that the most major challenge for existentialism is that of working out 'how to give man both his autonomy and his reality among objects, avoiding idealism without lapsing into a mechanistic materialism' (IOT: 46). He responds to this challenge by synthesizing the irreducible singularity of the lived experience with the universal in the human being, and by reconciling individual freedom with the notions of predestination and psychological oppression in a book about a man who suffered from a constitutional passivity and who found himself in a situation with very few options, but was nonetheless able to progress, through use of the means that were available to him, from being an insufficiently loved infant, to a slow learner, to the family idiot, to a ham actor, to the celebrated author of *Madame Bovary* and one of the most influential writers of his century. Moreover, this book aims to make the 'scandalous occurrence' of an idiot becoming a genius (FI I/IF I: 41/51) comprehensible by revealing the subjective sense of Flaubert's illness as an ingenious solution to an unbearable situation. It achieves this end by providing the reader with reconstructions of Flaubert's lived experience in the years leading up to his crisis that are, for the most part, based on a psychoanalytical reading of Flaubert's early literary works. *November*, the novella that Flaubert wrote two years prior to his crisis, is of central importance because Sartre believes it allows us to grasp how Flaubert experienced his situation as a living hell and to comprehend – through its disclosure of Flaubert's metaphysical attitude – his intention to become ill. The following passage illustrates how Sartre synthesizes an objective understanding of Flaubert's illness with the subjective comprehension of it that he reads Flaubert to 'incarnate' in his depiction of the pathological ataraxia (emotional disinvestment) and death of the hero of *November*:

> *Subjectively*, ataraxia simply manifests the disappearance of desire in the face of the mediocrity of the desirable ... and as desire defines man, it barely precedes burial. Besides the presentiment of death is merely the present ataraxia dreaming of itself, like an external consciousness of nothingness; *objectively*, on the other hand, ataraxia is merely anorexia, and this apathetic anorexia is a certain psychosomatic state which reproduces itself spontaneously and intentionally *in a certain man*. *Subjectively*, the journey toward death is merely the necessary relation of the microcosm to the macrocosm, the abolition of the first being the totalization of and the solution to the contradictions of the second; at issue

is a metaphysical attitude. *Objectively*, the foreseen and sought-after insanity expresses nothing about the relation of the individual to the world; it is the way that one individual, characterized by a certain anomaly, tries to resolve the contradictions that tear him apart.

(FI III/IF III: 630/1751–2)

The centrality of the subjective comprehension gained through engaging with Flaubert's literary works for Sartre's psychoanalytic interpretation of Flaubert's illness is clearly underlined in this passage, which shows how a purely objective understanding of it is incapable of appreciating how the choice to become ill makes sense for Flaubert as form of social suicide and a means to escape from a world he has no desire to live in.

Some may worry that Sartre's analysis of Flaubert's neurosis overestimates the capacity of Flaubert's intention to change his bodily relation to the world.[16] But this concern seems less appropriate regarding Sartre's analysis in *The Family Idiot* than it might be in relation to his earlier descriptions of magical behaviour for the main reason that it reveals an almost overwhelming amount of evidence for the view that Flaubert's illness was his neurotic solution to the problems he faced. Any reader of *The Family Idiot* would, I believe, have to agree with Hazel E. Barnes that its interpretation of Flaubert's illness 'so well supported' by Flaubert's writings that 'this part of the book is the most effective in making the reader feel that Sartre's Flaubert is close to that real man whom we can never know directly' (1981b: 211). Plus, Sartre is not alone in recognizing how Flaubert's nervous illness was instrumental to his becoming a great writer. Enid Starkie, for example, describes how Flaubert's perpetual convalescence allowed him to devote himself to his works, noting that Flaubert claims to have once written 'almost continuously for thirty-six hours' (1967: 214), and even B. F. Bart – who is almost certain that Flaubert suffered from epilepsy – ventures that Flaubert 'had perhaps unconsciously sought illness as a relief from a life he loathed being forced to live' (1967: 96–7). But it was not by some 'happy' chance or unconscious motivation that Flaubert became ill in Sartre's view, because Flaubert already comprehended his intention to become a *'man-failure'* when he fell at his brother's feet that night in 1844, even if he did not know it (FI IV/ IF III: 43/1812), and Sartre's psychanalytic readings of Flaubert's literary works – especially those written prior to his first attack – reveal a profound comprehension of his illness as his means to become the loser who wins by living in the imaginary.

Imaginary lives

As a sustained study of Flaubert's choice to live an imaginary life, *The Family Idiot* develops an important theme from *The Imaginary*: the dangerous potential of the imagination to ensnare the very freedom it makes possible. An understanding of this dangerous potential leads Sartre to propose that people may be divided into 'two great categories' depending on whether they choose to lead a real life or an imaginary one (I: 146/282). He argues that the choice to lead an imaginary life does not merely express a preference for different objects of experience than those that are available in reality but a preference for a radically different form of experience too. So, people who live imaginary lives in Sartre's view do not strive to replace the mediocre content of real life with an imaginary richness and beauty *despite* the fact that it is imaginary, they also choose it partly *because* it is imaginary and because they find the feelings and conducts associated with experience in the imaginary mode preferable to those associated with the perceptual mode. The choice to live an imaginary life is therefore a choice to be 'in' the imagination, to exist in another, private world, cut off from the real world of risk and opportunity that we share with others. The choice to live an imaginary life is a radical flight from being in this world and everything that comes with it: its 'character *of presence*', the kind of actions and reactions it demands of us, the overwhelming richness of perceptions, the independence of real objects and others, as well as 'the very way that our feelings have of developing' (I: 147/282).

This claim that the experience of imaginary objects must take place in the imaginary mode of consciousness is key to understanding Sartre's theorization of the choice to lead an imaginary life as one that is often associated with serious psychopathological conditions, such as schizophrenia. For what follows from it is that imaginary objects do not only appear to be poor substitutes for real ones for 'us', the people who choose to lead real lives: *being* a poor substitute for the real objects they aim at is what characterizes imaginary objects ontologically. The imaginary object is an object born of a desire for the 'real thing' that it is also essentially incapable of satisfying. Hence, Sartre describes the function of imaginary objects in lived experience as that of 'deceiving desires momentarily in order to exacerbate them' and likens their effect to that of sea water on thirst (I: 126/241). If this is correct, though, the choice of an imaginary life appears to be incomprehensible – how can the choice to live in an inherently dissatisfying state make sense? Who 'in their right mind' would make such a choice? Sartre resists the move to dismiss the preference for an imaginary life as one devoid of all logic. An important clue as to why he does so is to be found in his statement that although imaginary objects may be nothing but essentially impoverished, inherently dissatisfying appearances, they nevertheless provide us with an invitation flee from this world and all its constraints into an 'anti-world' with as many or as few constraints as we choose to put in it (I: 136/261). This indicates how an imaginary life may hold an irresistible appeal to those who find themselves trapped in hopeless situations because the imagination gives them the opportunity to experience their choices as having *something like* the desired effects in the imaginary. The choice of an imaginary life can therefore be comprehensible as the desperate choice of a subject to flee from a full, rich world in which their choices count for nothing into a dull, dry, meticulous, empty one in which their choice is everything.

The Imaginary argues that the pathological choice of an imaginary life can be comprehended, and *The Family Idiot* shows that it can. It makes Flaubert's illness comprehensible by explaining how Flaubert saw only two ways out of his unbearable situation: suicide or literature, but literature was not an option that he could actively choose because he was incapable of acting in defiance of the wishes of his family. It explains how Flaubert's illness can be interpreted as passive form of aggressive defensiveness that enables him to survive his situation by analysing how Flaubert develops his own comprehension of his situation and the options that are available to him. It is by writing the *November* that Flaubert first begins to 'realize' his intention to end his real life through relaying the story of the unnamed hero who manages to kill himself by ataraxia – by not caring enough about his life to do the things he needs to do to sustain it, such as eat. By killing off his alter-ego in the imaginary, then introducing a second narrator to complete his tale and immortalize him as one who was 'too great' for this world, Sartre reads Flaubert to evince his comprehension his intention to flee from this life in which he only suffers through a form of suicide that enables him to live on in 'another life' in which he can write and make believe that he is the loser who wins.

Thus, Sartre's psychoanalytic method takes important dimensions of Flaubert's lived experience to be incarnated in his literary works and uses them to facilitate a comprehension of his choice to lead an imaginary life as his solution to the problem posed by his unliveable life. By engaging with the experiences afforded by Flaubert's literary works and Sartre's relaying of them, the reader of *The Family Idiot* can, in theory, bypass the mediations of others' (Sartre's and Flaubert's) reflective thoughts and gain a direct apprehension of the sense of Flaubert's lived experience in the imaginary. Then, they can draw upon this comprehension to interpret Flaubert's nervous attacks, and subsequent withdrawal from bourgeois social life, (subjectively) as an original strategy for self-preservation *and* (objectively) as self-destructive behaviour that is symptomatic of psychological oppression.

A true novel: Knowing *through* imagining?

While *The Family Idiot* appears to be aptly described as a sequel to *The Imaginary* insofar as it shows how an imaginary life can be comprehended as a choice, the instrumental role Sartre assigns to imagining in the context of a work that aims to communicate knowledge of Flaubert appears to stand in tension with one of the key tenets of *The Imaginary*: that we cannot learn anything by imagining. However, the apparent tension between Sartre's theory in *The Imaginary* and his practice in *The Family Idiot* dissolves once we appreciate how his early theory of the imagination can accommodate his later understanding of selves as dialectical objects.[17]

Let us begin by clarifying Sartre's conception of the relation between the imagination and knowledge in *The Imaginary*. As Robert Hopkins points out, when Sartre states that we cannot learn from imagining, he should not be read to mean that we cannot learn *anything* whosoever since imagining can, at the very least, teach us 'about our ability to imagine things' (2011: 100). Indeed, given Sartre's commitment to a distinction between lived comprehension and knowledge, the statement that 'one can never learn from an image what one does not know already' (I: 10/27) is perhaps best interpreted to mean that we cannot gain any new knowledge about real objects by imagining them. So, I cannot, for instance, discover how many pillars the Panthéon has by imagining it because I can only find in my image of the Panthéon as many pillars as I put in it, based on the knowledge I already have. Imagining cannot yield any new discoveries concerning the objective features of its object because its object is necessarily absent and so cannot be observed; the only features to be found in imaginary objects are those that the subject puts in them.

However, Sartre explains the intuition that imagining enlightens us by showing that it typically furnishes us with some 'affective clarification' – i.e. a deeper comprehension of the subjective sense that objects have for us. This view is premised on the idea that our feelings behave in a similar way the face of the imaginary as they do in the face of the real. More specifically, constituting an imaginary object enables us to experience feelings that resemble the feelings we would feel in the presence of the real object it stands in place of, in certain desirable conditions.[18] Sartre illustrates this idea with the aid of a rather graphic example: vomiting out of disgust. He posits that if I form an image of a rotten plate of food, my knowledge of what this rotten dish is like provokes the affective sense of this object for me. As such, my image of the dish already 'knows (*connait*) itself at present as disgust with this dish' (I: 140/268–9) and does not deliver any new knowledge. But it does bring an 'affective dialectic' into my experience, as it allows the repugnance I feel in relation to this dish to respond to itself in the absence of the dish. A similar sort of dialectic is involved in perception, although the object has an entirely different function in each case. When I perceive a disgusting plate of food, my repugnance guides my disgust and leads me to 'discover in the real dish a thousand repugnant details', which may make me sick (I: 140/269), whereas when I imagine a disgusting plate of food, my disgust can also intensify to the point of sickness, but it does so '*of its own accord*' as it lacks the input from the object itself (I: 140/269). Hence, the object is indispensable to my feeling disgust in both cases, but in the former, it is as a stimulus and in the latter, it is as a '*witness*' (I: 140/269).

This illuminates what is distinctive about the feelings we experience in relation to imaginary objects in Sartre's view, which is that they are always anticipated and so never truly 'reactive'. Although he identifies 'constitutive' and 'reactive' layers within the imagining attitude, he argues that in most cases 'the affective factor is entirely exhausted in the constituent act' because the absence of the imaginary object means that 'the whole body' must actively collaborate in its constitution (I: 137/264). He urges us not to misinterpret the well-documented physiological changes that coincide with imagining – e.g. pupillary dilation and contraction, nausea, vomiting, salivation and erections – as reactions to the imaginary object since they form part of our effort to constitute it. Whatever spontaneous reactions we experience in the face of the imaginary object (if any) are incapable of revealing any new qualities in it: I can neither experience any new affects in relation to the dish I imagine, nor can I learn anything further about why it disgusts me, although I may be surprised that I managed to make myself sick '*because of nothing*' (I: 140/270).

So, it is always our love for absent loved ones that makes their face appear to us, not the other way around. Our feelings 'grope blindly at a moment in order to understand themselves'; they generate the intention to imagine a certain object they are associated with, so that they can become 'enlightened' through being connected with the knowledge we have of this object in our image of it (I: 141/271). Imaginings therefore allow us to clarify the affective sense objects have for us in our lived experience – or at least would have if they were experienced in 'the right' conditions – by reproducing the affective dialectic that constitutes the sense of them in Sartre's view. It is due to this capacity of imaginings to reproduce the affective sense of objects that Sartre employs them in *The Family Idiot*, where he aims to supply his readers with both the biographical facts about and an empathetic comprehension of their sense for Flaubert. As Flynn points out, it is Sartre's aim to communicate dialectical truths of becoming that explains his sometimes 'cavalier dealing with the facts' in his biographical works, as it makes him far less concerned with the truth of events as they actually happened than with the reproduction of the metaphysical attitude or the '"way of comprehending the comprehension" of the subject in question' (2014: 5). Indeed, Sartre calls attention to several minor 'factual errors' in *The Family Idiot* before dismissing their significance by asserting that his aim in *The Family Idiot* is 'to show a method and to show a man' (OIF/SIF: 111/93), which indicates that he sees the objective accuracy of the facts that are united in the self as less important than the principle of their unification – i.e. the comprehension that makes all of these facts make sense – since a self is a dialectical object, a totalization or a gestalt, which is irreducible to the pieces of knowledge it comprises.

An obvious challenge to Sartre's use of the imagination as a means of gaining an experience-based comprehension of a foreign experience is the view that imaginary experience cannot provide the subject with this kind of insight because it is not 'real' experience. L. A. Paul expresses this idea in the course of her argument for the view we should not base our decisions about whether to have a child, move to another country, study for a PhD, etc. on subjective projections of our current selves into possible futures because imaginary exercises such as this cannot provide us with a way knowing what experiences we have not had are like or how they may change us. When considering the question of whether we can understand what it is like to be a slave, a deaf person or a vampire, Paul argues that we cannot gain this sort of understanding without having had the relevant experiences of, for example, slavery, deafness or vampirism because these sorts of experiences instigate radical changes in the subject's lived situation, changes that make their experience different not only in terms content but also in terms of form or perspective. So, although it is perfectly possible to imagine having experiences that you have not actually had in Paul's view, she holds that it is impossible to imagine having experiences in which 'you' are other, which means that 'imagining isn't enough' to give you knowledge of what it is really like to be in a situation that is radically different from your own (2014: 8). And so, it follows that you cannot imagine experiences from another person's perspective because you have not had the relevant experience of *being* them.

Sartre can respond to this challenge by conceding that different subjective experiences are, by their very nature, fundamentally inaccessible to one another yet denying that this implies that it is impossible to gain an empathetic comprehension of how another subject makes sense of their situation by using the knowledge we have of their situation and how they responded to it as the basis for our incarnations of their experiences in the imaginary. The production of a new, imaginary experience formed on the basis of knowledge of objective biographical facts furnishes the empathizing subject with a comprehension of the dialectical sense of an experience for the original subject by way of a kind of affective 'deduction' of the reasons why the original subject responded to that experience in the specific way they did in Sartre's estimation. So, the role of empathetic imaginings in the context of his existential psychoanalysis is to deliver neither knowledge nor an experience that is the same as the original subject's but to yield a human comprehension of how the original subject must have made sense of certain objective facts. Accordingly, the naïve and possibly indefensible epistemological claim that one can gain knowledge of another's experience by imagining it cannot justifiably be attributed to Sartre.[19]

The central role of the imagination in Sartre's psychanalytical studies has led some commentators to believe that he must have revised his earlier theory of the imagination because they appear to blur the sharp distinction between the imaginary and the real he insists upon in *The Imaginary*. Kathleen Lennon, for instance, reads Sartre's studies of Genet and Flaubert to take him closer to a Merleau-Pontyan understanding of the imaginary and the real as blended in experience because 'the imaginary of the self' in these works is treated like a 'dimension of the experienced body/world' (2015: 102). Jennifer Gosetti-Ferencei also reads Sartre's 'interpretations of literary works (by Flaubert, Saint-Genet, and others)' to signal his move away from his earlier position on the grounds that they introduce the notion of the 'possibilization of the real' – i.e. imaginings of possibilities that contrast with, but necessarily refer to, the real – which, she believes, contradicts Sartre's earlier view that the negation of the real is a condition for the imaginary act (Gosetti-Ferencei 2014: 439). While both Lennon and Gosetti-Ferencei are right to observe that Sartre's later biographical studies emphasize the potential of imaginary experiences to facilitate more profound empathetic understandings, this section has shown why it is mistaken to infer from this that he must have gone back on his earlier views about the ontology of the imagination. Sartre's biographical works use the imagination to enlighten us about the affective sense of their subjects' experience in a manner that is entirely compatible with the understanding of the imagination as a state in which consciousness produces an imaginary object out of nothing to experience something like the feelings that would coincide with the real presence of that object in certain conditions. Even the claim that imaginings can produce the affective dialectic that constitutes the sense of an object for another subject is consistent with this idea since the comprehension of another gained through experiences in the imaginary does not, in itself, provide us with any further knowledge. Rather, as knowledge is what animates imaginary objects on Sartre's account, knowledge can never be the result of an imaginary act; it is what enables us to 'read' the imaginary objects we create, just as our prior knowledge allows us to read objects we perceive. Further, although Sartre theorizes selves and histories as imaginary and real dialectical objects in his later work, he affirms that they exist only in the imaginary and that it is due to the existence of objects that serve as analoga for them in reality that they have an objective truth.

The aim to present knowledge of Flaubert in a form that can serve as a physical analogon for his self is why, I believe, Sartre takes great pains to present the results of years of intensive psychoanalytical, biographical, socio-political and historical research into Flaubert's life and times in the form of a 'true novel' (*roman vrai*) (IWS: 27, OIF/SIF: 112/94). Even though he maintains that the greatest part of human experience is comprehended without being articulated, and that its richness can never be captured by concepts, he nevertheless believes that it is possible to communicate objective biographical facts about Flaubert, along with their subjective sense, through a book like *The Family Idiot*, whose sentences are, like the sentences of a novel, 'soaked with imaging knowledge [*savoir imageant*]' (I: 66/132). At the very end of his career, then, Sartre aims to supply us with a textual basis for the re-totalization of another self in the imaginary and, accordingly, complete his solution to the problem of other minds by providing a demonstration of the psychoanalytical method that he believes enables us to overcome our epistemic alienation from our own selves and those of others.

7

The future of Sartrean existential psychoanalysis

So far, this book has emphasized the continuities between Sartre's theoretical writings and his psychoanalytical studies to highlight the latter as extensions of his philosophical work. This chapter suggests some possible expansions of his existential psychoanalysis into clinical psychotherapeutic practice. Let us pave the way for these by summarizing the relevant achievements of Sartrean existential psychoanalysis.

We have seen how Sartre's psychoanalysis represents the final phase of his longstanding project to solve the philosophical problem of other minds by revolutionizing our way of thinking about our 'selves'. His final work, *The Family Idiot*, completes this project. Through synthesizing biographical knowledge of Flaubert with a subjective sense of his reality, it aims to provide an analogon for Flaubert's self, which can reward readers who make the cognitive and emotional efforts required to imagine Flaubert as he is described with the opportunity to know him better than he knew himself, without ever having met him in person. Though this is a rather ambitious aim, we have seen that Sartre's theorizations of the self, knowledge, the imagination and of socio-material human reality support the possibility of its success in principle.

Further, by offering us a concrete example of how a text could, potentially, provide the basis for the 're-totalization' of another self in the imagination of the reader, *The Family Idiot* underlines the rich therapeutic potential that Sartre sees in language as a means of bridging the epistemological gap between 'subjects' and 'selves'. Although language can exacerbate our alienation from our selves – as the words 'thief' and 'idiot' do for (Sartre's) Genet and Flaubert respectively – Sartre holds that language allows us to directly communicate knowledge – including the knowledge others have of us – and indirectly communicate the subjective sense of our experience. This means that while the ontological gap between one person and other is unbridgeable, the epistemological gap is bridgeable by language because the world we each experience derives its meaningful structure from a language that is shared. Nothing meaningful precedes language for Sartre as the only meaning that experiences can have is one that is communicable through language. The acquisition of language pulls us out of the 'profound and solitary reality' in which we live our first years (SM/QM: 63/90) and plunges us into a shared world in which every object is infused with latent meanings, where we are never 'really alone' because our 'thoughts are communicable' (SG: 590/651). *The Family Idiot* pushes this understanding of language to its most radical conclusion in its attempt to show that 'everything' there is to know about someone can be communicated (OIF/SIF: 123/106). This is testament to Sartre's belief in the great therapeutic potential of language: in the context of successful biographies (and long acquaintances), it can serve as a salve for existential loneliness; in the context of clinical applications of existential psychoanalysis, it can provide a cure for psychological illnesses that have their source in the subject's epistemic alienation from their self.

Sartrean existentialism: A new metatheory

In *Sartre & Psychoanalysis: An Existentialist Challenge to Clinical Metatheory* (1991), Betty Cannon contends that replacing Freud's biological model of the mind with Sartre's existential ontology can resolve the crisis she identifies in psychoanalytic 'metatheory' – the theory about how and why psychoanalysis works – by making it possible to accommodate insights brought forward by the post-Freudian theorists on human psychological development and relational needs, which cannot be satisfactorily incorporated into a traditional Freudian theoretical framework. She also describes how adopting Sartre's existential approach to psychoanalysis can free practitioners of the obligation to explain psychological issues that are comprehensible in terms of experiences of past trauma, irresolvable conflicts and interpersonal failures in terms of an 'experience-distant' theory of unconscious drives. The discussion that follows builds upon Cannon's work by teasing out further implications for psychotherapy from the philosophical reconception of Sartre's psychoanalysis offered in this book. It also points out the potential for Sartre's existential psychoanalysis to address new challenges facing psychotherapists today. To start with, though, let us establish how Sartre's existential psychoanalysis can inform therapeutic practice.

Perhaps the most major advantage of grounding psychoanalytic practice in Sartre's existentialism is that it provides the therapist with a coherent theory of how therapeutic change occurs. As Cannon points out, neither Freud's biological metatheory nor Lacan's structuralist reinterpretation of it can adequately sustain a theory of positive, therapeutic change because they are both deterministic (1991: 34–5, 260–73). A problem that any deterministic psychoanalytic metatheory faces is that of accounting for how insight, or corrective emotional experiences, or the resolution of a transference neurosis,[1] or, indeed, any proposed cure *can* cure. If the ultimate source of human behaviour is taken to lie outside of consciousness, it is difficult to see how we can *do* anything to change the way it acts upon the subject. How can knowledge of my unconscious wish, for example, stop it from tormenting me? Although there is, perhaps, more promise in Lacan's later thought – which suggests that slight alterations in the subject's structuration within the symbolic order, facilitated by psychoanalysis, may allow them to transition from an 'abnormal' to a 'normal' mode of regulating their desire – it is unclear how exactly Lacan believes this can be achieved (E: 700/826, see also Cannon 1991: 272; Howells 1992: 338). As Sartre's existentialism construes human beings as the exception to the deterministic order and affirms that knowledge is realized through action, rather than through the possession of representations inside the mind, it offers a robust explanation of why self-knowledge is the instrument for therapeutic change.

Put simply, the self-knowledge that Sartrean existential psychoanalysis aims to deliver is 'transformative' because 'getting it' means that you cannot go on being as you were before.[2] A good illustration of how this works is Sartre's exposition of how Genet changes from being an aesthete to an artist through the process of writing *Our Lady of the Flowers*. He describes this process as being simultaneously a conversion, a detoxification and revelation of self for Genet. *Our Lady of the Flowers* is not merely a material 'witness' to Genet's 'cure', it 'concretizes it' by realizing Genet's knowledge of his original choice of Self through effecting its conversion, which 'makes and rejects itself, observes and knows itself [*se connaît*]' through his act of creating it (SG: 449/499). So, Genet gains self-knowledge through the act of writing a novel, and this transforms him in Sartre's view.[3]

We have already seen that Sartre's analysis of Genet is a philosophical-therapeutic application of existential psychoanalysis not a clinical-therapeutic one, and that Genet actually found it distressing to read *Saint Genet*. This shows that the difference between these two kinds of applications of existential psychoanalysis must be reflected by a difference in practice: the discovery of transformative self-knowledge through existential psychoanalysis is not a purely intellectual one. Sartre's description of psychoanalysis as 'a movement' that simultaneously 'uncovers a neurosis and gradually makes the subject capable of supporting it' ([1964] 2008/1972: 145/300) in 1964 indicates his awareness that transformative self-knowledge can only cure the analysand if it is discovered in the right way – through a process that provides the subject with intellectual and emotional resources to change their way of being. Although Sartre affirms that the testimony of the analysand must be 'decisive' in clinical applications of existential psychoanalysis (BN/EN: 745/620) and emphasizes the importance of affect in the discovery of self-knowledge in *Being and Nothingness*, he does not provide us with a clear picture of how existential psychoanalysis should be applied in a clinical setting there. His 1969 *Les Temps modernes* essay, 'The Man with a Tape-Recorder', does, however, provide us with some important clues as, here, he uses a transcript of a psychoanalytic dialogue recorded by an analysand (against the explicit wishes of the analyst) as the basis for criticizing some specific features of traditional psychoanalytic practice. Putting aside questions about the ethicality of the journal's controversial choice to publish this transcript and the extent to which Sartre could understand it as an instance of transference,[4] let us use Sartre's analysis of this transcript to construct a sketch of what he believes clinical psychoanalytic practice should be like.

The main target of Sartre's essay is the lack of reciprocity in the relationship between the analyst and analysand in traditional psychoanalysis, where, he believes, the analyst monopolizes the status of subject within it by treating the analysand as an object that they observe. Even though it is predominantly the analysand who speaks in traditional psychoanalysis, their speech is denied the status of praxis because it has no potential to instigate change within the relation as the analyst will not be affected by anything that the analysand says.[5] The analyst's assumed perspective of the expert and disinterested observer therefore has the effect of transforming the analysand's speech act into an object 'even as it is uttered' (MT/HM: 201/1815). Moreover, the physical positions of the two figures in this relationship effectively locks the analysand in the object position: he lies on the coach under the critical gaze of the analyst, who is seated upright in a chair behind him and shielded from his Look. The analysand must 'emancipate himself' by working towards the end of '*self*-discovery', Sartre writes; yet, this is extremely difficult to achieve through a process in which he experiences himself as a passive, dependent object, waiting to be cured by an impassive, distant subject (MT/HM: 201/1815). Sartre regards it as instructive that the man with the tape recorder's feelings of deep frustration and disempowerment in his relationship with his analyst develops to the point of crisis: the lesson we can learn from reading the transcript of a tragicomic exchange that, undoubtedly, puts an end to this therapeutic relationship is that psychoanalytic interpretations should be offered in the context of a long joint 'adventure' (MT/HM: 201/1815) – a process undertaken by *two* subjects united in their pursuit of the same goal. This leads Sartre to conclude that the knowledge that cures in psychoanalysis can only be gained through a relationship of reciprocity in which both parties look at one another and make themselves vulnerable to being judged, misunderstood and hurt.

In existential psychoanalysis, then, the (human-)expert-(dehumanized-)object dyad is replaced with that of two human beings engaged in a joint project, working face to face. Sartre's remark that the man with the tape recorder may find 'valid interlocutors in England or Italy' (MT/HM: 204/1818) supplies us with a more specific suggestion about what the pursuit of this joint project might look like in practice, as it is a clear allusion to Ronald D. Laing and others in London and Franco Basaglia and his colleagues in Gorizia. Cannon has taken up this suggestion by looking towards Laing's treatment of a homeless paranoid schizophrenic woman at the Milton Erickson Foundations Evolution of Psychotherapy Conference in Phoenix in 1980 for inspiration. Here, Laing makes a genuine effort to enter this women's phenomenal world to understand what the 'conspiracy' she perceives around her is like, and she responds by admitting that she does not believe that the conspiracy exists when she is not thinking about it but that other doctors tend to make her 'believe it again' (Laing 1985: 14:05–14:30). Cannon attributes the striking improvement in this woman's coherence during her discussion with Laing to the fact that the therapeutic relationship he developed with her evinced what Sartre would call 'positive reciprocity'. However, Cannon stresses that facilitating positive reciprocity does not entail any abdication of responsibility on the therapist's behalf; Laing does not collude with this woman's delusion in an effort to be her 'chum', but he does display a willingness to take the risks involved in entering into a genuine dialogue with her, as well as a readiness to offer a different kind of 'Look' than the original others, one which may enable her 'to look at her life anew and to begin to live in a radically different way' (1999: 47).

This kind of positive reciprocity might be considered a form of 'love' insofar as it represents a way of appreciating another for who they are, a curiosity about how they experience the world, as well as genuine desire to nurture their growth which does not seek to determine its direction.[6] Indeed, elsewhere, Laing has described how the therapist's 'love that recognizes the patient's total being, and accepts it, with no strings attached' can be integral to 'uniting the patient, in allowing the pieces to come together and cohere' ([1960] 1969: 165). The founder of person-centred therapy, Carl Rogers, also believes that a 'person who is loved appreciatively, not possessively, blooms and develops his own unique self' (1980: 23). Love is also written about in the psychoanalytic literature, where it is often considered part of the process of analytic change in virtue of offering the analysand new, corrective experiences that allow them to break problematic patterns of thinking and relating (see, e.g., Fosshage 2007). However, the kind of love offered by the existential psychoanalyst is distinct insofar as Sartrean existentialism conceives of love as a positive reciprocal relationship that supports the growth of *both* subjects, which means that neither can be reduced to a prop supporting the other's transcendence and both subjects experience themselves as equals within the relationship.[7] Hence, an existential psychoanalysis emphasizes the importance of the presence of the therapist's other human perspective as the 'objective' component that provides the necessary dialectical opposition to the empathetic 'subjective' component of the therapeutic relationship.

Cannon provides a helpful clinical illustration of how an empathetic engagement with the client's perspective can be 'opposed' with the presence of the therapist's in her discussion of her application of Sartrean existential psychoanalysis in her treatment of Martha, a psychotherapist in her early thirties, who was undergoing an acute personal crisis when Cannon began to treat her. Working with Cannon led Martha to the discovery that her original choice to be a 'marvellous mirror' *for others* had been made in response to her apprehension of parental love as being conditional on her provision of emotional labour. Cannon notes that empathetic resonance along Rogerian lines was important in the early stages of Martha's treatment, as it helped Martha to build the strength she required to cope with the anguish she experienced as she came to acknowledge the role her choice had played in bringing her to her current crisis. However, Cannon contends that empathetic resonance alone, without the challenge to 'face the ontological dilemma that all of us lack an ego or self in the substantive sense', would not have been sufficient to support Martha in her capacity to change through behaving in ways that were both new and uncomfortable for her: entering situations where she would be the centre of attention, sharing herself more freely with others, etc. (1991: 345). Martha's treatment came to an end when she started to act in ways that allowed her to make her self something other than what her situation had made her, to pursue a fundamental project of becoming a certain sort of person for herself, rather than a human mirror for others. Hence, the kind of love that an existential therapist aims to offer is one that both prizes the client as a human being *and* pushes them out of vicious cycles of hexis which prevents their choice from influencing their self-formation.

Sartrean existential psychoanalysis in practice

Psychodynamic psychotherapists today generally emphasize the presence of two subjects in the healing relationship and affirm that psychoanalytic interpretations should be collaboratively constructed (e.g. Lemma 2003: 86–91; Fosshage 2007: 328–30). However, Sartre's commitment to a phenomenological approach, his insistence upon reciprocity in the therapeutic relationship, and his conception of transformative self-knowledge as the goal of therapy mean that his existential psychoanalysis is more aptly classified as a mode of 'humanistic' psychotherapy – alongside person-centred, gestalt and other existential therapies – than a form of 'psychoanalysis proper'. Indeed, Cannon's application of Sartre's existential psychoanalysis in her treatment of Martha shows that while its 'subjective' component involves the application of typical psychoanalytic regressive techniques, they form just part of a multifaceted, heuristic approach, which means that the findings obtained through their application are also interpreted in a different way. Though many of Martha's difficulties could be explained in terms of psychoanalytic concepts, both classical – the Oedipal triangle between her, her father and her mother; the compulsion to repeat; transference – and post-Freudian – narcissistic issues, failed mirroring – Cannon does not do so. Instead, she interprets Martha's difficulties through an existentialist lens, which emphasizes not the 'regressive pull to a *real* earlier state of development' but Martha's lived comprehension that her original others did not provide her with the recognition she required to develop a viable fundamental project (Cannon 1991: 348).

It might be objected that Sartre's existential psychoanalysis ought not to be classified as a humanistic mode of psychotherapy because it treats the self as its object, whereas all humanistic therapies emphasize subjectivity and resist the 'view of the person as an object, to be seen objectively from an external vantage point that ignores the individual's existential reality' (Rice and Greenberg 1992: 197). However, we have seen that Sartre's construal of the self as a 'dialectical object' of human making means that the objective method his psychoanalysis employs does not view the person it analyses from a solely external vantage point. To the contrary, it replaces the distant, disinterested objectivity of the natural scientist with the 'subjective objectivity' of another human perspective, which seeks to comprehend how the analysand's experience of their situation drives their self-formation; it holds that the way to understanding a person's qualities, quirks and 'abnormalities' is via empathetic comprehension, not clinical observation. Accordingly, Sartre's existential psychoanalysis refuses to employ psychodynamic concepts – e.g. 'resistance', 'transference', 'defense', 'compromise' and 'conflict', etc. – and nosological categories – 'neurotic', 'psychotic', 'schizoid', 'narcissistic', etc. – in the way that all psychodynamic therapies do (Lacewing 2018: 97; see also Wallerstein 1990; Cannon 1991; Hough 2014: 76–106), as it takes this practice to presuppose a form of psychological determinism wherein unconscious mechanisms are regarded as the ultimate 'cause' of the subject's current problems.

We have seen that Sartre regards the belief that psychoanalysis can cure in the manner of the medical sciences to be based on the false assumption that psychopathological symptoms and abnormal behaviours can be traced back to mechanistic causes, which neglects the role of choice in shaping human experience and guiding human action. In this respect, Sartre's position is very close to Laing's. Laing articulates the existentialist criticism of the assumption of a scientific kind of objectivity in psychotherapeutic contexts when he states that the notion that knowledge of a person can be gained through the methodological depersonalization of 'the person who is the "object"' of the investigation … is just as pathetic a fallacy as the false personalization of things' (Laing 1969: 24, cf. SM/QM: 157/218).[8] This quote is taken from Laing's pioneering study of schizophrenia, *The Divided Self: An Existential Study in Sanity and Madness*. As the title suggests, this work was deeply inspired by existentialist philosophy, especially Sartre's.[9] While Laing does not deny that biochemical elements may factor into the development of schizophrenia, his chief aim in this work is to show that the subject's social milieu plays a far greater role in precipitating the illness than any other factor. This view stood in stark contrast with the psychiatric orthodoxy at the time, which drew a firm distinction between 'neuroses', or affective disorders, and 'psychoses' on the grounds that the former result from an excess or deficit of normal, 'sane' emotions, while the latter are characterized by 'insane' behaviours that can only be explained by the subject's mind not working in the 'normal' – i.e. rational – way.[10] Schizophrenia was typically held up as the paradigm of psychosis (CW XIV: 196–204). Perhaps the most famous articulation of this view comes from Karl Jaspers. As he puts it: 'The most profound distinction in psychic life seems to be between that which is meaningful and *allows empathy* and what is in its particular way *ununderstandable*, "mad" in the literal sense, schizophrenic psychic life' (Jaspers [1913] 1963: 577). Although Jaspers' approach to psychiatry was phenomenological, he believed that the bewildering strangeness of schizophrenic experience precludes us (sane people) from gaining a subjective understanding of it through empathy, which led him to conclude that the only way to understand it is by assuming an objective stance that looks for causal explanations.

Without denying that 'praecox feeling', the profound sense of the inaccessibility of schizophrenic experience, is a major obstacle for clinicians striving to empathize with the schizophrenics they treat, Laing counters the conception that schizophrenia is inherently 'ununderstandable' by offering numerous powerful illustrations of how schizophrenics' disordered speech becomes understandable once efforts have been made to interpret it from within the schizophrenic's specific situation. Rather than taking schizophrenia to be beyond the scope of human understanding, Laing places it on the continuum of human ways of being by portraying the 'insane' schizophrenic position is a progression from the 'schizoid' position, which is 'sane' but neurotic and, possibly, pre-psychotic or 'prodromal'. By emphasizing the continuities between these two positions and the understandability of the latter as a withdrawal from a situation that deprives the subject of the things that provide others with metaphysical comfort – e.g. a sense of purpose, belonging, of being loved – Laing provides us with a perspective from which we can glimpse at least some of the salient features of the 'inner world' of the schizophrenic – an empathetic point of entry if you will.

The affinities between Laing's and Sartre's understandings of psychopathology run deep. This is confirmed by Sartre's Foreword to a selection of his works, edited and introduced by Laing and fellow psychiatrist D. G. Cooper, *Reason and Violence: A Decade of Sartre's Philosophy, 1950–1960*, where he goes out of his way to express his approval of the editors' attempt to establish an existential approach to treating mental illness in their other works. Significantly, he affirms that, like the editors, he believes that mental illness is a strategy invented by 'free organism, in its total unity' for living in an unliveable situation (1964: 7). Moreover, Laing and Cooper's remark that Sartre's *Saint Genet* serves as prototype for a 'clinical biography' (Laing and Cooper 1964: 26) shows that it is highly likely that Laing looked to Sartre's application of his existential psychoanalysis as a model for how to interpret mental illness. This, coupled with the fact that, in the course of his depiction of the schizoid position in *The Divided Self*, Laing describes the schizoid's experience of the world as 'a prison without bars' (1969: 79) – the very same phrase that Sartre uses to describe the situation that drove Genet to neurosis (SG: 69/85) – indicates that Laing's study of schizoid and schizophrenic positions in *The Divided Self* represents a valuable resource for psychotherapists seeking more specific directives on how to analyse their clients' situation, behaviour and speech along Sartrean-existential lines. However, Laing stresses that this study is not a 'direct application of any established existential philosophy' (1969: 9), and while he does not detail the differences between his existentialist position and Sartre's, I believe that it is important to bring some of these out here to provide a provisional indication of how a specifically Sartrean existential approach would depart from Laing's.

Initially, the most significant difference between Laing's and Sartre's approaches appears to lie in their vision of the goal of psychotherapy. For Sartre, it is transformative self-knowledge whereas, for Laing, it is 'ontological security'. It is important to note that Laing strips the term 'ontological' of its existential-philosophical connotations and uses it in an empirical manner to describe a subject's sense of their own being. 'Ontological security' therefore denotes the state of experiencing oneself as a real, living person, whose being is stable, whole and temporally continuous (1969: 39). 'Ontological insecurity' denotes the opposite: a profound uncertainty about the reality of the self, its stability and the boundaries between it and the world, and it is what lies at the heart of schizophrenia according to Laing. But he also maintains that a key feature of schizophrenia spectrum states is that they exist 'in the light' of the existential truth of the human condition that 'sane' minds are shielded from (1969: 27), which is to say that they are characterized by an acute awareness of ontological selflessness. So even though, in the context of Sartrean existentialism, 'ontological security' would be impossible for any human being, whose ontological selflessness means that their definitive existential characteristic is anguish – i.e. a form of ontological insecurity – Laing's empirical use of 'ontological' means that the two thinkers are actually in agreement on the point that schizophrenics are not subject to the 'healthy' delusion of an inner self that protects 'normals' from paralysing anguish (see TE: 46–8/79–82). This also means that Laing's conception of the goal of psychotherapy is much closer to Sartre's than it initially appears to be, as is most apparent in Laing's description of the relation of the schizoid subject to their self as a 'vicious circle', whose overall effect is to prevent the subject from living because their preoccupation with trying to affirm the existence of a self that they experience as unreal, insubstantial and divided precludes them from entering into meaningful 'creative' relationships with others (1969: 88).

The most important differences between Laing's and Sartre's therapeutic approaches are therefore to be found in the particulars of interpretation. So, let us now look to Laing's analysis of the ostensibly meaningless 'schizophrenese' (Laing's term) of Julie, a chronic schizophrenic patient. This analysis is preceded by a 'clinical biography' that chronicles the development of her illness and sets the stage for Laing's interpretations of how Julie's speech communicates her terror of truly relating to others. For example, Julie states: 'This child's mind is cracked. This child's mind is closed. You're trying to open this child's mind. I'll never forgive you for trying to open this child's mind. This child is dead and not dead' (1969: 202). Laing takes these remarks to betray Julie's wish to remain in her isolated state, which seems to her to be much safer than that of being in relations with others. The paradox in the last sentence is particularly telling in Laing's view because it conveys Julie's thought that 'by remaining in a sense dead, she can be not dead in a sense, but if she takes responsibility for being "really" alive, then she may be "really" killed' (1969: 202). The Sartrean existential analyst would, I believe, agree with Laing on all this but they would depart from Laing on the meaning of Julie's pronouncements that she has the power to be anything she wants: 'I'm Rita Hayworth, I'm Joan Blondell. I'm a Royal Queen. My royal name is Julianne' (1969: 203). Laing emphasizes the contrast between Julie's claims to complete control over her being and her lack of 'freedom, autonomy, or power in the real world' and infers from this that she is 'a girl "possessed" by the phantom of her own being', which suggests that her consciousness is 'inhabited' by a foreign force, albeit a very familiar one (1969: 203). The Sartrean analyst would agree with Laing on the significance of the contrast between Julie's imaginings and her reality, but rather than follow Laing in inferring that she is, in some sense, 'possessed', they would interpret Julie's avowed beliefs in her ability to be anything she desires as behaviour that attempts to 'crystallize' her imaginings and as part of her project to keep the imaginary cover she draws over her reality intact.

Another difference between a Sartrean and a Laingian approach is to be found in Laing's interpretation of Julie's paranoid belief that he was stealing her thoughts, which Laing articulates in syllogistic form:

> She is thinking thoughts a, b, c.
> I express closely similar thoughts a1, b1, c1.
> Therefore, I have stolen her thoughts. (1969: 199)

Laing deems Julie's accusation of his having her brains in his head to be 'completely psychotic' (1969: 199). And of course, when it is articulated in this form, Julie's conclusion does not follow from her premises. But Laing does not do full justice to the understandability of Julie's position here, seemingly because he takes analytical logic as the gold standard for assessing the rationality of a belief: Julie's belief that he can steal her thoughts is 'completely psychotic' because it cannot be supported by analytical logic. Because the Sartrean existential analyst replaces analytical logic with dialectical reason, though, they would be able to go further than Laing in comprehending Julie's belief from her perspective. They would be able to see how for Julie, who lives in an imaginary world where phenomena such as thought broadcasting, thought stealing, thought insertion are everyday occurrences, her conclusion is not entirely unsupported by her experience. Further, if we can comprehend how the alternative to Laing being able to steal her thoughts – i.e. ontological solitude – is too terrifying for Julie to countenance, then we can see how this would give her a strong motivation to regard her view that Laing steals her thoughts as being rooted in a kind of argument from 'best explanation'.

These two examples highlight what I believe to be the two main ways that Sartre's interpretive approach would differ from Laing's: it would draw on Sartre's theory of how the imaginary functions as an alternative to reality in various psychopathological conditions and it would use dialectical reasoning to uncover the human motivations for 'irrational' beliefs and behaviours. There is also a third way in which Sartre's interpretations would depart from Laing's that is worth calling attention to here, which concerns the family. While both thinkers underline the importance of subject's family to their self-formation, Laing, at least in *The Divided Self*, puts the larger sociological issues 'in parentheses' on the grounds that they are not of 'direct and immediate relevance' to the question of why any individual becomes psychotic (1969: 180).[11] Sartre, however, raises no doubt as to 'the priority of institutions' in his psychoanalysis, which regards the family as 'a certain individual manifestation of the family structure appropriate to such and such a class under such and such conditions' (SM/QM: 61/87).

Existential principles for integrative psychotherapy

'Integrative psychotherapy' does not denote a specific mode of psychotherapy but rather an international movement that strives to overcome the limitations of 'single-school' approaches to psychotherapy, as well as the lack of constructive dialogue between these schools in the twentieth century (Goldfried et al. 2011). Although many psychotherapists have not given up their allegiance to a single school, the vast amount of evidence suggesting that the different modes of psychotherapy taught by each of these schools are equally effective (Frank and Frank 1993; Wampold et al. 1997; Luborsky et al. 2002), coupled with that finding that psychotherapy is generally effective (Lambert 2013), has led to an increased scepticism in the field about the possibility 'of finding any one psychotherapy that can deal with all psychological and relational problems' (Goldfried et al. 2011: 289). Consequently, an integrative approach to psychotherapy has been hailed as a 'zeitgeist' in the field (Castonguay et al. 2015: 365) and even as the sixth 'paradigm' or 'force' in psychotherapy – following psychoanalysis, behaviourism, humanistic-existential approaches, various 'transpersonal' approaches and social justice (Fleuridas and Krafcik 2019).

Even though integrative psychotherapy is thought to have been motivated in part by the proliferation of psychotherapeutic schools (Norcross 2005), the movement has led to further proliferation, with numerous integrative psychotherapies being established in recent years, including, for example, Multimodal Therapy (Lazarus 2005), Cyclical Psychodynamics (Wachtel 1997), Cognitive Analytical Therapy (Ryle and Kerr 2002), Dialectical Behaviour Therapy (Linehan 1993), Cognitive-Behavioural Assimilative Therapy (Castonguay et al. 2004), Mindfulness-Based Cognitive Therapy (Teasdale et al. 2000) and Assimilative Psychodynamic Therapy (Stricker and Gold 1996). Furthermore, as a 'promiscuous "mix and match"' of interventions and techniques has been found to produce poor outcomes (Albeniz and Holmes 1996: 569), therapists who seek to engage in integrative practice without aligning themselves with any particular school of integrative psychotherapy face the problem of which 'pathway' to choose. At present, there are four established pathways to psychotherapy integration: atheoretical, effectiveness-based 'technical eclecticism'; the 'theoretical integration' of two or more therapies; 'assimilative integration', which supplements a primary therapy with specific elements from other psychotherapeutic systems; and the atheoretical 'common factors' approach, which emphasizes the therapeutic impact of factors shared across psychotherapeutic modalities over those that distinguish them (Castonguay et al. 2015).

Altogether, this means that the task of navigating the many routes to psychotherapy integration is one of the greatest challenges facing psychotherapists today. The aim of this section is not to present Sartre's existential psychoanalysis as an integrative (existential-psychoanalytic) psychotherapy that is somehow 'better' than others, nor to propose it as another pathway to psychotherapy integration. Rather, it is to indicate how integrative therapists of all stripes may look to Sartre's existential psychoanalysis for new principles to enhance their practice. Precisely because it is a heuristic method, without any fixed principles of practice, but which is rooted in a single, coherent existentialist theory, it can provide psychotherapists with theoretical principles that support their integrative practice, which can also acknowledge the value of a plurality of psychotherapeutic techniques as well as the centrality of 'common factors' to a positive psychotherapeutic outcome.

To offer a specific example, let us consider how Sartre's existential psychotherapy could help practitioners of existential-integrative therapy. Kirk J. Schneider has developed a methodological framework for existential-integrative psychoanalysis, partly in response to the ambivalent reception of existential psychotherapy in the profession. He reports that he finds the reasons for ambivalence expressed in the 'mixed reaction' of psychotherapy students who are, on the one hand, profoundly moved by existentialist insights into the human condition and, on the other, perplexed about how to translate them into therapeutic interventions (2007: 1). As part of his project to provide a clear framework for an existential-integrative approach, Schneider outlines both its conception of consciousness and of psychopathology in a sketch that spans just twelve pages. This sketch of the theoretical basis of existential-integrative psychotherapy also attempts to unite the thought of a range of thinkers as diverse as behaviourist B. F. Skinner, post-Freudian 'self psychologist' Heinz Kohut, and Christian existentialist Paul Tillich, whose views about the nature and reality of the self are at least *prima facie* incompatible. Thus, unless the existential-integrative psychotherapist engages in extensive further reading and takes on the difficult task of reconciling the ideas of the various thinkers cited in Schneider's sketch, they can only look to his hypothetical seven-level model of consciousness and condensed account of the existential goal to 'maximize' freedom as the theoretical basis for their practice. Like Schneider's approach, Sartrean existential psychoanalysis has the capacity to be both 'complementary to' and 'integrative of' other psychotherapeutic modalities (2007: 3), since its only essential practical feature is the presence of positive reciprocity in the therapeutic alliance. But it has the advantage of being able to supply therapists with a rich, coherent psychological theory, built upon the insights Sartre won through a long career studying consciousness.

Now we have seen how Sartre's existential psychoanalysis can help theoretical psychotherapy integration, but can it do anything for atheoretical approaches? In short, I believe it can by supplying them with a flexible theoretical basis to support their integrative style. Atheoretical integrative approaches run the risk of reducing the effectiveness of the very techniques they select for their effectiveness when they extract them from their theoretical context. As Safran and Messer note, the attempt to extract common principles of practice can lead one to 'lose sight of important features of the overall therapeutic system and the process through which it works' (Safran and Messer 1997: 143). Although research over the last few decades certainly supports Bruce E. Wampold's (2001) conclusion that the factors common to all established modes of psychotherapy make a greater contribution to client outcome than specific techniques (Lambert and Barley 2001), the conclusions of such studies are not fine-grained enough to serve as a guide for psychotherapy practice (Fromme 2011). The growing evidence for the efficacy of common factors cannot, therefore, be held up as evidence for the dispensability of specific techniques. To be sure, the therapeutic relationship or 'alliance' between therapist and client is the quintessential common factor across all modes of psychotherapy, and large-scale studies of client outcome indicate that a strong alliance catalyses positive therapeutic outcome and may even be a curative factor in its own right (Lambert and Barley 2001; Flückiger et al. 2018). But this does not imply that the *same kind* of alliance is effective across the board, for all clients. Recent meta-analyses point to an association between the satisfaction of the humanistic 'core conditions' of the therapeutic alliance – i.e. therapist empathy, unconditional positive regard and congruence – and positive treatment outcome (Elliot et al. 2018; Farber et al. 2018; Kolden et al. 2018); yet, the alliance and the specific techniques that therapists employ are, as Lundh observes, partly overlapping categories since 'the use of technique for the purpose of helping another person achieve certain psychological goals' is what sets the therapeutic relationship apart from other interpersonal relationships (2017: 61). Therapists working within different modalities can satisfy the core conditions while also conceiving of their role within the relationship differently and behaving differently as a consequence: cognitive-behavioural therapists will *direct* clients to more 'adaptive' cognitions, person-centred therapists will be *nondirective*, psychodynamic therapists will *interpret* their client's unconscious communications, etc.

Further, the finding that the person of the therapist plays a significant role in determining the outcome of psychotherapy[12] points to the need for therapists to possess a robust theoretical framework that gives them confidence in their approach and makes it meaningful for them. The dominant explanation for the phenomenon of 'therapist effect' in the psychotherapeutic literature is that the most effective, 'expert' therapists possess the ability to produce theoretically coherent conceptualizations of their clients' difficulties (Betan and Binder 2010). One author even proposes that the 'route to maximum effectiveness for any therapist' is to experience the therapy they practise as *theirs* by serving as a means through which they can express their own 'deeply held view of the human condition' (Simon 2006: 343). I submit that Sartre's existential psychoanalysis provides therapists with the theoretical tool they need to produce coherent case conceptualizations and to work in ways that allow them to express their existential views, without constraining them in the methods they choose to treat and build their relationships with their clients.

By way of concluding this discussion of how Sartre's existential psychoanalysis can provide principles for integrative psychotherapy, it is important to illustrate how it is compatible with the application of therapeutic techniques other than those of traditional psychoanalysis. To my mind, it is clearly compatible with the application of techniques from Transactional Analysis (TA), a school of psychotherapy founded by Eric Berne (1910–70), whose treatment for depression has recently been manualized (Widdowson 2016). TA has its roots in psychoanalysis but uses simplified terms such as 'Adult', 'Child', 'script', 'game' to enhance communication and empower clients (Stewart and Joines 2012: 8). It also recognizes, as Sartre's mature existentialism does, how habitual forms of thinking can trap subjects in vicious cycles of behaviour that prevent their choice from influencing their process of self-formation. It theorizes these habitual forms of thinking as ready-made 'life scripts', which are either forced upon subjects or taken up by them in the course of their socialization. The goal of TA is autonomy,[13] which it proposes can be gauged by the extent to which subjects can be themselves or 'off script' when they are with others. Through the systematic analysis of transactions, TA strives to make clients aware of their life scripts so that they can abandon them and 'get-on-with' living in the present (Stewart and Joines 2012: 123). The use of the tools honed by transactional analysts to identify scripts and to liberate people from them can be supported by a case conceptualization along Sartrean-existential lines, as a rigid adherence to a script can be interpreted as a form of defensive aggressiveness that places the subject in 'prison without bars'.

A helpful clinical illustration of TA is provided by Mark Widdowson in his study of the treatment of Alastair, a forty-two-year-old senior executive who suffered from anxiety and depression. In the tenth session, Alastair was invited to explore the origins of his sense that 'he should be different to who he was' (2014: 69), which the therapist took to represent part of Alastair's life script – specifically, his 'Don't Be You' injunction. Alastair recounted occasions during his childhood when he felt 'not good enough' and remarked that although he no longer felt this way, he feared that he was not liked by others. The therapist then brought this feeling into the 'here and now' by asking Alastair what it was like to 'be in therapy with someone who he felt disliked him', to which Alastair responded by stating that he had no reason to think he was disliked by his therapist and 'lots of reasons to think the opposite' (2014: 69). This example highlights some core characteristics of TA practice: the identification of 'scripty' feelings, the analysis of transactions between therapist and client, and the therapist challenging the client to re-evaluate his life script, as well as providing a protective environment in which the client feels permitted to transcend 'the programming of the past' (Berne 1964: 162). This manner of analysing a client's lived experience and challenging their beliefs from another human perspective would be justified by a Sartrean-existential conceptualization of Alastair's case that works to comprehend his 'Don't Be You' injunction as part of the strategy he developed to cope with his situation.

Existential e-therapy

Psychotherapists and psychoanalysts today must negotiate ever-increasing demands for 'e-therapy', that is, therapy through electronic forms of media. As I am writing this book during the world crisis of the Covid-19 pandemic, the inability of therapists to deliver in-person care, combined with the fact that anxiety and depression appear to be common psychological reactions to the pandemic (Rajkumar 2020), has meant that this demand has been experienced by many as an urgent need. Although large-scale clinical trials assessing the effectiveness of various e-therapies have yet to be conducted, evidence suggests that face-to-face therapy and e-therapy are similarly effective in treating clients' symptoms (Backhaus et al. 2012; Hilty et al. 2013; Norwood et al. 2018). However, therapists continually rate the effectiveness of e-therapy as lower and report that they find it much harder to develop strong alliances with the clients they treat via electronic media (Norwood et al. 2018; Cataldo et al. 2021).

In her book-length study of computer-mediated psychoanalysis and psychotherapy, psychoanalyst Gillian Isaacs Russell argues that while e-therapy is useful in situations where in-person care cannot be provided, it should be recognized as a poor substitute for face-to-face therapy because mediating the therapeutic relationship invariably degrades it. Russell's argument for her pessimistic view of e-therapy is mainly built upon her understanding of the role of 'presence' in the therapeutic relationship. In brief, Russell takes the goal of psychotherapy to be to 'establish an authentic sense of self' (2015: 134) and she conceives of the self as the unity of the body-mind, whose integrity is determined by the extent to which the subject experiences herself as a whole, bounded, agential being in the world. Accordingly, Russell argues that a person's sense of self is inextricably linked to 'presence', understood as a subject's sense that they are a discrete, spatiotemporally situated being capable of realizing their intentions through actions that alter their environment in ways that can win them recognition from others. The mere illusion of presence or 'telepresence' that characterizes computer-mediated relations can never offer clients a satisfactory substitute for real presence in therapy, since shared space is the condition for truly being with, and being vulnerable before, another. In face-to-face therapy, the *potential* to 'kiss or kick' the therapist is *there*, in the room. This potential is of the upmost importance to the end of self-discovery for the client in Russell's view as it represents the client's potential to test their therapist's 'capacity to bear the impact of their love and hate in the flesh and not protected by the barrier of the screen' (2015: 181).

Without denying that people can comprehend one another much more easily when they are 'co-present', Sartre's existentialism provides grounds for (cautious) optimism about the potential to develop effective computer-mediated therapeutic relations for the main reason that it denies that people's selves are really present 'in' their bodies to begin with. While Russell views therapy as a process 'directed toward patients becoming able to know themselves and their feelings, to feel fully present inside and outside, to be whole selves' (Russell 2015: 148), Sartre's ontology places the self outside the subject and denies that it can ever be unified with the subject who continually creates it. Further, as the goal of Sartre's psychoanalysis is transformative knowledge of the self, gained through an awareness and acceptance of the self as the objective product of the ongoing dialectic between the subject and the world, the electronic mediation of the therapeutic relationship does not represent an insurmountable obstacle to the attainment of that goal. However, a Sartrean psychoanalytic approach would emphasize the importance of appreciating how the therapist and client's joint adventure involves different possibilities, limitations and risks when it is undertaken through an electronic medium. Although e-therapy removes certain possibilities and risks, it introduces new ones: the client may, for example, surreptitiously record the therapy session and then share it out of context. Kicking and recording are both potential ways to wound the therapist, but the key difference between them from a Sartrean perspective is that they each attack a different analogon for the therapist's self. Kicking assaults the physical body, while producing and sharing the recording assaults the virtual one – i.e. the collection of information and images that stand for the self in cyberspace. As the virtual body is arguably more important to the therapist's professional reputation and esteem than their physical body, e-therapy may involve greater risk to the therapist's self than in-person therapy.

This may provide an important clue about the solution to the puzzle posed by the disparity between clients' generally positive and therapists' generally negative evaluations of videoconferencing therapy (VCP) (Cataldo et al. 2021).

One proposed explanation for the finding that the working alliance in VCP is inferior to that in face-to-face therapy but VCP and face-to-face therapy are equally effective is that increased 'client empowerment' in VCP compensates for the inferior alliance (Norwood et al. 2018: 805). This suggests that the lack of 'co-presence' may be compensated by a more balanced relationship, more conducive to positive reciprocity. Indeed, Cataldo and colleagues conclude from their literature review of the therapeutic relationship in VCP that VCP may be more cognitively demanding for therapists, who have to work around the new (tele)presence, lower levels of confidence and reduced control over the environment enveloping the therapeutic relationship, which suggests that clients may have to do more to support their therapists emotionally (2021: 9). Findings that clients tend to feel less inhibited and are more likely to disclose personal information when therapy is delivered electronically (Jerome & Zaylor 2000; J. Simpson et al. 2001; Himle et al. 2006) may therefore be interpreted as the fruit of greater reciprocity between therapist and client in electronically mediated therapeutic relationships. Altogether, this supports the view that functions of face-to-face therapy can be 'potentially analogued' (Walther and Hancock 2005), so long as both parties are prepared to trust and support one another when they work with one another this way. If this is correct, then Sartre's existential psychoanalysis lends itself to practise through various forms of electronic media because it interprets the human body as one analogon for the self among others and supplies us with tools to analyse the ways that other objects can function as analoga for selves.

Suggestions for further research

This book has shown that Sartre's development and applications of his psychoanalytic method enabled him to complete his original response to the problem of other minds and to refine his existentialist conception of the self. This conception aims to revolutionize our understanding of the self-other relation and, thereby, provide the basis for more profound empathetic understandings of existential loneliness, anguish and psychological oppression, as well as of the role of the imagination in self-formation. In this final section, I wish to highlight some avenues for future inquiry opened by this exposition of the philosophical significance of Sartre's existential psychoanalysis, but which could not be explored within the scope of this book.

The first and perhaps most important of these concerns Sartre's understanding of the role of the imagination in the precipitation of psychological illnesses, which he takes to be characterized by a pathological preference for the imaginary over the real, one which is objectively 'mad' but subjectively comprehensible as a strategy for surviving in an unliveable situation. This leads him to endorse Laing's view that schizophrenia ought to be reconceived of as a comprehensible response to a specific social situation. A cursory glance at the criteria for schizophrenia provided in the fifth edition of the *Diagnostic and Statistical Manual of Mental Disorders* (DSM-5), however, shows that the mainline psychiatric view of the illness has not changed significantly since the 1960s, when Laing described it as the view that schizophrenics 'suffer from some inherited predisposition to experience and to act in a predominantly meaningless way, and that an unknown genetic defect acts in some as yet undetermined biochemical-endocrinological-organic manner to produce a change' (Laing 1964: 186).[14] The definitive characteristics of schizophrenia listed in the DSM-5 are (1) delusions, (2) hallucinations, (3) 'disorganized speech (e.g. frequent derailment or incoherence)', (4) 'grossly disorganized' or 'catatonic' behaviour, and (5) other 'negative symptoms', such as 'avolition' or diminished capacity for emotional expression, with the presence of either (1), (2) or (3) being necessary for diagnoses (American Psychiatric Association 2013: 99). From this, we can see that what defines schizophrenia from a medical perspective are its negative features: namely, the lack of reason, will and/or stable connection with reality, which dispose the subject to act in ways that are devoid of meaning. And yet the status of schizophrenia as a meaningless biological disease appears to be belied by the continued failure of the 'medical model' to treat it well,[15] which was one of the main reasons for Laing's (1964) denial that it should be treated as a somatic disease.

Recent developments in the field of phenomenological psychiatry suggest that there is a growing recognition of the value of phenomenological approaches to the study of psychopathologies in the English-speaking world.[16] Josef Parnas and Peter Handest have, for example, offered a detailed study of the anomalous experience reported in the prodromal phases of schizophrenia to highlight how an understanding of the positive, subjective features of the illness represents an 'embarrassing psychopathological lacuna', which, they believe, blinds clinicians the first symptoms of the illness (2003: 121). By attending to the subjective features of schizophrenia – e.g. a profound sense of alienation from others and the world, a sense of the self as unreal, fragmented experience, and impaired higher cognitive function – phenomenological researchers have identified two core abnormalities in schizophrenic experience: exaggerated self-consciousness or 'hyper-reflexivity' and the dissolution of the first-person perspective at the pre-reflective level (Uhlhaas and Mishara 2007; Parnas and Sass 2011). This has led them to conceive of schizophrenia as a pathology of the self, which has already delivered promising results: self-pathologies have been found to be effective in discriminating schizophrenia-spectrum diagnoses from others (Parnas et al. 2005) and predictive of new schizophrenia-spectrum disorders (Parnas et al. 2011).

Now, although Sartre's early work on the ontogenesis of the self is often cited in passing in the phenomenological literature on schizophrenia, scant attention has been given to his theorization of schizophrenia as a pathology of the imagination.[17] But Sartre's later conception of the self as an imaginary dialectical object could provide the basis for a new, 'self-centred' approach to treating schizophrenia that could enable analysts to go beyond establishing the general structures of schizophrenic experience towards gaining a comprehension of its 'metaphysical tenor' for individual schizophrenics. Parnas and Handest hint at this potential in their summary of Peter's transition from prodromal schizophrenia to schizophrenia, where they note that Peter progressively infuses his self with more imaginary content through delusions that they note have a 'metaphysical taint' that is specific to schizophrenia in virtue of involving the subjectivization of the world – i.e. the placement of the self at the centre of the universal system of meaning rather than just a personal one – as well as an acute sense of selflessness (2003: 131). This paradoxical excess and deficiency of self in schizophrenic experience also makes it amenable to interpretation through Sartrean psychoanalysis, which can work to uncover its particular dialectical sense for individual schizophrenics in a way that could provide important clues about how their illness functions as a solution for them.

A second potential avenue for future research concerns Sartre's revelation of the family as an agency of psychological oppression. As Sartre sees it, aspects of the broader social context are intensified and reinterpreted within the family unit: the social microcosm within the macrocosm. As each individual's family represents their point of entry into the social macrocosm and provides them with the first framework for interpreting their social being, an individual's mode of insertion into the social microcosm of the family is taken to have a significant bearing on the way they perform within the macrocosm. Hence, Sartre's psychoanalysis concentrates on 'the process by which a child groping in the dark, is going to attempt to play, without understanding it, the social role which adults impose upon him' (SM/QM: 60/85). Through its concentration on the politics of looking as it is figured within the family, it can appreciate both the alienation from self we experience when we try to make ourselves a certain object *for others for ourselves* – that is, when we try to be who we want to be – and the deeper, more disempowering form of it we experience when we try to make ourselves a certain object *for others for others* – when we try to be who our parents (and other significant others) want us to be based on the social norms and expectations they have internalized – a way of being that Sartre believes can literally drive people mad and which he thinks characterizes the experience of psychological oppression.

Although Webber notes that Sartre's interpretation of Genet's family as an 'immediate instrument' for the wider society is limited in that it neglects to attend to the way that social prejudicial ideas tend to be both perpetuated and reinterpreted within families over generations via specific family rituals, stories, expectations and behavioural styles (Webber 2018: 202), Sartre's attention to Flaubert's proto-history – i.e. Flaubert's parents' family backgrounds – shows that the most developed form of his existential psychoanalysis does attend to this and can therefore help therapists interpret clients' situation in terms of both the social macrocosm and social microcosms. For example, Sartre argues that the critical Look Flaubert received from his father due to his learning difficulties condemned him to experiencing himself as a passive object in his relations with others for the rest of his life. But he also offers an explanation of why Dr Flaubert was so infuriated by his second son's prolonged illiteracy, which draws on a discussion of Dr Flaubert's background and which reveals him as a man with a point to prove ever since his employment as a surgeon enabled him to become a first-generation member of the middle class. Hence, Sartre's explanation of his anger: 'out of seven children, four are dead and one of the living has no brain. What he loved in Gustave was his own spermatic power; if the pretty little boy is brainless from birth, that success becomes a failure' and the paterfamilias is 'unmanned' (FI I/IF I: 357/369). Gustave's learning difficulties are thus interpreted by his father as a wound to *his* pride due to the specific way that the social class and gender expectations he has internalized shape his outlook.

This highlights the centrality of the politics of looking as it is played out within the family to a subject's self-formation as well as how experiences of personal distress and interpersonal conflict can be imbued with social meanings that subjects may not be aware of. The psychological oppression that occurs within the microcosm of family is therefore connected, in Sartre's view, to the structures of domination and control within the macrocosm, but not in any simple way. Psychological oppression within the family unit may drive subjects to self-harming hexis as it does in the cases of Genet and Flaubert, but it may also conceivably drive them to sadistic hexis too. People who are psychologically oppressed by their family but occupy positions of privilege within their society may, for example, try to compensate for the feelings of inferiority they experience in the microcosm by exploiting their membership in oppressor groups in the macrocosm, as Lucien, the protagonist of *The Childhood of a Leader*, appears to do. I believe that a greater understanding of the dynamics between the psychological oppression of individuals within the family and the structures that support the oppression of groups within society could furnish valuable insights into how prejudicial ideas are internalized and perpetuated, and the extent to which familial factors can protect individuals from or increase their vulnerability to them.

A third avenue for further investigation that is opened by this study of Sartre's existential psychoanalysis also concerns the politics of looking. Cannon identifies different categories of experience of the Look, noting that it can be experienced through actual looks but also through words and touches or the absences thereof, since all these are ways through which others can communicate the value we have for them. People may have been deprived of certain categories of the Look and not others and Cannon notes that it is important for therapists 'to discover which category of the Look wounded the child or which kind of response was denied to him' (1991: 113). If, however, our capacity to Look is partly determined by our general outlook, which partly determined by our situation, this could impair therapists in their capacity to provide their clients with the alternative Look that allows them to see their selves in a new light. We have seen an example of this in Chapter 5, where Sartre is shown to have been blinded to the positive dialectical counterparts to Flaubert's misanthropy and misogyny. Although Sartre appears to have been unaware of the biases that limited his capacity to see certain aspects of Flaubert, he may have been more aware of how his own metaphysical attitude tainted his perspective had he himself been analysed by another. But whether existential analysis can uncover the prejudices individuals harbour in ways that allow them to counter them remains an open question.

This leads to my fourth and final, and most tentative, suggestion, which is that the existentialist approach to 'reading' objects as analoga for selves could, potentially, be extended beyond bodies and texts[18] to any object through which a subject makes their mark on the world, including the *corpus delicti* or body of the crime. Sartrean existential psychoanalysis may offer a way of accounting for what many expert criminal profilers already do but which remains relatively undertheorized. Expert criminal profiler John Douglas is often asked about how he develops such specific descriptions of likely suspects by examining the crime scene alone. His answer is that 'if you want to understand Picasso, you have to study his art. If you want to understand a criminal personality, you have to study his crime' (Douglas and Olshaker 1995: 366). Douglas conceives of his approach to understanding the criminal mind as the inverse of the one generally adopted by mental health professionals who start from personality theories. His team start by examining behaviour, then they make inferences about personality from that perspective, which is to say, they derive their ideas about the subjective from what is objectively given, as Sartrean psychoanalysis does. While rivalling personality theories can constrain the thought of profilers (Kocsis 2007), existential psychoanalysis is not another personality theory. It teaches us that if we want to be able to predict how someone will act with some degree of accuracy, we need to know what their projects are, not what their personality type is. As Sartre writes of Genet, we can try to reduce the vices of a criminal to a 'psychological defect' but to do so would be to ignore their being as 'an absolute consciousness which approves of itself and chooses itself' (SG: 588/649) – their human being, which is also ours. Sartre's existential psychoanalysis strives to show us that we are entirely capable of comprehending criminal, mad and morally monstrous human beings if we have the courage to accept that it is only because we have made different choices that their qualities are not ours.

Notes

Introduction

1. To my knowledge, there has been no book-length treatment of Sartre's relationship with psychoanalysis from a philosophical perspective in either French or English. Betty Cannon's book *Sartre and Psychoanalysis: An Existentialist Challenge to Clinical Metatheory* is the only book-length study of Sartre's psychoanalysis in English. As the title suggests, it approaches Sartre's psychoanalysis from a clinical perspective, with a view to instigating developments inspired by it in therapeutic practice.
2. Sartre did, however, make a genuine attempt at self-analysis when he was writing his autobiography, *Words* (1964). During this time, he also asked Pontalis to analyse him, but Pontalis refused on account of their long friendship (Hayman 1986: 363–4).

Chapter 1

1. See Avramides (2001: 1–18), Dreyfus and Tayler (2015: 1–26) and Ryle (2009: 1–13) for discussions of Descartes' tremendous influence on the picture of our relation to the world, others and ourselves that is typically taken for granted in Western society.
2. The last lines of 'Intentionality: A Fundamental Idea of Husserl's Phenomenology' gesture towards the view that there is no self within consciousness; *The Transcendence of the Ego* offers a rigorous argument for this view, aspects of which are further developed in *Being and Nothingness* (see, especially, Pt. 2, Ch. 1); and, throughout his career, Sartre maintains that consciousness does not have contents or an interior life, that it is irreducible to a self and that the self is an object for consciousness (SG: 589/650; IWS: 11; OIF/SIF: 117/100).
3. Not all pure reflection is phenomenological in Sartre's view (TE: 23/48), although all genuine phenomenological reflection is pure. The performance of the phenomenological reduction facilitates a form of pure reflection that yields apodictic certainty concerning the form of the consciousness reflected on for Sartre. But his understanding of the phenomenological reduction differs from Husserl's in important respects. Notably, Husserl presents it as a method that

enables him to apprehend *himself* 'purely', 'as Ego', with his 'own pure conscious life', 'in and by which' the whole objective world exists for him ([1931] 1960: 21), whereas Sartre views it as a reduction to consciousness 'purified' of anything apart from its being as an intentional relation to its object.

4   Husserl distinguishes between the *epochē* and the phenomenological (or transcendental) reduction. He describes the former as the bracketing of 'naturalist' claims that rest on the assumption of the 'General Thesis according to which the real world about me is at all times known not merely in a general way as something apprehended, but as a fact-world *that has its being out there*' (Husserl [1913] 2002: 56), and the latter as the leading back from constituted phenomena towards the constituting, that is, transcendental consciousness, understood as a '*self-contained system of Being*' (Husserl [1913] 2002: 95). But this distinction is not upheld neatly by Sartre in *the Transcendence of the Ego*, which presents the *epochē* and the phenomenological reduction as one and the same. After he writes *The Transcendence of the Ego*, though, Sartre discovers that the *epochē* and the phenomenological reduction are distinct reductions, abandons the Husserlian idea that the *epochē* is a prerequisite for the phenomenological reduction, and performs some phenomenological reductions from within the 'natural attitude' (Flynn 2014: 80).

5   Husserl later outlines how he arrived at this discovery as follows: 'If I put myself above all this life and refrain from doing any believing that takes "the" world straightforwardly as existing – if I direct my regard exclusively to this life itself, as consciousness of "the" world – I thereby acquire myself as the pure ego, with the pure stream of my *cogitationes*' (Husserl [1931] 1960: 21).

6   As all reflection involves a shift from pre-reflective to reflective consciousness, it invariably '*modifies* spontaneous consciousness' (TE: 13/32). Indeed, no reflection upon spontaneous consciousness can truly yield knowledge of it, since even pure reflection introduces 'a division within consciousness insofar as its structure makes of consciousness an *object* to itself' (Richmond 2004: xix–xx).

7   Although Sartre does not explicitly describe pure reflection in these terms in *The Transcendence of the Ego*, he affirms that the 'I' of the Cartesian *cogito* is 'not apodictic' (TE: 15/35) and attributes the failure of Husserl's reflection on the 'I think' to deliver an accurate picture of the self-consciousness relation to its impurity (TE: 15/35). In *Being and Nothingness*, he describes the phenomenological form of (pure) reflection that he believes yields apodictic evidence in detail (Pt. 2, Ch. 2: §3).

8   In phenomenology, the term 'intentional' does not mean the same thing as 'willed'; rather, it denotes the essential feature of consciousness as an awareness, as always being 'of' or 'about' something. For Sartre specifically, intentionality also implies that consciousness depends on its objects for its own existence because it exists only through its relation to them, by always going beyond itself towards them, without being anything in itself or having any 'inside' ([1939] 2002/1990: 383/10).

9   For his early interpretation of Husserl's phenomenology (as well as his later critique of it in *Being and Nothingness*), Sartre is indebted to Martin Heidegger. His early rendering of intentionality may be considered Heideggerian insofar as it interprets the Husserlian consciousness as a 'consciousness-in-the-world' ([1939] 2002/1990: 383/11), whose fundamental relation to its objects is pragmatic. Thomas R. Flynn observes that Sartre's early (mis)interpretation of Husserl's phenomenology seems to respond to Heidegger's main objection to Husserl's phenomenology – namely, that it construes our primary relation to the world in a theoretical manner rather than a practical one – 'in advance' (2014: 64).

10 Contrary to Sartre's claim that Husserlian phenomenology is concerned with 'de facto problems' (TE: 4/17), Husserl holds that phenomenology is '*not as a science of facts*' but '*a science of essential Being*' that aims to establish '"knowledge of essences" (*Wesenserkenntnisse*) and *absolutely no "facts"*' through its assumption of a transcendental attitude that 'purifies' the phenomena of everyday experience ([1913] 2012: 3). Further, while Sartre affirms that phenomenology grants us access to a 'real' consciousness (TE: 4/18), Husserl regards his phenomenology as 'a theory of essential Being' that deals 'not with real but transcendentally reduced phenomena' ([1913] 2012: 4). All appearances that have been subjected to the process of transcendental purification via the *epochē* are 'non-realities' in Husserl's estimation because all of their connections with the 'real world' have been severed so that they may be studied not in 'their singular particularity' but in 'their essential being' ([1913] 2012: 4). Sartre's early misinterpretation of the aims of Husserl's phenomenology is explained by Sartre's later admission that he initially read Husserl as a metaphysical realist (IWS: 25).

11 Sartre's insistence that the being we each call 'I', '*with its personality*, is ... a centre of opacity' (TE: 8/25, emphasis added) overlooks the extent to which the self that survives Husserl's phenomenological reduction is scathed. As Dan Zahavi puts it, Husserl's transcendental ego is both 'pure' and 'poor' (2014: 83); it is a self stripped of all the factors that individuate it, and so it does not resemble anything like the personal, historical, character we each call 'I'. Although, to my mind at least, Sartre's phenomenological argument against the existence of a transcendental ego still holds for the ego that appears within Husserl's phenomenological attitude – which is merely as a formal correlate to the flux of experiences that replace one another – insofar as it is only discovered through a reflection that extends beyond an instant of pre-reflective experience.

12 As Sarah Richmond suggests, it is likely that Sartre intended to exploit the potential of the title, *The Transcendence of the Ego*, for a double reading, since this work aims to both establish the self as a transcendent object for consciousness and convince his readership to 'transcend' the mistaken conception of the self that the Cartesian philosophical tradition has imposed upon us (2004: x).

13 In *The Transcendence of the Ego*, Sartre describes anguish as a 'fear of oneself' that he believes to be 'constitutive of pure consciousness' (TE: 49/83). In *Being and Nothingness*, he characterizes it as freedom's apprehension of itself (BN/EN: 79/74).

14 Although we might be tempted to interpret 'consciousness of consciousness' as a 'knowledge of knowledge', Sartre urges us to resist the idea that the non-positional consciousness that consciousness has of itself is a form of knowledge (BN/EN: 10/18). Knowledge, for him, can only ever be knowledge of objects, so '*knowledge of consciousness*' could only ever describe 'a consciousness that is complete in itself and directed toward something that it is not' (BN/EN: 10/18).

15 By the time he writes *Being and Nothingness*, Sartre believes Husserl misunderstood the 'essential character' of intentionality and this is what led him to locate part of the self inside consciousness in a move which turns consciousness away from the world and back into itself. Rather than returning to 'the things themselves' as promised, Sartre reads Husserl's phenomenology to revert to the orthodox view that our cognitive powers cannot reach beyond our subjective representations of things to the things themselves. On this basis, Sartre criticizes Husserl for having become a 'phenomenalist' (*phénoméniste*) who dissolves objects of consciousness in thought, for never passing 'beyond the pure description of appearance as such' and for locking consciousness inside the *cogito* (BN/EN: 121/109).

16 Kenevan also acknowledges problems with her proposed modification. In particular, she notes that the possibility of such a spilt appears to reinstate the notion of there being two worlds: one of inner appearances and one of outer reality, which is precisely what Sartre tries to reject through his interpretation of intentionality. This leads her to conclude that the problem of authentic self-consciousness may be part of a broader problem associated with the very notion of a 'non-positional awareness of existence that is more basic than what is given through intentional objects' (1981: 208).

17 I borrow this term from Matthew Ratcliffe, who proposes that our sense of reality, in combination with our sense of belonging, '*is* the "world" that we take for granted in the natural attitude' (2012: 482). Support for Sartre's understanding of the centrality of a stable sense of self for psychological wellbeing can be found in phenomenological studies which show that a loss of the usual sense of self ('depersonalization') typically coincides with a compromised sense of reality ('derealization') in schizophrenia. See Laing (1969), Uhlhaas and Mishara (2007), Parnas and Sass (2011), Sass and Ratcliffe (2017) and Ch. 7 of this volume for further discussion.

18 An 'internal negation' for Sartre denotes 'a relation between two beings, where the one that we deny in relation to the other qualifies the other, at the heart of its essence, precisely by its absence' (BN/EN: 249/211). Hence, all relations of consciousness take the form of internal negations in his view because consciousness is a nothingness that depends on objects that *are not it* for its own

existence. For a clear and helpful exposition of the function of internal relations in Sartre's phenomenological ontology, see Morris (2008: 43–6).

19 Indeed, Sartre once characterized *Being and Nothingness* as an 'eidetic analysis of self-deception' (Sartre as quoted by Cumming [1981: 61]). Simone de Beauvoir also states that *Being and Nothingness* is largely a study of 'the serious man and his universe' (EA/MA: 46/60), where the term 'serious' refers to a particularly deplorable form of bad faith. For a further discussion of this view, see Howells (1988: 14–26).

20 To name but a few book length studies of bad faith in English: *Bad Faith, Good Faith and Authenticity in Sartre's Early Philosophy* (1995) by Ronald Santoni; *Good Faith and Other Essays: Perspectives on a Sartrean Ethics* (1996) by Joseph Catalano; and *Sartre Explained: From Bad Faith to Authenticity* (2008) by David Detmer.

21 This is with the notable exceptions of Betty Cannon's observations in *Sartre & Psychoanalysis* and Jean-Pierre Boulé's analysis of Sartre's own search for authenticity in *Sartre, Self-Formation and Masculinities*.

22 Social characteristics such as 'waiter', 'waster', 'judge', 'dentist', 'Jew' and 'woman' are 'unrealizables' for the existentialist philosopher because consciousness cannot be anything in-itself for-itself. 'As I exist for myself', Sartre writes, 'I am no more a teacher or a café waiter than I am handsome or ugly, Jewish or Aryan, witty, vulgar or distinguished' (BN/EN: 685/572), for it is only when I am objectified in the eyes of another than I take on such characteristics. Beauvoir also presents femininity as an 'in-itself that is unrealisable' (SS/DS: 595/ II: 401).

23 Indeed, the location of Sartre's analysis of conducts of bad faith at such an early stage in the work, prior to the analysis of human sociality in Part III, has been recognized as a major source of confusion and misunderstanding concerning the function of bad faith in the secondary literature (Eshleman 2008a).

24 Matthew Eshleman, however, suggests that analogy between the attitude of bad faith and the natural attitude is helpful in comprehending the former, which he characterizes as a 'natural' overestimation of the power of language to define us (2008a).

25 Sartre states that there are two ways that we can attempt to flee anguish: through trying to apprehend oneself either 'as *an Other*' or 'as *a thing*' (BN/EN: 84/78).

26 'Conflict is the original meaning of being-for-the-Other' (BN/EN: 483/404).

27 Sartre's examples of conducts of bad faith in the second chapter of *Being and Nothingness* are considered in isolation from the rest of the subject's life and, as Robert Solomon points out, with the possible exceptions of the discussion of a case of a frigid woman borrowed from Wilhelm Stekel's *La femme frigide* (BN/EN: 96–7/88–9) and the analysis of sadness (BN/EN: 105–6/95–7), they are neither based on real experience nor phenomenological (2006: 155–63). Rather, they are all illustrations of proposed prototypical conducts of bad faith.

28 The 'nature' we have for others escapes us and is 'unknowable as such' (BN/EN: 360/302).
29 Beauvoir develops the concept of seriousness by considering its social function, which leads her to affirm that serious people are dangerous because they are dogmatic in their views. It is 'natural', she writes, for the serious man to make himself a tyrant because by contriving to ignore 'the subjectivity of his choice, he pretends that the unconditioned value of the object is being asserted through him; and by the same token he also ignores the value of the subjectivity and freedom of others, to such an extent that, sacrificing them to the thing, he persuades himself that what he sacrifices is nothing' (EA/MA: 49/65).
30 This view that the moustache is a marker of a bourgeois brand of bad faith for Sartre appears to be confirmed in the final volume of *The Family Idiot*, where Sartre insists that the garbs and the aesthetic of the bourgeoisie are part of the intricate cover that the whole class has collectively fabricated to conceal their responsibility, hatred and self-hatred from themselves (FI V/IF 3: 230/249).
31 Sartre affirms that the object that I am for others is 'not an image cut off from me and vegetating within a foreign consciousness' but a being that is 'perfectly real'; it is 'my *being-outside*', not in the sense that it comes to me 'from the outside', but in the sense that is it 'taken up' by me and 'recognized as my outside' (BN/EN: 388/325).
32 As Moran sees it, a 'report' has an explanatory structure, it is 'grounded in evidence' and does not necessarily imply the reporter's commitment to its truth, whereas an 'avowal' does not require an explanatory structure or evidential basis as it is simply 'the expression of one's own present commitment to the truth of the proposition in question' (2001: 86).
33 See O'Brien (2003: 376–82) for further discussion of the need for Moran to specify the epistemic model that his account of self-knowledge employs.
34 Moran suggests that psychoanalysis cures by allowing the analysand to (re)discover the avowal route to self-knowledge. He illustrates this point by emphasizing the crucial therapeutic difference between a merely 'intellectual' acceptance of a psychoanalytic interpretation in the context of psychoanalytic treatment – which is usually considered a form of 'resistance' – and the process of 'working-through' – which yields a full, felt apprehension of the truth of an interpretation and effects a change in the analysand's mental life as a whole. This, for him, signals that the key aim of psychoanalysis is to provide the analysand with 'self-knowledge that obeys the condition of transparency' (2001: 89–90).

Chapter 2

1 Although notable exceptions to this rule include Webber (2018, 2009), Catalano (2010) and Lennon (2015).

2   The kind of creatures that philosophers generally refer to as 'zombies' are different from the creatures of the same name in popular culture in the important respect that they do not seem to be mindless (Kirk 2019). Outwardly, 'philosophical zombies' – or, rather, philosophy's zombies – function exactly as ordinary human beings do but the conscious experience that accompanies human functioning is absent in them. So, as David Chalmers puts it, there is 'nothing it is like' to be this sort of zombie (1996: 95).

3   No major philosopher has provided a serious, sustained defence solipsism. Bertrand Russell writes that the logician Christine Ladd Franklin was an avowed solipsist, but he does not report the details of her argument for this view, which he dismisses on the grounds that it is 'psychologically impossible to believe' ([1948] 2009: 161).

4   The argument from analogy was a popular response to the epistemic problem of other minds throughout the twentieth century. See, for example, Ayer (1946), Hampshire (1952), Hyslop and Jackson (1972) and Russell (2009), and there has been at least one recent attempt to reinforce it (Sollberger 2017).

5   For an informative discussion of this point, see Hyslop (1995: Ch. 1).

6   As the argument from analogy does not solve the epistemological problem of other minds, its popularity and persistence are most likely due to two other factors. The first is that attempting to justify an inference to other minds appears to be the best means of responding to the epistemological problem of other minds from the first-person perspective (Chalmers 1996). Second, the argument from analogy also offers an intuitive solution to *another* problem about other minds: the 'descriptive' problem, which is concerned with describing the processes through which we actually come to attribute minds to others, but not with whether these processes provide sufficient rational justification for our doing so.

7   An attitude of resignation is, perhaps, one of the most common responses to the problem of other minds in contemporary philosophy. The recent resurgence of interest descriptive problem of other minds – which questions how we actually acquire knowledge of other minds but brackets concerns about the justification of such knowledge – has, for example, been interpreted as part of a general trend of 'leaving behind traditional epistemological concerns with radical scepticism' (Avramides 2019).

8   This is with the exception of Heidegger, who is criticized, in the main, for his proposal that '*Mitsein*' or 'being-with' is the fundamental form of human relation, which Sartre believes to be contradicted by the phenomenology of social experience (BN/EN: 340–4/286–9).

9   I am indebted to Emmy van Deurzen and Clair Arnold-Bakers' depiction of the process of intentionality (2018: 31) for my depiction of Sartre's conception of the structure of consciousness's relation to the other-as-object.

10 Shame is the primary form of being-for-others in Sartre's view because relating to others-as-objects requires bad faith: I must constantly employ 'ruses' to distract myself from the certainty that others can look at me in order to ensure that they remain objects for me (BN/EN: 402/336).

11 Sartre does explicitly state whether he is referring to others as subjects or objects at numerous points, though (BN/EN: 352–3, 376–7, 397–402/296–7, 315–16, 332–7).

12 In his fifth Cartesian meditation, Husserl observes that what appears to another cannot be given to me since then 'it would be merely a moment of my own essence [*qua* subject of experience], and ultimately he himself and I myself would be the same' ([1931] 1960: 109). Sartre reiterates this point in his statement that 'the only consciousness that can exist [for me] without in any way apprehending or refusing me' and, thereby, being part of the structure of my consciousness 'is not a consciousness isolated somewhere outside the world, but my own' (BN/EN: 387/324).

13 Further evidence that Sartre is not attempting to supply a positive metaphysical result in response to the epistemological problem of others minds in his chapter 'The Other's Existence' is his admission that it is possible to experience shame when nobody is in fact there, looking. His examples of shame even have this possibility worked into them since they depict shame as being triggered by the perception of objects that refer to the other-as-subject: 'the convergence of two eyeballs towards me', the rustling of branches, the movement of a curtain, the sound of footsteps, a farmhouse at the crest of a hill, etc. (BN/EN: 353/297). It follows from this that the solipsist's nightmare is a possibility: all the eyes that look at me could be artificial; there may never actually be anybody at the other end of the Look I experience.

14 Perhaps the most often quoted line of Sartre's is that spoken by the character Garcin towards the end of *Huis clos*: 'Hell is ... other people!' (2000: 223). Certainly, Sartre's depictions of human interactions in *Being and Nothingness* emphasize the misery of relations lived in bad faith (Webber 2011), but his later work also attends to positive authentic relations, such as love and solidarity (see Chapter 3). So, interpersonal relations need not be hellish in Sartre's view, although they often are.

15 Jesse M. Bering defines 'epistemic social anxiety' as any 'negative affective state that is associated with someone else knowing about – or threatening to know about – the self's undesirable attributes' (2008: 4), and so it has more in common with 'shame' in the ordinary sense of the term, insofar as its object is the self as a *shameful* object, which Sartre construes as a derivative of the 'pure' shame of oneself as an object that he concentrates on (BN/EN: 392/328). See Dolezal (2017) for a helpful analysis of 'pure' Sartrean shame as the basis for negative socially mediated affects.

16 See Morris (1998) for a discussion of the view that Sartre construes knowledge narrowly as empirical knowledge in *Being and Nothingness*.

17 As Wittgenstein denies that his philosophy yields discoveries because it is focused exclusively on improving the way we represent what we already know (see 2009: §401–2), it is difficult to justify its claim to 'therapeutic' status, since this rules out the possibility that it can cure through the enlightenment of the subject. Peterman suggests that it is possible to provide a 'rough and ready' justification for Wittgenstein's therapeutic method through 'an appeal to one's own experience of thinking through and helping others think through philosophical problems' (1992: 121). Although a fully satisfactory justification would need to supply empirical evidence in support of Wittgenstein's hypothesis that the viewpoints that give rise to traditional philosophical problems impair our ability to live and that the provision of alternative viewpoints can improve our ability to live. I am unaware of any empirical investigations into this hypothesis.
18 Psychoanalysis is often classified as an 'insight-orientated' therapy. Traditionally, insight into the unconscious has been viewed as 'the sine qua non of psychoanalysis' and 'the most powerful agent' of its curative process (Blum 1979: 43). Some psychoanalytic therapists today may dismiss the view that insight is the most important or even a necessary factor in engendering therapeutic change, though, as more emphasis tends to be placed on the curative power of therapeutic relationship, narrative and the provision of corrective emotional experiences (Lemma 2003: 73–93).
19 The psychoanalytic unconscious is distinct from the kind of 'automatic', 'procedural', 'implicit', 're-attentive', or 'nonconscious' processes involved in language acquisition, depth perception, facial recognition, etc., which are often referred to collectively as the 'adaptive unconscious' in cognitive and social psychology today (Wilson 2002), for the main reason that psychoanalysis is principally concerned with unconscious thoughts that it regards as having a central role in the generation of psychopathological symptoms.
20 In this case study, Freud discovers that it is only when he reiterates his clinical interpretation in the course of an interpretation of the Rat-Man's projection of a trait of his father onto him – i.e. an episode of 'transference' – that the Rat-Man could accept it because it enabled the Rat-Man to re-experience the affect that belonged to 'the very episode from the past which he had forgotten, or which had only passed through his mind unconsciously' within the context of the therapeutic relationship 'as though it were new' (CW X: 199).
21 Like the behaviourists, Sartre rejects the view that there is anything inside consciousness and he interprets behaviour in terms of the 'situation', but he criticizes the behaviourists for having lost sight of the meaning of the situation, which is determined by the subject's projects (BN/EN: 399/333).
22 Although Richmond translates 'compréhension préontologique' as 'pre-ontological understanding', I use the term 'pre-ontological comprehension' here to emphasize

the point that it involves the intuitive grasp of the sense of the object as an experiential Gestalt as opposed to a theoretical understanding, which necessarily abstracts from what is pre-reflectively comprehended.

23 Sartre's early reading of Henri Bergson's *Les données immediates de la conscience*, translated as *Time and Free Will*, was a major source of inspiration for his conception of human being as a flight into the future (Hayman 1986: 186; Flynn 2014: 22–3). Breeur even interprets Sartre's pre-reflective consciousness as a radicalization of Bergson's idea of duration (2001: 178).

24 This dyad is not without psychoanalytical precedent. Indeed, the distinction Freud makes between the ego and the 'ego ideal' or super-ego is analogous to that which Sartre sets up between self and Self in the important respect that it makes a 'contrast between what is real and psychical, between the external world and the internal world' (CW XIX: 36). However, rather than functioning as a kind of 'conscience' that enforces internalized social standards, the Sartrean Self haunts consciousness by continually making it aware of the gulf between it and the Self it strives to be.

25 'Cathexis' is an economic concept in Freudian psychoanalysis that refers to the 'psychical energy' that mental representations of the instincts possess and which some analysts believe connects psychoanalysis to the field of neurophysiology (Laplanche and Pontalis 1973: 62–5).

26 In his 1926 *Encyclopaedia Britannica* entry on 'Psycho-analysis', Freud makes it clear that psychoanalysis construes instincts as the ultimate source of human behaviour. He states that 'psycho-analysis derives all mental processes (apart from the reception of external stimuli) from the interplay of forces, which assist and inhibit one another, combine with one another, enter into compromises with one another, etc.' and that all of these forces are 'originally in the nature of *instincts*' and therefore have an 'organic origin' (CW XX: 265). In his essay on 'The Claims of Psycho-analysis to Scientific Interest', he also states that he regards the concept of 'instinct' as being 'on the frontier between the spheres of psychology and biology' (CW XIII: 182).

27 *Le Mystère en pleine lumière* is the title of Maurice Barrès' 1926 novel.

28 Because it posits the Other as an object from the very beginning, Freud's metapsychology has an epistemological problem about Others: Freud admits as much when he states that our assumption of consciousness in other persons must rest upon an inference from analogy and so 'cannot share the immediate certainty which we have of our own consciousness' (CW XIV: 165).

29 In Chapter 3, we shall see that the objectivity of the Sartrean existential psychoanalyst is a special, dialectical objectivity, which differs significantly from the objectivity of the natural scientist.

Chapter 3

1. I follow Jonathan Webber in distinguishing between Sartre's 'initial' and 'mature' forms of existentialism (2018, 113–30). I take the former to find its fullest articulation in *Being and Nothingness* (1943) and the latter in the *Critique of Dialectical Reason* (1960).
2. Sartre's terms 'being-for-itself' and 'being-in-itself' carry much the same sense as Hegel's terms 'being-for-self' and 'being-in-itself' in *Phenomenology of Spirit*, where they are used to designate the two essential aspects of the appearance of an object or the internal relation between consciousness and an object that constitutes a moment of consciousness. However, Hegel construes this relation as a relation of knowledge (Hegel 1977: §82), rather than a relation of being, which is what ties Hegel's phenomenology to an idealist metaphysic in Sartre's view.
3. Kojève's interpretation of Hegel's work was a source of inspiration for Sartre. Although Sartre did not attend Kojève's famous lectures on Hegel's *Phenomenology of Spirit* in the 1930s (Flynn 1997: 24), he frequently refers to the published version of them, *Introduction à la lecture de Hegel* (*Introduction to the Reading of Hegel*), in his *Notebooks for an Ethics* (1992/1983: 17, 56, 58–9, 62, 64, 68–9, 71–2, 90, 164, 452/24, 62, 64, 68–9, 73, 97, 172, 467).
4. Hegel regards consciousness as the 'immediate existence of Spirit' because it is through being consciousness (of objects) that 'Sprit becomes object because it just is this movement of becoming an *other to* itself' (1977: 21). Consciousness is thus but a moment of Spirit in the Hegelian system; hence, the consciousness of an individual counts for very little in his picture of reality.
5. 'Objective' is placed in 'scare quotes' here because, as we shall see, Sartre's dialectical notion of objectivity is different from scientific objectivity in that it does not exclude subjectivity.
6. Sartre describes Hegel's identification of knowledge with its object as 'Hegelian dogmatism' (CDR I/CRD I: 21–2/141).
7. Sartre believes that his synthesis of the insights of Hegel with those of Kierkegaard allows him to offer what he takes to be essentially 'the same reproach' to Hegel as Marx (SM/QM: 13/20). See McBride (1991: 74–80) for an informative discussion of Sartre's interpretation of Marx's political philosophy.
8. Hazel E. Barnes translates Sartre's 'matérialisme réaliste' as 'realistic materialism' (1981a: 662), rather than 'realist materialism' as Alan Sheridan-Smith does (CDR I: 29). I follow Barnes's translation here because Sartre's endorsement of a materialist position in his mature work does not also commit him to metaphysical realism.
9. The validity of psychoanalysis's claim to scientific status remains the subject of much critical dispute. Some commentators deny that psychoanalysis meets the

criteria for a scientific discipline (Wittgenstein 1969; Popper 1983; Grünbaum [2002] 2015); others contend that psychoanalysis is, or at least has the potential to be, a science (Wallerstein 1986; Petcocz 2015; Lacewing 2018); while others argue that it should be categorized as a form of hermeneutics (Habermas [1968] 1971; Ricœur 1970) or a development of common-sense psychology (Gardner 1995).

10 Freud's note that his topographical conception of the psyche 'has *for the present* nothing to do with anatomy' in his essay on 'The Unconscious' strongly suggests that he envisions that developments in scientific technology will permit us to connect the mental apparatus it identifies to particular regions of the body (CW XIV: 175).

11 See, for example, SS/DS, Fanon ([1952] 1986), Beauvoir (1972/1970), Bartky (1990), Liebow (2016) and Manstead (2018).

12 For example, Bartky observes that the way society treats psychologically oppressed persons is similar to the way in which psychiatrist R. D. Laing proposes schizophrenic children are treated by their parents: 'professing love at the very moment they shrink from their children's touch' (Bartky 1990: 31).

13 In 1975, Sartre affirms that the war initiated the 'great change' in his thinking (IWS: 12).

14 Sartre argues that the young Flaubert forces his emotions 'just the young Baudelaire did' in *The Family Idiot* (FI II/IF II: 27/679), which suggests that he did not reject all the conclusions of his earlier study and that his experience of analysing of Baudelaire's childhood informed his approach to Flaubert's.

15 The notion that transcendence could become trapped in a circular movement allows Sartre to account for the so-called compulsion to repeat without making recourse to unconscious instincts. The hypothesis of a repetition compulsion is deployed by psychoanalysts to explain why subjects put often themselves into the same sorts of distressing situations time and time again but believe these situations to be 'fully determined by the circumstances of the moment' (Laplanche and Pontalis 1973: 78). Laplanche and Pontalis also observe that disagreement among psychoanalysts about which instincts are responsible for the compulsion to repeat is the source of a great deal of confusion in the psychoanalytic literature. As Cannon points out, from an existentialist perspective, the compulsion to repeat may be 'reconceived as a desire for the security of the known over the fearful confrontation with a self who never *is* but is instead always in the process of *becoming*' (1991: 317).

16 Sartre maintains that Baudelaire's dandyism expresses his membership in an imaginary 'suicides' club', which allows him to think of himself a member of an elite group of artists whose existence was justified in advance, in a way that excuses him, in his mind, from action and interaction (B: 146/136).

17 Sartre tells us that Genet's whirligigs employ the same pattern of circular sophistry as The Argument of Epimenides, which goes, 'Epimenides says that Cretans are

liars. But he is a Cretan. Therefore he lies. Therefore all Cretans are not liars. Therefore he speaks the truth. Therefore Cretans are liars. Therefore he lies' and so on (SG: 332–3/371).

18 *Being and Nothingness* describes 'instants' as 'marvellous moments in which the prior [fundamental] project collapses into the past in the light of a new project which arises on its ruins' (BN/EN: 621/520-1). But Sartre abandons the notion that subjects can be liberated from their original choice by the time he writes *Saint Genet*, where he states that he distrusts 'illuminations' since what we often take for discoveries are familiar thoughts that we have not yet recognized (SG: 406/453) and speaks instead of 'conversions' and the assumption of new behavioural ways of interpreting the original choice, which may be more or less 'adaptive' (see, e.g., SG: 49–52, 425, 449/63–6, 473, 499, and Webber 2018: 125–30 for discussion).

19 Nor, arguably, was hell other people for earlier Sartre since the sadomasochistic circles that characterize human relations in *Being and Nothingness* are a result of bad faith (Cannon 1991: 99; Webber 2011).

20 For example, Sartre describes the struggle of the proletariat as a 'circle of hell' on account of their progress being continually undone by the bourgeoisie's modification of prices (CDR II/CRD II: 45/55).

Chapter 4

1 Aspects of Achille-Clèophas and Caroline's relationship that become more understandable in the context of an 'exceedingly incestuous' marriage (FI I/IF I: 80/89), include: Achille-Clèophas sending Caroline back to boarding school and only permitting her to leave on the eve of their wedding (FI I/IF I: 76/85), and Caroline not displaying any signs of vexation when her husband paid a visit to a former mistress and left her standing outside, in the street, with their children (FI I/FI I: 87–8/96–7).

2 Sartre notes that, 'thanks to analysts', the tendency of a deprived childhood towards repetition with other children is well documented and so, 'if the former orphan who had recovered an incestuous father could succeed in creating an ameliorated version of her own childhood with a child of her own sex' (FI I/IF I: 81/90), she could supplement her images of own unhappy childhood with images of her daughter's happy one. He also takes the fact that Caroline gave her name to her daughter as further evidence for this view.

3 Some may worry that Sartre's choice to blame the mother for the son's misfortunes may be more a consequence of patriarchal logic than of dialectical reason. Additionally, Sartre admits in an interview that he does not like Flaubert's mother (OIF/SIF: 114/96), so there could be reason to assert that Sartre's negative

assessment of Caroline Flaubert's mothering is a case of the investigator finding what he is looking for. However, as we shall see below, Sartre holds Flaubert's father (who in the same interview Sartre admits to liking) equally accountable for Flaubert's constitution because he *could have* saved him but did not, which shows that Sartre is also critical of the male parent.

4   Sartre notes that 'even the most lucid critics' have been duped into thinking that Flaubert's portrayal of Dr Larivière has only one dimension (FI I/IF I: 440/454, see, for example, Bart 1967: 6). Had Flaubert simply wanted to paint an admirable portrait of this physician, Sartre contends that he would have introduced him at any juncture other than the one he did: when it is too late to save Emma's life. To the question of what Dr Larivière actually does in the novel, Sartre's answer is that he makes a grand entrance, makes a correct diagnosis, humiliates his colleague, then flees from the scene. Thus, Sartre concludes that this portrait of Dr Larivière is 'black and white' (FI I/IF I: 443/457).

5   Lest the term 'Golden Age' should seem deceptively positive, Sartre assures us that, in reality, it was most probably 'a period of rather gloomy estrangement' in which Gustave experienced the 'the intermittent presence and rather lukewarm tenderness of an overworked father' (FI I/IF I: 348–9/360).

6   The scientific reason for this cruel experiment was to settle once and for all the question that had troubled the Academy: whether a human and an ape could produce offspring. However, M. Paul also has less 'honourable' motivations: pride (he had made a bet that he could pass and ape off as a man) and revenge (the slave girl he locks in the room with the orangutan had previously rejected his sexual advances) (EW/OJ: 89/256–7).

7   In the conclusion of this tale, Flaubert abruptly switches from the third person to the second person. Speaking directly to the reader, he writes: 'You probably insist on a conclusion, don't you?' (EW/OJ: 102/272) – a technique he will famously use again at the beginning of *Madame Bovary*.

8   In *The Family Idiot*, Sartre refers to the process of self-formation as '*personalization*' (FI II/IF II: 8/658). But I use the term self-formation in this study for consistency.

9   The two other strategies Sartre suggests render the subject's original relation to the world unreal. The first interprets the nonassimilable aspect as a reproach of another (which may be false or flawed), while the other projects the nonassimilable aspect onto others (FI II/IF II: 5/655).

10 Sartre uses the image of a spiral to describe the totalizing movement of self-formation: '[W]e might well conceive of this movement in a three-dimensional space as a multicentered spiral that continually swerves ... making an indefinite number of revolutions around its starting point' (FI II/IF II: 7/657).

11 Although Sartre views Caroline Commanville's claim that Flaubert once obeyed Pierre the chef when he asked him to '[r]un to the kitchen ... and see if I'm there'

as a fabrication (*IF* I: 17–19/*FI* I: 7–9), the evidence indicates that little Gustave suffered from what Sartre calls a 'disease of truth' (*maladie de la Vérité*) (FI I/IF I: 156/164).

12 Sartre shows that Flaubert's preference for motherly women is reflected by his infatuations with Elisa Schlésinger and Louise Colet, who were both mothers and older than he (FI II/IF II: 52/704).

13 This choice of comparison is not random, as Sartre's 1954 adaption of Alexandre Dumas' play, *Kean*, explores the idea that people may be drawn to acting because it allows them to experience 'ideal' emotions, which are less ambiguous and more aesthetically appealing than those of everyday life.

14 Against the criticism that it may be improper to speak in terms of a 'vocation' in relation to someone so young, Sartre notes the zeal with which Gustave launched all his energies into his project to become a great actor – building by himself a miniature stage and compiling a repertoire of nearly thirty plays in just two years – and concludes that if he thrust himself into this venture, it is because 'it gave him something he was looking for, though without knowing it' (FI II/IF II: 120/775).

15 Here, 'crisis' refers to Flaubert's first attack at Pont-l'Evêque. Although Sartre sometimes also refers to this event as a 'fall' (see, e.g., FI IV/IF III: 111/1883), to avoid confusion with Flaubert's first Fall (from the graces of his father), Flaubert's first attack will only be referred to as his crisis.

16 Critics who agree that Flaubert's illness was most likely epilepsy include Enid Starkie (1967: 116), Geoffrey Wall (2006: 138) and Timothy Unwin (2004: 49). Notably, Benjamin F. Bart, in his attempt to settle the matter, submitted his report of Flaubert's symptoms to Dr Arthur Ecker, a clinical professor of neurological surgery at The Upstate Medical Center, Syracuse, New York, who confirmed the diagnosis of epilepsy (1967: 753–3n).

17 Sartre does, of course, also describe Flaubert's illness as a 'neurosis', but we shall see that Sartre does not offer this term as a 'diagnosis' but, rather, as part of an attempt to offer a precise description of the form of 'stress' that characterizes Flaubert's self-formation from 1844 onwards.

18 Sartre remains committed to the view that, in desperate situations, the body can be magically 'raised to the level of behaviour' (STE/ETE: 51/99), which he first argued for in his *Sketch for a Theory of the Emotions*. In *The Family Idiot*, Sartre interprets Flaubert's first attack in 1844 as an instance of 'magical behaviour' through which he 'turns his back danger so that it will be annihilated' (FI IV/IF III: 43/1812).

19 If we are to take Maxime Du Camp's word for it, Gustave's later attacks literally refer to the first, as he recalls that Flaubert would habitually cry 'Drop the reins; here comes the wagoner, I hear the bells! Ah! I see the lantern of the inn!' (FI IV/IF III: 15/1783). This, among other factors, including the less sudden nature of the later attacks, leads Sartre to conclude that the moment of the first attack is the only one

that counts, as this was when 'the neurosis is chosen, structured, realized' and that the purpose of the later attacks is merely to reaffirm this choice (FI IV/IF III: 16/1785). Flaubert's referential attacks say: *'I'm still just as sick'* and defend him against feelings of guilt by reconfirming his illness (FI IV/IF III: 119/1891).

20 Sartre argues that 'Loser Wins' (*Qui perd gagne*) is Flaubert's life-philosophy, which allows him to establish enough 'hope in the depths of [his] desperate soul' for him to continue to live (FI V/IF 3: 7/13).

21 Sartre cites many examples of this kind of generalization in *Agonies* and *Diary of a Madman* (*Mémoires d'un fou*) (FI III/IF III: 422–4/1536–9). Numerous instances are also discoverable in *November*, such as: 'I was exactly what all of you are, a certain man, living, sleeping, eating, drinking, laughing, wrapped up in himself' (Nov/OJ: 19/770, see also 24/774, 28/777).

22 'Neurotic literature' is in 'scare quotes' here, as Sartre does not consider *Madame Bovary* a morbid work that is underserving of its canonical status but, rather, as emerging from a specific historical moment in which 'neurosis was the royal road to the production of a masterpiece' (FI V/IF 3: 33/41).

23 In *What Is Literature?* Sartre theorizes the function of literature as the author's 'appeal' to the reader's 'freedom' (WL/QL: 122/163).

24 Sartre regards the great success of Darwin's work, *On the Origin of Species* (1859), as being partly due to the ideology of the ruling class, who approved of both its mechanistic approach and its popularization of 'two deliciously inhuman and pessimistic ideas, the struggle for life and the survival of the fittest' (FI V/IF 3: 236/256).

25 –Je hâte la dissolution de la matière!
   –Je facilite l'éparpillement des germes!
   –Tu détruis, pour mes renouvellements!
   –Tu engendres, pour mes destructions!
   –Active ma puissance!
   –Féconde ma pourriture! (Flaubert 1951: 188)

26 Notably, two of Flaubert's most famous protagonists respond with revulsion at first sight of their offspring: Emma Bovary turns her head away from her new born daughter (MB: 80/406), and Frédéric Moreau sees only 'a yellowish-red object … [that] had an unpleasant smell and was emitting loud wails' when he first looks upon his son (SE/ES: 419/506).

27 Sartre argues that Flaubert deflects his disgust about satisfying his sexual needs with prostitutes in his correspondence with Louise Colet by employing a distinctly bourgeois kind of misogyny. Flaubert is not embarrassed about attaining 'dissolute pleasures on the cheap', he maintains, because his ideology allows him to project his shame of his needs onto the female who is degraded and whose body is 'on the market' (FI V/FI 3: 341/367).

28 The fact that Flaubert presents the god-like physician, Dr Larivière, devouring a hearty meal at Homais's house immediately after he retreats from the dying Emma Bovary's bedside lends further support to Sartre's claim that Flaubert's portrayal of his father through this character is ambiguous (FI I/IF I: 441/445 and see note 4 above).

29 It may be contested that what Djalioh feels for Adèle cannot be categorized as masochistic devotion because he sexually assaults her and kills her at the end of the tale; yet, it is worth noting that Djalioh, who is only half-human, may not have been aware of the consequences of his actions and that he kills himself immediately after his crime.

30 At one point Mâtho cries about Salammbô: 'I need her! Its killing me ... I would like to sell myself and become her slave' (S: 42/82).

31 Although Justin is aware that he is insignificant to Emma Bovary, he takes pleasure in cleaning her boots (MB: 167/463) and feels 'an immeasurable sorrow' after her death (MB: 303/602).

32 Louise's love is described as 'both as pure as religion and as violent as hunger' (SE/ES: 272/335).

33 *A Simple Heart* reads like a hagiography, as the protagonist, Félicité, has apparitions of the both the Virgin Mary and the Holy Spirit, leads a life of devotion and dies a supernatural death. Bart notes that Félicité attains 'effortlessly' the sanctity that Flaubert's Saint Julien could accomplish only by enduring 'unbearable pains' (1967: 697). Sartre too recognizes Flaubert's presentation of Felicité's simplicity as admirable since she 'puts her genius into life' and does not reason but '*understands* [*comprend*] because devotion itself is a kind of understanding' (FI I/FI I: 321/332).

34 At the end of the first part of *Madame Bovary*, during Emma's first spell of depression, meals sicken her because 'it seemed to her that all the bitterness of life was served up to her on her plate' (MB: 59/385) and she begins drinking vinegar 'to lose weight' (MB: 60/386). Further, after Emma is rejected by her first lover, Rodolphe, she despairs about having to eat a meal with her husband (MB: 183/513).

35 Romantic devotion seems to lead to self-destruction too. To explain this, Sartre suggests that Flaubert's black saints appear to be made of 'such delicate stuff ... that they transform into infinite torture what for insensitive natures might be pleasure', so it is unlikely that the object of their affection will be able to understand them (FI I/IF I: 424/437-8). For example, Ernest is the object of Mazza's devotion, but we are told that *he* is not an 'exceptional soul' (EW/OJ: 103/275). Equally, all of Emma Bovary's lovers seem to be unworthy of her. Mâtho and Salammbô appear to be well matched, but their brief relationship ends in calamity when Mâtho is captured, tortured and killed by the people of Carthage and Salammbô dies of shock after witnessing it (S: 275-82/458-69).

36 Sartre uses the term '*class literature*' to designate 'a literature subservient to the needs of the upper classes' (FI V/IF 3: 273/296).

37 There is no English equivalent of 'déclassement' (IF 3: 531). Cosman translates it as 'changing class' (FI V: 499).

Chapter 5

1 Sartre recalls his delight in reading *Madame Bovary* as a child even though he was oblivious to its 'poisonous', adult significance (W/M: 37/49). He also suggests that he holds Flaubert partly accountable for his own, possibly neurotic, attitude towards writing when he states that the noxious, 'ancient bile of Flaubert' he devoured as a youth led him to confuse 'literature with prayer' and make a 'human sacrifice' of it (W/M: 113/146–7).

2 Other critics who find noting coincidental about Sartre's concentration on Flaubert include Julian Barnes (1982) and Leon S. Roudiez (1982).

3 In particular, it seems that Sartre intended to comment on the 'ugliness' of Flaubert's choice of verbs in connection with the sense of temporal vagueness he creates in his works (Notes: 188/176).

4 In an oft-cited passage from a letter to Louise Colet, Flaubert states: 'What seems beautiful to me, what I should like to write, is a book about nothing, a book dependent on nothing external, which would be held together by the internal strength of style, just as the earth, suspended in the void, depends on nothing external for its support; a book which would have almost no subject, or at least in which the subject would be invisible, if such a thing is possible' (1982/1980: 213/31).

5 Tony Tanner's classic study, *Adultery and the Novel: Contract and Transgression* (1979), illustrates how many of the novels of the nineteenth century that have since been canonized concentrate on the theme of adultery.

6 Earlier on in *November*, the narrator affirms that the sufferings of the soul 'don't kill you' and that only suicide can deliver one from them (Nov/OJ: 98/828).

7 Emma observes with intrigue the way that a woman at the ball drops her fan, then artfully drops a note into the hat of the gentleman who kneels to pick it up for her (MB: 47/372–3).

8 Mary Orr proposes that *Madame Bovary* is, specifically, *Cinderella*-in-reverse: Emma 'pretends to be Cinderella for the night by refusing to allow Charles to dance with her, as if she were single once more' and the tragedy implied by this formula is further compounded by the fact that 'the "bad" fairy godmother of fate' allows her to taste of the kind of life she dreams of after she is married, not before (Orr 2000: 37).

9   Sartre argues that this statement does not merely capture one of Flaubert's literary motifs, but a belief that is lived by the author as a 'permanent subject of anguish kept alive by self-loathing', caused by contrast between the grand ambition he is instilled with as a member of the Flaubert family and his lived sense of inadequacy (FI I/IF I: 551/570).
10 No English translation of this play exists. It is worth noting that Sartre also refers to it in *Being and Nothingness* to illustrate his notion of bad faith because it commences from our transcendence only to then 'imprison us suddenly within the narrow limits of our *de facto* essence' (BN/EN: 99/91).
11 This is a reference to the one of the two fictional Giants created by François Rabelais in his series of novels *La vie de Gargantua et de Pantagruel* (*The Life of Gargantua and of Pantagruel*). 'Pantagruelizing', as a verb in Sartre's use, refers to the act of viewing something from the perspective of a giant and abstaining from making negative moral judgements about the things one witnesses.
12 Sartre investigates Flaubert's laughter in detail in *The Family Idiot*, especially in sections: 'The Mirror and Laughter' (FI II/IF II: 23–32/674–84) and 'Laughter as the Fundamental Structure of the Garçon (or the Sadism of the Masochist)' (FI III/IF II: 144–95/1251–1303).
13 Sartre deduces that at some point between 1837 and 1838 Flaubert would have wanted to consult a priest and that he quite probably did. However, Sartre asserts that priests during this period of triumph for bourgeoisie would have been aware of their unpopularity and would have had little interest in converting the son of a 'family of freethinkers'; hence, any advice he received is likely to have been dull and uninspiring (FI I/IF I: 513–14/530–1). Such an experience, he suggests, may have left Flaubert with a grudge against priests because they failed to provide him with a satisfactory alternative to the scientism of his father.
14 In his notes for the fourth volume, Sartre also indicates that he intends to compare Emma's writing to Léon to Flaubert's own experience of writing love letters to a woman he did not love (Notes: 187/176).
15 The character of Dussardier in this novel may be considered Flaubert's mouthpiece for his despair over the political situation at this time. Towards the end of the work, he cries out: '[I]f only people would make the effort! If people were sincere, we could get on alright together! But they're not!… And there's no remedy, no way out, everybody's against us … If it goes on like this, it'll drive me mad! I'd like to get killed!' (SE/ES: 434/522).
16 What separates the committed (*engagé*) writer from the uncommitted (*désengagé*) writer, according to Sartre, is that the former 'knows that words are action', that 'to reveal is to change and that one can reveal only by planning to change' (WL/QL: 14/28).

17 'Confirmation bias' is the term used in the psychological literature to refer to the phenomenon whereby individuals unwittingly seek out and/or interpret evidence in ways that inappropriately bolster beliefs or hypotheses whose truth is in question in favour of their extant beliefs (Nickerson 1998).
18 Sartre's bibliographers describe how Sartre caused a scandal in 1966 by claiming to hold Flaubert and Edmund de Goncourt responsible for the repression that followed the 1871 Paris Commune (Contat and Rybalka 1970: 428).
19 Flaubert offers us literary descriptions of these two other possibilities for women through his depictions of Félicité, the servant in 'A Simple Heart', and Rosannette, a kept woman in *A Sentimental Education*.
20 Hazel E. Barnes (1981b: 364–5) and Mary Orr (2000) have uncovered feminist sentiments in Flaubert's literature.

Chapter 6

1 More exactly, Sartre proposes that the matter for the imaginary object is affectivity and, sometimes, also the feeling of bodily movements in Part II of *The Imaginary*.
2 We know, for example, that the way people say things is often, if not always, more important than what they say in facilitating our comprehension of their meaning. Albert Mehrabian and Susan Ferris's frequently cited quantitative study found that 'the combined effect of simultaneous verbal, vocal, and facial attitude communications is a weighted sum of their independent effects – with the coefficients of .07, .38 and .55, respectively' (1967: 252). This is the source of the famous '7-38-55' formula that aspirational politicians and businesspeople are instructed to bear in mind when thinking about how they can enhance their ability to communicate the 'right' messages to others.
3 Lacan describes his approach to psychoanalysis as a 'return to Freud' but many scholars view this 'return' as a structuralist reinterpretation of Freud (e.g. Cannon 1991; Zafiropoulos 2010).
4 Sartre now recognizes no 'unconscious' *apart from* what is lived and comprehended but unknown because it has not been articulated. We may interpret Sartre's acceptance of *a version* of the unconscious here as the culmination of a long 'conversion' to a more Freudian view of consciousness since, while no substance and no 'thing' is ever granted entry 'into' the Sartrean consciousness, its clarity is continually reduced. In 1940, Sartre defines consciousness as 'transparent to itself' (I: 6, 26, 72/19, 57, 143). In 1943, though, he describes consciousness as 'translucent' rather than transparent (BN/EN: 84, 89, 116/78, 82, 104, *passim*). Then in 1969, he affirms that consciousness is a 'lived experience' (*le vécu*) and a 'presence to itself' that is 'so opaque and blind before itself that it is also an

absence from itself' (IOT: 50), from which point he accepts opacity as a feature of consciousness. Nonetheless, he preserves his notion of (preontological) comprehension into his mature existentialism, where it is theorized as 'a silent adjunct to lived experience, a familiarity of the subjective experience with itself, a way of putting components and moments in perspective but without explanation' (IF III: 1544/FI III: 429).

5 According to Lacan, a significant factor contributing to the independence of human knowledge from the field of desire, relative to other animals, is their 'fetalization' – i.e. the premature birth of the human being as evinced by the human neonate's motor uncoordination and anatomically incomplete pyramidal system (E: 78/97) – since this creates the conditions for the formation of the infant's desire for unification with their body as imaged. So that, even prior to their entry into language, human beings' 'organic inadequacy' disposes them 'paranoiac knowledge', which is his term to describe the way that, developmentally, human knowledge is acquired only through an imaginary – and false – 'objectifying identification' with the self-other (E: 91/111), which the subject must anxiously protect from all the evidence that threatens to undermine it.

6 Lacan argues that instead of satiating the subject's desire to overcome her feelings of alienation, her unification with her self will further alienate her from her desire because it is a unification with the other that she mistakes for herself. Hence, he compares it to treating a limp by amputating the affected leg (E: 379/454).

7 Sartre observes that the anxiety associated with the Jewish complex takes a special form: unlike psychaesthenics who are plagued by fears that they might commit atrocious or obscene acts, a Jew with the Jewish complex lives in fear that she will conform to the negative stereotype others have of her. The fear of behaving like a Jew therefore overdetermines her behaviour according to Sartre, but it overdetermines her 'from the inside' because she allows it to, because she inauthentically plays at *not being a Jew* in response to it (1948/1954: 95/115).

8 It should be noted that Freud explicitly rejects the theory of complexes that he associates with the Swiss School of psychoanalysis, although he accepts that the term 'complex' can sometimes be indispensable in descriptive summaries of psychological states (CW XIV: 29–30).

9 Sartre describes the function of literary text as a physical analogon in the experience of the reader as follows: 'an entire world appears to me as imaged through the lines of the book ... and this world encloses my consciousness, I cannot disengage, I am fascinated by it' (I: 168/326).

10 Although this use of the term 'metaphysics' is consistent with Sartre's use of it in *Being and Nothingness*, where it is presented as being concerned with the reasons for being – the 'why' of it – rather than what being is (BN/EN: 801/667) and his view that each individual develops their own metaphysics to interpret the world as meaningful (BN/EN: 782/650).

11   Sartre excludes poetry from his conception of literature because he believes that poetic language lacks specific referents. He likens the poet's use of language to painter's use of colour as the poet uses language to construct an art-object to behold but, by refraining from attaching specific meanings to her words, the poet surrenders them to ambiguity and so they become 'words-things' (WL/QL: 8/22). Thus, though painters and poets may present a hovel, Sartre contends that only a literary author can describe it and make it seem like 'a symbol of social injustice and provoke your indignation' (WL/QL: 4/16).

12   While Sartre does not explicitly state that the affective sense of objects is a function of the subject's metaphysical attitude in *What Is Literature?* he does endorse a Beauvoirian view of metaphysics as a 'living effort to embrace from within the human condition in its totality' as opposed to 'sterile discussion about abstract notions which have nothing to do with experience' (WL/QL: 171/222). And I believe that this, taken together with Sartre's singling out D. H. Lawrence's works for their potential to convey the affective sense of objects that constitutes 'their deepest reality' for the fictional observer-subject while seeming only to describe their physical properties in *The Imaginary* (I: 69/139), and his discussion of how psychoanalysis reveals the 'metaphysical tenor' of qualities of objects (BN/EN: 782/650), justifies the ascription of this view to him.

13   Structuralism is an intellectual movement that may be characterized by the aim to provide scientifically rigorous analyses of social multiplicities and complex systems, a tendency to privilege whole systems over their individual elements, and a focus on language as an objective structure with its own rules of operation and means of signification. In various ways, structuralism seeks to expose the ubiquitous and multifarious effects of socio-political structures, systems of power and domination, and what Barthes calls 'the arrogant antiphrastical recriminations of good society' in people's everyday lives (Barthes 1977: 148/1994: 45).

14   Sartre emphasizes the role of the author's and the reader's freedom in his discussion of the literary work when he states: '[T]he unique point of view from which the author can present the world to those freedoms whose concurrence he wishes to bring about is that of a world to be impregnated always with more freedom' (WL/QL: 47/70).

15   In *The Imaginary*, Sartre explains that the 'primary reason' why the world of imaginary objects cannot truly constitute an alternate reality is that they are not 'individualized' through their concrete relations with all the other objects in their environment as real objects are (I: 135/260).

16   Despite championing Sartrean existentialism as a metatheory for psychotherapeutic practice, Cannon regards Sartre's concept of magical behaviour as the residue of an 'overly rationalist strain in his early philosophical thinking' because, while she accepts that emotions result from (pre-reflective) choice of being and cannot

therefore be described as something one undergoes, she denies that emotions are a magical way of changing the world through changing the subject's experience (1991: 352).

17 Sartre's comments about the relation between *The Imaginary* and *The Family Idiot* in later interviews indicate that he stands by the theory he put forward in the earlier work. In one interview, for example, he suggests that *The Family Idiot* is a development of *The Imaginary* that reflects the shift in his philosophical interests as he matured (IWS: 15). In another, he says that *The Imaginary* sought 'to prove that imaginary objects – images – are an absence', while *The Family Idiot* studies 'imaginary persons – people who like Flaubert act out roles' (IOT: 53).

18 The conditions in which it is possible to feel the way one wants to feel about the object of the imaginary act may be impossible in real life, hence Sartre's contrast between imagining punching one's enemy with really punching one's enemy. The former is enjoyable while the latter is not because, in the imaginary, this act will either not draw blood or will draw 'just as much' as one wants, but this is something one cannot control in reality (I: 146/281).

19 Sartre's conception of empathetic imaginings is, I believe, close to Matthew Ratcliffe's conception of radical empathetic experiences insofar as they are 'self-affecting' in virtue of resulting from the empathizing subject's suspension of their own metaphysical attitude and, hence, their openness to the experience of the world as having possibilities and meanings *for another* (2012: 488).

Chapter 7

1 A transference neurosis is the unconscious projection of qualities of a significant person from one's past – typically a parent figure – onto a person in the present, which leads the subject to react to their own projections, rather than the actual behaviour of the person in the present. Transference neuroses are reported to occur frequently in psychotherapeutic contexts, where they are often viewed by therapists, or at least psychoanalytical and psychodynamic therapists, to provide an invaluable opportunity to 'work through' the client's past issues in the present.

2 I borrow this concept of knowledge from David J. Kahane who argues that feminist knowledge is 'transformative' because 'getting it' means that you can no longer see or live your life in the same way (1998: 216–17).

3 Creative writing cures Genet but not Flaubert, in Sartre's estimation, because Genet's writing fails where Flaubert's succeeds. Instead of furnishing him with an experience in the imaginary that feels more real than his daydreams, writing *Our Lady of the Flowers* makes Genet's dream present on the page before him as a signification and, thereby, delivers his self to him as an object. So, as he writes,

Genet does not continue to feel the feelings that his imaginings produce in him as he hopes to, he 'ceases to feel' and 'knows that he *did* feel' (SG: 459/510). As he works to assume the role of a God-like creator, he 'connects with himself as a real creator of an imaginary world'; as he strives to lose himself in imaginary, he discovers his self as 'a man and a captive'; as he seeks refuge in lofty, proud solitude, he becomes suddenly aware of his yearning for others; as he describes the characters he creates out of nothing, he realizes that he needs readers to give them flesh (SG: 480/533–4). Writing his first novel therefore pulls him out of his onanistic inversion. Creative writing does not have the same effect on Flaubert, though, because Flaubert's alienation from his self is more total. Genet's solution to his unliveable life was to distract himself from desire for love by making it his project to be evil and unlovable, but his writing makes him confront that desire by objectifying his intention to connect with others. Flaubert's solution to his unliveable life, however, is to annihilate his self in his experience, which means that his writing only pushes his project of '*imaginarization*' to the limit (FI II/IF II: 265/926); it allows him to continue dreaming by crystallizing his imaginary self. *November*, for example, allows him to imagine himself as a 'cosmic child' who 'does not love because nothing of what *exists* is worth the trouble of loving'; it covers rather than reflects his real self as a child who lacks the love he longs for (FI II/IF II: 258/919).

4   The issue of *Les Temps modernes* in which the transcript and Sartre's analysis of it were published also contains responses from eminent psychoanalyst J.-B. Pontalis and B. Pingaud, two editorial board members who disagreed with the journal's decision to publish the transcript and resigned because of it. In his response, Pontalis contends that Sartre's interpretation of the transcript in his essay betrays a fundamental misunderstanding of psychoanalysis. Indeed, because Sartre lacked first-hand experience of psychoanalysis in a clinical setting, he could not fully understand the phenomenon of 'transference' – the client's projection of qualities they associate with 'original others', such as parents and siblings, onto the analyst. Nonetheless, Cannon rightly observes that we can appreciate that Sartre's understanding of transference is limited and still recognize that his existentialist perspective allows him to offer insights on the transcript that Freudian perspective cannot deliver (1991: 319).

5   It should be noted here that Sartre appears to be basing his criticism on a classical model of psychoanalysis that many psychoanalysts had already moved away from. D. W. Winnicott (1949), Paula Heimann (1950) and Margaret Little (1951), for example, had all published influential pieces emphasizing the importance of 'countertransference' – how the analyst is impacted by the client – as a tool in the work of psychoanalysis. Further, it should be noted that even the neutrality of the classical psychoanalyst is not indifferent or uncaring stance but a 'nonjudgemental' one (Eagle and Wolitzky 1992: 119).

6   The family therapist, Salvadore Minuchin, describes the positive changes he witnessed in the woman during her conversation with Laing as an effect of 'love' (Laing 1985: 52:45).

7   Kate Kirkpatrick notes that the Sartrean concept of reciprocity 'should not be called "Sartrean" without caveats' for the reason that Beauvoir was first to develop this concept (2019b: 30). Beauvoir's conception of love as a relation between two independent subjects is perhaps most apparent in her discussion of why love cannot flourish in the context of a traditional heterosexual marriage, where the husband does not invite his wife to 'transcend herself with him' but instead 'confines her to immanence' and the hexis of housework, which only supports his transcendence (SS/DS II: 481/256).

8   Laing is, however, much more willing to acknowledge the continuities between his existential analytic approach and Freud's than Sartre. He states that Freud was a 'hero', who had the courage to descend into 'Underworld' of the troubled psyche and survived to bring back the knowledge upon which modern psychoanalytic practice is based, and he urges psychotherapists and psychologists to explore this Underworld further 'without using a theory that is in some measure an instrument of defence' (Laing 1969: 25).

9   Laing points out that he is also indebted to Kierkegaard, Jaspers, Heidegger, Binswanger and Tillich for existential understanding of schizophrenia. However, Sartre is cited more than any of these other philosophers in *The Divided Self* – on eight separate occasions (1969: 39 n., 47, 52, 84–5, 94 n., 95, 120), including one in which Sartre's discussion of the difference between the 'real' and the 'imaginary' self is quoted at length (1969: 84–5).

10 In clinical psychiatry, 'psychosis' is used as a catchall for a broad range of illnesses whose origin may be either organic, such as general paralysis, or obscure, such as schizophrenia. In the narrower field of psychoanalysis, though, 'psychosis' denotes psychopathologies that are characterized by a disturbance in 'the relation to reality', such as delusional disorders, schizophrenia, paranoia, melancholia and mania (Laplanche and Pontalis 1973: 370).

11 As Laing's thought progressed in the 1960s and 1970s, he placed increasingly more emphasis on the role of society in 'madness'. Hence, in his note to the Pelican edition of *The Divided Self* in 1964, he notes that he was 'still writing in this book too much of Them, and too little of Us' ([1965] (1969): 11).

12 Studies suggest that the person of the therapist contributes more to the variation in psychotherapy outcome than the specific form of treatment delivered (approximately 5 per cent) and, on average, most effective therapists were twice as effective as least effective therapists (Baldwin and Imel 2013; Johns et al. 2019).

13 TA's founder, Eric Berne (1910–70), characterizes the autonomous person as one who possesses *awareness*, 'the ability to see a coffee pot or hear the birds sing in one's own way, and not the way one was taught' (1964: 158); *spontaneity* or

'liberation from the compulsion to play games and have only the feelings one was taught to have' (1964: 160); and capacity for genuine *intimacy*, which is 'much more rewarding than games' (1964: 162).

14   Although the DSM-5's recognition that the rates of schizophrenia are higher in urban environments and 'for some minority ethnic groups' (American Psychiatric Association 2013: 103) demonstrates some acknowledgement of socio-cultural predisposing factors.

15   Antipsychotic drugs remain the primary treatment for schizophrenia in the UK and the United States. However, a significant proportion – up to 40 per cent – of schizophrenics treated with antipsychotic drugs respond poorly and continue to display moderate-to-severe psychotic symptoms (National Institute for Health and Care Excellence 2014: 29).

16   With the notable exception of Laing and his colleagues, the continental phenomenological psychiatric tradition has had little influence on the Anglophone one until recently. For a discussion of this point, see Uhlhaas and Mishara (2007) and Parnas and Sass (2011).

17   Parnas and Sass, for instance, acknowledge the view that the presence of the self in experience is 'precisely that of an absence (as Sartre often implies)' before going on to state they endorse an alternative view that there is a sense of self in all experience (Parnas and Sass 2011: 527). The view of the self that Parnas and Sass endorse is Zahavian in the sense that it posits the presence of a minimal subjective self in all experience. Although Zahavi acknowledges his debt to Sartre for his view, he is critical of Sartre on the grounds that he cannot account for the first-person perspective (2000: 56–64). However, in Chapter 1, I have shown that Sartre's account of the body *as consciousness* has the first-person perspective built into it, which makes Sartre's position much closer to Zahavi's than Zahavi recognizes and, hence, also compatible with the phenomenological conceptions of schizophrenia as a pathology of the self discussed in this chapter, so long as the pre-reflective sense of selfness is clearly distinguished from the self which can only be present to consciousness as an object.

18   In his study of existentialism, Webber suggests that theoretical texts can be telling for the existential psychoanalyst too. While such texts may not be capable of providing the same kind of insight into their author's metaphysics as literary texts, they nevertheless result 'from the author's pursuit of their chosen values, where this pursuit is more or less tempered by social influences' (Webber 2018: 207). Through the production of a theoretical text, the author aims to make a contribution to knowledge by redressing what they see as an absence. So, at the very least, it could serve as an indication of what appeared to them as a 'lack' and an opportunity for them to be the person who did something about it.

References

Albeniz, A. and J. Holmes (1996), 'Psychotherapy Integration: Its Implications for Psychiatry', *British Journal of Psychiatry*, 169: 563-70.
American Psychiatric Association (2013), *Diagnostic and Statistical Manual of Mental Disorders*, 5th edn, Washington (DC): American Psychiatric Publishing.
Askay, R. and J. Farquhar (2006), *Apprehending the Inaccessible: Freudian Psychoanalysis and Existential Phenomenology*, Evanston: Northwestern University Press.
Avramides, A. (2001), *Other Minds*, London: Routledge.
Avramides, A. (2019), 'Other Minds', in E. N. Zalta (ed), *The Stanford Encyclopedia of Philosophy*. Available online: https://plato.stanford.edu/archives/sum2019/entries/other-minds/ (accessed 12 June 2020).
Ayer, A. J. (1946), 'Other Minds', *Proceeding of the Aristotelian Society, Supplementary Volumes*, 20: 188-97.
Backhaus, A., Z. Agha, M. L. Maglione, A. Repp, B. Ross, D. Zuest, N. M. Rice-Thorp, J. Lohr, and S. R. Thorp (2012), 'Videoconferencing Psychotherapy: A Systematic Review', *Psychological Services*, 9 (2): 111-31.
Baldwin, S. A. and Z. E. Imel (2013), 'Therapist Effects: Findings and Methods', in M. J. Lambert (ed), *Bergin and Garfield's Handbook of Psychotherapy and Behavior Change*, 6th edn, 258-67, Hoboken (NJ): John Wiley & Sons.
Barnes, H. E. (1981a), 'Sartre as Materialist', in P. A. Schilpp (ed), *The Philosophy of Jean-Paul Sartre*, 661-84, La Salle (IL): Open Court Publishing Company.
Barnes, H. E. (1981b), *Sartre & Flaubert*, Chicago: The University of Chicago Press.
Barnes, J. (1982), '"Double Bind": Review of *The Family Idiot* by Jean-Paul Sartre and *Sartre and Flaubert* by Hazel E. Barnes', *London Review of Books*, 10 (4): 22-4.
Barnes, J. ([1984] 2009), *Flaubert's Parrot*, London: Vintage Books.
Bart, B. F. (1966), 'Art, Energy, and Aesthetic Distance', in B. F. Bart (ed), *Madame Bovary and the Critics: A Collection of Essays*, 73-105, New York: New York University Press.
Bart, B. F. (1967), *Flaubert*, New York: Syracuse University Press.
Barthes, R. ([1977] 1994), 'The Death of the Author', in *Image - Music - Text*, trans. S. Heath, 142-8, London: Fontana/Collins/'La mort de l'auteur', in *Œuvres complètes III 1968 - 1971*, 40-5, Paris: Éditions du Seuil.
Bartky, S. L. (1990), *Femininity and Domination: Studies in the Phenomenology of Oppression*, London: Routledge.
Beauvoir, S. (de) ([1946] 2005), 'Literature and Metaphysics', trans. V. Zaytzeff and F. M. Morrison, in M. A. Simons (ed), *Simone de Beauvoir: Philosophical Writings*,

269–77, Illinois: University of Illinois Press/'Littérature et métaphysique', *Les Temps modernes*, 1 (7): 1153–63.

Beauvoir, S. (de) [1947, abbreviations: **EA/MA**] (1948/1947), *The Ethics of Ambiguity*, trans. B. Frechtman, New York: Citadel Press/*Pour une morale de l'ambiguïté*, Paris: Éditions Gallimard.

Beauvoir, S. (de) [1949, abbreviations: **SS/DS**] (2011/1976), *The Second Sex*, trans. C. Borde and S. Malovany-Chavallier, London: Vintage Books/*Le deuxième sexe*, 2 vols, Paris: Éditions Gallimard.

Beauvoir, S. (de) (1962), *The Prime of Life*, trans. P. Green, London: Penguin Books.

Beauvoir, S. (de) (1963), *Force of Circumstance*, trans. R. Howard, London: Penguin Books.

Beauvoir, S. (de) ([1972] 1970), *Old Age*, trans. P. O'Brian, London: André Deutsch and Weidenfeld and Nicolson/*La viellesse*, Paris: Éditions Gallimard.

Beauvoir, S. (de) ([1981] 1984), *Adieux: A Farewell to Sartre*, trans. P. O'Brian, London: Penguin Books.

Berg, W. J. (1982), 'Preface', in W. J. Berg, M. Grimaud, and G. Moskos (eds), *Saint/Oedipus: Psychocritical Approaches to Flaubert's Art*, 7–11, Ithaca: Cornell University Press.

Bering, J. M. (2008), 'Why Hell Is Other People: Distinctively Human Psychological Suffering', *Review of General Psychology*, 12 (1): 1–8.

Bernasconi, R. (2006), *How to Read Sartre*, London: Granta.

Berne, E. (1964), *Games People Play: The Psychology of Human Relationships*, London: Penguin Books.

Bernfeld, S. C. (1951), 'Freud and Archeology', *American Imago*, 8 (2): 107–28.

Betan, E. J. and J. L. Binder (2010), 'Clinical Expertise in Psychotherapy: How Expert Therapists Use Theory in Generating Case Conceptualizations and Interventions', *Journal of Contemporary Psychotherapy*, 40 (3): 141–52.

Blackburn, S. (2005), *The Oxford Dictionary of Philosophy*, Oxford: Oxford University Press.

Blum, H. P. (1979), 'The Curative and Creative Aspects of Insight', *Journal of the American Psychoanalytic Association*, 27: 41–65.

Boulé, J.-P. (2005), *Sartre, Self-Formation and Masculinities*, Oxford: Berghahn Books.

Breeur, R. (2001), 'Bergson's and Sartre's Account of the Self in Relation to the Transcendental Ego', *International Journal of Philosophical Studies*, 9 (2): 177–98.

Brown, F. (1982), 'Sartre's Last Chance', *New York Review of Books*, 4 February. Available online: https://www.nybooks.com/articles/1982/02/04/sartres-last-case/ (accessed 25 June 2021).

Cannon, B. (1991), *Sartre and Psychoanalysis: An Existentialist Challenge to Clinical Metatheory*, Kansas: University Press of Kansas.

Cannon, B. (1999), 'Sartre and Existential Psychoanalysis', *The Humanistic Psychologist*, 27 (1): 23–50.

Castonguay, L. G., C. F. Eubanks, M. R. Goldfried, J. C. Muran, and W. Lutz (2015), 'Research on Psychotherapy Integration: Building on the Past, Looking to the Future', *Psychotherapy Research*, 25 (3): 365–38.

Castonguay, L. G., A. J. Schut, D. E. Aikins, M. J. Constantino, J.-P. Laurenceau, L. Bolough, and D. D. Burns (2004), 'Integrative Cognitive Therapy for Depression: A Preliminary Investigation', *Journal of Integrative Psychotherapy*, 14 (1): 4–20.

Catalano, J. S. (1974), *A Commentary on Jean-Paul Sartre's 'Being and Nothingness'*, Chicago: The University of Chicago Press.

Catalano, J. S. (1996), *Good Faith and Other Essays*, Lanham: Rowman & Littlefield.

Catalano, J.S. (2010), *Reading Sartre*, Cambridge: Cambridge University Press.

Cataldo, F., S. Chang, A. Mendoza, and G. Buchanan (2021), 'A Perspective on Client-Psychologist Relationships in Videoconferencing Psychotherapy: Literature Review', *JMIR Mental Health*, 8 (2). Available online: https://mental.jmir.org/2021/2/e19004 (accessed 8 June 2021).

Caws, P. (1992), 'Sartean Structuralism?' in C. Howells (ed), *The Cambridge Companion to Sartre*, 293–317, Cambridge: Cambridge University Press.

Chalmers, D. J. (1996), *The Conscious Mind: In Search of a Fundamental Theory*, Oxford: Oxford University Press.

Charmé, S. Z. (2020), 'Existential Psychoanalysis', in M. C. Eshleman and C. L. Mui (eds), *The Sartrean Mind*, 251–63, London: Routledge.

Collins, D. (1980), *Sartre as Biographer*, Cambridge (MA): Harvard University Press.

Contat, M. and M. Rybalka (1970), *Les Écrits de Sartre: Chronologie, bibliographie commentée*, Paris: Gallimard.

Coorebyter, V. (de), '*The Transcendence of the Ego:* Reasoning and Stakes', trans. N. Bojko, in M. C. Eshleman and C. L. Mui (eds), *The Sartrean Mind*, 129–40, London: Routledge.

Cumming, R. D. (1981), 'To Understand a Man', in P. A. Schlilpp (ed), *The Philosophy of Jean-Paul Sartre*, 55–85, La Salle (IL): Open Court Publishing Company.

Descartes, R. (1997), 'Meditations on First Philosophy', trans. E. S. Haldane and G. R. T. Ross, in E. Chávez-Arvizo (ed), *Descartes: Key Philosophical Writings*, 123–90, Hertfordshire: Wordsworth Editions Limited.

Detmer, D. (2008), *Sartre Explained: From Bad Faith to Authenticity*, Chicago: Open Court.

Deurzen, E. (van) (2012), *Existential Counselling and Psychotherapy in Practice*, 3rd edn, London: Sage Publications.

Deurzen, E. (van) and C. Arnold-Baker (2018), *Existential Therapy: Distinctive Features*. London: Routledge.

Dolezal, L. (2017), 'Shame, Vulnerability and Belonging: Reconsidering Sartre's Account of Shame', *Human Studies*, 40 (3): 421–38.

Doubrovsky, S. (1995), 'Sartre's *La Nausée*: Fragment of an Analytical Reading', in C. Howells (ed), *Sartre*, 49–57, London: Longman Group Limited.
Douglas, J. and M. Olshaker (1995), *Mindhunter*, London: Arrow Books.
Dreyfus, H. and C. Taylor (2015), *Retrieving Realism*, Cambridge (MA) and London: Harvard University Press.
Eagle, M. N. and D. L. Wolitzky (1992), 'Psychoanalytic Theories of Psychotherapy', in D. K. Freedheim, H. J. Freudenberger, J. W. Kessler, S. B. Messer, D. R. Peterson, H. H. Strupp, and P. L. Wachtel (eds), *History of Psychotherapy: A Century of Change*, 109–58, Washington: American Psychological Association.
Edwards, M. (2021), 'Sartre and Beauvoir on Women's Psychological Oppression', *Sartre Studies International*, 27 (1): 46–75.
Elliott, R., A. C. Bohart, J. C. Watson, and D. Murphy (2018), 'Therapist Empathy and Client Outcome: An Updated Meta-Analysis', *Psychotherapy*, 55 (4): 399–410.
Eshleman, M. C. (2008a), 'The Misplaced Chapter on Bad Faith, or Reading *Being and Nothingness* in Reverse', *Sartre Studies International*, 14 (2): 1–22.
Eshleman, M. C. (2008b), 'Bad Faith Is Necessarily Social', *Sartre Studies International*, 14 (2): 40–7.
Eshleman, M. C. (2020), 'Introduction', in M. C. Eshleman and C. L. Mui (eds), *The Sartrean Mind*, 1–7, London: Routledge.
Fanon, F. ([1952] 1986), *Black Skin White Masks*, trans. C. L. Markmann, London: Pluto Press.
Farber, B. A., J. Y. Suzuki, and D. A. Lynch (2018), 'Positive Regard and Psychotherapy Outcome: A Meta-Analytic Review', *Psychotherapy*, 55 (4): 411–23.
Flaubert, G. [1857, abbreviation: **MB**] (2004/1951), *Madame Bovary: Provincial Manners*, trans. Margaret Mauldon, Oxford: Oxford University Press/'Madame Bovary: Mœure de province', in A. Thibaudet and R. Dumesnil (eds), *Flaubert: Œuvres*, vol. 1, 325–645, Paris: Librairie Gallimard.
Flaubert, G. [1862, abbreviation: **S**] (1977/1976), *Salammbô*, trans. A. J. Krailsheimer, London: Penguin Books Ltd./ *Salammbô*, Paris: Éditions Gallimard.
Flaubert, G. [1869, abbreviations: **SE/ES**] (2000/1965), *A Sentimental Education*, trans. D. Parmée, Oxford: Oxford University Press/*L'Éducation sentimentale*, Paris: Éditions Gallimard.
Flaubert, G. (1926), *The Complete Works of Gustave Flaubert*, trans. F. Brunetière, vol. 7, London: Privately Printed.
Flaubert, G. (1951), *Flaubert: Œuvres*, vol. 1, ed. A. Thibaudet and R. Dumesnil, Paris: Librairie Gallimard.
Flaubert, G. (1973), *Flaubert: Correspondance*, vol. 1, ed. J. Bruneau, Paris: Éditions Gallimard.
Flaubert, G. (1980), *Flaubert: Correspondance*, vol. 2, ed. J. Bruneau, Paris: Éditions Gallimard.
Flaubert, G. (1982), *The Letters of Gustave Flaubert (1830–80)*, ed. and trans. F. Steegmuller, Oxford: Picador.

Flaubert, G. [abbreviation: **EW**] (1991), *Early Writings: Gustave Flaubert*, trans. R. Griffin, Lincoln: The University of Nebraska Press.

Flaubert, G. (1991), *Flaubert: Correspondance*, vol. 3, ed. J. Bruneau, Paris: Éditions Gallimard.

Flaubert, G. [abbreviation: **OJ**] (2001), *Œuvres de jeunesse*, Paris: Éditions Gallimard.

Flaubert, G. [abbreviation: **Nov**] (2005), *November*, trans. A. Brown, London: Hesperus Press.

Fleuridas, C. and D. Krafcik (2019), 'Beyond Four Forces: The Evolution of Psychotherapy', *Sage Open*, 9 (1). Available online: https://journals.sagepub.com/doi/10.1177/2158244018824492 (accessed 29 June 2021)

Flückiger, C., A. C. Del Re, B. E. Wampold, D. Symonds, and A. O. Horvath (2012), 'How Central Is the Alliance in Psychotherapy? A Multilevel Longitudinal Meta-Analysis', *Journal of Counselling Psychology*, 59 (1): 10–17.

Flückiger, C., A. C. Del Re, B. E. Wampold, and A. O. Horvath (2018), 'The Alliance in Adult Psychotherapy: A Meta-Analytic Synthesis', *Psychotherapy*, 55 (4): 316–40.

Flynn, T. R. (1997), *Sartre, Foucault and Historical Reason: Toward an Existentialist Theory of History*, vol. 1, Chicago: The University of Chicago Press.

Flynn, T. R. (2014), *Sartre: A Philosophical Biography*, Cambridge: Cambridge University Press.

Fosshage, J. L. (2007), 'Searching for Love and Expecting Rejection: Implicit and Explicit Dimensions in Cocreating Analytic Change', *Psychoanalytic Inquiry*, 27 (3): 326–47.

Frank, J. D. and J. B. Frank (1993), *Persuasion & Healing: A Comparative Study of Psychotherapy*, 3rd edn, Baltimore: The Johns Hopkins University Press.

Fretz, L. (1992), 'Individuality in Sartre's Philosophy', in C. Howells (ed), *The Cambridge Companion to Sartre*, 67–99, Cambridge: Cambridge University Press.

Freud, S. [1900, abbreviation: **CW IV**] (1953), *The Standard Edition of the Complete Psychological Works of Sigmund Freud: The Interpretation of Dreams (First Part)*, vol. 4, trans. J. Strachey, London: The Hogarth Press.

Freud, S. [1900–1, abbreviation: **CW V**] (1953), *The Standard Edition of the Complete Psychological Works of Sigmund Freud: The Interpretation of Dreams (Second Part) and on Dreams*, vol. 5, trans. J. Strachey, London: The Hogarth Press.

Freud, S. [1901–5, abbreviation: **CW VII**] (1953), *The Standard Edition of the Complete Psychological Works of Sigmund Freud: A Case of Hysteria, Three Essays on Sexuality and Other Works*, vol. 7, trans. J. Strachey, London: The Hogarth Press.

Freud, S. [1906–8, abbreviation: **CW IX**] (1959), *The Standard Edition of the Complete Psychological Works of Sigmund Freud: Jensen's 'Gradiva' and Other Works*, vol. 9, trans. J. Strachey, London: The Hogarth Press.

Freud, S. [1913–14, abbreviation: **CW XIII**] (1955), *The Standard Edition of the Complete Psychological Works of Sigmund Freud: Totem and Taboo and Other Works*, vol. 13, trans. J. Strachey, London: The Hogarth Press.

Freud, S. [1914–16, abbreviation: **CW XIV**] (1957), *The Standard Edition of the Complete Psychological Works of Sigmund Freud: On the History of the Psycho-Analytic Movement, Papers on metapsychology*, and *Other Works*, vol. 14, trans. J. Strachey, London: The Hogarth Press.

Freud, S. [1917–19, abbreviation: **CW XVII**] (1955), *The Standard Edition of the Complete Psychological Works of Sigmund Freud: An Infantile Neurosis* and *Other Works*, vol. 17, trans. J. Strachey, London: The Hogarth Press.

Freud, S. [1923–5, abbreviation: **CW XIX**] (1961), *The Standard Edition of the Complete Psychological Works of Sigmund Freud: The Ego and the Id* and *Other Works*, vol. 19, trans. J. Strachey, London: The Hogarth Press.

Freud, S. [1925–6, abbreviation: **CW XX**] (1959), *The Standard Edition of the Complete Psychological Works of Sigmund Freud: An Autobiographical Study, Inhibitions, Symptoms and Anxiety, the Question of Lay Analysis* and *Other Works*, vol. 20, trans. J. Strachey, London: The Hogarth Press.

Fromme, D. K. (2011), *Systems of Psychotherapy: Dialectical Tensions and Integration*, New York: Springer.

Gardner, S. (1995), 'Psychoanalysis, Science, and Commonsense', *Philosophy, Psychiatry, & Psychology*, 2 (2): 93–113.

Ginot, E. (2009), 'The Empathic Power of Enactments: The Link between Neuropsychological Processes and an Expanded Definition of Empathy', *Psychoanalytic Psychology*, 26 (3): 290–309.

Goldfried, M. R., C. Glass, and D. Arnkoff (2011), 'Integrative Approaches to Psychotherapy', in J. C. Norcross, G. R. VandenBos, and D. K. Freedheim (eds), *History of Psychotherapy*, 2nd edn, 269–96, Washington: American Psychological Association.

Goldthorpe, R. (1992), 'Understanding the Committed Writer', in C. Howells (ed), *A Cambridge Companion to Sartre*, 140–77, Cambridge: Cambridge University Press.

Gosetti-Ferencei, J. A. (2014), 'The Mimetic Dimension: Literature between Neuroscience and Phenomenology', *The British Journal of Aesthetics*, 54 (4): 425–48.

Greenberg, L. (2008), 'Emotion and Cognition in Psychotherapy: The Transforming Power of Affect', *Canadian Psychology*, 49 (1): 49–59.

Grimaud, M. (1982), 'Conclusion: *Oedipus Sanctus*: Psychology and Poetics', in W. J. Berg, M. Grimaud, and G. Moskos (eds), *Saint/Oedipus: Psychocritical Approaches to Flaubert's Art*, 203–31, London: Cornell University Press.

Gross, D. S. (1985), 'Sartre's (Mis) Reading of Flaubert's Politics: An Unacknowledged Dialectic of Misanthropy and Utopian Desire', *Yale French Studies*, 68: 127–51.

Grünbaum, A. ([2002] 2015), 'Critique of Psychoanalysis', in S. Boag, L. A. W. Brakel, and V. Talvitie (eds), *Philosophy, Science, and Psychoanalysis: A Critical Meeting*, 1–36, London: Karnac Books Ltd.

Habermas, J. ([1968] 1971), *Knowledge and Human Interests*, trans. J. J. Shapiro, Boston: Beacon Press.

Hampshire, S. (1952), 'The Analogy of Feeling', *Mind*, 61 (241): 1–12.
Hatzimoysis, A. (2011), *The Philosophy of Sartre*, Durham: Acumen Publishing Limited.
Hayman, R. (1986), *Writing against: A Biography of Sartre*, London: Weidenfeld and Nicolson.
Hegel, G. W. F. (1977), *Phenomenology of Spirit*, trans. A. V. Miller, Oxford: Oxford University Press.
Heimann, P. (1950), 'On Counter-Transference', *International Journal of Psycho-Analysis*, 31: 81–4.
Hilty, D. M., D. C. Ferrer, M. B. Parish, B. Johnston, E. J. Callahan, and P. M. Yellowlees (2013), 'The Effectiveness of Telemental Health: A 2013 Review', *Telemedicine and E-Health*, 19 (2): 444–54.
Himle, J. A., D. J. Fischer, J. R. Muroff, M. L. Van Etten, L. M. Lokers, J. L. Abelson, and G. L. Hanna (2006), 'Videoconferencing-Based Cognitive-Behavioral Therapy for Obsessive-Compulsive Disorder', *Behaviour Research and Therapy*, 44: 1821–9.
Hopkins, R. (2011), 'Imagination and Affective Response', in J. Webber (ed), *Reading Sartre: On Phenomenology and Existentialism*, 100–17, London: Routledge.
Horton, S. (2017), 'The Authentic Person's Limited Bad Faith', *Sartre Studies International*, 23 (2): 83–97.
Howells, C. (1988), *Sartre: The Necessity of Freedom*, Cambridge: Cambridge University Press.
Howells, C. (1992), 'Conclusion: Sartre and the Deconstruction of the Subject', in C. Howells (ed), *The Cambridge Companion to Sartre*, 318–52, Cambridge: Cambridge University Press.
Howells, C. (2011), *Mortal Subjects: Passions of the Soul in Late Twentieth-Century French Thought*, Cambridge: Polity Press.
Hough, M. (2014), *Counselling Skills and Theory*, 4th edn, London: Hachette UK.
Hume, D. ([1739–40] 2000), *A Treatise of Human Nature*, ed. D. F. Norton and M. J. Norton, Oxford: Oxford University Press.
Husserl, E. ([1913] 2002), 'Consciousness as Intentional Experience', trans, J. N. Findlay, in D. Moran and T. Mooney (eds), *The Phenomenology Reader*, 78–108, London: Routledge.
Husserl, E. ([1913] 2012), *Ideas: General Introduction to Pure Phenomenology*, trans. W. R. Boyce Gibson, London: Routledge.
Husserl, E. ([1931]1960), *Cartesian Meditations: An Introduction to Phenomenology*, trans. D. Cairns, Dordrecht: Springer Science + Business Media.
Husserl, E. ([1936] 1970), *The Crisis of the European Sciences and Transcendental Philosophy: An Introduction to Phenomenological Philosophy*, trans. D. Carr, Evanston: Northwestern University Press.
Hyslop, A. (1995), *Other Minds*, Dordrecht: Kluwer Academic Publishers.
Hyslop, A. and F. Jackson (1972), 'The Analogical Inference to Other Minds', *American Philosophical Quarterly*, 9: 168–76.

Jaspers, K. [1913] (1963), *General Psychopathology*, trans. J. Hoenig and M. W. Hamilton, Chicago: The University of Chicago Press.

Jerome, L. W. and C. Zaylor (2000), 'Cyberspace: Creating a Therapeutic Environment for Telehealth Applications', *Professional Psychology: Research and Practice*, 31: 478–83.

Johns, R. G., M. Barkham, S. Kellett, and D. Saxon (2019), 'A Systematic Review of Therapist Effects: A Critical Narrative Update and Refinement to Review', *Clinical Psychology Review*, 67: 78–93.

Kahane, D. J. (1998), 'Male Feminism as Oxymoron', in T. Digby (ed), *Men Doing Feminism*, 213–35, London: Routledge.

Kail, M. (2006), *Simone de Beauvoir: philosophe*, Paris: Presses Universitaires de France.

Kenevan, P. B. (1981), 'Self-Consciousness and the Ego in the Philosophy of Sartre', in P. A. Schilpp (ed), *The Philosophy of Jean-Paul Sartre*, 197–210, La Salle (IL): Open Court Publishing Company.

Kirk, R. (2019), 'Zombies', in E. N. Zalta (ed), *The Stanford Encyclopedia of Philosophy*. Available online: https://plato.stanford.edu/archives/spr2019/entries/zombies/ (accessed 21 June 2020).

Kirkpatrick, K. (2017), *Sartre on Sin: Between Being and Nothingness*, Oxford: Oxford University Press.

Kirkpatrick, K. (2019a), *Becoming Beauvoir: A Life*, London: Bloomsbury.

Kirkpatrick, K. (2019b), '"Master, Slave, and Merciless Struggle": Sin and Lovelessness in Sartre's *Saint Genet*', *Sartre Studies International*, 25 (1): 22–34.

Kocsis, R. N. (2007), 'Schools of Thought Related to Criminal Profiling', in R. N. Kocsis (ed), *Criminal Profiling: International Theory, Research, and Practice*, 393–404, Totowa (NJ): Humana Press.

Kojève, A. ([1947] 1969), *Introduction to the Reading of Hegel: Lectures on the Phenomenology of Spirit*, trans. J. H. Nichols, Ithaca and London: Cornell University Press/*Introduction à la lecture de Hegel: Leçons sur la Phénoménologie de l'Esprit professées de 1933 à 1939 à l'École des Hautes Études réunies et publiées par Raymond Queneau*, Paris: Éditions Gallimard.

Kolden, G. G., C. C. Wang, S. B. Austin, Y. Chang, and M. H. Klein (2018), 'Congruence/Genuineness: A Meta-Analysis', *Psychotherapy*, 55 (4): 424–33.

Kruks, S. (1995), 'Simone de Beauvoir: Teaching Sartre about Freedom', in M. A. Simons (ed), *Feminist Interpretations of Simone de Beauvoir*, 79–96, Pennsylvania: The Pennsylvania State University Press.

Lacan, J. [1966, abbreviation: **E**] (2006/1966), *Écrits: The First Complete Edition in English*, trans. B. Fink, New York: W. W. Norton & Company/*Écrits*, Paris: Éditions du Seuil.

Lacewing, M. (2018), 'The Science of Psychoanalysis', *Philosophy, Psychiatry, & Psychology*, 25 (2): 95–111.

Laing, R. D. ([1960] 1969), *The Divided Self: An Existential Study in Sanity and Madness*, London: Penguin Books.

Laing, R. D. (1964), 'Is Schizophrenia a Disease?' *International Journal of Social Psychiatry*, 10 (3): 184–93.

Laing, R. D. ([1965] 1969), 'Preface to the Pelican Edition', in *The Divided Self: An Existential Study in Sanity and Madness*, 11–12, London: Penguin Books.

Laing, R. D. (1985), [Videotaped Clinical Presentation] 'Evolution of Psychotherapy', Phoenix, AZ: Milton H. Erickson Foundation. Available online: https://search.alexanderstreet.com/preview/work/bibliographic_entity%7Cvideo_work%7C1865889 (accessed 4 June 2021).

Laing, R. D. and D. G. Cooper (1964), 'Introduction', in R. D. Laing and D. G. Cooper (eds), *Reason and Violence: A Decade of Sartre's Philosophy, 1950-1960*, 9–27, London: Routledge.

Lambert, M. J. (2013), 'The Efficacy and Effectiveness of Psychotherapy', in M. J. Lambert (ed), *Bergin and Garfield's Handbook of Psychotherapy and Behavior Change*, 6th edn, 169–218, Hoboken (NJ): John Wiley & Sons.

Lambert, M. J. and D. E. Barley (2001), 'Research Summary on the Therapeutic Relationship and Psychotherapy Outcome', *Psychotherapy: Theory, Research, Practice, Training*, 38 (4): 357–61.

Laplanche, J. and J.-B. Pontalis (1973), *The Language of Psychoanalysis*, trans. D. Nicholson-Smith, London: Karnac Books.

Lazarus, A. A. (2005), 'Multimodal Therapy', in J. C. Norcross and M. R. Goldfried (eds), *Handbook of Psychotherapy Integration*, 2nd edn, 105–20, Oxford: Oxford University Press.

Lemma, A. (2003), *Introduction to the Practice of Psychodynamic Psychotherapy*, Chichester: John Wiley & Sons Ltd.

Lennon, K. (2015), *Imagination and the Imaginary*, London: Routledge.

Levin, H. (1972), 'A Literary Enormity: Sartre on Flaubert', *Journal of the History of Ideas*, 33 (4): 643–64.

Levy, L. (2020), 'Anguish and Bad Faith', in M. C. Eshleman and C. L. Mui (eds), *The Sartrean Mind*, 186–97, London: Routledge.

Liebow, N. (2016), 'Internalized Oppression and Its Varied Moral Harms: Self-Perceptions of Reduced Agency and Criminality', *Hypatia: A Journal of Feminist Philosophy*, 31 (4): 713–29.

Linehan, M. M. (1993), *Cognitive-Behavioral Treatment of Borderline Personality Disorder*, New York: The Guilford Press.

Little, M. (1951), 'Countertransference and the Patient's Response to It', *International Journal of Psych-Analysis*, 32: 32–40.

Luborsky, L., R. Rosenthal, L. Diguer, T. P. Andrusyna, J. S. Berman, J. T. Levitt, D. A. Seligman, and E. D. Krause (2002), 'The Dodo Verdict Is Alive and Well – Mostly', *Clinical Psychology: Science and Practice*, 9 (1): 2–12.

Lundh, L. G. (2017), 'Relation and Technique in Psychotherapy: Two Partly Overlapping Categories', *Journal of Psychotherapy Integration*, 27 (1): 59–78.

Madhusoodanan, S., Ting, M. B., Farah, T., and Ugur, U. (2015), 'Psychiatric Aspects of Brain Tumors: A Review', *World Journal of Psychiatry*, 5 (3): 273–85.

Malcolm, N. (1958), 'I. Knowledge of Other Minds', *The Journal of Philosophy*, 55 (23): 969–78.

Manstead, A. (2018), 'The Psychology of Social Class: How Socioeconomic Status Impacts Thought, Feelings, and Behaviour', *The British Journal of Social Psychology*, 57 (2): 267–91.

Manser, A (1987), 'A New Look at Bad Faith', in S. Glynn (ed), *Sartre: An Investigation of Some Major Themes*, 55–70, Aldershot: Avenbury.

Mauron, C. (1962), *Des Métaphores obsédantes au mythe personnel: Introduction à la psychocritique*, Paris: Librairie José Corti.

May, R. (1983), *The Discovery of Being: Writings in Existential Psychology*, New York: W. W. Norton.

McBride, W. L. (1991), *Sartre's Political Theory*, Bloomington: Indiana University Press.

McDowell, J. (1998), *Meaning, Knowledge, and Reality*, Cambridge (MA): Harvard University Press.

Meehl, P. (1995), 'Commentary: Psychoanalysis as Science', *Journal of the American Psychoanalytic Association*, 43: 1015–21.

Mehrabian, A. and S. R. Ferris (1967), 'Inference of Attitudes from Nonverbal Communication in Two Channels', *Journal of Consulting Psychology*, 31 (3): 248–52.

Mill, J. S. ([1865] 1872), *An Examination of Sir William Hamilton's Philosophy*, 4th edn, London: Longman, Green, Reader and Dyer.

Mirvish, A. (2020), 'Sartre and Gestalt Psychology', in M. C. Eshleman and C. L. Mui (eds), *The Sartrean Mind*, 65–74, London: Routledge.

Moati, R. (2019), *Sartre et le mystère en pleine lumière*, Paris: Les Éditions du Cerf.

Moran, R. (2001), *Authority and Estrangement: An Essay on Self-Knowledge*, Princeton: Princeton University Press.

Morris, K. (1998), 'Sartre on the Existence of Others: On "Treating Sartre Analytically"', *Sartre Studies International*, 4 (1): 46–62.

Morris, K. (2008), *Sartre*, Oxford: Blackwell Publishing.

Mouchard, C. (1971), 'Un roman vrai', *Critique*, 27 (2): 1029–49.

National Institute for Health and Care Excellence (2014), *Psychosis and Schizophrenia in Adults: Treatment and Management*. Available online: https://www.nice.org.uk/guidance/cg178/evidence/full-guideline-490503565 (accessed 4 June 2021).

Neu, J. (1988), 'Divided Minds: Sartre's "Bad Faith" Critique of Freud', *The Review of Metaphysics*, 42 (1): 79–101.

Nickerson, R. S. (1998), 'Confirmation Bias: A Ubiquitous Phenomenon in Many Guises', *Review of General Psychology*, 2 (2): 175–220.

Norcross, J. C. (2005), 'A Primer on Psychotherapy Integration', in J. C. Norcross and M. R. Goldfried (eds), *Handbook of Psychotherapy Integration*, 2nd edn, 3–23, Oxford: Oxford University Press.

Norwood, C., N. G. Moghaddam, S. Malins, and R. Sabin-Farrell (2018), 'Working Alliance and Outcome Effectiveness in Videoconferencing Psychotherapy: A Systematic Review and Noninferiority Meta-Analysis', *Clinical Psychology & Psychotherapy*, 25 (6): 797–808.

O'Brien, L. (2003), 'Moran on Agency and Self-Knowledge', *European Journal of Philosophy*, 11: 375–90.

O'Shiel, D. (2019), *Sartre and Magic: Being, Emotion and Philosophy*, London: Bloomsbury Academic.

Orr, M. (2000), *Flaubert: Writing in the Masculine*, Oxford: Oxford University Press.

Overgaard, S. (2012), 'Other People', in D. Zahavi (ed), *The Oxford Handbook of Contemporary Phenomenology*, Oxford: Oxford University Press.

Parnas, J. and P. Handest (2003), 'Phenomenology of Anomalous Self-Experience in Early Schizophrenia', *Comprehensive Psychiatry*, 44 (2): 121–34.

Parnas, J., P. Handest, L. Jansson, and D. Sæbye (2005), 'Anomalous Subjective Experience among First-Admitted Schizophrenia Spectrum Patients: Empirical Investigation', *Psychopathology*, 38 (5): 259–67.

Parnas, J. and L. Sass (2011), 'The Structure of the Self in Schizophrenia', in S. Gallagher (ed), *The Oxford Handbook of the Self*, 521–46, Oxford: Oxford University Press.

Parnas, J., A. Raballo, P. Handest, L. Jansson, A. Vollmer-Larsen and D. Saebye (2011), 'Self-Experience in the Early Phases of Schizophrenia: 5-Year Follow-Up of the Copenhagen Prodromal Study', *World Psychiatry: Official Journal of the World Psychiatric Association (WPA)*, 10 (3): 200–4.

Paul, L. A. (2014), *Transformative Experience*, Oxford: Oxford University Press.

Peterman, J. F. (1992), *Philosophy as Therapy: An Interpretation and Defense of Wittgenstein's Later Philosophical Project*, Albany (NY): State University of New York Press.

Petocz, A. (2015), 'The Scientific Status of Psychoanalysis Revisited', in S. Boag, L. A. W. Brakel, and V. Talvitie (eds), *Philosophy, Science, and Psychoanalysis: A Critical Meeting*, 145–92, London: Karnac Books Ltd.

Pontalis, J.-B. ([1969] 2008), 'Reply to Sartre', trans. J. Matthews, in *Between Existentialism and Marxism: Jean-Paul Sartre*, 220–220, London: Verso.

Pontalis, J.-B. (1985), 'Editor's Preface: Freud Scenario, Sartre Scenario', trans. Q. Hoare, in J.-B. Pontalis (ed), *The Freud Scenario*, vii–xviii, London: Verso.

Popper, K. (1983), *Realism and the Aim of Science*, London: Hucheson.

Pritchard, D. (2009), 'Knowledge, Understanding and Epistemic Value', *Royal Institute of Philosophy Supplement*, 64: 19–43.

Rajkumar, R. P. (2020), 'COVID-19 and Mental Health: A Review of the Existing Literature', *Asian Journal of Psychiatry*, 52: 1–5.

Ratcliffe, M. (2012), 'Phenomenology as a Form of Empathy', *Inquiry: An Interdisciplinary Journal of Philosophy*, 55 (5): 473–95.

Rice, L. N. and L. S. Greenberg (1992), 'Humanistic Approaches to Psychotherapy', in D. K. Freedheim, H. J. Freudenberger, J. W. Kessler, S. B. Messer, D. R. Peterson,

H. H. Strupp, and P. L. Wachtel (eds), *History of Psychotherapy: A Century of Change*, 197–224, Washington (DC): American Psychological Association.

Richmond, S. (2004), 'Introduction', in *The Transcendence of the Ego*, trans. S. Richmond, vii–xxviii, London: Routledge.

Ricœur, P. (1970), *Freud and Philosophy: An Essay on Interpretation*, trans. D. Savage, New Haven: Yale University Press.

Rogers, C. (1980), *A Way of Being*, Boston: Houghton Mifflin Company.

Roditi, E. (1950), 'Review of *Baudelaire*', *Poetry*, 77 (2): 100–3.

Rorty, A. O. (1972), 'Belief and Self-Deception', *Inquiry: An Interdisciplinary Journal of Philosophy*, 15: 387–410.

Rothfield, L. (1992), *Vital Signs: Medical Realism in Nineteenth-Century Fiction*, Princeton (NJ): Princeton University Press.

Roudiez, L. S. (1982), 'Flaubert, for Instance?' *The French Review*, Special Issue, 7: 68–78.

Russell, B. ([1948] 2009), *Human Knowledge: Its Scope and Limits*, London: Routledge.

Russell, G. I. (2015), *Screen Relations: The Limits of Computer-Mediated Psychoanalysis and Psychotherapy*, London: Routledge.

Ryle, A. and I. B. Kerr (2002), *Introducing Cognitive-Analytic Therapy: Principles and Practice*, Hoboken (NJ): John Wiley & Sons, Inc.

Ryle, G. ([1949] 2009), *The Concept of Mind*, London: Routledge.

Safran, J. D. and S. B. Messer (1997), 'Psychotherapy Integration: A Postmodern Critique', *Clinical Psychology: Science and Practice*, 4 (2): 140–52.

Santoni, R. E. (1995), *Bad Faith, Good Faith and Authenticity in Sartre's Early Philosophy*, Philadelphia: Temple University Press.

Santoni, R. E. (2008), 'Is Bad Faith Necessarily Social?' *Sartre Studies International*, 14 (2): 23–39.

Sartre, J.-P. ([1938] 1965/1981), *Nausea*, trans. R. Baldick, London: Penguin Books/*La Nausée*, in *Jean-Paul Sartre: Œuvres romanesques*, 8–210, Paris: Gallimard.

Sartre, J.-P. ([1939] 2002/1990), 'Intentionality: A Fundamental Idea of Husserl's Phenomenology', trans. J. P. Fell, in D. Moran and T. Mooney (eds), *The Phenomenology Reader*, 382–4, London: Routledge/'Une idée fondamentale de phénoménologie de Husserl: l'intentionnalité', *Jean-Paul Sartre. Situations philosophiques*, 9–12, Paris: Éditions Gallimard.

Sartre, J.-P. [1939, abbreviations: **CL/EC**] (1960/1981), 'The Childhood of a Leader', trans. L. Alexander, in *Intimacy*, 130–220, Aylesbury: Panther Books/'L'Enfance d'un chef', in *Jean-Paul Sartre: Œuvres romanesques*, 314–88, Paris: Gallimard.

Sartre, J.-P. [1939, abbreviations: **STE/ETE**] (1962/1995), *Sketch for a Theory of the Emotions*, trans. P. Mairet, London: Routledge/*Esquisse d'une théorie des émotions*, Paris: Herman.

Sartre, J.-P. [1939, abbreviation: **TE**] (2004/2003), *The Transcendence of the Ego*, trans. S. Richmond, London: Routledge/*La transcendance de la ego. Esquisse d'une description phénoménologique*, Paris: Librairie Philosophique J. VRIN.

Sartre, J.-P. [1940, abbreviation: **I**] (2005/2004), *The Imaginary: A Phenomenological Psychology of the Imagination*, trans. J. Webber, London: Routledge/*L'imaginaire. Psychologie phénémonologique de l'imagination*, Paris: ÉditionsGallimard.

Sartre, J.-P. [1943, abbreviations: **BN/EN**] (2018/1943), *Being and Nothingness: An Essay on Phenomenological Ontology*, trans. S. Richmond, London: Routledge/*L'être et le néant. Essai d'ontologie phénoménologique*, Paris: Éditions Gallimard.

Sartre, J.-P. ([1946] 1948/1954), *Anti-Semite and Jew*, trans. G. J. Becker, New York: Schoken Books/*Réflexions sur la question juive*, Paris: Éditions Gallimard.

Sartre, J.-P. [1947, abbreviation: **B**] (1975/1950), *Baudelaire*, trans. M. Turnell, New York: New Directions Publishing Co./*Baudelaire*, Paris: Éditions Gallimard.

Sartre, J.-P. ([1947] 2000), 'Huis Clos', trans. S. Gilbert, in *Huis Clos and Other Plays*, 181–223, London: Penguin Books.

Sartre, J.-P. [1948, abbreviations: **WL/QL**] (2001/1948), *What Is Literature?* trans. B. Frechtman, London: Routledge/*Qu'est-ce que la littérature ?* Paris: Éditions Gallimard.

Sartre, J.-P. [1952, abbreviation: **SG**] (2012/1952), *Saint Genet: Actor and Martyr*, trans. B. Frechtman, Minneapolis: University of Minnesota Press/*Saint Genet, comédien et martyr*, Paris: Éditions Gallimard.

Sartre, J.-P. [1960, abbreviations: **SM/QM**] (1963/1983), *Search for a Method*, trans. H. E. Barnes, New York: Vintage Books/*Questions de méthode*, Paris: Éditions Gallimard.

Sartre, J.-P. [1960, abbreviations: **CDR I/CRD I**] (1976/1985), *Critique of Dialectical Reason I: Theory of Practical Ensembles*, trans. A. Sheridan-Smith, London: NLB/*Critique de la raison dialectique précédé de questions de méthode, Tome I: théorie des ensembles pratiques*, Paris: Éditions Gallimard.

Sartre, J.-P. (1964), 'Foreword', in R. D. Laing and D. G. Cooper (eds), *Reason and Violence: A Decade of Sartre's Philosophy, 1950–1960*, 7–7, London: Routledge.

Sartre, J.-P. [abbreviations: **W/M**] (1964/1964), *Words*, trans. I. Clephane, London: Penguin Books/*Les Mots*, Paris: Éditions Gallimard.

Sartre, J.-P. ([1964] 2008/1972), 'Kierkegaard: The Singular Universal', trans. J. Matthews, in *Between Existentialism and Marxism: Jean-Paul Sartre*, 142–69, London: Verso/'L'Universel singulier', in *Situations philosophiques*, Paris: Éditions Gallimard.

Sartre, J.-P. [abbreviation: **IOT**] (1969), 'Itinerary of a Thought', *New Left Review*, 58: 43–66.

Sartre, J.-P. [1969, abbreviations: **MT/HM**] (2008/1969), 'The Man with the Tape-Recorder', trans. J. Matthews, in *Between Existentialism and Marxism: Jean-Paul Sartre*, 199–205, London: Verso/'L'Homme au magnétophone', *Les Temps modernes*, 274: 1813–19.

Sartre, J.-P. [abbreviation: **IF I**] (1971), *L'Idiot de la famille: Gustave Flaubert de 1821 à 1857*, vol. 1, Paris: Éditions Gallimard.

Sartre, J.-P. [abbreviation: **IF II**] (1971), *L'Idiot de la famille: Gustave Flaubert de 1821 à 1857*, vol. 2, Paris: Éditions Gallimard.

Sartre, J.-P. [abbreviation: **IF III**] (1971), *L'Idiot de la famille: Gustave Flaubert de 1821 à 1857*, vol. 3, Paris: Éditions Gallimard.
Sartre, J.-P. [1971, abbreviations: **OIF/SIF**] (1977/1976), 'On *The Idiot of the Family*', trans. P. Auster and L. Davies, in *Sartre in the Seventies: Interviews and Essays*, 109–32, London: André Deutsch Limited/'Sur « *L'Idiot de la famille* »', in *Situations, X: politique et autobiographie*, 91–115, Paris: Éditions Gallimard.
Sartre, J.-P. [abbreviation: **IF 3**] (1972), *L'Idiot de la famille: Gustave Flaubert de 1821 à 1857*, vol. 3, Paris: Éditions Gallimard.
Sartre, J.-P. (1978a), 'Justice and the State', in *Sartre in the Seventies: Interviews and Essays*, trans. P. Auster and L. Davies, 172–97, London: André Deutsch Limited.
Sartre, J.-P. (1978b), 'Self-Portrait at Seventy', in *Sartre in the Seventies: Interviews and Essays*, trans. P. Auster and L. Davies, 3–92, London: André Deutsch Limited.
Sartre, J.-P. [abbreviation: **IWS**] (1981), 'An Interview with Jean-Paul Sartre', in P. A. Schilpp (ed), *The Philosophy of Jean-Paul Sartre*, 5–51, La Salle (IL): Open Court Publishing Company.
Sartre, J.-P. [abbreviation: **FI I**] (1981), *The Family Idiot: Gustave Flaubert 1821–1857*, vol. 1, trans. C. Cosman, Chicago: The University of Chicago Press.
Sartre, J.-P. ([1983] 1984/1995), *War Diaries: Notebooks from a Phoney War*, trans. Q. Hoare, London: Verso/*Carnets de la drôle de guerre*, Paris: Éditions Gallimard.
Sartre, J.-P. [1985, abbreviations: **CDR II/CRD II**] (1991/1985), *Critique of Dialectical Reason, Volume II (Unfinished)*, trans. Q. Hoare, London: Verso/*Critique de la raison dialectique, Tome II (inachevé): L'intelligibilité de l'histoire*, Paris: Éditions Gallimard.
Sartre, J.-P. (1986), 'Conversations with Jean-Paul Sartre: August–September 1974', in S. de Beauvoir (ed), *Adieux: A Farewell to Sartre*, trans. Patrick O'Brian, 131–445, London: Penguin Books.
Sartre, J.-P. [abbreviation: **FI II**] (1987), *The Family Idiot: Gustave Flaubert 1821–1857*, vol. 2, trans. C. Cosman, Chicago: The University of Chicago Press.
Sartre, J.-P. [abbreviation: **FI III**] (1989), *The Family Idiot: Gustave Flaubert 1821–1857*, vol. 3, trans. C. Cosman, Chicago: The University of Chicago Press.
Sartre, J.-P. [abbreviation: **FI IV**] (1991), *The Family Idiot: Gustave Flaubert 1821–1857*, vol. 4, trans. C. Cosman, Chicago: The University of Chicago Press.
Sartre, J.-P. (1992/1983), *Notebooks for an Ethics*, trans. D. Pellauer, Chicago: The University of Chicago Press/*Cahiers pour une morale*, Paris: Éditions Gallimard.
Sartre, J.-P. [abbreviation: **FI V**] (1993), *The Family Idiot: Gustave Flaubert 1821–1857*, vol. 5, trans. C. Cosman, Chicago: The University of Chicago Press.
Sass, L. and M. Ratcliffe (2017), 'Atmosphere: On the Phenomenology of "atmospheric" Alterations in Schizophrenia-Overall Sense of Reality, Familiarity, Vitality, Meaning, or Relevance (Ancillary Article to EAWE Domain 5)', *Psychopathology*, 50 (1): 90–7.
Schneider, K. J. (ed) (2007), *Existential-Integrative Psychotherapy: Guideposts to the Core of Practice*, London: Routledge.
Searle, J. R. (1992), *The Rediscovery of the Mind*, Cambridge (MA): The MIT Press.

Simon, G. M. (2006), 'The Heart of the Matter: A Proposal for Placing the Self of the Therapist at the Center of Family Therapy Research and Training', *Family Process*, 45 (3): 331–44.

Simons, M. A. (1986), 'Beauvoir and Sartre: The Philosophical Relationship', *Yale French Studies*, 72: 165–79.

Simpson, J., S. Doze, D. Urness, D. Hailey, and P. Jacobs (2001), 'Telepsychiatry as a Routine Service – The Perspective of the Patient', *Journal of Telemedicine and Telecare*, 7: 155–60.

Soll, I. (1981), 'Sartre's Rejection of the Freudian Unconscious', in P. A. Schilpp (ed), *The Philosophy of Jean-Paul Sartre*, 583–604, La Salle (IL): Open Court Publishing Company.

Sollberger, M. (2017), 'The Epistemological Problem of Other Minds and the Knowledge Asymmetry', *European Journal of Philosophy*, 25 (4): 1476–95.

Solomon, R. C. (2006), *Dark Feelings, Grim Thoughts: Experience and Reflection in Camus and Sartre*, Oxford: Oxford University Press.

Starkie, E. (1967), *Flaubert: The Making of the Master*, London: Penguin Books.

Stewart, I. and V. Joines (2012), *TA Today: A New Introduction to Transactional Analysis*, 2nd edn, Chapel Hill (NC): Lifespace Publishing.

Stone, R. V. (1981), 'Sartre on Bad Faith and Authenticity', in P. A. Schilpp (ed), *The Philosophy of Jean-Paul Sartre*, 246–56, La Salle (IL): Open Court Publishing Company.

Strawson, G. ([1994] 2010), *Mental Reality*, 2nd edn, Cambridge (MA): The MIT Press.

Stricker, G. and J. R. Gold (1996), 'Psychotherapy Integration: An Assimilative, Psychodynamic Approach', *Clinical Psychology: Science and Practice*, 3 (1): 47–58.

Stroud, B. (1994), 'Kantian Argument, Conceptual Capacities, and Invulnerability', in P. Parrini (ed), *Kant and Contemporary Epistemology*, 231–52, Dordrecht: Kluwer Academic Publishers.

Tanner, T. (1979), *Adultery in the Novel: Contract and Transgression*, Baltimore: The Johns Hopkins University Press.

Teasdale, J. D., Segal, Z. V., Williams, J. M. G., Ridgeway, V. A., Soulsby, J. M., and Lau, M. A. (2000), 'Prevention of Relapse/Recurrence in Major Depression by Mindfulness-Based Cognitive Therapy', *Journal of Consulting and Clinical Psychology*, 68: 615–23.

Tilby, M. (2004), 'Flaubert's Place in Literary History', in T. Unwin (ed), *The Cambridge Companion to Flaubert*, 14–33, Cambridge: Cambridge University Press.

Uhlhaas, P. J. and A. L. Mishara (2007), 'Perceptual Anomalies in Schizophrenia: Integrating Phenomenology and Cognitive Neuroscience', *Schizophrenia Bulletin*, 33 (1): 142–56.

Unwin, T. (2004), 'Flaubert's Early Work', in T. Unwin (ed), *The Cambridge Companion to Flaubert*, 34–50, Cambridge: Cambridge University Press.

Wachtel, P. L. (1997), *Psychoanalysis, Behavior Therapy, and the Relational World*, Washington (DC): American Psychological Association.

Wall, G. (2006), 'The Invisible Man: An Essay on Flaubert and Celebrity', *The Cambridge Quarterly*, 35 (2): 133–50.

Wallerstein, R. S. (1986), 'Psychoanalysis as a Science: A Response to the New Challenges', *The Psychoanalytic Quarterly*, 55 (3): 414–51.

Wallerstein, R. S. (1990), 'Psychoanalysis: The Common Ground', *International Journal of Psychoanalysis*, 71: 3–20.

Walther, J., G. Gay, and J. Hancock (2005), 'How Do Communication and Technology Researchers Study the Internet?' *Journal of Communication*, 55 (3): 632–57.

Wampold, B. E. (2001), *The Great Psychotherapy Debate: Models, Methods, and Findings*, Mahwah (NJ): Lawrence Erlbaum Associates Inc., Publishers.

Wampold, B. E., G. W. Mondin, M. Moody, F. Stich, K. Benson, and H. Ahn (1997), 'A Meta-Analysis of Outcome Studies Comparing Bona Fide Psychotherapies: Empirically, "All Must Have Prizes"', *Psychological Bulletin*, 122 (3): 203–15.

Webber, J. (2009), *The Existentialism of Jean-Paul Sartre*, London: Routledge.

Webber, J. (2011), 'Bad Faith and the Other', in J. Webber (ed), *Reading Sartre: On Phenomenology and Existentialism*, 180–94, London: Routledge.

Webber, J. (2018), *Rethinking Existentialism*, Oxford: Oxford University Press.

Widdowson, M. (2014), 'Transactional Analysis Psychotherapy for a Case of Mixed Anxiety & Depression: A Pragmatic Adjudicated Case Study – "Alastair"', *International Journal of Transactional Analysis Research*, 5 (2): 66–76.

Widdowson, M. (2016), *Transactional Analysis for Depression: A Step-By-Step Treatment Manual*, London: Routledge.

Wider, K. (1997), *The Bodily Nature of Consciousness: Sartre and Contemporary Philosophy of Mind*, Ithaca: Cornell University Press.

Williford, K. (2011), 'Pre-Reflective Self-Consciousness and the Autobiographical Ego', in J. Webber (ed), *Reading Sartre: On Phenomenology and Existentialism*, 195–210, London: Routledge.

Wilson, T. D. (2002), *Strangers to Ourselves: Discovering the Adaptive Unconscious*, Cambridge (MA): The Belknap Press of Harvard University Press.

Winnicott, D. W. (1949), 'Hate in the Countertransference', *International Journal of Psychoanalysis*, 30: 69–75.

Winnicott, D. W. (1971), *Playing and Reality*, London: Routledge.

Wittgenstein, L. ([1953] 2009), *Philosophical Investigations*, 4th edn, trans. G. E. M. Anscombe, P. M. S. Hacker, and J. Schulte, London: Blackwell Publishing Ltd.

Wittgenstein, L. (1968), 'Notes for Lectures on "Private Experience" and "Sense Data"', *Philosophical Review*, 77 (3): 275–320.

Wittgenstein, L. (1969), *Preliminary Studies for the "Philosophical Investigations," Generally Known as the Blue and Brown Books*, 2nd edn, Oxford: Blackwell Publishing.

Yalom, I. D. (1980), *Existential Psychotherapy*, New York: Basic Books.

Zahavi, D. (2000), 'Self and Consciousness', in D. Zahavi (ed), *Exploring the Self: Philosophical and Psychopathological Perspectives on Self-Experience*, 55–74, Amsterdam: John Benjamins Publishing Company.

Zahavi, D. (2014), *Self & Other: Exploring Subjectivity, Empathy, and Shame*, Oxford: Oxford University Press.

Zafiropoulos, M. (2010), *Lacan and Lévi-Strauss or the Return to Freud (1951–1957)*, trans. J. Holland, London: Routledge.

Index

analogon 158–61, 167, 169, 198–9, 180, 181
anguish 2, 16–18, 20–1, 22, 26, 28–31, 33, 39, 88, 190
antipsychiatry 127
Anti-Semite and Jew (Sartre) 165
Arnold-Baker, Clair 47n
argument from analogy 42–4
Askay, Richard 65
authenticity
  anguish as a prerequisite for 16–17, 21, 26, 28–9
  in self-formation 27, 33, 34, 127

bad faith 27–9
  as distinct from the natural attitude 19
  of Flaubert and his first readers 124
  implicit in the assumption of a truly objective or 'desituated' perspective 130
  as an obstacle to self-knowledge 54
  and oppression 80, 85–6, 165
  and the puzzle of self-deception 56, 59–60
  in Sartre's reading of Freud 57
  in self-formation 30–4, 84
Barnes, Hazel E. 72n, 92–3, 95, 97, 99, 107, 136, 153n, 173
Barnes, Julian 131n, 132
Barrès, Maurice 63n
Bart, Benjamin F. 95, 110n, 145, 173
Bartky, Sandra Lee 80–1, 81n
Baudelaire (Sartre) 33–4, 83–4, 87, 162
Baudelaire, Charles 33, 60, 83–4, 137
Beauvoir, Simone (de) 2–4, 6, 32, 80, 82–5, 88, 153, 168–9
Being and Nothingness (Sartre)
  bad faith in 19, 27–30, 33
  critique of Freud 54–60
  description of existential psychoanalysis 54, 78, 184
  and dialectical reason 67–8, 70, 134
  discussion of Flaubert 131
  influence of Hegel 69, 82
  on the possibility of taking up a new fundamental project in 141
  and the problem of other minds 3, 41, 46, 66, 88, 158
  and Sartre's theory of the self 2, 7, 22–3, 35
  theorization of consciousness 26
being-for-others (objective embodiment) 23–5, 47, 49, 105
Bergson, Henri 61n
Bering, Jesse M. 51n
Berne, Eric 196, 196n
black saint(s) 122–3, 123n, 144–5
Boulé, Jean-Pierré 27n
Bourget, Paul 60–1
Breeur, Roland 61n

Cannon, Betty 27n, 163, 182–3, 185–7, 203
A Case of Hysteria (Freud) 76
Catalano, Joseph 27n, 41n
Chalmers, David 42n, 43n
Charmé, Stuart Z. 57
Chevalier, Maurice (entertainer) 160
'The Childhood of a Leader' (Sartre) 30, 33, 203
cogito 9–10, 36, 49
comprehension
  in applications of existential psychoanalysis 88, 187, 201
  of Flaubert's lived experience 91, 97, 102, 114–15, 121, 139, 144, 166, 172–3, 175, 178
  and knowledge of a self 4, 82, 64, 171
  literature and 116, 131, 168, 170, 176, 179–80
  preontological 61
  Sartre's account of 60, 62–3, 67, 75, 78, 87, 162–3, 165

constitution
    of the ego 18–22
    Flaubert's 91–2, 95–6, 99–103, 107, 110, 146, 172
    of an image 177
    of the self (*see* self)
Coorebyter, Vincent (de) 15, 18–19
Critique of Dialectical Reason (Sartre)
    discussion of Flaubert 132
    introduction of a new form of rationality 67–8, 77, 134
    Sartre's revisions to his existentialism 3–4, 81, 170–1
    terminology 72–3, 83, 86, 116

Descartes, René 2, 7, 9, 36, 43
Detmer, David 57n
Deurzen, Emmy (van) 5, 47n
dialectic
    as a dialogical method 68
    of *The Family Idiot* 4, 136, 147–8, 178
    historical 3, 68–72, 75–6, 134, 171
    (Hegelian) Master-Slave 82
    between the subject and the world 70, 80, 177, 180, 198
dialectical objects 4, 74–5, 77–8, 89–90, 130, 176–8, 180, 187, 201
dialectical reason 3, 67–74, 77–9, 134, 166, 191–2
The Divided Self (Laing) 188–9, 192
Dolezal, Luna 51n
Dostoyevsky, Fydor 131

eidetic reduction 23, 65
ego
    Freudian 55–9
    Husserlian (transcendental) 9–12, 15
    Sartrean 2, 8, 12–25, 62n, 186
The Ego and the Id (Freud) 55, 58
engaged writing 148, 167
epochē 8–9, 8n, 19–20
Eshleman, Matthew 62n
e-therapy 197–9
The Ethics of Ambiguity (Beauvoir) 83
existential psychotherapy 5, 52–4, 187–92, 194–7. *See also* psychotherapy

faith (religious) 100–1, 105, 121, 145–6

The Family Idiot (Sartre) 1, 4–5
    achievements of 155–6, 171–3, 181–2
    aims of 90–1, 102, 178, 180
    analysis of Flaubert's literature 122, 137, 143, 146, 165, 169–70
    analysis of Flaubert's nervous crisis 109, 115, 126–7
    concept of Objective Spirit 116
    on constitution 92–3, 101, 146
    objectivity of 129, 131–2, 134–6, 147–51, 153–4
    as a re-totalization of Flaubert's self 160
    theorization of laughter in 143
    treatment of Flaubert's childhood 'stupors' and difficulties with language 123, 164–5
    treatment of freedom 79–80
    treatment of the imaginary 157–8, 173–6
Farquhar, Jensen 65
femininity 28n, 82, 103–5, 152–4
feminism 153–4
Ferris, Susan 161n
Flaubert, Achille 106, 112
Flaubert, Achille-Cléophas 92, 96, 99–100, 202
Flaubert, Caroline (junior) 106–7
Flaubert, Caroline (senior) 92–5
Flaubert, Gustave 4–5, 60, 90, 91–127, 129–56, 157, 160, 164–6, 169–76, 178–80, 181, 202–3. *See also The Family Idiot*
Flaubert's Parrot (Barnes) 132
Flynn, Thomas R. 11n, 155, 178
Franconay, Claire (performance artist) 160–1
Freud, Sigmund 2, 55–60, 62–6, 76–8, 82, 133, 162–3, 166–7, 182–3
fundamental project 61–2, 64, 86n, 110, 125, 141, 152, 186–7

Garçon, character of 108–9, 114, 143, 145
Genet, Jean 4, 84–9, 164–5, 179, 181, 183, 189, 202, 204. *See also Saint Genet: Actor and Martyr*
Goethe, Johann Wolfgang (von) 111
Goldthorpe, Rhiannon 149
Gosetti-Ferencei, Jennifer 179
Gross, David 147–8

Handest, Peter 200–1
Hegel, Georg Wilhelm Friedrich 2, 47, 69–72, 74, 82
Heidegger, Martin 11n, 47, 47n, 50, 61, 188n
Heimann, Paula 184n
hexis 81, 83, 86, 88–9, 186, 186n, 202
hodological space 81
human-reality 61–2, 75, 79
Hume, David 42
Husserl, Edmund 2, 8–12, 15, 17, 19, 47, 133
hysterical illness 110, 126

id 56
idealism 47, 69n, 70–2, 116, 172
imaginary 105–7, 142, 147, 157–8, 160, 167–8
   experience and knowledge 176–80
   objects 4, 18, 23, 74, 159, 160–1, 169, 174–7, 201 (*see also* dialectical objects)
   self (*see* self)
   'solutions' 108–9, 118, 120, 124–5, 141–2, 191
   worlds 137, 141, 167–70
The Imaginary: A Phenomenological Psychology of the Imagination (Sartre) 5, 157–8, 160, 174–6, 176n
imagination 1, 4, 140, 142, 147, 154, 157–8, 167, 176, 178–80, 181, 199
   pathology of 5, 174–5, 191–2, 200–1
   Sartre's treatment of Flaubert's relationship with 4–5, 95, 104–9, 114, 120, 123–7, 137, 147, 154, 157, 171, 173–6
internal negation 26, 48

Jaspers, Karl 188, 188n
'Justice and the State' (Sartre) 132
juvenilia (Flaubert's) 97, 136, 170

Kafka, Franz 32
Kahane, David J. 183n
Kenevan, Phyllis Berdt 15–17, 17n
Kierkegaard, Søren 71–2, 72n, 188n
Kirkpatrick, Kate 186n
Kojève, Alexandre 69, 69n

Lacan, Jacques 163–4, 166, 183
Laing, Ronald D. 81n, 185, 188–92, 200
The Legend of Saint Julian Hospitator (Flaubert) 113, 122, 149
Lennon, Kathleen 41n, 179
Levin, Harry 131
Lipps, Theordor 51
Little, Margaret 184n
the Look 23–4, 29, 47–9, 85, 105, 158, 184, 202–3

Madame Bovary (Flaubert) 4, 95, 102, 104, 108, 115, 123–5, 129, 132, 135–42, 144, 147, 149–52, 154–5, 170, 172
magical behaviour 111, 126, 173
Malcolm, Norman 44–5
Mallarmé, Stéphane 109–10
Marx, Karl 2, 71–2, 75, 79, 82
masculinity 153–4
materialism 71–2, 75, 82, 95, 99, 108, 116, 121, 172
May, Rollo 5
Mehrabian, Albert 161n
The Metamorphosis (Kafka) 32
Mill, John Stuart 42
Minuchin, Salvadore 185n
misanthropy 118–19, 124, 147–9, 154, 203
misogyny 118–20, 150–1, 153–4, 203
Moran, Richard 36–40
Morris, Katherine 52n

natural attitude 8, 19–21, 28
neobehaviourism 44–6, 49, 52
neurosis 4, 76, 81, 101, 106, 110–13, 115–18, 125, 164, 173, 183–4, 189
nonassimilable 102, 117, 125, 165
non-positional consciousness of consciousness 12–17, 25–6
November (Flaubert) 111, 140, 152, 172, 175

objective spirit 116–17
objectivity 49, 133–4, 187–8
oppression 87–8, 151, 153
   psychological 4, 80–4, 87, 127, 165, 172, 176, 199, 201–3
original choice 61–7, 70, 81, 84, 86–7, 102, 107, 126, 141, 147, 154, 166, 171, 183, 186
Orr, Mary 141n, 153n

Parnas, Josef 200–1
perverse sexuality 103–5
Peterman, James 53, 54n
phenomenological reduction 8–9, 11
  eidetic 23, 65
Pontalis, Jean-Bertrand 1, 5n, 62n, 184n
postromantics 117–19, 123–5, 135, 150
practico-inert 72–3, 116
praxis 72–3, 77, 89, 184
psychoanalytic metatheory 5, 59–60, 65, 182–3
psychosis 188, 188n
psychotherapy 5, 52–4, 89–90, 157, 181–99

Ratcliffe, Matthew 21n, 179n
reciprocity 87–8, 116, 184–5, 187, 194, 199
Richmond, Sarah 9, 15n
romanticism 108
Roudiez, Leon S. 131n
Russell, Bertrand 42n
Russell, Gillian Issacs 197–8

Saint Genet: Actor and Martyr (Sartre) 4, 84, 87–9, 164–5, 183, 189
Salammbô (Flaubert) 121
Santoni, Ronald 57n
Scheler, Max 51
schizophrenia 174, 185, 188–90, 200–1
Schneider, Kirk J. 194
The Second Sex (Beauvoir) 82–3
self 1–5, 141–2
  alienation from 50, 100, 105–6, 146, 164, 180–2, 201
  of another person (or the other-as-object) 2, 35–6, 54, 73–4, 87–90, 129–30, 157–62, 171, 180–1
  constitution of 3, 25, 70, 102, 161
  and freedom to choose 34, 62, 67, 79–83, 85–7, 107, 165, 174–5, 186, 204
  ideal (Moi/Self) 61–2, 62n, 64–7, 86–7
  imaginary 18, 158–62, 164, 201, 179–80
  reality of 15, 18, 24–6, 31–2, 34, 62–4, 160–1, 164, 190, 194
  Sartre's departure from standard model of the self 7–11
  Sartre's re-totalization of Flaubert's self 98, 100–9, 113–15, 119, 121–7, 129–30, 134–6, 147, 149, 151, 155, 172–6, 181, 202–3
  Sartre's revised account of the self (as a dialectical object) 22–6, 75, 130, 178, 187, 198–9
self-consciousness or positional consciousness of the self(-as-object) 10, 14, 16, 34, 48–50
self-deception 27, 29, 37, 55–7, 59–60, 121
self-destruction/-sabotage/-harm 80, 123, 175–6, 202
self-formation, process of 19, 21, 26–30, 30–5, 67, 78–80, 84, 86, 91–2, 102, 107, 109, 121, 126, 162, 165, 192, 196, 199, 202
self-in-progress 15–17, 21–2
self-knowledge 16, 21–3, 27, 31, 35–41, 63–4, 71, 102, 114–15, 158, 161, 164, 183–4, 187, 190
self-loathing/-hatred 96, 120, 124–5
selfness 11–12, 23, 35
sense of self and psychological illness 20, 197–201
A Sentimental Education (Flaubert) 122, 131, 148
seriousness 30–3, 32n, 143, 145
shame 2, 23, 27, 29, 47–51, 66, 85, 119–20
situation(s), impact on the subject 1, 4, 23–5, 28, 37, 40, 51, 54, 67, 78–9, 81–4, 111, 116, 141, 167, 175, 178–9, 186–7, 189, 197, 200, 202–3
  Emma Bovary's 142, 144–5, 151
  Flaubert's 92, 95, 99, 101–2, 113, 115, 119, 125, 127, 149, 172, 175
  Genet's 85–7, 189
  oppressive 81, 83, 86, 88, 164–5
  women's 82, 152
Sketch for a Theory of the Emotions (Sartre) 111n
Solomon, Robert 30n
Starkie, Enid 110n, 130, 138, 173
Stein, Edith 51
Stekel, Wilhelm 30n
Stroud, Barry 46
super-ego 57–9

The Temptation of Saint Antony (Flaubert) 120, 122, 135, 137
The Transcendence of the Ego (Sartre) 2, 8, 14–15, 17–19, 21, 23, 25, 28, 35
totalization(s) 70, 74–5, 78–9, 88–90, 127, 134, 161, 171–2, 178
　re-totalization 102, 116, 129, 158, 160, 162, 171, 180–1
Transactional Analysis 196

unconscious 19, 61, 84, 104, 133, 173, 195
　Freudian 30–1, 55–60, 77, 166–7
　Lacanian 163

Sartre's rejection of 55–7, 59–60, 65, 166, 182–3, 188

Wampold, Bruce E. 194
Webber, Jonathan 28, 57–8, 67n, 202, 203n
Widdowson, Mark 196
Williford, Kenneth 13–14
Winnicott, Donald 95, 184n
Wittgenstein, Ludwig 44, 52–3, 54n
Words (Sartre) 5n, 131–2

Yalom, Irvin D. 5

Zahavi, Dan 11n, 13, 201n

www.ingramcontent.com/pod-product-compliance
Lightning Source LLC
Chambersburg PA
CBHW062127300426
44115CB00012BA/1834